161 363186 9
AF804196
WITHDRAWN
Two week loan
Benthyciad pythefnos
WITHDRAWN

Evolution of the Economic System in Japan

Evolution of the Economic System in Japan

Juro Teranishi
The Institute of Economic Research
Hitotsubashi University
Japan

Edward Elgar
Cheltenham, UK • Northampton, MA, USA

338.952
T

© Juro Teranishi 2005

All rights reserved. No part of this publication may be reproduced, stored in a retrieval system or transmitted in any form or by any means, electronic, mechanical or photocopying, recording, or otherwise without the prior permission of the publisher.

Published by
Edward Elgar Publishing Limited
Glensanda House
Montpellier Parade
Cheltenham
Glos GL50 1UA
UK

Edward Elgar Publishing, Inc.
136 West Street
Suite 202
Northampton
Massachusetts 01060
USA

A catalogue record for this book
is available from the British Library

CARDIFF UNIVERSITY
-3 NOV 2005
PRIFYSGOL CAERDYDD

ISBN 1 84376 163 7
Printed and bound in Great Britain by MPG Books Ltd, Bodmin, Cornwall

Contents

Figures

Tables

Preface

The economic system of Japan stands at a crossroads. During the postwar high-growth period, the economic system was characterized by various 'Japanese-style' properties: life-time employment, the main bank system, a close government–private-sector relationship, and so on. Since the bubble period of the late 1980s and severe downturn of the economy in the 1990s, it has been undergoing drastic changes. This book deliberates how and why the economic system of the high-growth period emerged, and how and why it is going to change.

This is an English version of *Nihon no Keizai Shisutemu* (*Economic Systems in Japan*), published in 2003 by Iwanami-Shoten. The Japanese version was written in the midst of the serious deterioration of Japan's economic performance, unprecedented in the last fifty years. Partly for that reason, the introductory and concluding chapter devoted considerable space to explaining how such conditions as deflation and unemployment were related to the changes in the economic system, and what kind of concrete reform measures in the economic system were needed in order to improve the situation. While I firmly believe that the economic performance of the 1990s was closely related to the coordination failures caused by the mismatch between the existing economic system and exogenous conditions, it is one thing to conduct a historical analysis of the economic system and quite another to draw a picture of the future economic system. Thus, I have deleted most of the discussion of policy analysis and proposals for the future economic system. Instead, I focus on the implications of the analysis for understanding the long-term evolution of Japan's economic system and related controversies. (I have also updated and corrected some errors in the statistical tables.)

With respect to the preparation of this edition, I benefited from a critical reading of the manuscript by Larry Meissner. The discussion through e-mail with him on several conceptual issues was enormously helpful in clarifying my thinking. Bruno Dallago, Randal Morck, Hugh Patrick and Adrian Rixtel also were kind enough to read either parts or the whole of the preliminary English manuscript, and gave me useful comments.

The idea of writing a book on the economic system in Japan dates back to the 1970s, when I conducted a survey of existing literature on the analysis of the Japanese economy. That survey was published in *Keizai-kenkyu* in a series of articles during 1972–74, and part of it was published in English as 'A survey of Economic Studies of Prewar Japan' (*Japanese Economic Studies* 1 (2), Winter 1972–73).

Since then, I have spent almost four decades formulating my own view of the Japanese economic system. During this time, most of my research has been carried out in the academic atmosphere of the Institute of Economic Research, Hitotsubashi University. The stimulation, collaboration and encouragement I have experienced in this environment have contributed significantly to whatever academic value this book can claim.

I am grateful for the comments on the Japanese language version, either in the form of review articles in newspapers and journals or in letters. The review by Professor Takafusa Nakamura that appeared in Nikkei-Shinbun (9 March 2003) was quite encouraging, and so were pertinent and useful reviews by Kazuto Ikeo, Hirohisa Kohama, Kimihiro Masamura, Tatuya Nakamura, and Megumi Suto. Correspondence with Professors Shozaburo Fujino, Yujiro Hayami, Akiyoshi Horiuchi, Shigeru Ishikawa, Kenichi Miyazawa, Toshiyuki Mizoguchi, Miyohei Shinohara, Yuichi Shionoya, Shigeto Tsuru, Tsunehiko Yui and Mataji Umemura, as well as the late Shoichi Royama, were also highly appreciated.

Finally, I would like to express my sincere appreciation to my secretary Mayumi Okado for her help in preparing the manuscript.

20 September 2004
Juro Teranishi

PART I

1. Introduction

During the high-growth-period and subsequently, Japan's economic system has been characterized by various 'Japanese-style' properties: a firm system based on seniority wages and life-time employment, a bank-dominated financial system with an active role for main banks, heavy government involvement through industrial policy. Since the bubble period, and especially in the severe downturn of the economy during the 1990s, however, the system has been undergoing noticeable changes: the labor market is becoming more liquid, except for core employees at large firms; bank firm relationships are loosening, especially for large firms; the government has been obliged to reduce its control of the economy through deregulation.

This book deliberates how and why such an economic system, called a high-growth-period economic system in this book, emerged, and how and why it is going to change.

1.1 ISSUES ADDRESSED

With respect to the question of how the economic system emerged, we will examine how much the birth of the system owes to the gradual transformation of economic system since the prewar period, to the exogenous shocks delivered by the World War II, and to the transformation after the war. Views about these points are diverse.

Regarding the issue of prewar roots, it is often pointed out that many of the origins of Japanese-style characteristics could be traced back to the 1920 or even before. Features of the modern Japanese-style employment system, such as seniority wage, were gradually institutionalized after the 1920s (Chuma 1987 Odaka 1993): the financial system was bank dominated even before the 1920s (Ishii, 1997); industrial policy aimed at promoting heavy and chemical industries was intensified after World War I (Miwa, 1976). However, Okazaki (1993b) finds that the employment system of non-zaibatsu firms in the 1930s was not Japanese-style in the postwar sense; it was closer to neo-classical-type. Teranishi (1990) compares the financial systems of prewar and postwar Japan, and finds them quite different in the degree of utilization of market mechanisms.[1] Likewise, the emphasis on the role of banks in the prewar economy by Ishii (1997) stands in clear contrast with works such as Hoshi and Kashyap (2001), which draw attention to security-based financing of large firms.

The World War II, or the war during 1937 to 1945, on the other hand, converted the economic system into a highly controlled system, and various legislations enacted during the period in order to facilitate the economic control survived long after the end of the war, together with the bureaucrats experienced in economic regulations (Nakamura 1974). Noguchi (1995) contends that the high-growth-period economic system was established when various regulations were introduced toward 1940 as a preparation for 'total war', and calls the system '1940 system'.[2] Likewise, Okazaki and Okuno (1993) asserts that the high-growth-period economic system was finally established when a central-planning system based on the regulation of private firms was introduced toward the end of the war.[3]

These authors seem to be correct in pointing out the significant changes during the war that took place regarding the regulatory role of the government in the economy. With respect to other aspects of the economic system, however, especially concerning the evolution of the private sector, there are substantially different viewpoints that emphasize the transformation of the economy after the war. For example, Koike (1997) considers that the formation of firm-specific skills through regular job rotation began during the 1950s and became prevalent toward the end of the 1970s; Tsuda (1984) claims that a cooperative management–labor relationship did not exist at least until the end of 1946, and that practices such as long-term employment were gradually formed in the process of the process of severe labor disputes during the first decade after the war. Moreover, from the viewpoint of political economic analysis, some authors, such as Nakamura (1993a) and Hiwatari (1991), emphasize the importance of the class struggle[4] after the war. They claim that the postwar political and economic system was established around 1955, when the national wage campaign system (*shuntô*) was introduced,[5] giving rise to the cooperative labor–management relationship characteristic to the high-growth-period economic system.

This book will try to reconcile these diverse viewpoints through giving a coherent explanation of the process of the formation of the high-growth-period economic system. For this purpose, we utilize a broad framework that incorporates not only the changes in the role of the government in the economy but also the characteristics of the private sector, as well as the mechanism of interaction between the government and private sector. It will be shown that the process of the establishment of the high-growth-period economic system is composed of various phases that are characterized by significant interactions among these aspects, called sub-systems in this book, and that the process was completed during the 1950s.

We will also address ourselves to the question of why the high-growth-period economic system emerged. In this regard, some of conventional views claim that Japan has monotonically behaved so as to establish 'Japanese-style' economic system since she started construction of a new modern state. Representative and most influential hypotheses are Johnson (1982) and Dore (1973). Johnson (1982) discusses the evolution of the Japanese economic system as a simple-minded pursuit of a powerful developmental state. It is claimed that 'plan rationality' as opposed to market rationality was an invariable policy motif of the Japanese government since the mid-Meiji period. Likewise, Dore (1973) describes the formation of the Japanese-style employment system as a continuous and monotonic process of the cooperative 'organization-oriented' evolution since the late Meiji Period.[6]

In order to examine this monotonic transformation hypothesis, it is not sufficient to examine the evolution process of particular properties of an economic system such as a seniority wage system or industrial policy. Even if we find some embryonic form of particular properties, for example, nascent intervention in industrial promotion, this does not necessarily justify the statement that the economic system-building of modern Japan is characterized by a simple-minded pursuit of an economic system characterized by the property. It is essential to grasp with accuracy the full structure of the economic system existing during the prewar period comparable to the economic system in the high-growth-period, and to evaluate the importance of the embryonic forms of the properties in the system.

In this book, the views developed by Dore and Johnson are examined in a model that incorporates not only the economic system in the high-growth-period but also an economic system existing prior to it. It will be shown that the economic system existing prior to the high-growth-period, a system called the Meiji-Taishô economic system in this book, is quite different from the image conjured up by Johnson (1982) and Dore (1973), and that the emergence of the high-growth-period economic system is closely related to the vicissitudes of the Meiji-Taishô economic system.

With respect to the nature of the changes in the economic system that have been taking place since the late 1980s, we will examine how serious and deep those changes are and why they are occurring. Regarding the first question, during the recession in the 1990s there were arguments in favour of inflation targeting as an effective monetary policy to rehabilitate an economy plagued with deflation and lack of demand. Such a view presupposes that Japan has the same economic system and economic structure as before, so that the general price level is derived from the information set about the economic structure in the past shared by every agent; a time-consistent commitment by the monetary authority to some non-negative inflation rate is sufficient to coordinate the behaviour of the people and bring about a growth of demand.

However, it seems that the ongoing changes in the economic system are concerned not only with the role of the government *vis-à-vis* the market, or the degree of government regulation, but also with the transformation of the much broader dimension of the system, including the Japanese-style firm system and the bank–firm relationship as well as the mechanism of the government–private sector interaction. It is possible to consider that the structure of the economy was undergoing drastic changes, and there is no consensus about the emerging structure yet, so that people were not confident with the coordination of behaviour with each other: in other words, the assumption of sharing the same, stable information set about the economic structure did not hold.

In what follows, we will examine the question of how Japan's economic system is changing after the 1980s in a framework that incorporates not only the changing role of government but also the difficulties faced by the existing mechanism of interaction between the private sector and the government. It will be shown that the current structural changes are more wide-ranging than inflation-targeting theory envisages.

With respect to the question of why the Japanese economic system is changing, it is sometimes argued that the main drawback of Japan's current economic system lies in the lack of market discipline, so that structural reform in the form of liberalization and deregulation in various respects needs to be implemented in order to replace the system on the 'right' track. Quite often, this kind of assertion of structural reform, emphasizing liberalization and deregulation, reflects the view that the evolution of the Japanese economic system as a process of modernization or of convergence to some from of Western economic system or global standard system. In this view, the evolution of the economic system in Japan is simply a move from a pre-modern and backward system to a modern Western system, so that the high-growth-period economic system that is so 'Japanese' is simply a digression in the modernization process due to, for example, the heavy intervention in the economy by 'development-oriented bureaucrats'. Moreover, this view argues that recent globalization of the world economy in financial market activities and product market competition makes it inevitable that various economic systems converge, and that the current transformation of the high-growth-period economic system is nothing but a part of the global process of convergence among economic systems.

In this book, we will emphasize the mechanism of evolution of an economic system as an process of adaptation to the changes in conditions exogenous to the Japanese economy such as the technological gap with advanced countries, the stagnation and subsequent growth by neighbouring Asian countries, and the state of economic thought regarding the costs and benefits of government intervention in the economy. It will be shown that such a model is also useful in explaining the reason for structural changes that are currently taking place in the economic system of Japan. In other words, it is suggested that convergence to some global standard system is not the only hypothesis that explains the recent changes in the economic system of Japan. Needless to say, however, in order to judge whether or not Japan's current economic system is on the way to converging with some global system, considerable amount of research remains to be done, both theoretically and empirically.

1.2 ANALYTIC APPROACH

Next, let us explain the methodology or analytical framework for these issues in this book. The methodology has two characteristics: first, we will focus on the evolution not only of particular ingredients of economic systems but also of the whole economic system, in which each ingredient or property is institutionally interdependent with each other; and, second, we will examine the emergence and transformation of the high-growth-period economic system in a long-term evolution process of the economic system since the Meiji period.

Let us explain the first characteristic of our methodology. In order to capture the evolution of economic systems as a whole, an economic system in our framework is considered to be composed of three sub-systems. The first relates to the division of labor between the government and the private sector or the market, and is mainly concerned with the degree of government intervention in economic activities. The second is the sub-system within the private sector, and is related to the employment system, financial system, production system, and so on. The third sub-system captures the government–private-sector interaction regarding income-distributional impacts of government intervention in the economy. Government interventions in the economy, for whatever purposes (resource allocational, income redistributive or political), have a significant influence on the income distribution in the private sector. People in the private sector react to the intervention through organizing coalitions, and interacting with the government.

The third sub-sector, representation pattern at the government–private-sector interface, takes various forms depending on the pattern of government intervention as well as on the degree of factor mobility in the economy. When government intervention in the economy is confined to the supply of public goods to various regions, people tend to form coalitions depending on the geographical identity. When government intervention affects product and factor prices through industrial policy, people form coalitions such as labor unions or industrial associations depending on the degree of factor mobility. Quite often the formation coalitions is facilitated when people are united by a common ideology or social norms. In addition, incentives for people to form coalitions or to be involved in interest-group activities seem to be intensified whenever the state has strong power *vis-à-vis* the people, either politically or economically; People need to enhance bargaining power *vis-à-vis* the government through organizing coalitions.

Furthermore, in order to capture the dynamic changes of economic systems as a whole, we employ the following simple framework of evolutionary process of adaptation to changes of exogenous conditions. We will take up three exogenous conditions related to the historical evolution of the Japanese economic system. In the dimension of time, Japan was a latecomer in the circle of industrialized economies. In the dimension of space, the industrialization of Japan was an isolated catch-up process in the Far-East region.[7] Finally, in the dimension of economic thought, the notion of accepting and supporting government intervention in the economy gradually won popularity after Japan started its industrialization, and it retained its influence until Japan completed its catch up process. Generally speaking, adaptation to external conditions by an economy's endogenous institutions does not necessarily lead to a desirable economic system. Quite often, it results in an inefficient resource-allocation system with high economic costs (inefficiency of the economic system caused by economic mechanisms), an inadequate political and administrative system with high political costs (inefficiency of the economic system caused by political and administrative mechanisms) and disintegrated social norms of value judgments regarding representation of distributive interests at the government–private-sector interface. In such cases, it is necessary to resort to public policies of some kind in order to restore the system. If such policies are not successful, the economy stagnates and declines.

In terms of the three sub-system configuration, each sub-system is affected by the changes of exogenous conditions either directly or indirectly. Indirect influences occur because of the close institutional complimentarity between the sub-systems. While exogenous impacts are transmitted through institutional complementarity, adaptation to exogenous impacts is also carried out not only by the sub-system directly influenced by the impact but also indirectly by the other sub-systems, institutionally complementary.

Let us move on to the second characteristic of our methodology; namely, focusing on the long-term process beginning at the Meiji period. Japan started construction of a new modern state after the Meiji Restoration in 1868. New administrative, judiciary, taxation and education systems were introduced along with a socio-industrial infrastructure such as banking, transportation and communication systems. It is safe to say that a modern capitalistic system was established by around the early 1900s. For example, Ohkawa and Rosovsky (1973) call the period from the 1860s until the outbreak of the Russo-Japanese War in 1904 as the period of 'initial' modern economic growth, and consider that modern economic growth based on the absorption of Western technology was started thereafter (p. 3). Likewise, Ishii (1997) contends that the trial-and-error process of establishing modern industries (the Japanese version of on 'industrial revolution') was completed by the early 1900s, and the development based on a capitalistic system started thereafter; the recession in 1907, the first capitalistic recession caused by 'over-production' by the industrial sector, earmarks such a start.

It is important to note that the economic system established by around the early 1900s was significantly different from the one in the high-growth period. It was much more market based, and the intervention by the government was limited; although the firm system was already characterized by some kind of cooperative order, workers were highly mobile between firms; income and asset distribution was substantially unequal, and the zaibatsu and landlord systems provided the basic framework of economic life for the people. In this book, we will conduct a systematic comparison of this economic system, called the Meiji-Taishô economic system, with the high-growth-period economic system.

In other words, in analyzing the problem of the emergence and transformation of the high-growth-period economic system, we examine the evolution process of the economic system since Meiji period by focusing on two economic systems: the Meiji-Taishô economic system[8] and the high-growth-era economic system. The Meiji-Taishô economic system prevailed from the mid-1900s to mid-1920s, and is characterized by a market-based economy in the sub-system of the government–private-sector division of labor, a dominance of large shareholders in corporate governance and an indigenous industry financing by banks in the sub-system of the private sector, and a role for regional economies in representing distributional interests at the interface between the government and the private sector. A contribution to the development of the region where people lived, comprised a social norm, and people lobbied the government in order to realize policies favourable to their regions. The high-growth-period economic system prevailed during the mid-1950s to the mid-1980s, and was characterized by a pervasive role of government regulation in the sub-system of the government–private-sector division of labor, the Japanese-style firm system and the bank-dominant financial system in the sub-system of the private sector, and by inter-industrial interest representation at the interface between the government and the private sector. People recognized an instrumental value in the growth of the industry and firm to which they belonged, and lobbied the government to realize policies favourable to their industries.

Incidentally, the main reason for adopting the framework composed of two economic systems lies in the convenience of discussion about the emergence of the high-growth-period economic system: the framework makes it easier to shed light on merits and demerits of the existing hypotheses such as the wartime-shock hypothesis or the monotonic transformation hypothesis. There are additional two reasons for this. First, this book tries to draw attention to the fact that the high-growth-period economic system is not 'the Japanese economic system'. What is called Meiji-Taishô economic system in this book is an abstract concept to summarize a phase of an economic system that evolves continuously over time, just like the concept of high-growth-period economic system. It is, however, sufficiently distinct from the image of the Japanese economic system that is associated with the postwar 'economic miracle'. In order to draw a future design of the economic system in Japan, it is useful to learn from the experience in the past that is different from the postwar economic success.

Second, this book intends to re-evaluate the difficulties and policy muddles faced by the prewar economic system during the 1920s and the 1930s. Most of the recent historical analysis of Japan by economists tend to treat the World War II as a purely exogenous variable, or simply as a disaster that suddenly overlook the economy that was enjoying a rapid recovery from the World Depression during the mid 1930s. There is no need to say that such a big issue as World War II is beyond the scope of simple economic analyses. It is at the same time difficult to deny, however, that there is some factor related to the nature of the socio-economic system before the war, which needs analyses participated by economists. An analysis of the emergence and the fall of the Meiji-Taishô economic system in this book is expected to serve as a preliminary step in this direction.

1.3 THE ELEMENTS OF GROWTH

Let us give a brief review of the growth of the Japanese economy as a background for the following discussion. During the period analyzed in this book, the Japanese economy experienced a relatively high rate of economic growth, as evidenced by an increasing share of world GDP (Table 1.1). This high growth rate occurred not only during the high-growth-period economic system, but also in the years of the Meiji-Taishô system. Japan's share of world GDP increased by a factor of 1.8 between 1870 (2.43 per cent) and 1938 (4.38 per cent). This is almost comparable to the United States, whose share increased by a factor of 2.2, from 9.39 per cent to 20.69 per cent.

Any coherent analysis of Japan's system needs to explain not only postwar high growth but also the prewar transformation from a poor agrarian economy to an industrial leader in Asia. The high growth of the postwar period is due to the growth of the industrial sector manufacturing and mining), while prewar growth was in both the industrial and primary (agriculture, fishery and forestry) sectors. Tables 1.2 to 1.5 provide data on the growth and composition of GDP, and on employment composition.

The growth rate of the industrial sector has invariably been high throughout the century after 1889 (Table 1.2). However, in the prewar period, the contribution of primary-sector growth to total-GDP growth (Table 1.4) is high because of its large share in total GDP (Table 1.3). Furthermore, a very large part of the non-primary sector (the industrial and service sectors) comprised activities closely related to agriculture and other indigenous industries. A typical example is silk

Table 1.1 Percentage composition of GDP of Japan and Asian countries in world GDP

	UK	US	Asia (total)	Asia			Total of world 56 countries
				China	Japan	Other Asia	
1870	9.13	9.39	38.74	17.87	2.43	18.44	100
1900	9.55	16.92	29.76	14.09	2.71	12.96	100
1913	8.40	20.28	25.75	11.78	2.70	11.27	100
1938	7.34	20.69	24.79	10.33	4.38	10.08	100
1960	5.68	25.61	19.82	7.42	4.62	7.78	100
1970	4.62	23.67	22.13	6.94	7.66	7.53	100
1980	3.97	22.97	25.03	7.92	8.45	8.66	100
1990	3.66	21.38	31.96	11.98	8.97	11.02	100

Notes: Composition of real GDP in Geary-Khamis dollar at 1990 prices. (The Geary-Khamis method is a method of multi-country GDP comparison, now widely used in projects such as the ICP of the United Nations. The purchasing power parity dollar in this method is close to the one obtained by the Paasche index.) The number of countries for each region are: Western Europe 12; Western Offshoots (US, Canada, Australia and New Zealand) 4; South Europe 5; East Europe 7; Latin America 7; Asia 11; and Africa 10. 'Other Asia' includes Bangladesh, Myanmar, India, Indonesia, Pakistan, the Philippines, Korea, Taiwan and Thailand. The Asia's (and China's) share in 1870 is higher than now. This is reasonable. Asia's share in 1820 was much higher, and, even more so in the eighteenth century. The recent figure for Japan's share is significantly low in the Geary-Khamis method compared with the figures based on the current dollar value. The reason for this is not clarified.

Source: Calculated from Maddison (1995).

manufacturing, a leading manufacturing industry before the 1930s; production of cocoons comprised a major part of farm activity in many prefectures. The data in Table 1.5 show that more than 30 per cent of the gainfully employed worked in such indigenous industries of then on-primary sector.

The relatively high growth rates of agriculture during the period of the Meiji-Taishô system, 1.66 per cent during 1901–10 and 1.62 per cent during 1911–20, are significant factors in the analysis of the welfare and socio-political implications of the economic system. In other words, in order to arrive at a coherent explanation of the evolution of the economic system in Japan, it is necessary to focus not only on the high growth of manufacturing during the high-growth-period system but also on the sound and stable growth of agriculture and related indigenous industries during the Meiji-Taishô system.

There have been varying views of the relationship between agri-

Table 1.2 Growth rate of real GDP, by sector (per cent)

Year	Primary	Industry	Service Sector	Con- struction	Infra- structure	Total
1889–1900	1.37	5.91	3.16	5.35	9.06	2.92
1901–10	1.66	5.82	1.55	4.17	10.30	2.62
1911–20	1.62	6.40	4.26	2.30	8.74	4.13
1921–30	0.75	4.82	0.44	6.33	6.79	2.41
1931–38	1.30	8.88	3.64	9.47	2.85	4.86
1956–60	3.34	16.18	7.83	12.56	13.69	9.30
1961–70	2.10	14.50	9.25	11.85	10.98	10.12
1971–80	–0.29	5.37	5.72	2.93	3.62	4.83
1981–87	0.71	5.21	4.32	1.73	4.08	4.19

Notes: Annual compound rates calculated from seven-year moving averages. Prewar figures are in 1934–36 prices; postwar are in 1985 prices. Infrastructure includes transportation, communications, and public utilities.

Source: Minami (1992).

Table 1.3 Sectoral composition of real GDP (per cent)

Year	Primary	Industry	Services	Construction	Infra- Structure
1888	41.5	8.1	46.3	2.6	1.5
1900	34.6	11.3	47.5	3.5	3.1
1910	31.5	15.4	42.8	4.0	6.3
1920	24.7	19.0	43.2	3.4	9.7
1930	20.9	24.0	35.6	4.9	14.6
1938	15.9	32.4	32.3	6.9	12.5
1955	16.7	12.6	54.0	8.5	8.2
1960	12.6	17.1	50.4	9.9	10.0
1970	5.9	25.2	46.6	11.5	10.8
1980	3.6	26.5	50.7	9.6	9.6

Notes: Annual compound rates calculated from seven-year moving averages. Prewar figures are in 1934–36 prices; postwar are in 1985 prices. Infrastructure includes transportation, communications, and public utilities.

Source: Minami (1992).

culture and industry in early Japan development. Ohkawa (1972) emphasized their concurrent growth, and Nakamura (1971) drew attention to the balanced growth of the modern and indigenous sectors, prior to World War I. This view is also endorsed by Hayami

Table 1.4 Contribution to GDP growth by sector (per cent)

Year	Primary	Industrial	Services	Others
1888–1900	17.8	19.3	50.6	12.3
1901–10	20.8	29.2	26.8	23.2
1911–20	11.0	26.5	44.0	18.5
1921–30	7.1	42.4	7.0	43.5
1930–38	4.9	50.5	25.4	19.2

Note: This table shows the share of GDP growth in Table 1.2 accounted for by each sector, so each row adds to 100%. Others include construction, transportation, communications and public utilities. Prewar figures are in 1934–36 prices; postwar are in 1985 prices.

Source: Minami (1992).

Table 1.5 Distribution of gainfully employed by sector (per cent)

Year		Non-primary	
	Primary	Modern	Indigenous
1891–95	66.1	2.9	31.0
1901–05	64.0	4.7	31.3
1911–15	60.7	7.6	31.7
1911–25	49.2	11.7	39.1
1931–35	46.4	12.1	41.5

Source: Nakamura (1985).

(1973). On the other hand, Smith (1959) and Nakamura (1966) emphasized the role of agricultural growth during the pre-Meiji period, and argued that the accumulation of savings and transformation of the labor market provided the precondition for modern growth. Both views are correct: agriculture and indigenous industries started growing before the Meiji restoration of 1868, particularly from the early 19th century, and this growth continued until World War I.

The high rate of growth in the high-growth-period economic system is usually explained not only by exogenous factors such as the widened technological gap with Western economies and the large pool of cheap labor in rural areas, but also by endogenous institutional mechanisms such as the effectiveness of industrial policy, Japanese-style employment practices, and the informational efficiency of the main bank system. In Chapter 7, I argue that, among those endogenous institutional mechanisms, the most important was a mechanism that provided incentives to behave with a long time horizon and to implement relation-specific investments. The high rate of growth in the Meiji-Taishô economic system, on the other hand, is usually explained by exogenous factors such as the diffusion of agricultural technology and expansion of domestic and overseas markets in the case of agriculture, and the technological and labor-market factors common to the high-growth period in the case of industry. In addition to this, I will suggest that there were also endogenous institutional mechanisms that are characteristic of the Meiji-Taishô economic system such as skill formation by tenant farmers and the mobilization of human resources to corporate management.

In the following chapters, Chapter 2 explains basic analytical framework of this book. Chapters 3 to 5 analyze the emergence, mechanism, and transformation of the Meiji-Taishô economic system. Chapters 6 to 8 provide discussion on the emergence, mechanism, and transformation of the high-growth-period economic system. Chapter 9 summarizes the major propositions set out in this book.

NOTES

1. Hoshi and Kashyap (2001) also find differences in the financial systems, although I do not agree with some aspects of their analysis (Teranishi 2003a).
2. The war with China began in 1937, and the Pacific War in 1940.
3. The recent assertion by Dower (1999) that the postwar Japanese economic system is a SCAPnese (combination of SCAP and Japanese) system, emphasizing the continued regulation on the economy by the occupation forces, is considered to be along similar lines.
4. The rekindling of labor disputes after the war is closely related to the reform activities implemented by the occupation force that include not only legitimization of labor unions but also thorough-going land reform and *zaibatsu* dissolution.
5. At the same time, the dominance of the Liberal Democratic Party was established. Nakamura calls this system as '1955 system'.
6. Gordon (1993) draws attention to the monotonic nature characteristic of the hypotheses of Johnson and Dore.
7. Abramoviz (1990) and Crafts and Toniolo (1996) consider that the economic development of Europe after World War II until the oil shock period was also a catch-up process. The catch-up of Japan was different from the European case in that it was economic growth based not only on utilizing imported foreign technology but also on selective acceptance of a Western-type transformation of social and cultural systems. The concept of modern economic growth in Kuznetz (1966) captures these two aspects well.
8. Earlier, I called this system the Taishô system (for example, Teranishi 2000), but Meiji-Taishô is preferable because it includes part of the Meiji period (1868–1912).

2. Analytical framework

To analyze the evolution of Japan's economy since the late 19th century, the concept of an economic system is used. An economic system or institution is defined as the set of rules that constrain the economic behavior and interactions of economic agents. The rules are formal – that is, determined through legislative processes and formal contracts – and informal, such as customs and behavioral patterns. For example, tax rates and tax standards are formal rules, while the main bank system is an informal rule.

A rule becomes a rule as an institution (that is, part of the economic system) when most people do not want to change it. In other words, the economic system is a bundle of rules in equilibrium configurations.

An economic system evolves either as a response to the changes in exogenous conditions or endogenously through interactive mechanisms. During the period when the changes in exogenous conditions are slow, this process can be sufficiently stable to give the system in a specific period its own name. That is done in this book: I name two identifiable economic systems in the evolution of Japan's economic system.

In this analysis, Japan's economic system is composed of three sub-systems, and changes in the system have taken place in the context of three exogenous conditions present for most of the time since Japan began to modernize. The framework's general characteristics are given in the first section. This is followed by presentation of the sub-systems. Next, the two evolutionary phases of Japan's economic system that most concern us are introduced and related to the sub-systems. Then, the exogenous conditions are discussed. Finally, brief overviews of each of the two economic systems are presented.

2.1 CHARACTERISTICS OF THE FRAMEWORK

Evolution is intrinsic to an economic system: the failure of an incumbent system to adapt successfully, or at all, ultimately leads to its replacement. Systems have costs, and tracking those costs is key to identifying the health of the system and, thus, the pressure for changes. All this takes place in a specific intellectual climate and set of social norms, both of which also change. This section looks at these three characteristics of the framework.

2.1.1 Evolution

When a sufficiently large number of economic agents come to have incentives to change existing rules and institutions, and they devote resources to that purpose, a process of evolution is started. Thus, new rules can take the place of old ones, and become part of the economic system when equilibrium is attained through an interactive process among economic agents. This kind of theory of institutional evolution is extensively investigated in North (1990a) in the context of transaction cost theory, and is given a game-theoretic summary in Aoki (2001).

There are incentives to change rules or institutions in three cases: when the economic costs of the existing rules are too high, when the political costs are too high, and when the rules become incongruent with prevailing social norms and value judgments or are perceived as inappropriate to a new norm. Changes in economic and political costs, and of social norms and value judgments, occur as a response to changes in conditions. These can be exogenous or generated from within the system as it evolves.

Economic costs are too high when following the rules results in an inefficient allocation of resources or a malfunctioning of the growth mechanism. Political costs can be too high because of inefficient government administration or a wasteful political regime. In these two cases, because the profits or political benefits (more votes or political support) of rule change are expected to be greater than the opportunity costs, reformers have an incentive to devote resources to rule-changing activities.

A change of rules is a dynamic process in the sense of a shift of an equilibrium to a new equilibrium. It is characterized by strategic complementarity (that is, incentives for an agent to follow a rule increase as more agents adopt the rule) and entails considerable time and resource costs. Moreover, the rationality of individuals is by no means perfect, and markets are plagued with asymmetrical information and incompleteness, so that a state of multiple equilibrium is a common outcome. Therefore, even when significant effort has been devoted to defining and instituting the rule change, the result might not be what was expected. Quite often a dynamic evolutionary process results in a sub-optimal equilibrium.

Although institutions to some extent have their own self-correcting mechanisms, it is not always appropriate to leave institutional reform to endogenous evolutionary mechanisms alone. Public policy to complement the endogenous mechanism is definitely needed in many situations. One such case arises because an economy, plagued with high economic and political costs and lax social norms and value judgments, tends to lose in international competition among economic systems. Relatedly, North (1981) argues that a state with inefficient property rights tends to be less prosperous than one with stronger rights; high enforcement costs of contracts and distortion of the incentive system result in high transaction costs, and hence inefficient resource allocation.

A discussion of public policy cannot avoid the normative issue of what is a desirable economic system. The literature on social choice has accumulated vast theoretical results regarding the efficiency of resource allocation and distributive fairness. The aim of this book requires a more pragmatic approach, however.

2.1.2 Political Costs

I examine economic costs arising mainly from allocational inefficiency, political costs arising mainly from income distributional conflicts, and changing social norms and value systems separately for each of the model's sub-systems. This should enable us to identify the areas and direction of reform that reduce economic and political costs to an internationally competitive level and lead to broadly agreeable social norms and values.

Thus, the notion of political costs in this book stands in the following relationship with the concept of costs in the transaction-cost theory of politics proposed by North (1990b) and Dixit (1996). Defining transaction costs as costs of measuring and enforcing agreements, North argues that, compared to economic markets, political markets are far more prone to inefficiency from transaction costs. This is because it is extraordinarily difficult to measure what is being exchanged in political markets and, in consequence, to enforce agreements.

Dixit, applying this transaction-costs theory of politics to the actual contracts between constituents and legislators, and between legislators and agencies implementing policies, argues that principal–agent problems like opportunistic behavior are liable to occur, and this consequently makes the adoption of inefficient policies likely.

Costs in the transaction-costs theory of politics are those associated with inefficient political and administrative activities, while the concept of political costs in this book refers to costs in the form of losses in resource allocation, both static and dynamic, incurred by an inefficiently working political and administrative system within an economic system. Specifically, it is suggested that such resource costs arise mainly through malfunctioning of the government–private-sector interface regarding income-distributional conflicts. To what extent these resource costs are caused by transaction costs in a North–Dixit sense is left as an open question.

2.1.3 Social Norms and Intellectual Climate

The sustainability of an economic system is quite often influenced by the strength of the social norms and value system. In this connection, note that all societies have social norms of some sort, and their existence means costs for individuals in the sense of restricting the range of possible activities and value judgments.

Through an examination of free-rider problems in collective action, Olson (1965) maintains that the larger the size of a group, the more likely it is that collective action fails, because the benefit for an individual member of the group gets smaller, while the costs of maintaining the group rise. North (1981) criticizes this and emphasizes that ideology or social norms play a role in preventing free-rider problems, and bring about successful large-group behavior. To the extent that the participants believe the system fair, the costs of enforcing the rules and property rights are enormously reduced by the simple fact that the individuals will not disobey the rules or violate property rights even when a private costs/benefit calculations would not make such action worth while (North 1981). In other words, ideology or social norms have the power to preclude private-profit-pursuing behavior, and to let people serve the public interests of a socio-economic system. Social norms could be substitutes for laws and their enforcement mechanism.

2.2 THE THREE SUB-SYSTEMS

In order to analyze the transformation of Japan's economy over time, a broad framework is necessary. However, the existing literature on the economic system of Japan, in particular that of the high-growth period, has focused either on private-sector characteristics such as the Japanese-firm system and the main-bank system, or on government behavior, often characterized as developmental, such as policy-based lending. To get a complete picture, both sectors, and their interaction, are important. Hence, in this analysis, the economic system is composed of three sub-systems. Their basic features are presented in Table 2.1.

Table 2.1 Sub-systems in the economic system

Government–market division of labor	
	This is mainly concerned with the modality and degree of government intervention in economic activities, ranging from predominantly relying on market mechanisms to extensive intervention (including 'developmental government').
Government–private-sector interface	
	This captures government and private-sector interaction, especially regarding income-distributional effects of government intervention in the economy. The interactions involve interest groups formed by class, region, industry, etc.
Private sector	
	This relates to the economic system within the private sector, such as corporate system, the financial system, employment system, production system, and so on.

Each sub-system is affected by changes in exogenous conditions and state variables directly, and, because of the close institutional complimentarity among the sub-systems, indirectly. Adaptation is thus a response to both direct impacts and the adaptations of the other sub-systems. In other words, these sub-systems interact – indeed, the second sub-system is about interaction. Government intervention in the economy for whatever purposes (resource allocation, income redistribution, political) affects income distribution in the private sector. People in the private sector react to the intervention by organizing coalitions, and interact with the government.

Representation at the government–private-sector interface depends on the pattern of government intervention, as well as on the degree of factor mobility in the economy. When government intervention is confined to the supply of public goods to various regions, people tend to form coalitions depending on geographical identity. When intervention affects product and factor prices through industrial policy, people form coalitions such as labor unions and industrial associations. Quite often, coalition formation is facilitated when people are united by common ideology or social norms.

2.2.1 Government–Market Division of Labor

The extent to which the economic system should rely on market signals or government involvement is a central theme of political economy. Government involvement is expressed not only in directives (regulation and administrative guidance) but also in the government's share of the economy (expenditures, including transfer payments, production, and ownership). This section looks at three factors that largely determine the division of labor and at historical trends in the extent of government involvement.

2.2.1.1 Factors affecting the division

The division of labor depends on three factors: the degree of market failure, the state of economic thought with respect to market failures, and the behavior of the bureaucratic system.

Market failure arises from the inability of the market to 'optimize' income distribution and from various market imperfections caused by such factors as technological externality, increasing returns to scale, and asymmetric information. The actual degree of failure is dependent on the growth phase of an economic system. For example, an economy in catch-up – that is, being able to grow quickly simply by adopting existing technologies and management practices from the rest of the world – tends toward a supply shortage of skilled labor and industry-level information owing to strong externality. In such an economy, weakening of traditional community mechanisms regarding mutual assistance and group activity can reduce the effectiveness of reputation accumulated through repeated transaction, possibly giving rise to serious agency problems.

The extent to which government intervenes in the market is determined not only by the actual degree of market failure but also by the state of economic thought – in particular, the consensus on what sorts of economic policies are appropriate. In other words, the realized market failure and the degree of government intervention do not necessarily correspond exactly. This is because the supply of public goods and government intervention is subject to government failures, and the evaluation of the relative costs of market failures and government failures depends crucially on the state of economic thought and value judgments.

Economic thought – including theoretical and policy-prescriptive – has had significant influence on income–distribution issues such as redistribution policy and the role of the welfare state. The remarkable increase in government intervention after World War II, in terms of both expenditure and regulation, is attributable in large part to intellectually vigorous advocates of alternatives to capitalist and free-market models.

Interventionists were aided by the general public perception that the Great Depression of the 1930s was due primarily to a failure of the capitalist system, the belief that interventionist policies were instrumental in ending the Depression (for example, the New Deal in the United States), and the seeming success of socialism and communism. Keynsian economics was a driving force for the role of government in economic stabilization after World War II. To this was added a general move by advanced economies toward becoming welfare states. (This originated in the social security system of Bismarck's Germany and the National Insurance Act in Britain before World War I, and became mainstream through the implementation of comprehensive and centralized welfare programs proposed in 1942 by the Beverage Report.) Further, the emergence of a Third World and the promotion of developmental Big Push policies to implement import substitution spread government intervention through developing countries during the 1950s and 1960s.

Thus, from advocacy and historical events, new social attitudes emphasized the costs of market failures and approved government intervention.

The degree of government intervention in the economy is affected by the behavior of the bureaucracy. It is often pointed out that bureaucracy has an endogenous expansion mechanism. Thus, the law of expansion of state activities put forward by Wagner (1892) emphasizes the extension of state activities regarding culture and welfare. Then there is the displacement effect noted by Peacock and Wiseman (1961), emphasizing the weakening of tax resistance at the time of social crisis such as a war or an economic panic. The power balance between the bureaucratic class and the private entrepreneur class has also been a factor affecting the degree of government intervention, a major factor in the case of Japan.

2.2.1.2 Trends in government involvement

Starting with the Great Depression and militarization in the 1930s, the 20th century witnessed significant expansion of government intervention in economies world-wide. This had two aspects: the share of government spending and regulation. Both have seen increases in countries with advanced, market-based economies since the 1930s, if not earlier.

Kaizuka (1984) investigates expenditure data with respect to the postwar period, and finds that (1) the expansion of government expenditures is due not only to transfer payments but also to other expenditures, and (2) the increase was caused by expansion of expenditure not only on pure public goods such as military and general government services but also on quasi-public goods and private goods. Such an expansion of expenditures for other than social transfers suggests that increased concerns over market failures caused extension of government activities into areas of private-goods production during the period.

2.2.2 Government–Private-sector Interface

The effects of government intervention regarding income distribution are different depending on the modality of intervention. People generally seek interventions with outcomes favorable to themselves. They do this individually or, quite frequently, through collective action in the form of coalitions or groups. Coalitions can be based on various identities: classes, industries, ethnic groups, religions, regions, and so on. What is important here is that the pattern of representation of distributional interests differs considerably depending on the pattern of intervention. This is because the specific impact on income distribution is a function of the pattern of intervention.

When government intervention is directed only to the supply of pure public goods, as dictated by the classic liberal view of the role of government, the intervention need not have much impact because the exclusion principle does not apply to pure public goods. However, people may form coalitions based on regions. Thus, for example, they may lobby to have a park close to their residence. When government intervention extends to other public goods, or to private goods, the incentive for interest representation through regional coalitions becomes stronger, and competition for public goods among regions intensifies.

When government interventions involve such areas as income redistribution, industrial policy, and macro stabilization policy, there are different effects on income distribution among various industries and classes. In such cases, the pattern of coalition representing distributive interests depends on the mobility of economic factors among industries. Whenever there are immobile factors specific to each

industry, people form a coalition based on the industry to which they belong, while coalitions based on the class to which people belong are formed when all factors are mobile among various industries.

During Japan's high-growth period, the skill of labor was largely firm– or industry–specific, so representation of distributive interest at the government–private-sector interface was based on industry. In the socio-democratic system in Europe, labor is mobile, although functionally fixed, so representation is based on class. Box 2.1 develops the concept of coalition formation more fully.

BOX 2.1 COALITION FORMATION

As is well known in international trade theory, a policy that raises the output price of a particular industry has a positive distributional effect on the economic factor intensively utilized in the industry, whenever economic factors are freely mobile among industries. The positive effect is enjoyed by all the people who own the factor, not only in the industry but in other industries. Therefore, in this case people form coalitions depending on the factor they own, irrespective of the industry they belong to, and lobby against those who own other factors. In other words, under the condition of perfect mobility of economic factors, interest representation based on class, determined by the ownership of economic factors, prevails.

Conversely, when each industry has factor– specific factors immobile among sectors, a policy that raises the price of a particular industry has a positive distributional effect on the factor specific to the industry, and a negative effect on the factors specific to other industries. In this case, coalitions representing distributional interests are formed according to the industry to which people belong and give rise to inter–industrial distributive conflicts rather than class conflicts.

Let us examine this point further by comparing the Heckscher – Ohlin model and the specific–factor model in trade theory.

The Heckscher – Ohlin model assumes perfect factor mobility. Further, assuming that there are two industries (1 and 2) and two factors of production (capital and labor), and that industry 1 uses labor more intensively than industry 2, it is shown that an increase in the price of industry 1

relative to that of industry 2 will cause an increase in wage rates and a decrease in profit rates.
Moreover, the increase in wage rates is proportionally greater than the increase in the price of industry 1's output (Stolper - Samuelson Theorem). In other words, when factors are perfectly mobile, a policy that increases the price of labor- intensive production benefits workers in that industry. Capitalists lose and the interests of workers and those of capitalists diverge. Under such conditions, a coalition of labor and capital for the protection of the industries cannot be realized. A rise in wages benefits workers in capital- intensive industries, and labor as a whole has an incentive to lobby the state against the interests of capitalists as a whole. Representation of distributive interests by economic classes is a natural outcome in this case.

When an economy is composed of 'pure' workers and 'pure' capitalists, only distributive conflicts emerge between the workers and capitalists as a class. When, instead, each economic agent earns both wage and profit income, distributive conflicts are governed by the capital- labor ratio of median voters, provided that wage income is evenly distributed. When, for example, the capital- labor ratio of the median voter is lower than the average capital- labor ratio (the national endowment ratio), a policy favorable to capital accumulation may not be adopted (Alesina and Rodrick, 1994).

The specific-factor model, on the other hand, assumes one factor, say capital, is perfectly mobile between industries while the other, say labor with industry-specific skills, is specific to each industry. An increase in the price of the output of industry 1 relative to that of industry 2 causes a shift of capital from industry 2 to industry 1. Output of industry 1 rises, and that of industry 2 decreases. The profit rate on capital increases, but proportionately less than the rise in price of output 1, implying a decline in the real rate of profit in terms of output 1's price and a rise in real rate of profit in terms of output 2's price. In this case, it is not possible to say if the capitalists are better off or worse off. However, workers with skills specific to industry 1 are clear beneficiaries. This is because the real profit rate in terms of the output 1 price falls, so that the rise in incomes of workers with industry 1 specific skills is proportionately more than the rise in the output 1 Price. Since the output 1 price rises relative to the output 2 price, the real income of workers with industry 1 specific skills increases unambiguously. Conversely, it can be shown that the real income of workers with industry 2 specific skills definitely falls. In other words, immobile and industry-specific factors of production definitely benefit from a policy that increases the output price of the industry that uses these in abundance.

Workers with industry- specific skill therefore have an incentive to form a coalition to lobby for policies favoring their industry. Since the workers in other industries are clear losers from such policies, there tend to be significant conflicts of interest among industries using workers with industry-specific skills. Industry-based representation of distributional interests is a reasonable institutionall arrangement in this case. Because the gains of capitalists in real terms are ambiguous and depend on the deflator, it is not certain that capitalists would form a coalition with workers. However, managers with industry-specific skills would join with workers, and it is natural to assume that lobbying is conducted on an inter-industry basis. For more discussion on this point, refer to Nelson (1988, p. 803), Mayer (1984), and Baldwin (1984).

The term 'intermediate organization' is sometimes used to denote the private-sector coalitions at the government–private-sector interface. The term was used originally by Tocqueville as a generic expression for such organizations as churches, political associations, jury systems, and the like, which complement the working of democracy. Inoki (2001) uses the concept to denote organizations to complement the working of a market system, such as NGOs, labor unions, management associations, consumer groups, and so on. The interface between the government and the private sector has become an active area of research. Box 2.2 gives a brief overview of existing literature on the role of intermediate organizations and interest group politics.

BOX 2.2 INTEREST GROUP POLITICS

This book tries to incorporate the behavior of intermediate organizations such as regional communities and industrial associations with the working of economic systems. In the existing literature the role of intermediate organizations at the interface between the government and the private sector has been analyzed under the heading of the role of interest groups in the endogenous determination of policies.

Becker (1983) is the influential work in this area. Utilizing the concept of political influence function that determines policies with political pressure as inputs, he analyses the mechanism and effects of non-cooperative competition for political influence by pressure groups. The basic stance behind his assertion is the recognition that the preference of voters is not a crucial independent force in the political process. Such a stance provides a clear contrast to a series of macroeconomic analysis that the employs medium voter theorem in analyzing the effects of income distribution on the political determination of macro policies, such as Alesina and Rodrik (1994) and Persson and Tabellini (1990).

Binswanger and Deininger (1997) applies Becker's model to the agrarian policy, arguing that political outcomes in an agrarian economy are by and large a consequence of political bargaining among interest groups. Krueger (1992), however, maintains that although group interaction influences political decision process, it was the ideological environment that sanctioned discrimination against agriculture in developing economies.

Interest group politics is also examined in broader frameworks. Ranis and Mahmood (1992) analyses such an issue with respect to a comparison of economic development between East Asia and Latin America. The relationship between political and administrative organization and interest group politics is examined by Laffont (2000) by use of contract theory. Further, in a political science framework, Alesina and Rosenthal (1995) studies the relationship of policy determination and partisan politics.

2.2.3 Private Sector

The private-sector sub-system evolves through an interactive process among private economic agents who, usually, optimize under the rules of the game and are ready to devote resources to changing rules whenever they find it worthwhile. Such a process of evolution is dependent on exogenous conditions as well as various state variables such as levels of knowledge and education, social infrastructure, distribution of wealth, and so on. In addition, it is important to note that the process involves interaction with other sub-systems owing to the institutional complementarity among sub-systems. This is developed more fully later.

2.3 THE ECONOMIC SYSTEMS

From the beginning of Japan's modern era in the mid-19th century to the present day, its economic system has evolved through two identifiable phases. These are the Meiji-Taishô system and the high-growth-period system.

The existing literature has focused mainly on a comparison of the postwar, high-growth period system with the wartime system. However, for a full understanding of the high-growth system the comparison must be broader. There are several reasons for this. For one, the exogenous conditions that framed the working of the high-growth period system originated earlier, during the late 19th century. In addition, the wartime system clearly was not sustainable, and it was imposed.

Thus, to add to understanding of the high-growth system and what might follow it, this study concentrates on comparing it to what I call the Meiji-Taishô economic system. That system, established by the early 1900s, was significantly different from the one in the high-growth period. The major features of each, in relation to the three sub-systems outlined above, are presented in Table 2.2.

As the comparison shows, the Meiji-Taishô system was much more market based, and intervention by the government was limited. Although the firm system was already characterized by some kind of cooperative order, workers were highly mobile between firms. Income and asset distribution was substantially unequal, and zaibatsu and landlords provided the basic framework of economic life of the people.

The interface between the government and private sector is quite different. In the earlier system, a contribution to the development of the region where a person lived constituted a social norm, and people lobbied the government in order to realize policies favorable to their regions. In the later system, people recognized an instrumental value in the growth of the industries and firms to which they belong, and lobbied the government to realize favorable policies to their industries.

Table 2.2 Characteristics of Japan's economic systems

Sub-system	Meiji-Taishô economic system	High-growth-period economic system
(Peak time period)	Mid-1900s to early 1920	Mid-1950s to 1980s
Government–Market division of labor	Market mechanism	Government intervention
Government–Private sector interface	Inter-regional	Inter-industrial
Private sector	Large shareholders	'Japanese-style' firms
	Banks finance indigenous industries	Bank-centered financial system

The differences between the two systems can be related in large part to the enormous shocks delivered by war and its aftermath. Militarization of the economy in the 1930s and 1940s meant discontinuous changes in the economic system, including introduction of new traits. In addition, postwar reforms, including zaibatsu dissolution and land reform laid the groundwork for substantial equality of both assets and income. The result was a significantly different economic system after the war.

Both the Meiji-Taishô and high-growth-period systems emerged through interactive processes among a broad strata of people. In other words, they are systems consciously chosen by the people. The Meiji-Taishô system become a coherent system during the first decade of the 1900s and gave way to the militarization of the 1930s. It was established to implement the building-up of the new socio-economic system after the Sino-Japanese War (1894–95) and the Russo-Japanese War (1904–05) on two foundations: the rise of nationally integrated markets and promulgation of the Meiji Constitution (1889) with the subsequent implicit agreement regarding the division of labor between the government and the private sector. The high-growth-period system was established to pursue postwar catch-up on two foundations: the accomplishment of postwar reforms and the establishment of what is commonly called the 1955 system (a working democracy despite the government being continually controlled by just one party, the Liberal Democrats (LDP) beginning in 1955).

In comparison, the developmental (*shokusan kôgyô*) economic system during the early Meiji period (1870s) was an impatient attempt at a big-bang catch-up implemented by a government concerned with establishing its power base both domestically and *vis-à-vis* possible Western encroachment. Likewise, the wartime system from the mid-1930s to the mid-1940s was organized by the military and related bureaucrats. (The wartime period for Japan can be dated from July 1937 when the invasion of China was begun.)

In other words, before establishment of the Meiji-Taishô system, the design and monitoring of the economic system were left solely in the hands of bureaucrats and politicians, based on the interests of *hanbatsu*. *Hanbatsu* is a fief-based political coalition; the senior leaders of the Meiji government were drawn almost exclusively from the former feudal ruling class, primarily lower-level samurai, and dominated by members from two specific fiefs (*han*). Even the main taxpayers, farmers and landlord were excluded from political decision-making. After the 1889 promulgation of the constitution and the opening of the Diet, however, not only farmers and landlords but also newly rising manufacturers and merchants could participate in system design and establishment. Likewise, after 1945, decision-making regarding the economic system was opened up to a broad strata of constituents including women, labor unions, and left-wing parties.

Moreover, the systems were regarded by economic agents at the time as sustainable for a reasonable time span, and they behaved with that sustainability in mind. Sustainability is attained only when the players believe that each does not have incentives to change the rules. Such a belief is shared only when economic and political costs do not change drastically and there is a stable social norm. Without a belief in sustainability, it is difficult to achieve a stable macroeconomy and growth because investment behavior is a complex process that is possible only with such a belief.

For both systems, the socio-political environment provided favorable conditions for establishment of an agreed interface between the government and the private sector regarding distributive conflicts. Moreover, both were established on relatively stable exogenous conditions (discussed in the next section). These are basic conditions for the emergence of the belief in the sustainability of the economic systems.

2.4 EXOGENOUS CONDITIONS

The dynamic changes in Japan's economic system have taken place in the context of three exogenous conditions present for most of the time since Japan began to modernize. This section examines the long-term trend and effects of these conditions, which are presented in Table 2.3.

Table 2.3 Exogenous conditions framing the evolution of Japan's economic systems

- Japan was playing 'catch-up' until the mid-1970s to around 1980.
- Japan was the only Asian country to industrialize significantly until the Asian Tigers began to emerge in the 1980s.
- Government intervention in the economy was not accepted during the period before World War I. It came to be accepted from the time of World War II until around 1980.

The Meiji-Taishô system was established and prospered under conditions of the stagnation of other Asian countries and Japan's catch-up industrialization as a latecomer. Because of the prevalence of economic thought that emphasized free competition, the economic system was characterized by extensive reliance on market mechanism. It was followed by the high-growth-period economic system, which approved and emphasized the role of government in the economy. The Meiji-Taishô system fell into crisis when difficulties encountered in the catch-up process increased economic costs significantly and the spread of economic thought emphasizing market failures resulted in a policy muddle and, hence, serious coordination failures.

The high-growth-period system is now obliged to retreat or adjust as these exogenous conditions have undergone drastic change. As catch-up was completed, other Asian countries achieved rapid growth, and economic thought shifted from the role of the government to emphasis on the free-market mechanism, the system's economic costs increased considerably. Contributing to the rising costs were neglect of comparative advantage and failure of the financial system to evolve successfully from being dominated by the banks. In addition, the move to global marketism is now causing large political costs. Captured by the vested interests of existing industries and their regulators, the government–private-sector interface has become significantly costly, giving rise to inadequate political and administrative responses to rapidly changing technological circumstances.

2.4.1 Isolated Catch-up in East Asia

The evolution of the economic system in Japan has been considerably influenced by its location and historical timing: isolated catch-up in East Asia. This is reflected in two important characteristics of Japan's economic system since the 1920s, especially during the high-growth period. First is the rise of a dual structure, which was manifested in a significant wage differential between large firms and small and medium firms. The other is the emergence of a quasi-autarchic – 'full-set' – industrial structure in the sense of having all types of modern industries, irrespective of factor endowment and technology.

To demonstrate isolated catch-up, Table 1.1 (p.11) shows the changing shares in the world economy of Japan, China, other Asian countries, the UK and the United States. Japan had a rising share from the 1870s until the 1970s, while China and the rest of Asia as a group had declining shares. Subsequently, China and other Asian countries have increased their shares. This is because a rapid catch-up occurred in many of these countries, partly the result of adoption of incentive policies, and partly from investment by Japan and other developed countries.

The engine of international convergence – catch-up – is usually technology transfer from advanced (leader) to less-advanced (laggard) countries. For laggards, the technological age of its capital stock is much greater than the chronological age, while for leaders the technological and chronological ages are the same. This means a leader's embodied technological progress is limited by the advance of knowledge over the life of its capital instruments, while a laggard can make a large leap by substituting modern equipment for instruments that were possibly already obsolete when installed (Abramovitz 1986, 1990). According to Abramovitz, the speed of convergence depends on the social capability of the laggard and the degree of technological congruence between the laggard and the leader.

Catch-up has occurred as the influence of the epoch characterized by the explosion of technological knowledge since the mid-18th century has diffused the world over, primarily from advanced countries. The diffusion has usually been associated with modernization of socio-economic structures, including changes in industrial structure, institutions and social norms. The notion of modern economic growth advanced by Kuznets (1966) conceptualizes such a phenomenon. The economic development of Japan was also catch-up growth in this sense.

2.4.1.1 When did catch-up end?

For the purposes of this book catch-up is concerned only with technological levels. The most detailed econometric study puts the end of catch-up in the 1970s, and this is consistent with other approaches. Specifically, Jorgenson and Nishimizu (1978), using an aggregate growth-accounting model during 1952–74, found that by 1973–74, the level of Japanese technology overtook that in the United States (although there still remained a substantial gap between the two countries in output per unit of labor, due to the difference in capital intensity of production). Jorgenson, Kuroda and Nishimizu (1987) applied a similar method to the disaggregated model of production accounts comprising 30 industries. They found that the Japanese manufacturing industries belonging to raw material processing and the intermediate goods manufacturing sector closed the technology gap with the United States by 1979; three light manufacturing industries (lumber and wood products, miscellaneous manufacturing industries, and precision instruments) also closed the gap by that time. Although some productivity gaps still remain with respect to some of the light manufacturing and investment goods manufacturing, the gap is expected to be reduced in the near future. Overall, they conclude that by 1979 Japan was no longer a latecomer in technology.

The attitude of the government regarding technology is also significant. The government had an active policy to promote technology imports to facilitate catch-up. In addition, foreign exchange rationing, which existed for an extended time after World War II, was used to facilitate technology imports. The regulation was considerably relaxed from the end of the 1960s, and finally completely liberalized in 1980. (See Goto 1993, and Odagiri and Goto 1996, for more on the rationing.)

2.4.1.2 Dual structure

The rise of a dual structure was manifested in the significant wage differential between large firms and small and medium firms (SMEs). Catch-up was implemented mainly by large firms in the modern sector. Since the utilization of foreign technology required skilled industrial labor, which was not abundant, partly because of under-development of higher (college) and vocational education, large firms undertook on-the-job training (OJT) and other measures from the 1920s. In contrast, firms in the indigenous sector and SMEs relied mostly on unskilled labor, which was elastically supplied from the rural areas, and so was an unlimited supply, as in Fei and Ranis (1964) and Lewis (1955). In this way, the dual structure emerged during the 1920s.

With the rise of an internal labor market for skilled labor in large firms, labor markets became segmented. The excess demand for skilled labor and the excess supply of unskilled labor resulted in wage differentials between large firms on the one hand, and SMEs and the indigenous sector on the other.

In producing modern manufacturing goods, large firms relied on skilled workers and managers, but at the same time hired large numbers of unskilled workers. Their products, still relatively low in quality compared with Western firms, found markets in Japan as well as neighboring Asian countries. During the interwar period, access to Asian markets was quite frequently impeded by the well-established colonial structure and by competition from equally low-cost (low-wage) producers. Large firms, however, expanded their market utilizing their strong marketing and information resources (Howe 1996).

Initially, the dual structure attracted public attention mainly because of the need for social policy for the indigenous sector, which suffered seriously through the credit crunch during the Showa depression (1930–31). After recovery of the economy in the mid-1930s, the 'rationalization' (modernization) of SMEs in export industries was emphasized from the viewpoint of foreign exchange shortages. It was after World War II that the dual structure became highlighted as a major economic problem from the viewpoint of an anti-monopoly movement against large firms and the social inequality issue regarding the differential wage structure. Shinohara (for example, 1962) and other leading economists at the time emphasized this viewpoint, as did the 1957 issue of the Economic Planning Agency's annual White Paper on the economy.

Promulgation of the Basic Law for Small and Medium Enterprises (*Chûshô Kigyô Kihon Hô*) in 1963 was the landmark for this. The situation is quite similar to the protection policy for agriculture, where rice-price policy after 1960 came to be implemented from the viewpoint of 'correcting' the income differential between agriculture and non-agriculture.

After the 1970s, the dual structure, or SME problem, changed from being a social policy issue to one of adjusting inter-industrial interests, giving rise to legislation to prevent entry by large firms into areas dominated by incumbent SMEs. These include the restriction of large-scale retailers (*Daikibo Kouriten Hô*) in 1973 and restricting the activity of large firms (*Bunya Chôsei Hô*) in 1977.

Industries with a large number of SMEs, such as consumer goods, distribution and commerce, and construction, obtained huge rents from the interest-representation system because of their strong political influence. The behavior of these industries, however, became the target of criticism by consumers and the new middle class during the second half of the 1980s, leading to a significant rise in the political costs of the high-growth-period system.

2.4.1.3 'Full-set' industrial structure

Another important effect of isolated catch-up was the emergence of a quasi-autarchic – 'full set' – industrial structure in the sense of having all types of modern industries, irrespective of factor endowment and technology. This emerged in three stages.

First was the impact of World War I. The cessation of imports of heavy and chemical products from Europe triggered an unexpected boom in establishing new firms in steel, shipbuilding, electric machinery, and chemicals – a process termed secondary import substitution. Moreover, exports of munitions-related goods to Europe and the United States flourished. As a result, by 1918 Japan was equipped with a full set of heavy and chemical industries, probably without any consideration to comparative costs and international division of labor.

Second was the conscious move toward autarchy. World War I made Japanese policy-makers aware of the possible consequences of total war. In the event of such a war, it was feared that import of commodities and foreign technology would become extremely difficult. Moreover, it had been very difficult to get access to foreign technology through inward foreign direct investment, primarily because potential investors simply did not have much information about, or interest in, Japan.

Foreign direct investment (equity held by the rest of the world) was 2.2 per cent of total equity in 1910, 0.4 per cent in 1920, and 1.0 per cent in 1930 (Fujino and Teranishi 2000). In March 1931, the share of foreign capital in manufacturing was just 0.49 per cent, and this was primarily because of investments in machinery (which included electrical and transport) where the share was 1.60 per cent. Elsewhere it was quite low: metals 0.05 per cent; chemicals 0.03 per cent; food 0.04 per cent; public utilities (gas and electricity) 0.004 per cent; and other manufacturing 0.28 per cent. It was just 0.12 per cent in mining and 0.02 per cent in commerce. (Data from Nihon Kogyo Ginko 1948.)

Japanese firms established all the basic industries, eventually giving rise to an autarchy. During the 1930s, such a move, forming block economies, was also a common tendency in Western countries. The motivation for self-sufficiency, however, was most articulated in the case of Japan because of its geographical location. Germany and Italy also tried to establish autarchy, but their policy was *ad hoc* and dilettantish. Trade between the two increased remarkably after 1927, and for both it declined with the United States (Toniolo 1980).

The third stage resulted from the fact that the heavy and chemical industries inherited from the war economy were protected and maintained after World War II within the government–private-sector interface based on inter-industrial interest representation. As is shown in Chapter 4, the effective functioning of the interface was possible only when most of the intermediate goods were produced domestically; in other words under the full-set industrial structure.

The formation and maintenance of the full-set structure is shown in Table 2.4. The share of manufactured products in total imports declined from 49 per cent in 1892 to 22 per cent in 1925. It is surprising that the low level of the manufactured-product import ratio, which attracted public attention during the early 1990s as evidence of excessive protection of consumer industries, actually originates as early as 1925.

On the other hand, the share of machinery in total exports increased steadily from zero around 1920 to more than 70 per cent after the 1980s. In other words, Japan produced most of its manufactured goods domestically during the 60 years from the early 1920s to the 1980s and restricted imports mainly to foods, raw materials and fuels.

There seems no doubt that the full-set industrial structure worked effectively during the wartime economy and immediately after World War II when world trade was inactive. The structure was effective in eliminating bottlenecks and enhancing economies of scope. However, it is apparent that the structure has become significantly costly. First, there are resource-allocation costs arising from the maintenance of industries that do not have international comparative advantages. Second, the government–private-sector interface, closely related to the structure, has begun to incur serious political costs in the form of inefficient political and administrative decisions in the face of trade friction and the emergence of non-inter-industrial interests.

2.4.2 Acceptability of Government Intervention in the Economy

The second half of the 20th century witnessed unprecedented expansion of government intervention in economies. The expansion of government intervention in the economy occurred in two ways: spending and regulation. Both became significant.

There was a world-wide increase of the share of government spending in GDP (Table 2.5). For Japan, the share increased from a less than 10 per cent level in 1885 and 1923 to more than a 30 per cent level during World War II (31.6 per cent in 1940), and especially during the 1980s.

Table 2.4 Manufactured products import ratio (manufactured product import/total imports) and export ratio of machinery (export of machinery/total exports)

Year	Product import ratio (%)	Export ratio of machinery (%)
1892	49	0
1902	36	0
1912	36	1
1925	22	1
1935	22	7
1958	23	22
1960	23	23
1962	26	25
1964	26	29
1966	23	38
1968	27	44
1970	30	46
1972	30	48
1974	24	45
1976	22	53
1978	27	57
1980	23	55
1982	25	56
1984	30	60
1986	42	74
1988	48	74
1990	50	75
1992	50	75
1994	52	76
1996	61	74
1998	48	73

Note: Data before the war in yen and after the war in dollars. Manufactured products include machinery, chemical products, metal products, textiles, re-imports and special products, and (non-monetary use) gold. Total imports are the sum of foods, raw materials, fuels and manufactured products.

Source: Data before WWII are obtained from Yamazawa and Yamamoto (1979) and Yukizawa and Maeda (1978), and after WWII from *Tsû-shô Hakusho* (various issues).

The rise of the share during the wartime period owes much to the expansion of military expenditures, while after 1960 it is primarily from social transfers, although other expenditures also increased.

The world-wide increase in government intervention was caused by:

1. an aggravation of market failures such as monopolistic firm behaviour due to increasing returns to scale, agency costs due to the separation of ownership from control, and unemployment problems

Table 2.5 Percentage share of government expenditures in GDP

	1870	1923	1937	1960	1980	1998
Total expenditure						
Australia	18.3	16.5	14.8	21.2	31.6	32.9
Belgium		13.8	21.8	30.3	58.6	49.4
France	12.6	17.0	29.0	34.6	46.1	54.3
Germany		14.8	34.1	32.4	47.9	46.9
Italy	11.9	11.1	24.5	30.1	41.9	49.1
Japan	9.1	8.3	25.4	17.5	32.0	36.9
Netherlands	9.1	9.0	19.0	33.7	55.2	47.2
Norway	5.9	9.3	11.8	29.9	37.5	46.9
Sweden	5.7	10.4	16.5	31.0	60.1	58.5
UK	9.4	12.7	30.0	32.2	43.0	40.2
US	7.3	7.5	19.7	27.0	31.8	32.8
Average	10.0	11.9	22.4	29.1	44.3	45.0
Standard deviation	3.9	3.2	6.6	5.0	10.1	8.0
	1880	1910	1930	1960	1980	1990
Social transfers						
Australia	0.0	1.1	2.1	7.4	12.8	15.4
Belgium	0.2	0.4	0.6	13.1	30.4	29.7
France	0.5	0.8	1.1	13.4	22.6	27.8
Germany	0.5	n.a	5.0	18.1	25.7	21.2
Italy	0.0	0.0	0.1	13.1	21.3	24.5
Japan	0.1	0.2	0.2	4.0	11.9	16.1
Netherlands	0.3	0.4	1.2	11.7	28.3	31.7
Norway	1.1	1.2	2.4	7.9	21.0	23.0
Sweden	0.7	1.0	2.6	10.8	25.9	21.3
UK	0.9	1.4	2.6	10.2	16.4	16.8
US	0.3	0.6	0.6	7.3	15.0	16.3
Average	0.4	0.7	1.7	10.6	21.0	22.2
Standard deviation	0.3	0.4	1.4	3.7	6.0	5.5

Notes: Total expenditures are sum of social transfers (spending on pensions, welfare, unemployment compensation and health) and other expenditures of the central and local governments. For Belgium, Italy and the Netherlands the data do not include local government until 1937.

Source: Crafts (2000). The 1870 statistics for Japan were for 1885, obtained from Ohkawa and Shinohara (1979), Table A1 and A4.

due to price rigidities;

2. the development of economic theory regarding the working of

markets and related changes in economic thought;
3. a self-expansion of bureaucratic organizations.

The second factor, interacting with the first factor and the effects of the Great Depression, is especially important: an overwhelming momentum toward government intervention arose primarily from the diffusion and social acceptance of economic thought that approved and advocated government intervention.

In prewar Japan after World War I, although the actual degree of government intervention remained rather low, the belief that some sort of intervention was necessary in order to alleviate distributive conflicts and enhance the international competitiveness of industries was increasingly shared by the people, and collective action based on such a belief and expectations about the realization of the belief came to shake the society to its foundation.

Overall, in the postwar period, the share of government expenditure in Japan has not been high internationally, but the total level of intervention was high until into the 1980s. The reason is that Japan has been very interventionist when it comes to regulating the activities of industries, and this is so even though the actual degree of market failure has not been large compared to the prewar situation. This was partly because bureaucrats strongly believed in the effectiveness of developmental regulations, and partly because the weakening of the private sector's bargaining power gave the bureaucrats room to indulge in interventionist policies.

Postwar industrial policy was implemented by means of a competition-prevention policy, quantitative rationing, and price controls, as well as through measures that affected government budgets such as tax exemption, tariff policy, and the explicit supply of subsidies. Government regulation was most prevalent in catching-up countries, including postwar Japan.

2.4.2.1 Effects of intervention

The expansion of government activities beyond the role of a provider of pure public goods has significant effects on economic systems because it makes it necessary to have an interface – intermediate organizations– between the government and the private sector to adjust income-distributive conflicts. Redistributive policies through social transfers have direct effects on income distribution. Industrial policies give rise to policy-induced rents, so economic agents treated favorably can obtain a return greater than the market rate. Economic stabilization policies affect prices, wages and the exchange rate, thus entailing a significant influence on income distribution.

When the role of government is confined to the provision of public goods, regional economies usually play the role of an intermediate organization, because the distributive influence of public-goods supply is more or less even among people in the same region. However, when the activity of the government expands beyond this boundary, the influence becomes uneven, depending on factor endowments and industries. People are induced to form coalitions to manipulate the government so as to realize policies favorable to particular coalitions.

In postwar Japan, such an intermediate organization was established for each industry. That is, the government–private-sector interface was organized so as to represent inter-industrial interests. Government agencies (*genkyoku*) and industrial associations, each specific to a particular industry, played the role not only of the conduit of information between the government and industries but also of the interface regarding adjustment of distributive interests. People organized industrial associations to realize greater rent opportunities for the industries they belonged to, and the government took care of their demands through agencies established for each industry.

Industrial policy was applied to influence competitive conditions, and hence the level of value-added, of industries. When entry of new firms and imports of industry A are regulated, the resulting rents benefit the industry, both capital and labor. However, industry B, which uses the product of A as an input, loses, so B has an incentive to lobby. The system of *genkyoku* and industrial associations adjusted interests between the two industries. This is developed at greater length in Chapter 7.

In contrast, in many European and Latin American countries, coalitions are formed according to economic class determined by factor ownership. People lobbied the government as the working class or the capitalist class so as to realize policies favorable to their particular class. Minimum wages, incomes policy, taxation of capital, and, quite often, tools for macroeconomic stabilizations were utilized to adjust the distributive conflicts. The issue of why class did not become a basis for coalitions in high-growth-period Japan is returned to also in Chapter 7.

2.5 THE MEIJI-TAISHÔ ECONOMIC SYSTEM

The Meiji-Taishô economic system is market based, with corporate governance led by large shareholders and bank-dominated financing of the indigenous sector, and regional economies acting as intermediating organizations.

The system's marketism has two meanings. First was the limited role of government intervention. This was mainly through provision of basic infrastructure (highways, the main railways, harbors) and supply of pure public goods such as public safety (police, fire fighting, flood control), national security (military, foreign diplomacy), and the legal system (the judiciary). Second was the resistance and self-assertion of business leaders in both the modern and indigenous sectors against the Meiji government. The merits of the market mechanism were ardently advocated by some of Japan's leading 19th-century economists, such as Taguchi Ukichi (1855–1905). However, the market mechanism was respected mainly because of an emphasis on private initiatives rather than from the viewpoint of allocative efficiency.

The modern corporate sector relied mainly on financing through equity issues. Partly because the number of wealthy individuals was limited, firms were owned by a limited number of shareholders, and corporate control was implemented quite often on a consensual basis among the shareholders. Banks lent mainly to the commercial sector or to merchants who relent the money to the indigenous and agricultural sector, or invested it in stocks of modern corporations. Intermediation by banks was dependent on double intermediation through the role of merchants, so that the prevalence of large-shareholder–based corporate governance does not imply a small role for banks in financial flows.

The government–private-sector interface with regional economies as intermediate organizations was suitable to the system because government intervention was confined to the supply of public goods. In the political history literature, the working of this interface is usually called the 'mechanism for pumping benefits to the regions'. One must be careful, however, in understanding this phrase. It is true that politicians at the time were ardent in inviting central government investment in railways, roads, port facilities, and schools in their villages and towns. However, in two respects the mechanism was quite different from the behavior of today's politicians, called *zokugiin*. (These are Diet members who act for the interests of particular industries.)

First, because the living and economic activity of people was closely linked to regional economies and competition among regions put vitality into the national economy, a solicitation of government investment benefited not only a particular sector (such as the construction industry) but also inhabitants in the region as a whole. Second, leaders of regional economies, often called *meibôka* (men of reputation) devoted their own assets to the construction of industrial and social infrastructure in their regions. Indeed, one can still find schools and irrigation facilities constructed in this way. These projects were undertaken even as the *meibôka* were, through taxes, consciously financing central government expenditures both in social and industrial investment in other regions and in the building-up of military and economic strength. Of course central-government investment was beneficial to private business leaders, but they devoted considerable private wealth to the development of regions.

In other words, from the viewpoint of local leaders, soliciting central government investment was synonymous with the choice between donating money directly to the regional economy or indirectly through the central government budget (that is, paying national taxes and inducing expenditures for the sake of their regions). It was an issue of neither personal benefits nor of vote collection.

2.5.1 Periodization

Periodization of something that was continually evolving is problematic but, for purposes of the analysis, the system emerged in the 1890s, was at its height from just after the Russo-Japanese war until the Kanto earthquake (that is, 1906–23), peaking more or less with the 1919–20 boom, stumbling badly after 1927, and finally collapsing in the mid-1930s.

Comparing this periodization to others, it partially overlaps Japan's industrial revolution (Ishii 2000), which was characterized by a massive establishment of modern firms and is usually dated as 1886–1907, and the era of industrialization by the development of indigenous industries (*sangyô-ka no jidai*) dated at 1885–1914 (Nishikawa and Abe 1990). Nakamura (1971) refers to the period from World War I to the start of the Pacific War (Pearl Harbor) as one of 'unbalanced growth'. This relates to the discussion of dual structure (on which, see Nakamura and Odaka 1989).

Politically, its emergence overlaps the 'state building' period ending around 1901, and its peak and decline coincide with the period of Taishô democracy.

Banno (1982) considers that during 1901–13 (the *Keien*-period) when Katsura Taro, leader of the Chôshû-based fief group, and Saionji Kinmochi, president of the Seiyûkai political party, alternately organized cabinets, the Meiji constitution system, also called the 1900-*nen* system, was weakened, and party politics did not work adequately due to the dearth of government revenue and so on. Because of repression by the fief-power-based (*hunbatsu*) Meiji leaders, party politics did not develop as much as they might otherwise have done.

2.5.2 Brief Chronology

The Meiji-Taishô system was established by around 1900. It began to come together in the 1890s after the Matsukata deflation (early 1880s) and the failure of earlier developmental policy. The political events that set the stage for its arrival were promulgation of the Meiji Constitution in 1889 and opening of the Imperial Diet the following year. These marked a shift from *hanbatsu* power held by the members of the former samurai class that dominated the government, to a broader group, including budding political parties. Although the fief-power-based Meiji leaders still largely controlled the government, providing all but one prime minister until 1901, the Diet had the 'power of the purse' and used it.

Two key developments affected the system's formation. First, a national economy was emerging, with the beginning of fierce competition among regions shortly thereafter. This in part reflected the extensive transportation and communication investment already made by that time which connected each regional economy to the national center.

Second, a tacit agreement was reached between the Meiji government and the political parties. The government was pressing for a rapid build-up of military and economic strength (*fukoku kyôhei*) and the parties were supporting gradualism and an alleviation of the burden on the people (*minryoku kyûyô*). The private sector was willing to cooperate with the increase of military strength and to bear the tax burden, and the government left most economic activity to the free play of the private sector.

There followed a military build-up and an infrastructure building policy, called *Nisshin-nichiro sengo keiei* (post Sino-Japanese and Russo-Japanese war economic policy). This involved a marked expansion of government expenditures, so the period extending from after the Russo-Japanese war until World War I has been called an era of large government (Nakamura 1990) or the Big Push (Okazaki 1997). However, expenditures were confined to the military and to the supply of public goods, including subsidies for construction of local private railroads and some private goods, such as shipbuilding, including warships.

During its run, the system realized a reasonably high level of economic growth: 3.07 percent for real GNP during 1900–1920. The growth was brought about through competition among regions, and centered around agriculture and related indigenous industries. Landlords led the growth of agriculture through their dedication to diffusion of improved technologies including high-yielding rice varieties, water control and land improvement. At the same time, a fixed-rent system gave substantial incentive to tenants to invest. This was because the incremental income went to the tenant farmer, not to the landowner. Moreover, tenant farmers had significant control rights in the utilization of land.

Landmarks of the system's decline include the unsuccessful attempt to restructure the social order, which was led by *meibôka*, utilizing villages and townships as regional units of interest representation; the deterioration of a corporate governance system dominated by large shareholders, with a consequent surge of moral hazard and scandals; and initiation of an industrial policy by the government.

By the end of the 1910s, increases in the system's economic and political costs, as well as the disintegration of social norms, put the system into difficulties. Economic costs increased partly because the heavy and chemical industries, which had expanded during the World War I period due to the cessation of imports, were forced to face severe competition from Western producers, partly because the banking sector grew less stable due to a lack of asset diversification and partly because the agricultural sector lost growth momentum due to government policies unfavorable to the sector and a slow-down in technological progress. As the limitations of the system's economic capability came to the fore, the economy fell into secular stagnation in the 1920s.

Social norms also became lax. The motivation for social improvement with regional communities as its base became weaker as the growth potential of the agriculture and indigenous industries fell; and frequent tenant disputes reduced incentives for landlords to be agricultural entrepreneurs and regional leaders.

In March 1925 the Diet abolished the requirement that only those who paid more than a certain amount in taxes could vote and otherwise established universal suffrage for males over 25. The number of eligible voters substantially increased as a result, from 3.1 million in 1920 to 12.4 million in 1928. Tenants thus came to have equal political rights, but they lacked the economic and other power to lead the community. As support for the idea of community development with *meibôka* leadership as the social norm waned during the 1920s, bureaucrats took the lead in social reform with policies such as the *nôsangyoson kôsei undô* (reform movement of the rural sector).

The diffusion of skepticism and disbelief regarding the working of capitalism in economic thought magnified the social turmoil caused by the system's economic costs, thereby increasing the political costs. As feelings of identification with regional community weakened, people tended to assert the distributive interests of the classes and industries they belonged to.

The government tried to cope with this by resorting to a policy mix that was (1) neutral to class conflicts, (2) favorable to non-agriculture with respect to conflicts between agriculture and non-agriculture, and (3) favorable to light industries, trade, and financial firms with respect to the conflicts between them and the heavy and chemical industries. The key for implementation of this mix to be successful was the recovery of indigenous commercial and industrial activities.

However, reviving the indigenous economy was not fully congruent with the desire to return to the gold standard at the old parity. This necessitated a tight fiscal and monetary policy and meant an over-valued exchange rate. But successive governments wished to restructure the economy through weeding out weaker segments, and had faith in the classical autonomous adjustment mechanism helping to achieve this. Return to the gold standard came in January 1930, soon after the stock market crash in New York. The government policy of strengthening the banking system by reducing the number of banks, begun in 1928, contributed to a credit crunch that made the situation even worse for indigenous industries. Thus, one goal of economic policy eventually led to the bankruptcy of the policy mix being used at the government–private-sector interface to address distributive issues.

2.6 THE HIGH-GROWTH-PERIOD ECONOMIC SYSTEM

The high-growth-period economic system is characterized by extensive government intervention in the economy through regulations, Japanese-style firms, a bank-centered financial system, and representation of inter-industrial interests through *genkyoku*–industrial associations.

Government intervention took the form of industrial policy implemented mainly as controls on competition in each industry. Major tools were controls on entry, production, production facilities, and trade. Such measures as preferential tax treatment, rationing of foreign exchange, and policy-based financing were also utilized in order to influence private-sector activities through both subsidy effects and competition-preventing effects.

Interventions extended to the regional economies as well. Although autonomy of municipal governments was promoted politically — for example, through a change in the prefectural governor selection system from designation by the central government to local elections — the central government strengthened its control on the fiscal side. Tax revenues of local governments were strictly controlled with respect to the choice of tax objectives as well as tax rates. Municipal government bonds needed approval by the central government on an each-issue basis. Total expenditures were tightly controlled because the gap between revenue and expenditures was filled with unconditional lump-sum transfers from the central government, called tax-sharing grants *(chihô kôfuzei)*, and conditional grants, called special purpose grants (*kokko hojyokin*).

The Japanese-style firm system comprised autonomy of corporate managers through cross-shareholding and internal labor markets characterized by long-term employment and a seniority wage system. The bank-centered financial system implied a dominant role of banks both in mobilization of funds and corporate governance. It is well known there are institutional complementarities among these elements of the private-sector sub-sector, and the sub-sector was considered to have enhanced the efficiency of the economy through relation-based investment by employees and by group firms, as well as through informational efficiency by the main bank system.

The third pillar of the high-growth-period economic system was the sub-system of inter-industrial interest representation. Combined with the implementation of industrial policy, this sub-system played the role of adjusting policy-induced rents accruing to each industry through control of its competitive conditions. This was implemented by the *genkyoku*–industrial association system (each *genkyoku* was in charge of each industry). Owing to the input–output relationship among industries, as well as the full-set industrial structure in which most intermediary goods were produced domestically, this sub-system could influence the level of value-added among industries. The *shuntô* (spring labor offensive) system was complementary to this mechanism because the adjustment of inter-industrial wage levels enabled an effective sharing mechanism within internal labor markets.

2.6.1 Brief Chronology

The high-growth-period system was established by the mid-1950s, after implementation of postwar reforms and when the economy had restarted catch-up through an exploitation of the technological gap with Western countries, which had widened during World War II.

The reason for the introduction of government intervention was partly a reflection of widespread skepticism about the automatic adjustment mechanism of capitalism and concerns over the costs of market failures. Another reason was the continuity of the bureaucratic system, in which a majority of the bureaucrats in charge of wartime economic control survived and led the postwar catch-up. A reason no less important than these two was the drastic decline in the bargaining power of the private sector *vis-à-vis* the government. Especially important in this regard was the *de facto* default of wartime debts by the government, which drove major firms and banks into virtual bankruptcy, making room for bureaucratic intervention, especially in the banking sector. In addition, the turmoil of defeat and postwar reforms impoverished the wealthy class that had led the socio-economy before the war. Through zaibatsu dissolution, land reform and high inflation, the huge amount of financial assets and land held by the wealthy was virtually confiscated and dispersed.

The rise of a bank-centered financial system and the role of the main-bank system therein are also closely related to the decline of the private sector's power and the changes in the distribution of wealth. Banks on the verge of bankruptcy were put under bureaucratic control, and the disappearance of controlling shareholders due to wealth redistribution resulted in cross-shareholding in order to prevent unstable corporate governance.

In sum, the shock of war and defeat had an overwhelming influence on the economy not only in the sense of bureaucratic continuity but also of the weakening of the private sector and the drastic changes in wealth distribution, and these influences are still affecting Japan today.

From a macroeconomic viewpoint, the high rate of economic growth during the high-growth period owes much to the active import of foreign technologies, thereby exploiting the benefit of being a latecomer, and an ample supply of low-cost labor from agriculture. From an institutional viewpoint, the high growth rates are ascribed to informational efficiencies such as the monitoring mechanism of the main-bank system, coordination through government intervention in the catch-up process, and firm-and relation-specific investment by workers and related firms. In Chapter 7 it is argued that although it is undeniable that the first two contributed growth to some extent, the most important factor was the third. Through cross-shareholding among firms, managers and workers were given a wide range of autonomy, in effect the residual income and control rights normally accruing to shareholders. Although this reflected weak protection of outside investors, and ultimately caused inefficiency due to managerial entrenchment, leading to shirking and empire building, the system gave a strong incentive for managers, workers and related firms to invest in firm-specific skills. The high international competitiveness of Japanese manufacturing firms during the period owes much to this mechanism.

The high-growth-period system reached a historic crossroads around 1980 when the three exogenous conditions that had shaped the system for two decades changed simultaneously. First, the catch-up process was completed, and Japan entered a phase in which it needed to develop new technology and industry for itself. Second, economic thought took a turn toward marketism, which is supported by globalism based on IT development. Third, the rapid growth of other Asian countries made Japan's full-set industrial structure even more inappropriate.

The economic costs of the high-growth-period economic system rose sharply, especially in the financial sector. Increased technological uncertainty due not only to the completion of catch-up, but also to the world-wide move into a new technological phase, destabilized banks. Banks may a have comparative advantage in production of firm-level information, but they are not necessarily good at gathering and analyzing information about new industries and technologies. The absence of a proper division of labor between banks and markets, and the lack of a mechanism for risk transfer through capital markets aggravated the plight of banks further.

Bank destabilization from the mid-1990s directly reflect a shift in the needs of its traditional customers — the heavy and chemical industries that had led the high-growth era. These firms no longer needed huge amounts of new loans, or at least not from banks: increasingly they could tap international capital markets. The banks found themselves needing new customers, but without the tools, let alone experience, to select and monitor them properly. The banks' catch-up-oriented, full-set-style lending pattern had inhibited development of any meaningful skills in credit-risk analysis. Moreover, reliance on real estate collateral was supported by faith in rising land prices generally.

Underdevelopment of the capital market was partly due to the deficiency of the *genkyoku*–industrial association system, which was constrained by the vested interests of existing financial industries and failed to ride the wave of financial innovation swelling outside Japan. In Japan now, wealth is still dispersed widely mainly among aged retirees, who are not necessarily active in risk taking. This, together with the rise in participation costs in capital market, despite the fall of trading costs, has made it difficult to have a market-based financial system based directly on individual investors.

Political costs also increased considerably with regard to the government-private-sector interface.

First, as marketism developed and consumers' sovereignty came to be increasingly emphasized, the *genkyoku*–industrial association system, whose capability in interest adjustment is confined to inter–industrial interests, faced serious difficulties. In particular, consumers' criticism of the producer-dominated system became intense, especially when the yen appreciated drastically after 1985.

Second, an intensification of trade disputes brought out another limitation of the interface: the increased influence of foreign producers' interests and exchange-rate fluctuations made representation through *genkyoku*–industrial associations less effective. As a result, policy coordination outside the bureaucracy, especially within the Liberal Democratic Party, became an increasingly common practice, with the consequent activation of intermediation by *zokugiin* (loosely, special-interest politicians).

Third, public works are another aspect with which the existing interface cannot deal adequately. The allocation of public investment in local areas has become a serious political issue because it is at the intersection of three dimensional interests: inter-regional, inter-industrial (especially the construction industry and agriculture), and environmental.

Among those in the managerial class of large business firms and white-collar workers more generally, who had been dedicated proponents of the high-growth-period system, there arose growing skepticism about a scenario in which the growth of firms and industries was the means to economic and social prosperity. In other words, the producer sovereignty principle was being challenged by consumer sovereignty, and the major advocates of the latter (as the middle class) had been the main supporters of the former (as workers in large firms). The social acceptance of criticizing over-work and company-men is also closely related to the decay of social norms in this sense.

PART II

The Meiji-Taishô economic system

3. Emergence of the Meiji-Taishô economic system

The central elements of the Meiji-Taishô economic system were in place by around 1900. These comprised reliance on market mechanisms, representation of distributive interests by regional economies, corporate governance led by large shareholders, and indigenous industries financed by banks.

After achieving power with the 1868 Meiji Restoration, the new government's leaders set about building a strong state. One aspect of this is roughly summarized in a slogan of the time: *fukoko kyôhei* (rich country, strong military). 'Rich country' meant one with a large, growing tax base. Although a desire to avoid the fate of a semi-colonized China was universal, there was no consensus on the size of the military needed, or on the extent of involvement in neighboring territories. Further, many felt there should be greater, faster democratization. The dispute over national objectives, and how to pay for them, are major themes in Japan's political history during the last decades of the 19th century.

An 1870s foray into government-owned factories – as models of technology, rather than an indication of faith in the efficiency of government compared to markets – resulted in large deficits. In any case, it was clear the private sector was quite willing to avail itself of the opportunities provided by the privatization of government factories, and actively embarked on new businesses. Thus, there was never serious doubt that most economic activity would be left to the private sector, and so to the market mechanism.

Settling the national-objectives debate, and how to finance them, gave rise to a division of labor between the government and the private sector. The pursuit of national objectives was put in the hands of the government, and farmer-landlords assumed the role of financing government expenditures in exchange for freedom of economic activity. An epoch-making event in this was raising the land tax, introduced in the Diet held during 1898–99.

Further, there emerged a national linkage of financial and commodity markets owing to development of a transportation and communication infrastructure. This enabled representation of distributive interests by regional economies, giving rise to the 'mechanism of pumping benefits to regions' based on the 'positive policy (*sekkyoku-shugi*)' of the Rikken Seiyûkai, a political party formed in August 1900, henceforth referred to simply as Seiyûkai.

In short, through institutional complementarity, the various strands of economic and political development in the late 19th century had, by the end of the century, woven themselves into what I call the Meiji-Taishô economic system. By then the mobilization of savings held by large merchants and landlords had been completed, corporate firms had been established and were governed by large shareholders, and a system of financing capital formation through current savings by households had begun to function. This chapter investigates the process of the emergence of the system with respect to each of its sub-systems: the division of labor between the government and private sector, the interface between the two sectors, and the characteristics of the private sector.

Building the infrastructure of a modern economy was recognized as a necessary part of the Meiji government's overarching goal of maintaining Japan's independence. Thus, it moved to create a modern banking system and adopt a set of commercial laws and institutional forms modeled on those of the Western powers. This is well studied, but several aspects of the process and results are relevant to the emergence of the Meiji-Taishô system, and this chapter addresses them.

The chapter begins by looking at the mobilization of funds, a key requirement for both the government and private investors. The establishment of corporations, including issues related to managers and governance, is then addressed. Analysis of the emergence of the division of labor that characterized the Meiji-Taishô system, and of the linking of the regional and national economies that was the basis of the government–private-sector interface follows. The chapter concludes with a look at the wealthy as the system emerged.

3.1 MOBILIZATION OF ACCUMULATED SAVINGS

For the Meiji government, newly established in 1868, the biggest constraint was the shortage of funds for its activities. The government relied heavily on borrowing (*kaikei kiritsu-kin*) from merchants in the Kinki region (that is, Osaka, Japan's traditional leading merchant city) and the issue of inconvertible notes such as *dajyôkan-satsu*. Borrowing from abroad was not impossible, but the government took an extremely cautious approach in this regard. Foreign bonds were issued twice, in London, during early Meiji: 4,782,000 yen at 9 per cent in its third fiscal year (October 1869–September 1870) to finance railway construction between Tokyo and Yokohama, and 10,837,000 yen at 7 per cent in its sixth fiscal year (January 1873–December 1873) to finance part of the severance payments to samurai. After that, until 1899 there were no foreign bond issues.

The major revenue source was taxation of farmers. They, however, bitterly resisted the levying of the land tax. As a result, when the rate was set at 3 per cent of the land's value in 1873, the government promised to reduce it to 1 per cent when commodity tax revenue increased. In 1877 the rate was reduced to 2.5 per cent, but in 1884 the promise of a 1 per cent rate was officially withdrawn (Nakamura 1966, Appendix A).

While the government suffered from severe fiscal difficulties, there were a large number of merchants and landlords who had accumulated wealth from economic development during the Tokugawa period. In the turmoil toward the end of the period, some of this group went into decline, while others, and some newcomers, increased their wealth through government contracts or patronage. Those who particularly exploited close contacts with the government came to be called 'political merchants' (*seishô*).

The engine of economic growth in the Meiji period was started as merchants and landlords, as well as some former samurai, reacted shrewdly to the incentives arising from the new institutional environment. For large firms in modern industries, this gave rise to the firm system characterized by the leadership of large shareholders in corporate governance.

However, development of Japan's economy depended not only on modern industries but also on indigenous industrial activities. Many small and medium landlords and farmers established individually owned firms and engaged in various indigenous industrial activities. These individuals were the owners or clients of the many banks that sprang up in the 1870s and 1880s, and those banks that survived into the 20th century were an important part of the Meiji-Taishô system.

Establishment of a modern banking system was a priority of the Meiji government, both for its own fiscal purposes, to redeem non-convertible notes issued earlier, and to mobilize funds for investment.

3.1.1 Creation of the Banking Industry

Figure 3.1 shows the sources of banking sector funds from 1874 to

1913. Government funds are government deposits, borrowing from the government and the Bank of Japan, and bank notes issued by private national banks. Government deposits are mainly tax revenue temporarily kept in the vaults of banks that were in charge of government accounts. The national banks had the privilege of issuing bank notes, which can be regarded as zero-interest rate borrowing from the government. Banks also obtained fees for handling government accounts.

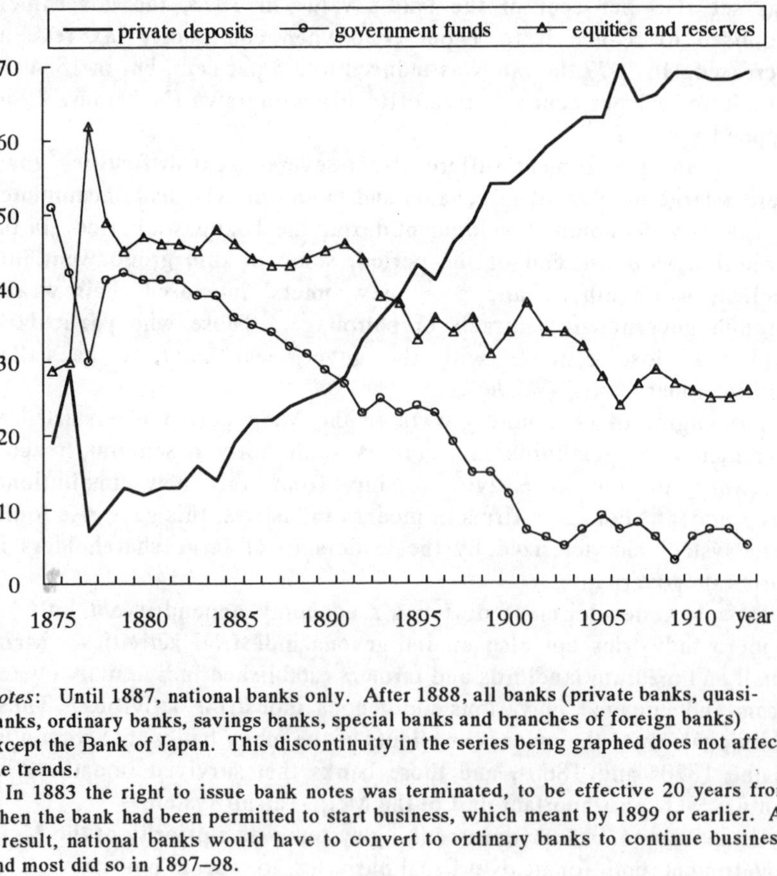

Notes: Until 1887, national banks only. After 1888, all banks (private banks, quasi-banks, ordinary banks, savings banks, special banks and branches of foreign banks) except the Bank of Japan. This discontinuity in the series being graphed does not affect the trends.

In 1883 the right to issue bank notes was terminated, to be effective 20 years from when the bank had been permitted to start business, which meant by 1899 or earlier. As a result, national banks would have to convert to ordinary banks to continue business, and most did so in 1897–98.

Source: Teranishi (1982, statistical appendix) calculated from data in various issues of *Ginko-kyoku Kin'yû Nenpô*.

Figure 3.1 Percentage composition of financing of the bank sector

A modern banking industry was created in the 1870s, but not without initial problems. Under the 1872 National Bank Act (*Kokuritsu-Ginkô Hô*), 40 per cent of bank equity had to be subscribed in specie and the remaining 60 per cent in non-convertible currency (*dajôkan-satsu*). Note issue was allowed up to 60 per cent of equity. Moreover, because of the requirements placed on note issue – they had to be convertible into gold – the privilege was of limited practical value. As a result, only four banks had been established by the end of 1874.

The Bank Act was revised in 1876 to relax reserve and convertibility requirements, making the right to issue notes valuable. The revision also allowed up to 80 per cent of equity to be subscribed in national bonds, including those issued to commute samurai stipends (*kinroku-kôsai*, severance bonds). Note issue was allowed up to 80 per cent of equity, and notes were required to be convertible into (inconvertible) government notes, not into gold. From 1876 to 1877, paid-in capital of national banks increased more than tenfold, and their number jumped from 5 to 26. (Another 125 banks were created in 1878–79, but these were smaller, so that paid-in capital increased only 77 per cent.) Note issue (graphed with government funds) also surged. By 1882 there had been more than a 14-fold increase in bank funds (capital, bank note issue, and deposits), over one-third of which was note issue.

An aim of the bank law's revision was to make it easier for former samurai to invest their assets (the severance bonds), and the equity of national banks was indeed mainly subscribed with the bonds: 86.4 per cent of bonds paid in as national bank capital comprised such bonds. However, it was rich landlords and merchants who took the lead position in bank establishment (Asakura 1961). Out of 48 banks for which the establishment process is clear, 20 were started under the leadership of merchants, 5 by merchants and landlords, 6 by merchants and former samurai, 16 by former samurai, and 1 by aristocrats. The last, the Dai-Jyugo Ginko (15th Bank), was informally known as the Peer's Bank. Of those founded by former samurai, 4 were virtually run by merchants. In 1888, former samurai and court nobles held 39 per cent of national bank equity and merchants, landlords and industrialists held 61 per cent. (Data from Teranishi 1982.)

The first four national banks that opened in 1874 also indicate the differences in the level of financial asset holding between landlords and merchants. Fourth National (Niigata Dai-Yon-Kokuritsu Ginko), founded with a total capitalization of 300,000 yen, was established in Niigata, a major regional city at the time, by large landlords, including two who invested 6,500 yen each. The rest of the equity was shared by 351 investors, which means an average of just over 800 yen each. In contrast, the Second National (Kanagawa Dai-Ni-Kokuritsu Ginkô) established by merchants engaged in foreign trade in Yokohama, raised its total capitalization of 250,000 yen from only 29 shareholders, with the top shareholder investing 50,000 yen, and the second largest 30,000 yen.

After the Bank of Japan was established in 1882, national banks, together with private and quasi-banks, were required to convert to commercial banks called ordinary banks (*futsû-ginkô*) or savings banks (*chochiku-ginkô*). The conversion was completed in 1899, and bank notes issued by national banks were redeemed.

3.1.2 Expansion of the Banking Industry

As Table 3.1 shows, in 1879, after establishment of national banks reached a pre-designated maximum determined by the total capitalization of the banks, there was a surge in the establishment of private banks (*shiritsu-ginkô*) and quasi-banks (*ginkô ruijikaisha*).

Some of the private and quasi-banks were founded by money lenders, and quite often they maintained their traditional business style after becoming banks. This also means that many quasi-banks engaged in activities such as warehousing and transportation. Most of the private and quasi-banks were established in centers of production of indigenous products such as tea, raw silk, and textiles, in reaction to the new profit opportunities created by the improvement of social infrastructures in transportation and communication and by the activity of national banks, such as transactions in documentary bills.

The 1880–85 surge in bank establishment was a surprise to the government, and there was no administrative or legal framework with respect to banks other than national banks. The government took an accommodating stance toward this working of market forces. At first, it left the licensing of new banks to the discretion of local offices, and then resorted to a completely *laissez-faire* policy of allowing banks without any official licensing. Therefore, private banks and quasi-banks in Table 3.1 are a mixture of banks authorized locally under the guidance of the Ministry of Finance, banks authorized only by local offices, and banks without any licenses.

'Some are capitalized with only several hundred yen, while others have capitalization on the order of several hundred thousand yen or even several million yen, whose scales of operation are comparable to those of national banks, and have enormous effects on regional economies' (Meiji-Zaisei-shi Hensankai 1927, p. 492). Most of these banks were officially authorized in 1890 when the Ordinary Bank Act

Table 3.1 Number of banks, 1874–1945

Year	Total	National banks[a]	Private banks	Quasi-banks	Ordinary banks and saving banks
1874	4	4	–	–	–
1877	27	26	1	–	–
1880	309	151	38	120	–
1883	913	141	199	573	–
1886	1,104	136	219	749	–
1889	1,084	134	255	695	–
1892	1,137	133	324	680	(c)
1895	1,041	133	(b)	(b)	908
1898	1,762	4			1,758
1901	2,334				2,334
1904	2,204				2,204
1905	2,178				2,178
1915	2,099				2,099
1925	1,670				1,670
1935	545				545
1945	65				65

Notes: Does not include special banks. See the source for other reservations and reasons this series may differ from others.

[a] There was a pre-designated maximum of 153 private banks. That number had been approved by 1879, so no more were allowed. There was a delay in the start of business by two banks, so the number actually opened at the end of 1879 was 151.

[b] None after 1892, see note c.

[c] None before 1893. In that year, 629 were established, most by converting from private- or quasi-bank status.

Source: Teranishi (1982, p. 35 and statistical appendix 5-1).

and Saving Bank Act were promulgated.

Table 3.2 compares national and private banks between regions with active indigenous production and other regions. It can be seen that, by type of bank, there is no significant difference in the ratio of lending to total assets (sum of net worth, private deposits, government deposits, and banknote issue) between the two types of regions. However, private banks were more active in basic banking – that is, lending – than the national banks. Moreover, private banks enjoyed relatively large private deposits compared to national banks.

Note that the private banks in the regions with indigenous production relied more on net worth (equity including reserves) than national banks anywhere and private banks in other regions. In other words, merchants and landlords in indigenous-production regions were active in investing in the banking business.

Table 3.2 Sources and uses of bank funds, by region, 1889

	Active[a]	Other[b]
	Lending	
National banks	46.6	46.1
Private banks	77.1	79.5
	Private deposits	
National banks	25.4	24.3
Private banks	32.1	41.7
	Government deposits	
National banks	16.3	6.9
Private banks	9.5	15.5
	Bank notes	
National banks	15.4	22.3
Private banks	–	–

Notes: Entries are percentages of total assets.

[a] Regions with active indigenous production. These are Hokuriku, Tokai and Tosan (the latter two are now called Chubu). All three are contiguous, more or less in the middle of Honshu.

[b] All other regions.

The share of capitalization by types of banks is as follows.

National banks	Private banks	Quasi banks	Region:
28.0	32.4	39.6	Active
65.7	23.5	10.8	Other

Source: Compiled by the author from data in various issues of *Ginko-kyoku Kin'yû Nenpô*.

3.1.3 Bank Borrowing in Perspective

Table 3.3 shows that the financing of modern industries, including manufacturing, relied mainly on equity capital in prewar Japan. The low level of retained earnings and high reliance on equity capital are even more prevalent during the 1890s (Teranishi 1982, p. 210, which provides data for before 1902).

The low dependence on bank borrowing has frequently been pointed out using piecemeal evidence. Table 3.3 confirms this point with a comprehensive data set. The low dependence on borrowing (including bills payable) does not necessarily mean a small role for banks in prewar Japan (Teranishi 2003b). Looking at the data for the total non-financial private sector (corporations, unincorporated businesses, and individual producers such as farmers and households) one sees a heavy reliance on borrowing (including billed discounted by banks).

Table 3.3 Percentage distribution of sources of funds, private sector, 1902–40

	Borrowings[1]	Bonds	Equities	Retained earnings
Large corporations in manufacturing				
1902–1915	18.9	9.0	56.0	16.1
1914–1930	16.3	13.2	48.6	21.9
1928–1940	17.1	12.3	53.4	17.2
Large corporations in modern industries				
1902–1915	10.0	8.6	61.8	19.6
1914–1930	11.7	15.9	55.0	17.4
1928–1940	13.7	20.9	53.3	12.1
Total non-financial private sector[2]				
1902–1915	64.9	4.2	26.1	4.8
1914–1930	53.5	6.6	33.2	6.7
1928–1940	44.4	11.9	40.7	3.0

Note: Percentage share of each item in the total of borrowing, bonds, equities and retained earnings.
Entries are percentages calculated from year-end data.
[1] For large corporations in manufacturing and modern industries, includes bills payable. For the total non-financial private sector, includes bills discounted by the banking sector.
[2] This is the corporate and individual sector in the flow of funds account at the macro level.

Source: Calculated from data in Fujino and Teranishi (2000).

The role played by the commercial sector provides a key to understanding the seemingly contradictory phenomenon of the corporate sector's low dependence on borrowing and the private and non-financial sector's high dependence on borrowing. Merchants (the commercial sector) were the major borrowers from banks (Teranishi 1982, p. 372). These funds were used either to invest in equities of large corporate firms or to lend on to small and medium enterprises and indigenous producers, including farmers.

Equities were often used as collateral for the loans. Banks never lent to small firms and farmers directly: in what is termed 'duplicated intermediation' (Teranishi 2000), the merchants intermediated between banks, small firms and farmers, utilizing their reputations with banks and information networks with respect to small firms and farmers. Merchants had extensive information accumulated through transactions: for example, through dealing in rice and fertilizer with small farmers, and in raw materials with small firms.

In other words, banks in the Meiji-Taishô system fulfilled an important role in financing industrial activities, in the sense of the quantitative flow of funds in the macroeconomy, although not necessarily in the sense of corporate governance (monitoring) of large firms (Teranishi 2003a).

The functioning of banks relied heavily on the reputational and informational role of merchants with respect to indigenous-sector financing and on the role of merchants as capital market-investors with respect to the modern sector. In this sense, the role of banks in the Meiji-Taishô economic system was qualitatively different from that of the high-growth-period, where banks, through mobilizing small savings of households, financed firms of all sizes directly.

3.1.4 Capital Market Efficiency

The high dependence of large corporation financing on equity capital does not necessarily mean the prewar capital market was efficient. Kataoka, Maru and Teranishi (1989) present a preliminary analysis of the informational efficiency of the stock market in the Meiji period. Using daily stock-price data from January 5 to December 29 1900, and monthly data from January 1898 to December 1903, of listed companies in the railroad and cotton spinning industries, it appears that the Meiji market was as efficient as the postwar market using the weak test of price randomness, but less efficient in terms of the semi-strong test regarding the effect of information about official discount rates and dividend payments. However, about 80 per cent of stock trading was done outside the stock exchanges (Hayashi 1963), so it is not easy to say anything conclusive about the efficiency of the stock market as a whole without further information. (For more on this point, see Shimura (1969), Shibagaki (1965), and Tsurumi (1983). Teranishi (1991, ch. 3) and Teranishi (1995a) also deal with the capability and limitations of prewar capital markets.)

3.2 ESTABLISHMENT OF CORPORATIONS

There were two waves of creation of corporations in the decades leading up to the emergence of the Meiji-Taishô system. Both are attributable to the emergence of new profit opportunities. Table 3.4 provides data.

Table 3.4 Capitalization and number of companies, 1887–97

Year	Firms[1]	Capital[2]
1887	2,038	67.9
1890	4,296	225.5
1894	2,104	148.4
1897	6,113	532.5

Notes:
[1] For 1887 and 1890, includes individually-owned firms.
[2] In million yen. For 1887 and 1890, this is authorized capital, not all of which was paid in. For 1894 and 1897 it is paid-in capital.

Source: *Teikoku-tôkei Nenkan*, each year.

The first occurred during 1887–89, centering on railroads and cotton spinning. In railroads, there were 46 applications to establish companies, 12 of which were licensed. In cotton spinning, starting with the reorganization of Mie Bôseki into a joint-stock company in 1886, modern firms with more than 10,000 spindles were established one after another: six in 1887, five (including Kurashiki Bôseki) in 1888, and five firms in 1889. Modern firms were also established in industries such as steel, cement, electricity, beer, sugar refinery, and paper manufacturing.

Another surge occurred during 1893–96, after the old Commercial Code became effective and the economy had recovered from the 1890 depression. Railroad construction enjoyed a second boom, centered on local short-distance lines. Many new firms were created in banking and cotton spinning, followed by heavy industries such as electricity, shipbuilding and steel.

Establishing a Commercial Code was an important goal in satisfying Western conditions for treaty revisions, as well as useful in its own right. (Japan had no tariff autonomy under the treaties signed when it was open to Western trade.) Thus, the Meiji government set to work. A German advisor serving as a professor at the Imperial University (the modern Tokyo University) produced a draft based primarily on French law, but also drawing on German and English law. At the same time, a Civil Code was being drafted, based largely on the French civil code. Both passed the Senate and the consultation by the Privy Council in 1890, but the Civil Code became embroiled in controversy, in part because of a backlash against what many felt was excessive

Westernization. As a result, the effective dates of both codes were postponed. However, some parts of the Old Commercial Code (*Shôhô*) became effective on July 1 1893. Most of these dealt with companies.

The New (Meiji) Commercial Code was drafted by a committee of three Japanese. It was passed by the Diet in 1899, taking effect on June 16 in that year. The drafting of the New (Meiji) Civil Code was started in 1893 by the deliberative council *hôten-chôsakai.* It was passed by the Diet partially in 1885, and fully in 1898. At the time of promulgation of the New Civil Code, the 1890 Civil Code, unenforced, was repealed (the New Civil Code became effective from June 16 1989).

3.2.1 Ownership Structure

Many of the new firms were family owned. Separation of ownership and management was also limited among stock companies: in 1900, 48 per cent of managers of 329 large companies were owner–executives (founder or his family) (Aonuma 1965). Stock ownership was also concentrated: in 1898, the number of stockholders per firm was fewer than 200 in 147 of 153 industries, and fewer than 50 in 104 industries (Imuta 1976b). Among the six exceptions were railroads, which averaged 736 shareholders.

The share of partnerships was also very high. Even in 1906, the number of joint-stock companies (4,300) was less than half the total number of corporations (9,400). However, they represented over 70 per cent of the capital. Many zaibatsu firms were not joint-stock companies until the 1930s, and it was only during the 1920s that the joint-stock company system became compulsory for the banking sector. This requirement was instituted in 1922 for saving banks, in 1923 for trust banks, and in 1927 for ordinary banks. Data on the legal structure of firms are in Table 3.5.

While family ownership is convenient and effective in mobilizing funds in the hands of entrepreneurial rich families, it is not usually effective in mobilizing funds of outside investors, especially small investors, because of the high agency costs entailed by the lack of information disclosure and insider control.

3.2.2 Liability

The government tried to cope with the deficiencies of family ownership through rules regarding liability.

Until the old Commercial Code became effective on July 1 1893,

Table 3.5 Legal structure and capitalization of firms

Year	Joint-stock companies		Limited partnership		Unlimited partnership	
	Number of firms	Average Capital	Number of firms	Average capital	Number of firms	Average capital
1896	2.6	138	1.7	17	0.3	37
1906	4.3	219	3.6	19	1.5	43
1916	7.5	279	7.5	21	3.2	60
1925	17.6	542	11.5	63	5.2	171
1925*	17.6	844	11.5	63	5.2	171
1935*	23.3	855	44.4	26	16.5	79

Notes: Number of firms in thousands, average capital in thousand yen.
Joint-stock company (*kabushiki-kaisha*), limited partnership (*gôshi-kaisha*), unlimited partnership (*gômei-kaisha*).
* Authorized capital, including unpaid-in portions.

Source: Nihon Tokei Kyokai (1988b, Table 15-5-b and 15-5-c).

even joint-stock companies were subject to unlimited liability, except for some categories of companies protected by special action. Thus, limited liability was applied to national banks, the Bank of Japan, the Yokohama Specie Bank, stock exchanges, rice trading associations, and Nihon Yûsen (the steamship company) by either special registrations or administrative regulations. Private banks were joint-stock companies with unlimited liability in principle until 1884, when limited liability was allowed.

The old Commercial Code (1893) adopted the Western system, requiring joint-stock companies to be limited liability. It also said that limited partnerships were to be composed of members with either limited or unlimited liability, and unlimited partnerships should consists of members with unlimited liability only. However, when the new code took effect on June 16 1899, the liability system was changed so that limited partnerships could not be established without some unlimited-liability members.

3.2.3 Voting Rights

The government put restrictions on the control rights of large owners. In the case of national banks after revision of the National Bank Act in 1886, for example, shareholders received one vote per share for the first 10 shares owned, one vote per 5 shares for the next 90 shares, and one vote per 10 shares over 100 shares. Likewise, under the articles of the shipping company Nihon Yûsen as revised in 1883, shareholders received one vote per share for the first 10 shares owned, but only one vote for each 5 additional shares. Table 3.6 has data on voting rights.

Table 3.6 Type of voting rights selected by newly formed companies, 1872–1900

1872–76	1877–85	1886–89	1890–92	1893–96	1897–1900	Type of voting rights
Firms selecting one vote per share as percentage of all firms in period						
50	6	15	31	61	76	
Number of firms, by type of voting						
3	2	12	5	63	26	One vote per share
–	–	8	1	2	–	Other[1]
2	14	15	1	20	2	Curtailment by simple declining ratio[2]
–	3	1	–	–	4	One vote per shareholder
1	15	42	9	18	2	Other curtailment
6	34	78	16	103	34	Total number of firms

Note: Entries are the number of firms in each time period filing articles (*teikan*) that indicate the type of voting system. The data were collected from an actual examination of documents in the 1970s, so they include only firms whose articles survived and were available.

[1] Includes variants of one vote per share.

[2] National-bank or Nihon-Yûsen type curtailment where, above specified levels, shares have less than one vote each. See text for a complete description.

Source: Imuta (1976a, p. 206).

The Commercial Code that became effective in 1893 made the one-share one-vote system the norm. In anticipation of this, restrictions were becoming less common in the early 1890s. However, the Code did allow restrictions on the voting rights of shareholders with more than 10 shares. Establishment of limited partnerships, which gave one vote to each partner irrespective of the amount of capital contributed, increased after 1893.

According to Imuta (1976a), restriction of voting rights was endorsed and recommended by the government during the Meiji period. In order to understand why restrictions on voting rights were introduced, it is important to note the role of former samurai in the newly established corporate system. The major investors in modern corporations were merchants and landlords. Most corporate managers, however, were former samurai.

3.2.4 Managers

The government was eager to mobilize the funds of rich merchants and landlords but, at the same time, it did not want to give much power to investors. There are several, non-conflicting, ways to look at this ambivalence.

Because many private-sector managers were former samurai, and the Meiji government was established primarily by samurai, in particular those below the top tier, it might not be far off the mark to conjecture that the government intended to protect the position of managers in modern corporations. That is, the government restrictions on investors *vis-à-vis* managers were mainly motivated by a desire to improve the economic conditions of former samurai who had lost their positions in the ruling class at the time of Meiji Restoration in 1868.

Another view stresses the fact that samurai had a value system that emphasized the social value of actual producers and managers compared with mere rentiers. Thus, Takahashi (1977, p. 15) notes that the former samurai in government highly valued service as an end in itself.

The extent of samurai as managers in the modern sector is illustrated by two studies. Morikawa (1980) presents detailed information about corporate managers at eight large zaibatsu who were not members of the zaibatsu family. Of the 76 managers who became board members before 1912, 63 per cent (48) were former samurai. In the case of 14 national banks with main offices in Tokyo, 63 per cent (39) of the 62 managers were former samurai, including all the managers of three banks. Tokyo had 16 national banks, but data are lacking for one, and the Fifteenth (Peers) Bank was an outlier because it was established exclusively by court nobility (who were not samurai). (Refer to Takahashi 1977 on these points.)

Box 3.1 ASSET HOLDERS IN THE TOKUGAWA PERIOD

Underlying the behavior of the former samurai class was a value system regarding occupation in the feudal period.

During the Tokugawa era there was a strict caste ranking among occupations. There were four categories: the highest was samurai, then farmers, then craftspeople (including manufacturers and engineers), and finally, at the bottom, merchants.

Members of the ruling class in feudal Japan were not asset holders. This is quite different from the European case, where the ruling class also had huge wealth. Most financial assets in Japan were held by merchants, and land was held by farmers – small cultivating farmers called *hyakushô* and emerging landlords. The ruling class had only taxation rights, and did not possess any substantial income-yielding property. Partly for this reason, investors' rights were not necessarily respected.

The *daimyo* (fief rulers) and other samurai borrowed heavily from merchants. The loan contracts were quite often cancelled by official decrees in order to restore the fiscal condition of the fief government, as well as to relieve samurai and peasants in poverty.

3.2.5 Leveraging

The government tried to make the most of the reputation of wealthy individuals to complement the lack of information about newly established firms. The practice of equity collateral-financing was a typical case. From around 1887, banks were increasingly involved in the business of lending to wealthy individuals by taking equity held by them as collateral. A landlord or a merchant, who bought stock in firm A with his own savings could borrow from the bank with the stock as collateral, and use the borrowed money to purchase stock in firm B. This mechanism facilitated equity investment by wealthy individuals, and enhanced the role of equity capital in financing corporate investment. Newly established firms had not built up a reputation nor were they able to provide much information about their trading position, so it was not easy for them to borrow from banks. The equity capital supplied through equity collateral financing functioned as a substitute for direct bank lending to the firms. This is another reason for the high reliance on equity financing of large modern corporations in Table 3.3.

The same mechanism explains why retained earnings in Table 3.3 are so low: individuals who borrowed from banks requested high dividend payments on their equity holdings in order to cover the interest costs of the borrowing.

The Bank of Japan (BOJ) promoted this mechanism. It accepted equity-collateral lending by commercial banks from 1885, and became more deeply involved at the time of the 1890 depression. As an immediate measure to restore bank liquidity, BOJ specifically approved the shares of Nihon Yûsen, Marine Insurance, and 13 railroad companies as collateral qualifying for bill discounting. Article 12 of the Bank of Japan Act actually prohibited loans with equity collateral, but utilizing discounting circumvented this. Although the actual function of the discounting was a close substitute for loans, it was considered an 'unavoidable expedient'. Such discounting continued to be an important practice until 1942, when a new Bank of Japan Law acknowledged the practice as a formal business.

Not all the money lent by BOJ to commercial banks was utilized for equity collateral-financing. Moreover, while the role of BOJ credit was significant during the 1890s, the commitment of commercial banks to such financing far outweighed BOJ bill discounting with equity collateral after around 1900. The share of lending with equity collateral to total lending of ordinary banks was 24.5 per cent during 1893–97 and 23.5 per cent during 1903–07, while the ratio of bill discounting by BOJ to total loans of ordinary banks was 23.2 per cent and 4.0 per cent, respectively, for example. Even though BOJ bill discounting with equity collateral had only a limited effect in alleviating the liquidity shortage of commercial banks, it cannot be denied that the policy promoted bank equity collateral-financing through an authorizing effect.

3.2.6 Corporate Governance Led by Large Shareholders

Corporate governance led by large shareholders in the Meiji-Taishô economic system emerged through a process of incentive provisions by the Meiji government, which intended to mobilize the wealth of landlords and merchants. In providing various incentives, the government took quite a flexible stance: it allowed banks to run subsidiary businesses like warehousing and transportation in order to make the most of the informational capability of merchants and industrialists; pyramidal ownership of a group of corporations was not negated, and instead of negating, the government introduced various devices regarding the liability system and voting rights in order to alleviate market failures arising from the ownership structure; the practice of equity collateral-financing was not prohibited, but rather promoted by Bank of Japan policy in order to compensate for the lack of reputation of newly established corporations.

Merchants and landlords, who had accumulated savings and acquired business skills during the economic growth that began in the early 19th century, reacted shrewdly to the new profit opportunities provided by the incentives and by the expansion of markets resulting from infrastructure development. The investment of their savings, together with bank borrowing through equity-collateral financing, resulted in the dominance of large shareholders in the ownership and control of new corporations in modern industries.

The realistic and flexible approach taken by the Meiji government was a natural response to the international political environment in East Asia and Japan's latecomer position. The severe tension with nearby China and an expansive Russia made the rapid build-up of military power backed by economic strength an urgent task for Meiji Japan. Under these conditions, establishing fully-fledged modern financial institutions was not necessarily the first priority. What was most important was to establish a system capable of mobilizing resources to support rapid economic and military expansion. In other words, Japan's policy at the time was not a big–bang approach of modernizing the economy all at once. Rather, a two-track approach was used: a gradual promotion of modern institutions while at the same time making the most of existing traditional practices (Teranishi 2003b).

A policy that emphasized maximum mobilization of resources, while leaving the traditional system in tact, naturally had costs. Serious agency costs caused by symbiotic bank–firm relationships, called the organ-bank problem, were one. Banks established to serve related firms or firm groups were called organ banks (*kikan-ginkô*), and the groups made use of interlocking ownership and directorships to retain tight control.

Further, corporate governance led by large shareholders provided the basis for a classic liberal system through assertion of the 'logic of the private sector' (*min no ronri*) against bureaucratic control. This logic was gradually converted into the 'logic of the strong' (*kyôsha no ronri*) in the 1930s, giving rise to problems related to monopoly and dominance by zaibatsu.

3.3 FROM 'DEVELOPMENT FROM ABOVE' TO A DIVISION OF LABOR

The Meiji-Taishô system is characterized by respect for private sector initiatives and the nature of the division of labor between the government and private sector with respect to the pursuit of economic and political goals. It was only 30 years after the Meiji Restoration, however, that such a characteristic emerged, and the private sector obtained a formal political voice in how to develop the national economy.

Until the late 1890s, it had not been agreed within the government how to apply as policy the well-known slogan for the objective of the Meiji government, *fukoku-kyôhei* (economic strength and military might). Rather, there was recurrent controversy among those asserting *kyôkoku-ron* (a military build-up), *fukoku-ron* (economic development), and *minryoku kyûyô-ron* (alleviating the burden on the people). The last group tried to stem both *fukoku-ron* and *kyôhei-ron*. Moreover, the controversy itself took place without consulting the opinion of taxpayers, or the private sector. 'For long after the Meiji Restoration, a pursuit for the policy of *fukoku-kyôhei* by the *hanbatsu* [Meiji] government was possible because of the exclusion of the landlords and farmers, who were the main taxpayers, from the decision-making process' (Banno 1971, p. 1). The promulgation of the Meiji Constitution in February 1889 and the opening of the Imperial Diet in November 1890 provided an opportunity to change the situation.

In fact, the main aim of the *jiyû-minken-undô* (freedom and private rights, or popular-rights movement) by landlords, farmers, and former-samurai groups from the 1870s lay in institutionalizing their voice by means of the Diet system. After opening of the Diet, however, neither the *minryoku kyûyô-ron* asserted by the political parties representing the interests of farmers nor the *fukoku kyôhei-ron* advocated by the Meiji leaders was realized. Instead, there was an unexpected stalemate, which was sustained for almost 10 years.

It was only after the bill for a land tax increase was approved and the Rikken Seiyûkai political party was organized (August 1900) that a pursuit of national objectives based on a newly agreed division of labor between the government and private sectors was resumed. The basic background for this was the continued growth in size and wealth of the class of merchants and industrialists, and the manifestation of their interests and power.

3.3.1 Conflicts within the Government Regarding State Objectives

The choice between *fukoku-ron*, economic development from above, and *kyôhei-ron*, military expansion, provoked a long-running controversy among the Meiji leaders, bureaucracy, and political parties, not only at the national level but also at the level of stability of regional economies and society.

First was the conflict regarding the early developmental policy (*shokusan-kôgyô*). It began with the establishment of the Ministry of Industry in 1870, and enjoyed its heyday after 1873 under the leadership of the Ministry of Internal Affairs, eventually entering a winding-up process as early as 1880. The first stage of the policy, characterized by the modeling of Western manufacturing by state factories and led by the Ministry of Industry, was cut back after political turmoil in 1873.

Saigô Takamori and Itagaki Taisuke resigned from the government after their advocacy of a military expedition against Korea, *kyôhei-ron*, was defeated in October 1873 by an assertion of the primacy of domestic economic development, *fukoku-ron*, advocated by Okubo Toshimichi. This was the first major split in the Meiji leadership.

Under Okubo, as Internal Affairs Minister, and Okuma Shigenobu, Finance Minister, the early developmental policy entered its second stage, emphasizing promotion of a variety of indigenous and light industries: subsidization of the establishment of private cotton-spinning companies, establishment of agricultural schools and experimental stations, and promotion of the establishment of national banks. The developmental policy, however, was abandoned after the assassination of Okubo in 1878 and the downfall of Okuma in the political turmoil of 1881. The new Finance Minister, Matsukata Masayoshi, privatized state enterprises and restricted state involvement in industrial activities that had mainly been implemented by the Ministry of Agriculture and Commerce.[1]

The early developmental policy played an important role in that the government took the risks of transplanting new manufacturing industries. Losses on these state projects, however, aggravated the fiscal deficit, so abolition of the policy was inevitable.

3.3.2 Deficits and Deflation

The overall fiscal deficits were caused by two events. First, the government had reduced the land tax rate in 1876; this is discussed below in the section on 'Conflict between State and Farmers'. Second, was high inflation (Table 3.7).

Table 3.7 Inflation rates, 1877–80

Annual percentage rates for	1877	1878	1879	1880
Agricultural products	15.0	13.0	25.2	11.5
Industrial products	1.6	8.0	11.5	20.2

The inflation, caused by the issue of non-convertible government notes to finance military expenditures regarding the civil war in 1877 (*Seinan-sensô*, generally called the Satsuma Rebellion in English) and by bank-note issue by national banks, decreased the real value of land tax revenue, the nominal value of which had been set as given percentages of land prices predetermined by the 1873 Meiji land tax reform.

Okuma attempted to cope with the government deficits by such measures as a foreign bond issue of 5 million yen and levying part of the land tax in kind (payment in rice) without success, and eventually succumbed to Matsukata, who favored the necessity of fiscal tightening through curtailment of developmental state projects and the redemption of non-convertible currencies. In the early 1880s Matsukata continued the tight fiscal policy started by Okuma which finally resolved fiscal deficits and realized redemption of non-convertible currencies. Another important objective was to stem the outflow of specie by lowering the price level. As shown below, the policy entailed serious deflation, which bears Matsukata's name.

Table 3.8 Deflation rates, 1881–85

Annual percentage rates for	1881	1882	1883	1884	1885
Agricultural products	11.3	–16.7	–21.4	–12.4	9.8
Industrial products	21.6	–9.2	–20.7	–10.9	–3.1

As a stabilization policy, the effectiveness of Matsukata's policy should not be exaggerated, because inflation had tended to stabilize before initiation of the policy. Also, the reduction of budget deficits by Okuma has been estimated as being approximately the same amount as that under Matsukata (Teranishi 1982).

The deflation increased tax revenue in real terms with respect to the land tax. Matsukata also shifted a significant part of the fiscal burden to local governments through the implementation of the 48th Decree, which had been promulgated by Okuma and Ito Hirobumi in 1880. This did three things: it raised local tax rates, shifted certain expenditures from the central government to the local governments, and abolished central-government subsidies of local public works. As a result, the budgets of local governments turned into deficits amounting to 9.1 million yen during 1882–84, which was close to one-third of the surplus of the central government, 28.50 million yen, during the same period (Teranishi 1982).

The political turmoil in 1873 was a conflict between *fukoku-ron* and *kyôhei-ron*, that is, between developmental policy and foreign-expedition policy, and that of 1881 was related to the dispute with respect to the methodology of *fukoku-ron*, that is, between development from above and growth based on the market mechanism.

3.3.3 Picking Policies

After the deflation caused by Matsukata's policy subsided around 1885, another conflict emerged within the government regarding governance of regional economies. Mikuriya (1980) explains the complicated structure of this conflict among interest groups as follows. The Ministry of Internal Affairs, dominated by those who came from the former Chôshû fief, advocated subsidizing local public works, which meant abrogation of the 48th Decree, in order to relieve local economies depressed by the deflation and to control municipal assemblies.

The Ministry of Finance, led by those who came from the former Satsuma fief, including Matsukata, at first opposed Internal Affairs from the standpoint of fiscal soundness, and then argued for financing local public works through establishing a new development bank. This idea provoked opposition from the Ministry of Agriculture and Commerce, also dominated by Satsuma people, who maintained that the main role of a new development bank should be to promote indigenous export industries.

With no concession by any ministry, the dispute was finally brought to a conclusion through the resignation of Maeda Masana in 1885. He had led the Ministry of Agriculture and Commerce plan. Maeda was re-instated in 1889 with a new plan for a development bank, which was close to the Ministry of Finance plan. Maeda's new plan, however, triggered opposition by Chôshû people, who suspected that a coalition between the Ministries of Finance and of Agriculture and Commerce might monopolize the rights and interests of the new bank, so Maeda was ousted again in 1890 by a cabinet led by Yamagata Aritomo, leader of the Chôshû group.

In the meantime, Internal Affairs proposed a new policy to transfer forests held by the central government to municipal governments in order to improve their fiscal conditions. The Minister of Agriculture and Commerce, Inoue Kaoru, who came from Chôshû, agreed with this. However, Inoue was obliged to withdraw support in 1890 when the Ministry of Finance campaigned against it, claiming it would not necessarily improve the fiscal condition of municipal governments.

3.3.4 Conflict between State and Farmers

The conflict among Meiji leaders and bureaucrats regarding state objectives was ostensibly a rivalry within the government sector. However, this reflected a rivalry between the government and farmers with respect to the financing and use of government expenditures.

At first, the demand by farmers and landlords was simply an alleviation of their tax burden, and this was manifested in *ad hoc* peasant uprisings. In 1877, the year of civil war in Kyushu (*Seinan-sensô*), and in the midst of frequent riots by dissident former samurai, the government was obliged to issue an Emperor's Notification reducing rates in a bid to pre-empt farmers joining the samurai. The land tax rate was decreased from 3 per cent to 2.5 per cent, and the maximum rate of local tax, which was stipulated as a fraction of land tax, was reduced from one-third to one-fifth of the land tax. The result was that local tax revenues were halved. Total reduction in revenues, central and local government combined, amounted to 15 million yen, which was virtually the maximum permissible limit (Banno 1983) in view of the size of total government expenditure, 91 million yen in 1880 (Table 3.9).

Table 3.9 Expenditures of central and local governments (million yen per annum)

	1880	1890	1900	1910	1920	1930	1940
Central government[1]	63	82	293	569	1,360	1,558	5,860
Local governments	28	42	133	288	963	1,775	3,123
Prefectures	13	21	52	87	285	478	1,461
Cities, towns villages[2]	15	21	79	165	663	1,274	1,661

Notes:
[1] General account only.
[2] Includes counties.
In the original source, local government entries are not equal to the sum of prefecture and cities, towns and villages, which they should be. It is not clear why this is the case.

Source: Nihon Tokei Kyokai (1988a, Tables 12-1-a and 12-14-a).

In addition, the government suffered from the decline in the real value of revenues resulting from inflation. This invites the conjecture that the actual aim of the deflationary policy implemented by Matsukata was to increase the real value of government revenues, that is, to transfer income from farmers and landlords to the government (Teranishi 1983). Inflation had already tended to stabilize before initiation of the policy.

In the private-rights movement (*jiyû-minken-undô*), the rivalry between the government and farmers regarding tax rates was converted into a controversy over state objectives. Farmers pressed for burden alleviation as a national policy, and this comprised one of the three pillars of the assertions in the democratizing movement, along with revision of the unequal treaties with foreign countries, and opening of an Imperial Diet.

After opening of the Diet in November 1890, the rivalry was succeeded by confrontation between Meiji leaders and the political parties. The parties, inheriting the *minken* spirit, asserted burden alleviation and small government, while the government, dominated by the *hanbatsu*-based oligarchs, emphasized a building-up of economic and military strength. The confrontation continued through the 1890s, and reached a deadlock because tax rate changes needed to be passed both by the lower house and the House of Peers. The demand for burden alleviation and small government policy was rejected by the Peers, which was composed primarily of former samurai and courtiers (although there was some representation of large taxpayers), and the demand for the policy advocating build-up of economic and military strength was rejected by the lower house, which was dominated by the parties (Banno 1971).

A resolution was triggered by the rise of merchants and industrialists as a new class to shoulder the tax burden, and the heightening of international tension in East Asia.

3.3.5 Taxing Businesses

As private-sector businesses increased in number and importance to the economy, they naturally were viewed as a source of tax revenue.

After the Sino-Japanese War (1894–95) the chambers of commerce in various cities and their federation (established in 1892) were confronted by the government with respect to the levying of business tax. The resistance by the chambers reached a climax in 1897, when 17 of them issued public statements against the new business tax. Reasons for their opposition were: there was room for a land tax increase in view of the rise in rice prices; the government should reduce expenditures further, especially the cost of the military build-up by the army; and merchants and industrialists had been subject to taxation of local business since 1875.

There are two things of note here: the expression of concern about the expansion of non-productive military expenditures, and, especially, the assertion of equal burden-sharing among farmers, merchants and industrialists. This was not so much opposition to being taxed, as an argument that introduction of business taxes could be agreed to only with an increase in the land tax rate. This was explicitly stated, for example in a public statement of the Osaka Chamber of Commerce reported in *Tokyo keizai zasshi* 181, February 8 1896.

Further, the policy recommendations by farmers and political parties, emphasizing burden alleviation and reduction of the land tax, became less forceful after the Sino-Japanese War when a national consensus to strengthen military and economic power was emerging. As international tension on the Asian continent was running high, military build-up was considered indispensable, and the parties had already expressed support for the strengthening policy at the Ninth Diet (1895–96). Moreover, since the land tax was still a major source of central government revenue, an increase in the burden on farmers was inevitable.

As a result, a bill creating a business tax was passed in 1896 as Act 33, and the land tax law was revised at the 13th Diet (1898–99), resulting in an increase in the tax rate of 0.8 percentage points, to 3.3 per cent. The government agreed the increase was to be temporary – five years. However, this agreement was not upheld.

The political parties, especially the Kenseitô (successor of the Jiyûtô), did not lose support among farmers and landlords even though they had agreed to raise the land tax. One reason was that a reassessment of land prices was carried out at the same time, resulting in a reduction of the land values used to compute the taxes. (For the effect of reassessment on political support, see Banno 1971.)

Another reason was introduction of the policy of siphoning off benefits to regions, especially by Kenseitô and its successor in 1900, the Rikken Seiyûkai (henceforth, simply Seiyûkai), through which local infrastructure was subsidized, compensating the raised tax burden on farmers and landlords.

Duties on imports were restricted by treaty, but indirect taxes were another source. The first Okuma cabinet (1898) resorted to extensive increases in taxes on liquor, tobacco and sugar. Even though it was the first cabinet organized by political parties (on June 30 1898), it was obliged to support a military build-up in order to gain acquiescence by the more authoritarian of the Meiji leaders, while adopting a policy of opposing the land tax increase.

3.3.6 Government–Private-sector Cooperation

Before the rise of merchants and industrialists, farmers and landlords were the only taxpayers. As farmers and landlords came to recognize this fact, their willingness or reluctance to pay taxes was closely related to their evaluation of state objectives. After merchants and industrialists became another important tax-paying class, however, a mechanism emerged in which decisions regarding state objectives, that is, how to allocate government expenditures, was separated from the decision of financing, that is, how to share the tax burden.

Although the Meiji economic system was not a world of lump-sum taxes, so that separation of the two decisions was not necessarily an optimal configuration, an agreed-on burden-sharing among taxpayers enabled the separation as a realistic arrangement. In this way, a consensus on the division of labor between government and the private sector was reached. Government was entrusted to allocate its expenditures at its discretion and to pursue state objectives through a political decision-making process; the private sector, while assuming the role of financing the expenditures, was allowed to engage in economic activities, more or less free of government interventions.

In this arrangement, the emphasis on the private-sector initiative was synonymous with use of market mechanisms. Moreover, the concurrent emergence of the system of siphoning off benefits to regions enabled taxpayers to monitor central government expenditures through representation of distributive interests by regional economies. From the viewpoint of political science, the emergence of such an agreement is considered to be a completion of the Meiji Constitution system. That is, democratization in the form of promulgation of the constitution in 1889 and opening of the Diet in 1890 was made institutionally compatible with the pursuit of state objectives emphasizing the build-up of military and economic strength (Banno 1971, p. 241).

Table 3.10 presents changes over time in the sources of central government revenue. Owing to the new business tax, central government revenue increased 2.1 per cent (4.4 million yen) in 1897. Revenue from the land tax increased 16.7 per cent (6.4 million yen) from 1898 to 1899. During the Russo-Japanese war (1904–05), the land tax, business tax and income tax rates were increased further, and an era of 'expensive government' arrived, as noted in Nakamura (1985). In 1904, land and business taxes were raised considerably because of the war. However, a new duty on imported rice was introduced to compensate farmers for the land tax increase.

Table 3.10 Central government, general account, revenue (million yen, per fiscal year)

Revenue from	1880	1890	1900	1910	1920	1930	1940
Taxes	55	66	134	317	730	835	3,653
Duties	3	4	17	40	69	105	144
State enterprises	2	9	40	129	328	438	499
Bonds and borrowing	–	–	44	4	76	38	1,282
All else	3	27	61	183	797	181	867
Total	63	106	296	673	2,000	1,597	6,445
			Taxes, detail by type				
Land tax	42	40	47	76	74	68	4
Income tax	–	1	6	32	190	201	1,489
Business tax	–	–	6	26	62	54	78
Liquor tax	6	14	50	87	164	219	285
Sugar tax	–	–	–	18	40	78	141
Other	7	11	25	78	200	215	1,656

Note: The total revenue of the central government is not equal to the total expenditure in Table 3.9. This seems to be due to the practice of deferred payments and receipt without formal loan contracts. (Figures of both tables are settlement accounts).

Source: Nihon Tokei Kyokai (1988a, Tables 12-1-a and 12-8-b).

3.4 LINKING REGIONAL AND NATIONAL ECONOMIES

In the sub-system of the division of labor between the government and the private sector, government intervention in private economic activities was kept at a minimum. The government did, however, allocate a significant part of its enlarged revenue to the supply of public goods, and this exerted a substantial influence on the distributive interests among people. Regional economies came to play the role of intermediated organizations at the government–private-sector interface, and represented the distributive interests of the people.

This section examines how regional economies were linked to the central (national) economy, and then shows how, with increased competition among regions, a mechanism of 'siphoning off benefits to the regions' (*sekkyoku-shugi*) emerged as a mechanism to represent distributive interests through intermediation by political parties.

3.4.1 Integration of Regional Markets

During the Tokugawa era, transportation of goods and people across regions was strictly regulated for military reasons. Moreover, bridges were not allowed across major rivers. Long-distance transportation was primarily by sea. In contrast, the Meiji government embarked on significant development of the transportation and communication systems, which had enormous effects on the distribution of population and economic activity. Tables 3.11 and 3.12 depict the growth of infrastructure.

With respect to transportation, the number of freight wagons and carts increased rapidly, reflecting the emphasis on road construction in government policy. The progress of marine transportation is illustrated by the increase in steamships and western-style sailboats. Development of railroads accelerated after 1885, and by 1900 most arterial routes were completed. With respect to communications, the telegraph was introduced in 1870 and the postal service in 1871. They spread rapidly throughout the country. Diffusion of the telephone system, introduced in 1890, was also remarkably fast.

The effect of developments in transportation are clearly seen in the lowering of marine freight charges on coal from Wakamatsu in northern Kyushu to Yokohama: from 3.17 yen per ton in 1876 to 1.65 yen in 1898. The price of freight for rice from Niigata to Osaka went from 112 yen per 100 *koku* in 1870 to 50 yen in 1883 (Yasuba 1979).

The improved communication and transportation networks, and lower freight charges, contributed to a convergence of goods prices and interest rates. This is illustrated in Figure 3.2, which uses changes in the coefficients of variation in prices and rates as an indicator of integration: a declining coefficient means convergence, and convergence is a measure of integration. The rice market was already relatively tied to the center, but prefectural variations nonetheless fell by half in the 1880s. The prefectural variations of the silk price decreased until 1890 but did not do so toward 1900. This seems to be related to the increased sensitivity to the quality of raw silk by the market as well as the growing difference in the quality among prefectures (During 1890 to 1900, the percentage of farms engaged in sericulture in total farm households increased from 19.9 per cent to 29.0 per cent, tapering off the thereafter, and the ratio of output of machine-reeled output to traditional *zaguri* silk increased from 0.74 to 1.30.)

Backed by the development of transportation and communication, the banking system, which began in 1876, quickly integrated local financial markets. The number of correspondence contracts increased from only

Table 3.11 Development of transportation system, 1870–1910

Year	Railroads			Road Vehicles		Coastal shipping	
	Nationals lines, operating (km)	Private lines, operating (km)	Passengers, national lines (millions)	Freight wagons (000)	Carts (000)	Steamships (000 tons)	Sailboats (000 tons)
1870	0	0	0	–	–	15	2
1875	61	0	2.8	1.7	116	42	9
1880	124	0	53.2	3.4	317	41	48
1885	270	217	26.1	14.5	474	60	53
1890	887	1,366	11.27	40.1	763	94	52
1895	954	2,731	18.76	70.1	1,043	341	45
1900	1324	4,675	31.46	120.6	1,322	543	–
1905	2414	5,232	31.03	125.5	1,356	939	–
1910	7837	823	1386.3	194.0	1,668	1,234	–

Note: Private railroads were mostly nationalized during 1906–10. Freight wagons were drawn by horses or oxen. Carts were drawn by people.

Source: Asahi Shinbun (1930).

Table 3.12 Development of communications network

	Mail	Telegraph		Telephone	
	Domestic pieces sent (million)	Cable length of (km)	Messages sent (000)	Cable length (km)	Calls made (000)
1871	1	75	20	0	0
1875	26	2,502	520	0	0
1880	68	6,762	2,030	0	0
1885	115	8,820	2,640	0	0
1890	224	11,314	4,210	50	30
1895	446	15,881	910	178	131
1900	740	27,489	16,230	763	666
1905	1,236	31,027	22,100	1,317	1,505
1910	1,509	39,030	28,640	2,606	5,584

Note: Cable lengths converted from *ri* (3.927 km) in source.

Source: Asahi Shinbun (1930).

one (between Tokyo Dai-Ichi Bank and Ono-gumi in Nagasaki) in 1876, to 338 in 1879, and to 1027 in 1880.

There was some convergence of deposit interest rates, although more so for minimum rates than for maximum rates. It could be conjectured that the minimum deposit rate in each prefecture represents rates of either the largest banks in the region or of banks with main offices in Tokyo or Osaka. Perceived as relatively safe, they did not need to offer as high a rate as a smaller, local bank. Because nation wide banks had no particular reason to offer different rates in different regions, they in effect set a national floor. The maximum rates represent the cost of funds for small and risky banks, reflecting deposit-market risks idiosyncratic to each prefecture.

Lending rates in each prefecture, both maximum and minimum, are related to the industrial risks peculiar to the region, and thus do not show any convergence. This is illustrated in Figure 3.3.

The available evidence seems to corroborate the fact that the integration of financial markets around the turn of the century occurred mainly in the form of linkage between each prefectural market and central markets in Tokyo or Osaka, rather than linkages among neighboring prefectural markets. Thus, prices and interest rates in the periphery converged to those of the center, not to some set of peripheral levels. And, of course, differences persisted for local reasons.

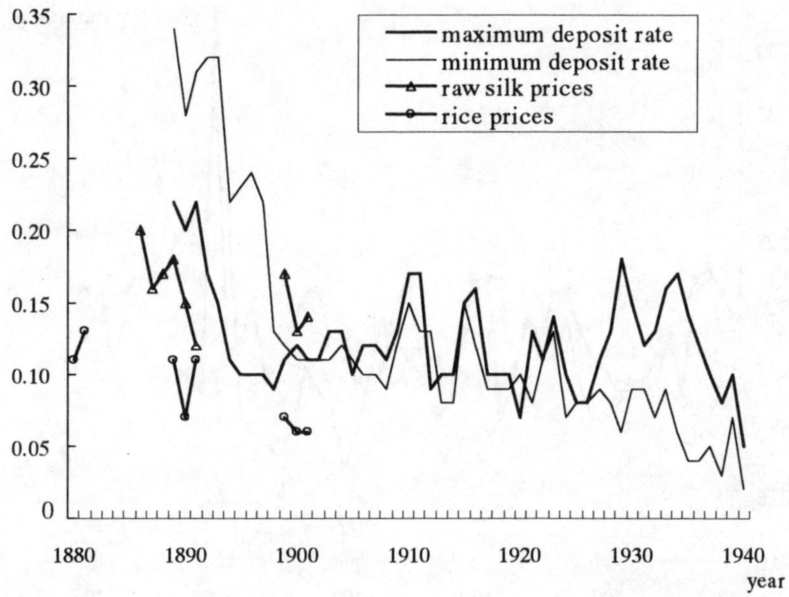

Source: Drafted by the author from data in various issues of *Teikoku Tôkei Nenkan* and Noda (1963).

Figure 3.2 Coefficient of variation in deposit rate and selected prices, 1880–1940

3.4.2 Representation of Distributive Interests

The impact of the integration of regional economies into the national economy was enormous, both economically and politically. Local producers who had segmented markets for their products came to compete intensively in the national and export markets. This, in turn, made the enhancement of competitive strength an urgent task for each region, invoked movements to invite the central government to invest in regional infrastructure. Regions began to vie fiercely for railroads, port facilities, roads and high schools.

Take Yamanashi prefecture as an example. Until the late 1880s undertakings by the central government regarding regional public works and school system encountered serious opposition from landlords, merchants and other local leaders (*meibôka*), arousing serious disputes between the prefectural assemblies they led and the prefectural administration controlled by the central government (Ariizumi 1980). This was

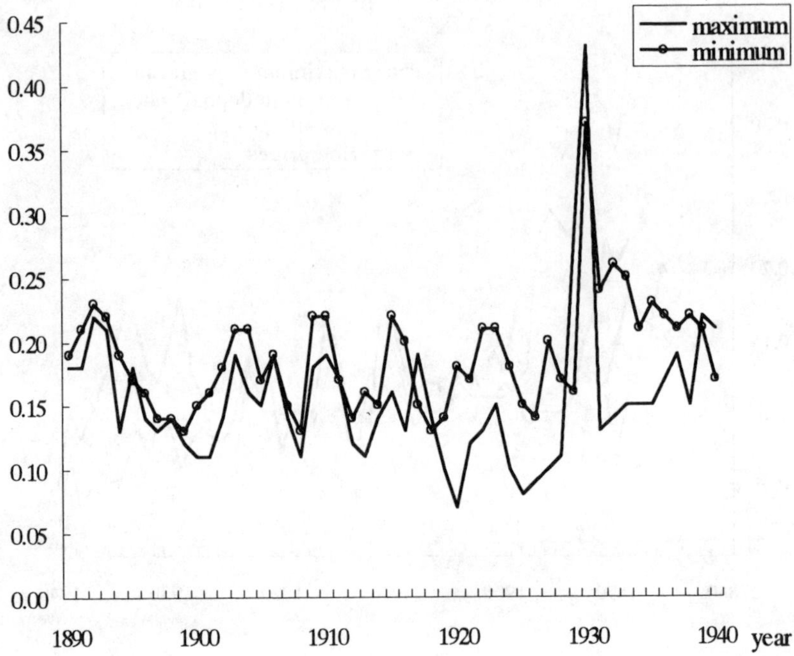

Source: Various issues of *Teikoku Tôkei Nenkan*.

Figure 3.3 Coefficient of variation in bank lending rates, 1880–1940

partly because local leaders hated to bear expenses allotted to the prefecture, partly because many of the undertakings were related to military and political activities, so that they were not directly beneficial to the regional economy, and partly because leaders were confident in their ability to promote regional society and economy by themselves. For example, many leaders who opposed establishment of prefectural schools operated private schools in order to bring up local youngsters in line with their own philosophy. Likewise, leaders were critical of the industrial policy of the central government, because they considered it hindered the development of private businesses.

From the mid-1890s, however, having become more conscious of competitors and economic differentials among regions, local leaders ceased to resist the policies of the prefectural administrators, and instead eagerly began to engage in the induction of central government investment in local infrastructure and to apply for subsidies for public schools.

In Yamanashi (immediately west of Tokyo in the mountains), merchants and landlords became quite intent on inviting construction of a railroad: extension of the Kôbu railroad to the prefecture. As a backdrop for such a movement, there was serious anxiety among Yamanashi leaders regarding competition in silk manufacturing: competitors in the Gunma prefecture (northwest of Tokyo) were expanding production rapidly utilizing the Jômô railroad, and in Nagano prefecture, which was served by the Chûzan railroad.

An additional reason for welcoming central government investment was the dearth of local financial resources due to the frequent occurrence of floods at the time. After the Meiji Restoration, the mountains in Yamanashi had been denuded by indiscriminate deforestation to obtain fuel used in manufacturing raw silk, tea and ceramics, and this resulted in widespread and frequent local floods (Ariizumi 1980).

3.4.3 Effect on Political Parties

The integration of regional economies into the national economy and the intense competition among regional economies had a significant influence on politics, especially on the behavior of political parties. In central government, political parties were confronting the Meiji leaders (*hanbatsu*). The parties' assertions concerning alleviation of the people's burden and curtailing government expenditures were becoming less persuasive as military expansion became inevitable in order to cope with international tension after the Sino-Japanese war. 'The people' in this context means farmers and landlords. It was necessary, however, for political parties to secure the support of merchants and industrialists and, at the same time, to request that they share the fiscal burden.

To handle this complicated situation and to balance supporting powers, in the late 1890s the Kenseitô resorted to the following policy mix.

1. With respect to merchants and industrialists, to levy a business tax at the central government level, but to keep the tax rate as low as possible by increasing land tax revenue.
2. With respect to farmers and landlords, to increase the land tax, but reduce the groups' burden by restricting the period of tax increase and reassessing land values used to compute the tax.
3. With respect to regional economies, to introduce a 'positive policy' (*sekkyoku-seisaku*) whereby each region could request that the central government provide benefits to the region in the form of infrastructure investment such as railroads, port facilities, and schools.

In other words, to compensate for the increased tax burden on landlords and merchants, political parties introduced a policy of siphoning off benefits to regions governed by them.

Hoshi Toru, a leader of Kenseitô, delivered an address on his canvassing tour at Sendai in September 1899, which is considered to be a monumental event in the history of party politics in Japan (Ariizumi 1983):

> Tôhoku seems to be backward compared with the south-western regions. What should we do for the future of Tôhoku? Should Tohoku resort to a feudal-style 'negative policy', or to a 'positive policy', suitable for the era of the new constitution? I believe there is no doubt that Tohoku should adopt a 'positive policy'. Economic development could not be realized without adequate transportation facilities. Equipped with advanced transportation, exports would increase, and both agriculture and commerce would develop. With respect to education, Tohoku is backward in both compulsory and higher-level education. It is necessary to increase higher-level public schools to catch up to the western areas. This is why Kenseitô has referred to the necessity of railroads, port facilities and higher-level education in its recent Diet resolution. Since such policies do not hurt any other regions and bring benefits to Tohoku, they are beneficial to the national economy.

The term 'positive policy' had been coined originally as a concept regarding state objectives, with the implication of simultaneous promotion of economic development and military expansion, as against a 'negative policy', which emphasized burden-alleviation and a choice between economic development and military expansion.

Simultaneous pursuit of multiple objectives makes expansion of government expenditures inevitable: the advent of the era of large central government. Kenseitô tried to obtain the support of regional leaders for its expensive policy, and proposed making regional economies intermediate organizations at the government–private-sector interface regarding distributional conflicts in the era of large government.

3.5 THE WEALTHY AS THE SYSTEM EMERGES

The modern economic development of Meiji Japan started as wealthy individuals invested in industries such as banking, cotton spinning, and railroads, and various indigenous industries. It is interesting to examine who were wealthy individuals at the time. Table 3.13 classifies 108 rich individuals according to the size of their wealth in 1902.

The majority of the 108 individuals are merchants and industrialists, with heads of major zaibatsu families – Mitsui, Mitsubishi (Iwasaki family), and Sumitomo holding top positions. Indigenous industries are well represented: 17 *kimono* merchants, 6 *sake* brewers, 4 in raw silk, and 3 others, for a total of 29 different individuals (one brewer also dealt in raw silk). There are 15 landlords, 3 of whom, including the 2 richest, also have other occupations. All of the 12 who are just landlords are classed under 15 million yen, with 6 in the 10-million class. There are 9 money-lenders, 3 in conjunction with other activities.

Wealth distribution was highly unequal. Looking at the individuals in Table 3.13, their combined wealth roughly aggregates to 1,336 million yen. For the same year, 1902, total financial assets held by the private sector have been estimated as 2,001 million yen (Fujino and Teranishi 2000) and the total value of land at 8,397 million yen (Nihon Ginko 1966). Thus, 13 per cent of private national wealth (financial assets plus land) was owned by just 108 individuals.

Data in Table 3.14 on the 1901 distribution of security holding among the middle and higher classes provides wider coverage than Table 3.13, albeit for only one, wealthy, city. Those included in the sample are merchants and industrialist who paid income tax – a small percentage of the total population – and thus the table somewhat overstates the share of holdings of the wealthier groups, although probably not by much. It could be said that, below the class of extremely rich family shown in Table 3.13, there was a large number of upper-middle class asset holders, mostly merchants and industrialists in the cities, and landlords.

Table 3.13 Wealthy individuals, 1902

Minimum assets[1]	Number in group	Occupation (industry) of individuals or name (if well-known or occupation unclear)
80	3	Iwasaki Yanosuke, Mitsui Hachiroemon, Iwasaki Hisaya.
60	2	Kônoike Zenuemon (banker), Sumitomo Kichizaemon.
30	3	Banker, money-lender, money-lender–real estate.
20	7	Landlord–charcoal merchant, money-lender landlord, raw silk merchant, *sake*-maker, shipbuilding, tea.
15	6	Banker (2), banker–foreign trade, *kimono* merchant (2); Iida Shinshichi.
10	26	Banker, *kimono* merchant (6), landlord (6), mining (2), money-lender (3), money-lender–*sake*-maker, paper merchant, rice merchant (2), *sake*-maker, white collar; Kagoshima Seibee, Takashima.
8	26	Banker (3), banker–*sake*-maker, banker–commerce, commerce, commerce–manufacturing, cosmetics merchant, foreign trade, *kimono* merchant, landlord (4), marine transportation (2), mining, money-lender, raw silk (2), sea products, *sake*-maker, tea–*kimono* merchant, Western clothing merchant; Tamura, Ishizaki.
6	13	Banker, cement contractor, cotton-spinning, court noble, fertilizer and salt merchant, *kimono* merchant (3), railway, white collar; President of Mitsui-Bussan (zaibatsu trading company), Kashima Seiuemon.
5	22	Banker (2), banker–*kimono* merchant, commerce–landlord, cotton yarn merchant, court noble, *kimono* merchant (3), landlord (2), marine transportation, mining (2), money-lender, rice merchant, *sake*-maker–raw silk, tobacco, warehouse; Kawakami Sashichirô.

Notes:
[1] Million yen.
The list includes 108 individuals. Within groups, occupations are alphabetical. Numbers in parentheses show how many individuals in the class engage in the occupation if it is more than one.

Source: Teranishi (1982), using data provided by Nakamura Masanori. The original data are two surveys of wealthy individuals.

Table 3.14 Distribution of securities by size of holdings, Osaka city, 1901

Percentage of Individuals	Percentage of Total holdings	Size of holdings (yen)
0.4	25.5	>300,000
14.0	62.2	20,000–300,000
85.6	12.3	<20,000

Notes: Securities are equities and bonds at market value.
The sample size is 12,368 merchants and industrialists who paid income tax.

Source: Ishii (1978).

NOTE

1. Matsukata was finance minister during 1881–92 and 1896–1900 (concurrently prime minister 1891–92 and 1896–98). Besides introducing a market-oriented development policy based on sound fiscal policy, he oversaw the integration of the financial and banking systems. He was the longest-lived of the first generation of Meiji leaders, staying active in government affairs until the early 1920s.

4. Mechanism and performance of the Meiji-Taishô economic system

The Meiji-Taishô system was one of classical free-competition capitalism, where owner-managers played an important role in corporate governance, an emphasis on the 'logic of the private sector' resulted in the economic activity of the private sector being free of government intervention, and local leaders led representation of distributive interests as well as the social and economic development of regions. Inheriting various indigenous elements and feudalistic status systems to some extent, it functioned as a sustainable system during the period before the beginning of pervasive government intervention and the aggravation of difficulties related to import substitution of heavy and chemical industries.

The chapter begins by looking at large shareholders and corporate governance, including an analysis of ownership structure. As illustrations of the market-based system, several topics are taken up: the establishment of the Industrial Bank of Japan, the nature and extent of government intervention, competition, and continued reliance on traditional forms. Regional economies, including the role of *meibôka*, and government investment, especially in railroads and education, are then analyzed. Next, institutional complementarity is discussed.

The economy's performance is then presented, with a discussion of contributing factors, including incentives in the tenancy system and domestic demand. The chapter concludes with a look at wealth and income distribution, and tenancy.

4.1 LARGE SHAREHOLDERS AND CORPORATE GOVERNANCE

Table 4.1 shows that in 1919, the first year for which suitable data are available, about three-quarters of the largest shareholders of the largest companies were individuals. Quite a few had significant influence on corporate activity through either direct participation in management or through exercising 'voice' as stockholders. Many, however, were simply portfolio (and thus passive) investors. Shareholders were relatively wealthy individuals, and thus only a small portion of the population.

Table 4.1 Large shareholders of large corporations (per cent)

Type of shareholder	1919	1936
Individuals	74.4	16.2
Banks	3.6	5.8
Insurance companies	0.9	10.2
Trust companies	0.6	0.9
Security companies	0.9	1.9
Other corporate firms	15.0	56.4
Others	4.5	8.7

Note: Distribution, by type of shareholder, of shares held by the 12 largest shareholders of 491 corporations included in *Kabushikikaisha-nenkan* (shôwa 12 nen) and *Kabushiki-nenkan* (shôwa 12 nen).

Source: Shimura (1969, p. 409).

BOX 4.1 ZAIBATSU

These are groups of firms in diversified areas controlled through a governance system with owner-families at the top. They emerged in the 19th century and were dissolved by the Occupation after World War II. Zaibatsu are commonly divided into three groups. The old zaibatsu were established during the Meiji period – before 1912, and often with roots much earlier. *Taishô* zaibatsu were created mostly in the 1910s and early 1920s, that is, during the Taishô reign (1912– 26). *Shinkô* zaibatsu were the new zaibatsu created primarily to take advantage of opportunities offered during the militarism of the 1930s, as discussed in Box 6.1.

The big four – Mitsui, Mitsubishi, Sumitomo and Yasuda – were old zaibatsu. Important Taishô zaibatsu are Asano, Kuhara, Okura and Suzuki. The term 'local zaibatsu' is often applied to diversified or (locally) large family-based business groups.

4.1.1 Ownership Structure

The ownership structure of large corporations was of three types: family, a small number of shareholders, and a large number of shareholders.

There were a large number of family-owned firms. Most were in a single business, or in closely related businesses, but many were quite diversified, and these family-based business groups are commonly referred to as zaibatsu (see Box 4.1).

Through an examination of the lists of wealthy individuals in local areas and histories of 16 local zaibatsu, Morikawa (1985) found that in 1912 most individuals with total assets of more than 10 million yen were portfolio investors, while the active business managers were in families with total assets of 0.5 million to 7 million yen. These local zaibatsu typically were managed by family members with a high level of education and with a flair for business.

However, family ownership does not necessarily mean family control. At first, zaibatsu were controlled either directly by family members or by head clerks (*bantô*). Gradually, however, the management system shifted toward utilization of highly-educated professional managers and of internal control mechanisms such as a holding company system or a divisional organization system (Okazaki 1999). In other words, the growth of zaibatsu, especially large ones, owes much to improvements in the management system and accumulation of managerial skill. This is discussed further in the next section.

Firms other than family-owned firms were controlled by either a small or a large number of shareholders.

Cotton-spinning was an important early industry, and the firms tended to be controlled by a small number of shareholders. According to data on 63 cotton-spinning companies in 1899, the average number of shareholder was 347, with the 10 largest owning 34 per cent of shares. Murakami (1970) shows that the large shareholders, generally about ten in number, had significant influence on the management of these firms either as managers or as shareholders.

Table 4.2 shows that 38.5 per cent of large shareholders in the industry were directly engaged in management at that time. It can be said that, in cotton-spinning, ownership and management were not completely separated, and a classical management style prevailed, although firms were usually not family owned. The industry did have family-owned firms: for example, Kishiwada Bôseki, the seventh largest firm as of 1914 (measured by production) was controlled by the Terada family.

Table 4.2 Percentage distribution of occupation of large shareholders

	1898	1913
Directors of cotton spinning companies	27.4	29.3
Directors of other companies	11.1	34.2
Merchants in textile and apparel	27.4	13.7
Other	34.1	22.8

Note: The sample is 866 individuals in the second half of fiscal 1898 and 269 in 1913 (first half).

Source: Murakami (1970, p. 98).

Table 4.3, derived from samples of large corporations, shows that owner-managers that were not founders or family-owners comprised 38 per cent of managers in 1900. Most of these previously were self-employed, mainly (90 per cent in 1900) as merchants (Aonuma 1965). Textile merchants becoming cotton-spinners are a typical example. In this sense, the case of cotton-spinning can be generalized as a case representative of corporate governance in the Meiji-Taishô economic system.

Table 4.3 Distribution of managers of large corporations by type (per cent)

Type	1900[a]	1928[b]	1936[b]
Founders and their relatives	10.9	8.8	10.6
Other owner–managers	38.1	8.6	4.4
Employee managers	51.0	82.6	85.0

Notes: Industries covered include mining, fishery, manufacturing, electricity and gas, transportation, commerce and insurance.

[a] The sample is 420 managers chosen from the 329 largest companies in terms of authorized capital.

[b] The sample is 500 managers chosen from about 125 largest companies in terms of sales revenue and authorized capital.

For each of the managers chosen, the career was checked by referring to *Jinji-kôshin-roku* or other sources.

Source: Aonuma (1965, p. 139).

Let us move on to the case of ownership by a large number of shareholders, and take railroad companies as the typical example (Imuta 1976a). According to Kataoka (1988), around 1900, shares held by the 10 largest shareholders of each railroad constituted about 20 per cent of total outstanding shares. The number of shareholders ranged from several hundred fro small local railroads to 3,000–5,000 for large railroads.

In such highly public companies, the shareholder meeting functioned quite effectively as a place for adjusting interests among shareholders. Through an examination of 16 historical cases of merger among railroad companies before nationalization in 1907, Kataoka shows that in many cases there were intense debates between shareholders for and against a merger, that none of the cases were settled by the use of majority rule at a shareholder meeting, and that in most cases representatives of both pro and con shareholder groups negotiated tenaciously to achieve a consensus. Moreover, managers were quite cooperative, and made great efforts to build consensus among shareholders.

Stockholders were significantly conscious of the market value of their stock and actively voiced their interests at the meeting. Except for the very large main railroads, railroad stockholders were mainly wealthy local leaders, so both those for and those against a merger had serious concerns regarding the externality of a merger on their regional economy. In the sense that both groups had common interests in the regional economy, mergers of railroad companies might be a special case. However, it seems rather likely that this kind of governance style, *à la* classical capitalism, could emerge when many modern corporations were run within a circle of a small number of wealthy families.

4.1.2 Zaibatsu and Professional Management

From very early in their existence, zaibatsu firms were keen to recruit high-ranking government officials as well as to hire young promising intellectuals, mostly sons of former samurai educated at leading universities, domestic and overseas, as top managers (Takahashi 1977).

In the Taishô and prewar Shôwa periods, they paid hired managers high basic salaries, with extraordinary bonuses for successful achievement. Large zaibatsu firms paid more from their profits to managers as a bonus payment than did non-zaibatsu firms, and less to stockholders as dividends. Thus, in 1922, with respect to a sample of 22 firms belonging to the four big zaibatsu (Mitsui, Mitsubishi, Sumitomo and Yasuda) and 65 other firms, manager bonuses as a share of profits were 5.3 per cent for zaibatsu firms and 4.8 per cent for non-zaibatsu firms, and the share of dividends was 77.8 per cent for zaibatsu, and 86.5 per cent for non-zaibatsu firms. With respect to the same sample in 1936, manager bonuses were 4.9 per cent for zaibatsu firms and 3.7 per cent for non-zaibatsu firms, and dividends were 57.3 per cent for zaibatsu firms and 63.8 per cent for non-zaibatsu firms. (Data from *Kabushiki Kaisha Nenkan* for the two years.)

It is true that some large zaibatsu were established by aggressive and active founders such as Iwasaki Yataro, Yasuda Zenjiro, Furukawa Ichibee, Asano Soichiro and Okura Kihachiro. However, the growth of zaibatsu after establishment owes a crucial debt to the managerial human resource procured from outside. For example, at Mitsubishi, after the death of founder Iwasaki Yataro in 1885, and his brother, Yanosuke in 1908, family involvement decreased. By the 1930s, when the family was headed by Koyata, the son of Yanosuke, its leadership became nominal, only a 'spiritual core'. At Mitsui, although some members of the main family held managerial positions, the other 10 families were excluded. At Sumitomo, the family never intervened in management.

Morikawa (1980) raises the following cases as evidence of the importance for managerial skill for zaibatsu growth,

1. Failure of Ono-gumi and Konoike to become zaibatsu owing to the lack of modern managerial resources.
2. Crisis within the Mitsui zaibatsu before hiring Nakamigawa Hikojiro as a top executive in 1891.
3. Stagnation of the Sumitomo zaibatsu before resignation of the traditional steward (*bantô*) in 1883, and modernization of the managerial system led by Suzuki Masaya, Kawakami Kinichi, and others. Nakamigawa was president of Sanyo Railway Company and, before that, a high-ranking government official. Suzuki was also a government official, and Kawakami came from the Bank of Japan. Led by a powerful modern-management team, Sumitomo subsequently successfully diversified away from copper mining.
4. Failure of the Furukawa zaibatsu in expanding outside copper mining after the death of Furukawa Ichibee in 1903, due to a complicated internal struggle among family members and top managers.

In other words, zaibatsu, especially those that became large zaibatsu, were not genuinely controlled by stockholders: rather, autonomy and motivation of managers had been assigned a great deal of importance. This is confirmed by the fact that, among zaibatsu firms, a long-term employment system (Okazaki 1991) and cross-shareholding (Teranishi 1994a) were already established in the 1930s. While zaibatsu firms came to exhibit traits of the Japanese-style firm system, it must be noted that most other firms retained traits of a corporate governance system characterized by classical stockholder control, where the controlling shareholders or owner-family exercised strong control.

CARDIFF UNIVERSITY PRIFYSGOL CAERDYDD

4.2 THE MARKET-BASED SYSTEM

Let us examine the working of a market-based economy from four angles: penetration of the 'logic of the private sector (*min no ronri*)', the level of government intervention, the degree of competition, and market imperfections.

4.2.1 Establishing the Industrial Bank of Japan

How 'the logic of the private sector' was realized – that is, how the interests and goals of the private sector came to be reflected in policy determination – can be well understood through examining the process of establishment by the government of an industrial bank. The discussion had been largely confined to a narrow circle of incumbent politicians and bureaucrats, and it had given rise to serious conflicts within the government, twice resulting in the abortion of plans – first in 1884 and again in 1890.

The first proposal, by Maeda Masana and the Ministry of Agriculture and Commerce, was motivated by the desire to rehabilitate the indigenous industries stricken by the Matsukata deflation. The idea of an industrial bank had been expressed by Matsukata Masayoshi. This was done within a comprehensive framework of banking sector development involving a plan for the division of labor among banks published in 1890 as an 'Explanation of establishment of a hypothec bank, security-collateral bank, and agricultural bank'. Namikata (1972) found that a similar plan was originally put together by the Ministry of Finance as a 'Plan for a security-collateral bank' before publication of Matsukata's idea.

In 1897 a third attempt, based on the concept of security-collateral banks in the Matsukata proposal, was made by two bureaucrats. One was Kaneko Kentaro, a bureaucrat-turned-politician, who served as Minister of Agriculture and Commerce during April–June 1898. The other was Soeda Juichi, of the Ministry of Finance, and its vice-minister during July–November 1898. He had drafted the Hypothec Bank Bill passed in 1896. Kaneko and Soeda almost succeeded in presenting a bill on an industrial bank before the Diet, but were forestalled because of the collapse of the cabinet in November 1898 for unrelated reasons.

Despite the 1897 adoption of the gold standard, overseas borrowing (capital imports) by the private sector was not easy, and attempts at foreign borrowing by railroad companies had failed, partly due to institutional defects such as absence of a law on collateralized corporate bonds. Kaneko and others aimed to import foreign capital efficiently through facilitating issue of collateralized corporate bonds by an industrial bank, enhancing bargaining power by unifying the import channel, and lowering interest rates with government guarantees.

Soeda and Kaneko resumed their attempt in early 1899 by organizing a 'Confederation for Establishing an Industrial Bank'. The purposes were, first, to support development of industries by means of a new bank for industry just like the Bank of Japan for commerce and Japan Hypothec Bank for agriculture, second to let ordinary banks specialize in commercial banking activities through the taking over by the new bank of the equity-collateral financing businesses, and third to promote economic development by carrying out foreign-capital-imports efficiently through a unified channel of the new bank.

The attempt evoked widespread controversy not only among bureaucrats, but also in a broader circle. The bill prepared by the bureaucrats generated heated opposition from the private sector. In particular, all the large banks such as Mitsui, Dai-ichi, Daisan, Dai-hyaku, Dai-jyûgo, and Mitsubishi were against the plan. The reasons were, first, unification of the foreign-capital-import channel would prevent them from entering foreign-capital related businesses and, second, lending to industries by the new bank might deprive them of customers. Opposition was so intense that the Finance Minister, Matsukata, was eventually obliged to give up presenting the bill to the 13th Diet (December 1898–March 1899) (Asai 1975).

The weekly business journal *Toyo keizai shipô* fiercely repeated its opposition to the bill in editorials (Asai 1983). The main grounds for opposition were that equity-collateral financing by ordinary banks and the Bank of Japan was more effective in promoting lending to support industrial activities than was establishing a new bank for such financing. Another leading journal, *Tokyo keizai zasshi*, also criticized entry of a new bank in security-collateral lending, and especially the subsidizing of business by the government.

Compared to these strong objections by large banks and leading journals, small and medium industrialists in the 'Federation for Establishing an Industrial Bank', who advocated establishment of the new bank, were far less powerful in their political influence.

The strenuous opposition was based on the 'logic of the private sector', maintaining the freedom of private-sector economic activities from government interventions. The private-sector's interests of course color its activities. Ishii (1983) points out that the private banks were rapidly expanding industrial lending activities with the support of the Bank of Japan, and that Amano Tameyuki of *Toyo keizai shinpô* opposed the bill to support Yamamoto Tatsuo, governor of the Bank of

Japan. The latter is not convincing, however, partly because Ishii does not provide evidence of the importance of the relationship between the two men.

Even after the bill creating the Industrial Bank of Japan (IBJ, Nihon Kogyo Ginko) finally passed the Diet in March 1900, it was two years before IBJ actually began operations on April 1 1902. In addition, criticism and resistance to IBJ's creation resulted in its being obliged to operate with severe constraints compared to the original vision. Thus, there was not even a clear statement that the specialization of the new bank was to be lending for the sake of industries. Also, there also was no government guarantee of debentures. Although Article 14 of the act creating IBJ stipulated that there be a subsequent special act for a government guarantee in carrying out foreign capital imports, this was not realized until 1905. There were restrictions on the types of loans.

Soeda, president of the new bank during 1902–13, expressed expansive hopes for the bank in a 1902 address, but in fact IBJ remained rather inactive until the World War I period. Its activities were largely confined to foreign-capital imports (borrowing in London), primarily for the purpose of capital exports to colonies and lending to businesses in areas similar to those of ordinary banks. In 1905 some limitations on loans were removed, some bill discounting was authorized, and the level of debentures allowed was increased from being five times to being ten times paid-in capital. From 1911 a series of revisions allowed IBJ to expand its range of discounting and mortgage businesses, including broadening the real estate collateral acceptable for loans, and documentary bills (bills of exchange with shipping documents attached, used in trade) and other services, more like an ordinary bank.

During 1902–13, the share of foreign-capital imports by IBJ was 18.1 per cent of total capital imports, and 41 per cent of the capital imported by IBJ was for export to colonies, which included Taiwan (from 1895) and Korea (from 1910, although within Japan's sphere of influence from 1905), as well as China and Manchuria. The share of lending to manufacturing stayed very low, at 13.5 per cent of total loans of the bank, even in December 1918. In this sense, resistance and opposition by large private banks had been by and large successful.

4.2.2 Nature and Extent of Government Intervention

Let us discuss how and to what extent the government intervened in the economic activities of the private sector. It is important to note that industrial subsidies of the central government were considerably curtailed and the emphasis of industrial policies had shifted to subsidization by local governments (Saito 1983), as shown in Table 4.4.

Table 4.4 Subsidies in support of industrial policies (million yen)

	1890	1900	1910	1920
Agriculture and Commerce Ministry[1]	1.2	11.6	14.7	46.7
Municipal governments[2]	0.3	2.8	11.1	40.9

Notes:
[1] Total expenditure of the ministry.
[2] Expenditures on industrial promotion.

Source: Asahi Shinbun (1930).

Sugihara (1995) notes that after the Russo-Japanese War municipal governments actively established exhibition centers of commodities, experimental stations for manufactured products, and technical schools. From examining their activities, he concludes the developmental policies implemented by local governments were characterized by promoting exports of indigenous industries within a regime of free trade.

Industrial policy as carried out by the central government was primarily provision of tax and subsidy incentives for the emerging heavy and chemical industries. Such incentives for the most part were provided with preset time limits. (See Miwa 1976 and Miyajima 1991 on this.) For example, a Special Tax Exemption for Important Manufacturing Firms (heavy and chemical industries producing material products) introduced in 1913 was applied only to new firms for three years after their establishment. The Act Encouraging Production of Dyes and Medicines enacted in 1915 guaranteed dividend payments of 8 per cent (of par value) by means of government subsidies, but this was limited to 10 years. However, after that guarantee expired in 1925, a new Act Encouraging Production of Dyes was enacted. It provided subsidies to producers of artificial indigo and high-quality dyes for six years with a ceiling of 4 million yen on the total amount. The exemption from income and business taxes for large steel producers, enacted by the 1917 Act Promoting the Steel Industry, had a time limit of 10 years.

Tariffs were not an important policy tool, partly owing to historical circumstances. Under the unequal treaties of the late Tokugawa period, Japan did not have full tariff autonomy until 1910. Autonomy was partly recovered in 1897, and after revision of tariff rates in 1906, fully recovered in 1910. Subsequently, use of tariffs as a tool of industrial policy was modest, in part because of belief in the efficiency of a free-trade regime. For example, tariff revision in 1910 was implemented mainly to secure tax revenue, and protection of industries was left to be considered 'as occasion arises'. (However, Yamazawa (1984) claims the real objective was protection of industries, and revenue needs was an excuse to avoid being criticized for acting against the free-trade principle.)

In sum, intervention in private economic activities by the government under the Meiji-Taishô system was not significant by any measure; developmental policy was implemented only by local governments; the provision of incentives through tax and subsidies was with predetermined time limits; and tariffs were not utilized as a measure to protect industries.

4.2.3 Competition

Next, let us examine how the competitive mechanism functioned in markets.

The competitive nature of the Meiji-Taishô system is underlined by the rise and fall in the number of banks, as shown in Table 3.1. The number began to decrease after 1901. This was not simply a process of closure or merger. Take 1902–19 as an example. The net reduction over the period was 333 banks. This was a result of 442 bankruptcies and 179 mergers (a gross loss of 621) and 285 newly established banks. Note that a considerable number of new banks were being established even as others failed. (The detailed figures do not tally with the overall total because of data inconsistencies in the sources, which are various issues of *Ginkô-kyoku Nenpô*).

Prices were quite flexible during the period. Interest rates on lending were perfectly market determined. With respect to deposit interest rates, there was an agreement on the maximum rate among members of the bankers' association in Osaka in 1901 and in Tokyo in 1902. This, however, did not function at all, partly because it did not have any punishment clause. An effective interest agreement with a punishment clause was introduced in 1918, but even then it was violated quite often.

With respect to manufacturing, cartel agreements to control output and prices were exceptional during the period. Out of 84 cartels existing in 1932, 7 were formed before 1914, 12 during 1914–26, and more than half (48) during 1930–32 after the shock of the return to the gold standard and enactment of the Controlling Important Industries Act (*Jyuyô-Sangyô Tôsei Hô*) (Takahashi 1933).

Up to the first half of the 1920s, the market share of zaibatsu was not very large. Thus, as an example, the share of the five largest banks, all zaibatsu affiliated, in total deposits and authorized capital, was not particularly large before 1930. This is shown in Table 4.5.

Table 4.5 Share of the five largest banks, 1900–1940

Year	Authorised capital	Deposits	Lendings
1900	4.0	17.8	11.9
1905	5.5	21.9	15.7
1910	8.5	21.5	17.2
1915	13.2	23.9	20.5
1920	18.4	26.9	20.9
1925	17.4	24.1	18.4
1930	23.5	36.5	29.5
1935	27.0	53.7	45.0
1940	31.5	52.3	56.8

Note: The percentage share of the five largest banks relative to all ordinary banks. The banks, by asset size, are Mitsui, Mitsubishi, Yasuda, Sumitomo and Dai-Ichi.

Source: Goto (1970).

4.2.4 Continued Reliance on Traditional Forms

While the Meiji-Taishô system was competitive, with flexible prices and interest rates and without significant obstacles to entry and exit, it was an economy full of potential for market failure due to asymmetric information (low levels of information disclosure) and high contract costs. In addition, there was a deficiency in institutional infrastructure, such as legal and accounting systems.

To prevent market failures, the system resorted to heavy use of traditional information and transaction networks. For example, in loan markets, the traditional informal-credit system played an important role for a long time. With respect to the farm sector, in 1888 the percentage share of borrowing from informal credit sources such as money-lenders and merchants was 92.8 per cent of total debts, while the share from modern financial institutions such as banks and credit cooperatives was 7.2 per cent. The share of informal credit remained more than half into the 1930s: 64.4 per cent in 1911 and 52.7 per cent in 1932.

A similar observation applies to manufacturing. In Tokyo and Kobe in 1932, the percentage share of borrowing from modern financial institutions was only 60.8 per cent, with the remaining 39.2 per cent borrowed from informal sources. Further, modern financial institutions such as banks utilized the borrower's reputation, as well as the transaction and information network of merchants, as much as possible.

4.2.4.1 Financing raw silk

Take the advance-payment financing system by wholesalers (*toiyasei maegashi kin'yû*) in raw silk production. ('Raw silk' is the filament unwound from the cocoon and wound into thin threads. It is thus an intermediate product between cocoon and yarn, and as such the process can be separated from growing cocoons.)

Silk producers borrowed part of their funds from raw silk wholesalers, and the rest from regional banks or branch offices of large city banks. The wholesalers borrowed from large banks in Yokohama, where raw silk was exported. Direct lending to producers by Yokohama banks was quite difficult due to a lack of information on possible borrowers (there were 91,751 silk-reeling factories in 1926). In contrast, the wholesalers had a vast network of information sources on the producers. Thus, even regional banks made their lending decision on the base of signaling by wholesalers – that is, following the lending behavior of wholesalers.

Due to the serious segmentation of regional loan markets, interest rates in the major cities were significantly lower than in other areas, so that, for raw silk producers, borrowing costs were cheaper from wholesalers than from regional banks, even with the spread taken by wholesalers. Moreover, the high reputation and large wealth of the wholesalers meant they could borrow for relatively long periods, and this enabled them, in turn, to offer loans to producers with a longer maturity than the term offered by regional banks. Wholesalers also financed producers by offering advanced payments, and when the advanced payment was not sufficient, producers borrowed the rest from regional banks. Producers used the fund to purchase cocoons from farmers, and repaid their borrowing when they sold the raw silk.

Advanced-payment financing was quite prevalent not only for raw silk but also for many other indigenous products, and remained so for a long period. According to a survey conducted by BOJ regarding the financing small of manufacturers and merchants in Osaka in 1914, the method of borrowing materials or funds from wholesalers in advance and paying with delivery of manufactured products was utilized in almost all cases. In other words, 'in almost all indigenous industries such as raw silk and textiles, financing of manufactures relied mostly on wholesalers, and banks had relationships only with wholesalers' (Watanabe and Nishikawa 1957).

4.3 REGIONAL ECONOMIES

When agriculture was the only taxpaying sector, conflicts between the interests of agriculture and state objectives were relatively straightforward – one-on-one, leaving aside factions within each. The rise of industrial and commercial sectors, however, changed the situation, and made it necessary to adjust distributive interests among various constituents. The rapid development of transportation and communication systems gave rise to a linkage between the central economy (Tokyo and Osaka) and regional economies. Among the latter, there occurred intense competition.

In this setting, the government–private-sector interface in the Meiji-Taishô system came to be formed with regional economies as coalition units – intermediate organizations – to represent the distributive interests of the people. Each regional economy aimed at socio-economic development under the leadership of wealthy landlords and merchants called *meibôka*. *Meibôka* and political parties, in which they participated, played an important role in the competition for inviting central government investment to regions.

Under these circumstances during the 1910s and 1920s there blossomed a variety of regional cultures as part of what an extensive literature calls 'Taishô democracy'. In developed regions with active indigenous production, there were movements to promote arts and literary education. This included cities and towns in Yamanashi, Nagano, Chiba and Ibaraki prefectures. There were adult education and free university movements in parts of Nagano, Niigata and Gunma prefectures. A new movement regarding the traditional short poem (*tanka*) was actively carried out in such prefectures as Nagano, Akita, Aomori and Iwate. The humanist campaign by writers associated with *Shirakaba* (a literary magazine launched in 1910) generated widespread reactions in various regions. The school houses and Western-style building of banks and commercial centers, erected during the Meiji-Taishô periods and often still standing in these regions, tell of the vigor and spiritual uplift of Taishô democracy.

4.3.1 *Meibôka*

Meibôka were wealthy merchants and landlords who became regional leaders. Many of them participated in the 'private-rights movement' during the 1870s and 1980s, and thereafter became absentee landlords, portfolio investors, or managers of commercial and industrial corporations. As a group they had three functions: maintaining rural order, participating in political parties, and advising and managing local industrial activity. The significant role they played in improving agricultural techniques is discussed later. It was rare that one particular *meibôka* played all three roles at the same time, though an individual might play different roles at different times. (The pioneering work on these functions was done by Tsutsui (1993), and his formulation is followed here. The word *meibôka* was first used in the late Meiji period, and after World War II it became a technical term in the socio-political analysis of the Meiji period.)

Meibôka collaborated with the government in reorganizing rural communities and were in charge of maintaining rural order. High-ranking officials of regional governments in the Meiji-Taishô system, such as prefectural governors, were designated and dispatched by the central government, and were under the control of the Ministry of Internal Affairs. Under such high-ranking officials, many *meibôka* took leadership roles in local governance as directors of governmental organizations, and heads of agricultural and industrial associations. Moreover, under the leadership of *meibôka*, cultivating landlords in villages and large owner-farmers became administrators of city and town halls (mayors, members of municipal assemblies) and thus were involved in administration and decisions.

Many *meibôka* participated in political party activities, and lobbied the central government for benefits for their region. Some became party politicians at the level of the central government, and others supported them through party activities in prefectural assemblies and local branches of political parties.

With regard to regional development, *meibôka* devoted considerable effort to promoting commerce and industry, and took a leadership role in the diffusion of new agricultural technology. More specifically, as landlords and merchants, they took an active role in establishing and advising new firms, often in modern industries, and assumed risks as managers and stockholders. An analysis of the behavior of the wealthy class in Niigata shows that, along with the many who became portfolio investors, there were *meibôka* who became entrepreneurs themselves and became committed to the growth of corporations not only as stockholders but also as managers (Tanimoto and Abe 1995).

Likewise, an examination of 16 local zaibatsu (defined as diversified business groups owned by families and operating in a small geographical area) by Morikawa (1985) finds three that were particularly active in taking risks introducing modern industries. These are Yasukawa (electric machines, 1915), Ishibashi (rubber soles for shoes, 1918; tires, 1931), and Toyota (automatic looms, 1918). All three exist as firms today: within a decade, and with the founding father's help, the second-generation Toyota shifted to automobiles. Yasukawa Denki is a leading maker of electric motors. Ishibashi is Bridgestone Tires.

4.3.2 Regional Economies at the Level of Towns and Villages

In the Meiji-Taishô system, prefectures were administrative units under the direct control of the central government through governors sent by the central government. In contrast, the heads of towns and villages were elected by local assemblies and were more or less autonomous. After the 1900s, in particular, the role of towns and villages as administrative units became quite important. Their budgets expanded because of increased responsibilities imposed by the central government, including the delegation of additional administrative duties. In addition, the role of regional communities and the indigenous village system weakened because of the development of transportation and penetration of the market economy (Mitani 1995). The rapid growth of the budgets of cities, towns, and villages, as compared to prefectures, is shown in Table 3.9 (p. 75). The ratio of the former to the latter doubled from 1.15 in 1880 to 2.33 in 1920.

The idea of regarding cities, towns, and villages as intermediate organizations is clearly seen in two policies carried out by the Hara cabinet (1918–21) of the Seiyûkai. These are the small-constituency system and abolition of the county system (*gun-sei*).

Initially, before 1900, a small-constituency system had been used for Diet elections, with 214 one-person districts and 43 two-person districts, for a total of 300 members. This had been recommended by Yamagata Aritomo, who considered small districts suitable to represent people's demand adequately and to reflect regional differences in the absence of national-level political parties. Beginning with the 14th Diet in 1900, constituencies were based on a large-district system. The system was expected to induce top-level *meibôka* at the national level to lead the maintenance of the social order, and thus to promote development of national-level political parties.

The influence of *meibôka* on the social order, however, tended to be weakened as the power structure diversified in the atmosphere of Taishô democracy. Hara Takashi (also known as Hara Kei) was particularly concerned about penetration of socialist ideology, and sought ways to stem socialist influence and to revive the role of traditional reputation in regional governance. The shift to small constituencies and abolition of the county system both reflect Hara's desire to make towns and villages core 'political intermediate organizations' (*seiji-ken*) in a government–private-sector interface based on regional economies. Under the Hara cabinet, the small-district bill was passed by the Diet in 1919, and the county system was abolished in 1921.

Together with the diversifications of both ideology and power structures, economic factors were crucially responsible for weakening governance based on *meibôka* leadership. Mitani (1995), on the other hand, considers that this governance system weakened through an endogenous political mechanism: the rise of political parties accelerated an emphasis on non–state interests such as the competitive induction of central government investment, and the emphasis of non-state interest resulted in the weakening of the social orders based on *meibôka*. He also notes that this endogenous mechanism is complemented by two exogenous factors: weakening of popular concern with international tensions, and the increase in the size of the electorate after the Russo-Japanese war as economic growth increased the number of taxpayers, and thus of qualified voters.

4.4 GOVERNMENT INVESTMENT IN REGIONS

The targets for induction of government investment in regions included not only industrial infrastructure such as railroads, port facilities and roads, but also cultural infrastructure including high-level schools. Let us examine this point in relation to the policies of the Hara cabinet (1918–21). Among four major policies – strengthening of national defense, promotion of education, encouragement of industrial activities, and improvement of transportation and communication – railroads and education were particularly epoch-making.

In a system with regional economies functioning as intermediate organization, railroads and education facilities were seen as public rather than private goods. Both railroads and high-level education were much more closely related to the total welfare of the inhabitants in each region than they are today. The benefits from the development of regional industries were enjoyed by many of the inhabitants, and the social success of individuals after graduating from regional high-level schools was considered to be an honor for the region.

4.4.1 Railroads

While the emphasis of previous railroad policies was on trunk lines, Hara's policy intended to improve local and branch railroads to regions.

The railroad-construction bill submitted to the 44th Diet in 1921 planned to build 149 feeder lines (plus 28 branch feeder lines) with a total length of 10,221 kilometers in 30 years. In 1920 the existing lines were 10,633 kilometers in length, so this was to be a near-doubling of the track. During 1920–30 operating national railway lines increased by 4,156 kilometers, much larger than the 2,878 kilometer increase during the preceding 10 years.

Motivated by his political aim to rehabilitate the *meibôka* order in towns and villages, Hara's emphasis on investment in local lines was based on his vision of the transportation system: long-distance transportation by coastal shipping and local transportation between ports and surrounding areas by rail. This vision had been in opposition to Goto Shinpei, who proposed investing in the conversion of the narrow-gauged railroads to broad-gauge, for military and economic reasons. The bill submitted by the Hara cabinet concluded the controversy, which had lasted over 10 years.

4.4.2 Education

With respect to education, Hara announced a 'Plan for Improving High-level Education' in 1918. (High-level education encompasses anything beyond grade 9, including colleges and universities, as well as high schools and assorted specialized schools.) It was a plan to expand the education system on an unprecedented scale, including the establishment of 29 public high-level schools (10 high schools, 17 specialized business schools and 2 specialized schools) in six years starting from 1919. At the same time, decrees on universities and on high schools were revised, resulting in a mushrooming of private universities and specialized schools (Ito 1993). Together with the expansion already scheduled before the plan, this meant that the number of high-level schools and their students increased drastically (see Table 4.6) (Monbusho 1966).

This aggressive policy was possible partly because of ample revenue resulting from the boom related to World War I, and partly because of strong demand for college graduates by large corporations. Moreover, the policy was supported by the vigorous desire of regions to have high-level education facilities. The expansion had significant effects.

Table 4.7, based on Aonuma's data, shows the composition of managers of large corporations classified by the regions they came from. In 1900, some 78 per cent of large-corporation managers came from the two major metropolitan regions (south Kanto (Tokyo) and Kinki (Osaka, Kobe, Kyoto)). In 1950 the figure is drastically lower at

Table 4.6 Increase in high-level schools and students, 1918–24

Year	High schools	Specialized schools (including business schools)	University
		Number of schools	
1918	8	96	5
1924	28	129	32
		Number of students in thousands	
1918	6.8	49.3	9.0
1924	15.5	59.7	42.8

Table 4.7 Regions of managers of large corporations (percentage distribution)

Region (from north to south)	1900	1950
Hokkaido	0.2	2.4
Tohoku	0.7	3.6
South-Kanto	2.1	5.2
North-Kanto	42.9	18.0
Hokuriku	2.6	7.2
Tozan	3.3	3.8
Tokai	1.2	7.6
Kinki	35.1	17.2
Chugoku	2.9	10.6
Shikoku	2.7	6.0
Kyushu	3.3	15.2
Overseas and unidentified	2.2	3.2

Source: Aonuma (1965, p. 94).

35 per cent. Those in managerial positions in 1950 had been at colleges or other high-level schools after around 1920, so the table shows one effect of improving educational facilities in non-metropolitan areas.

Comparing prefectures, the presence of high schools in the prewar period was an important factor in determining whether someone subsequently became a large-corporation manager. Aonuma (1965) determined this by conducting a cross-prefectural regression analysis with the ratio of large-corporation managers to total male births in 1920 as a dependent variable, and the ratio of primary-industry population to total population as an independent variable. Comparing the actual value of the dependent variable for each prefecture with the value forecast by the regression equation, four prefectures had actual values greater than forecast and six had smaller values. Among those that were greater that forecast, one (Shiga) borders Kyoto and the other three (Nagano, Okayama, and Kochi) had high schools. Those with lower values (Iwate, Tochigi, Gifu, Mie, Tottori, and Miyazaki) had no high schools or schools specialized in commerce and industry, only schools for agriculture.

4.5 INSTITUTIONAL COMPLEMENTARITY

There was institutional complementarity among the sub-systems of the Meiji-Taishô system in three respects.

Between the emphasis on the market mechanism and corporate governance by large shareholders. Marketism (emphasis on the market mechanism) in the system was synonymous with the autonomy of the private sector in its economic activities. The private economy was led by wealthy merchants and landlords, who established and governed modern corporations. Their capability and devotion to economic activities justified their autonomy.

Between the emphasis on the market mechanism and the government–private-sector interface based on regional economies. Because the autonomy of the private sector was emphasized, government involvement was confined to supply of public goods. The benefits of public goods were enjoyed more or less equally by all the inhabitants of a region, so the role of regional economies as intermediary organizations was a reasonable arrangement, and was congruent with the sub-system regarding the division of labor between the government and the private sector.

Between regional economies as intermediary organizations and indigenous industry being financed by banks. The development of regional economies was led by wealthy merchants and landlords, called *meibôka*, who invested in modern industries, including banks. Banks lent mostly to indigenous industries through intermediation by merchants.

4.6 PERFORMANCE

Growth from around 1900 to the early 1920s is characterized by advances in industrialization, expansion of agriculture and other indigenous industries, and dependence on domestic demand. (Data in this section are from LTES volume 1, that is, Ohkawa (1974) except as noted.)

The advances in industrialization are illustrated by the composition of not domestic product (NDP) and manufacturing (see Table 4.8).

Table 4.8 Advances in industrialization, 1900–1920

	1900	1920
All industry, as percentage of NDP	16.1	23.5
Specific industries as percentage of total manufacturing:		
Heavy and chemical industries	16.2	33.4
Textiles, including cotton-spinning, raw silk	36.3	34.3

Industrial growth owes much to the development of the various textile industries. Together they were the largest sector in manufacturing until the 1930s. Their share declined to 30.6 per cent in 1930 and 16.8 per cent in 1940. The doubling of the share of heavy and chemical industries reflects the World War I boom. Sources of growth in modern industries, which include textiles in this period, were the accumulation of capital stock and human capital, as well as technological imports.

Consumption grew quite rapidly in real terms, especially in the clothing sector, even as the share of consumption in income continued to decline, resulting in a steady increase in the saving rate (Nishikawa and Abe 1990). Increased saving was utilized in capital formation by firms; the main source of investment funds during the period had already shifted from the mobilization of accumulated savings to current savings out of income flow.

4.6.1 Contributing Factors

Skill formation and technology import played essential roles in economic development in prewar Japan. Their roles are briefly summarized here. They are extensively examined in such studies as Howe (1996), Saxonhouse (1974), Kiyokawa (1995), and Nakaoka, Ishii and Uchida (1986).

While there was an ample supply of unskilled labor, the accumulation of human capital was also considerable, owing to the rapid diffusion of education. As Table 4.9 shows, school attendance had reached 96 per cent in 1905 for elementary schools (first 4 grades until 1907, then 6 grades), and after 1900 increased rapidly at the medium level (basically, junior high school). At the beginning of industrialization, most of the labor force had no formal education, but the diffusion of schooling realized a rapid improvement in the quality of labor.

Table 4.9 School attendance ratio

Year	Elementary school	Medium level	High level
1885	49.6	0.8	0.4
1895	61.2	1.1	0.3
1905	95.6	4.3	0.9
1915	98.5	19.9	1.0
1925	99.4	32.3	2.5
1935	99.6	39.7	3.0

Note: Medium level includes junior high schools, women's high schools, and normal schools. High level is high schools, specialized schools, specialized business schools, colleges, universities, higher normal schools, and the like.

Source: Monbusho (1966).

Table 4.10 shows the average amount of schooling of the production-age population. This change was partly due to the expenditure devoted to elementary education by municipal governments out of their tight budgets, and partly to the enormous expansion of high-level education carried out by the central government during the Terauchi and Hara cabinet periods (1916–21).

Table 4.10 Average schooling of production-age population, 1888–1940 (in years)

1888	1900	1920	1940
1.1	2.0	4.3	6.5

Source: Godo and Hayami (1999).

Technological progress, a major source of growth in modern industries, relied heavily on the active import of technology. In particular, light industries (especially textiles) and public utilities were quite active in transplanting the latest technologies. (On technology choice in cotton textiles, see Saxonhouse 1985.) Despite these successes, however, it was by no means an easy matter for Japan to transplant advanced technologies in a short period. It is well known that technology transfer in the steel industry experienced repeated failures, especially regarding production of pig iron (see, for example Ono 1985). Similar stories apply to chemical industries, in which even zaibatsu firms hesitated about entry. In electrical machinery, Japan was barely able to catch up in the production of small products, and never succeeded in the production of high-quality large machines during the prewar period.

Although the share of agriculture in GDP declined steadily, from a historical perspective the growth rate of agriculture was unprecedentedly high during the period. Indigenous manufacturing and service industries also experienced high growth rates.

As Table 4.11 shows, growth in the GDP of primary industry (agriculture, forestry and fishery) accelerated after the mid-Meiji period, attaining its highest annual rates – over 1.6 per cent – during the first two decades of the 1900s. In terms of employment in agriculture, the average number of gainfully employed was 14,250,000 during 1901–05, and stayed at a similar level into the 1920s: 14,130,000 from 1921–25. In other words, the net outflow of agricultural labor was minimal, more or less equal to the natural increase within the sector, and there was no massive out-migration of farmers from agriculture to industry during the period 1901–25.

Table 4.11 Growth accounting of the primary sector (annual growth rate, in per cent)

Year	Production	Labor	Labor productivity	Technological progress
1889–1900	1.37	−0.03	1.40	0.96
1901–10	1.66	−0.33	1.99	1.11
1911–20	1.62	−0.56	2.18	1.10
1921–30	0.75	−0.04	0.71	0.55
1931–38	1.30	−0.28	1.58	1.03

Source: Minami (1992).

In the chemical industry, products such as soda ash, caustic soda, sulphuric acid, bleaching powder, animal oil and fats, menthol, Western paper, and fertilizer were products of modern industries, while things such as salt, indigo, lacquer, plant oil, camphor, wax and Japanese paper were products of indigenous industries. The total value of production of the 7 products in the latter category in the total of 15 products was 64.5 per cent in 1900 and 31.2 per cent in 1930 (Nishikawa and Abe 1990).

The number of gainfully employed in indigenous industries increased slightly, from 9,190,000 from 1901–05 to 10,480,000 from 1921–25 (Nakamura 1993b). Indigenous employment in service industries, construction, public utilities and financial industries is included, so occupations such as family-managed retailers, carpenters, plasterers, rickshaw men and small restaurant managers are included in the estimates.

The high rate of growth in agriculture and other indigenous industries is quite often ascribed to the diffusion of existing high-yielding varieties and cultivation technologies in rice production. The latter were advanced traditional techniques called the *Meiji-nôhô* (Meiji agricultural methods) used in western Japan, especially Kinki and northern Kyushu, during the Tokugawa period. Hayami (1973) presents econometric evidence to show that these diffused east and north during 1890–1920, and that the diffusion was saturated after around 1920. Table 4.11 reflects this process.

In this process, cultivating landlords and large farmers, called *rônô* (literally, old farmers) fulfilled important roles, especially in the first part of the period. Most of them were leaders of rural communities, *meibôka*, actively involved in seed-exchange meetings and lecture series on agricultural technology. The government also played a role in the formation of agricultural experimental stations, as did agricultural associations (*nôkai*) and industrial associations. Tsutsui (1993) notes that, from the mid-1890s to the early 1910s, the government in some cases used police power to coerce farmers into adopting new varieties and technologies.

While there is no denying that the diffusion of technology is an important reason for the high growth rate of agriculture and related indigenous industries, it must be noted that there are two other equally, or even more important, reasons for agricultural growth.

First is the linkage of regional economies with the central and foreign economies owing to development of transportation and communication. The linkage generated a considerable expansion of markets, both domestic and overseas, for agricultural products other than rice and for indigenous manufactured goods such as raw silk, tea and Japanese papers. Regions specialized in the production of such products, and competed fiercely with each other. 'In each region, a tendency toward specialization of production occurred, while at the national level, indigenous and agricultural products intensified the level of diversification owing to competition' (Takahashi 1976, pp. 94–95).

Through the process of competition and specialization, the area of cultivation of rice and other grains decreased until 1918 (but thereafter turned to an increase). This was because regions were eager to plant products in which they had comparative advantages. Such competition also occurred in manufacturing. Through an examination of the competition in the traditional-clothing industry, Abe (1989) shows that, until the 1920s, production centers competed fiercely to increase market share in domestic markets.

4.6.2 Incentives in the Tenancy System

Another important reason for agricultural growth lies in the incentive structure of agricultural production. The tenancy system was characterized by a high degree of residual income and significant control rights held by actual producers, the tenant farmers. As shown by the movement of the tenancy ratio in Table 4.12, the landlord system was established during the Tokugawa period, and reached its heyday around the 1910s. Some landlords cultivated their land with hired labor, but most land was rented to tenant farmers.

Table 4.12 Tenancy

Year	Per cent
1883/84	35.9
1887	39.6
1897	41.4
1908	44.9
1917	45.9
1927	45.3
1937	46.3
1940	45.7

Note: Entries are the share of total arable land rented by tenants.

Source: Nakamura (1993b).

Rent was fixed mostly as an amount of rice per unit of land in the case of paddy fields. For dry fields, contracts usually were in terms of rice or currency. This means the residual-income right was held by the tenant farmer. (Rents were sometimes reduced, especially in seriously poor crop years, but never increased above the contracted level in the good years.) Share tenancy or share cropping was very rare, and was confined to very underdeveloped or mountainous areas in peripheral prefectures such as Aomori, Iwate, Nagano, Kumamoto and Okinawa. There was also a system in which rent was determined after harvest (*mitori* or *kenmi*), but this was not common either.

Landlords took the movement to strengthen tenancy rights quite seriously. In particular, the parts of civil law related to the legal nature of land tenancy contracts (real property and credit contracts), was a focal point. The old Civil Code, promulgated in 1890 for enforcement from 1893, strengthened the position of tenants against landlords. The effective date of the 1890 Code was postponed for a variety of reasons, and then it was decided to start a new code. The new Civil Code, which became effective in 1898, favored landlord rights. For example: the old code stipulated that when a tenant had rented land for more than 30 years, he obtained the right to rent permanently; this was not part of the new code.

Whatever their formal legal status, tenant farmers enjoyed not only the residual-income right but also a substantial degree of control-rights regarding rented land. With respect to farming methods, most contracts required the agreement of landlords before any significant change in use was undertaken – such as planting fruit or mulberry trees in a paddy field, for example. Apart from that, however, tenants generally had control over the choice of crops, inputs of fertilizers, and the marketing of harvested crops. Even re-renting (sub-letting) of land and other transactions in tenancy rights were popularly undertaken (*Kosaku-kankô ni kansuru Chôsa-shiryô*, March 1924, pp.49–50).

Endowment of both residual-income and control-rights gave tenant farmers strong incentives to invest in land-specific skills such as irrigation control and land improvement. Such behavior resulted in a rise in productivity, and seems to comprise an additional reason for the high growth of agriculture under the Meiji-Taishô system.

4.6.2.1 Fixed-rent tenancy vs share tenancy

The fixed-rent tenancy of Japan stands in contrast to the share-tenancy system elsewhere in East Asia. Both regions are affected by the summer southwest monsoon, with its high rainfall potential. Thus, both regions belong to Monsoon Asia, and both produce rice with family-based farming (Oshima 1987). So why the difference?

One possible reason is absolute poverty in East Asia: poor peasants prefer share tenancy in order to avoid the risk of a bad harvest. It is difficult to show that East Asian peasants were generally poorer than prewar Japanese farmers, however. For example, in the 1930s the wage level of unskilled workers in Japan was said to be lower than that in India.

A second possible reason is differences in the enforcement costs of contracts. Noting that share-tenancy contracts are more difficult to enforce, Otsuka, Chuma and Hayami (1992) argue that because of the close human relationship and reputational ties in a rural community, enforcement costs of tenancy are low in East Asia. However, this does not explain the difference with Japan, which also had rural communities with close ties.

It seems to me that one of the most important reasons for adoption of the fixed rent system is that it enhances the incentive of the farmer to produce as much as possible. Landlords, *meibôka*, were eager to develop their regional economies. As part of this, they actively engaged in the promotion of new technology in rice production, such as land improvements, water management, and adoption of new rice varieties. Because it is very difficult to monitor the acquisition of new technology and skill by individual tenants, the best way is to confer substantial income and control rights on the tenant and to assume the less-successful adapters will be winnowed out by an inability to meet the fixed rent, to be replaced by a tenant that can. In other words, to achieve development, landlords chose a fixed-rent tanancy system, and tried to maximize the accumulation of land-specific skill among the direct producers (tenants).

4.6.3 Domestic Demand

The economic growth of the Meiji-Taishô system relied mainly on domestic demand, especially consumption. Although the share of exports to GDP was rising steadily, it was still low, except for the World War I period. The effects of the expansion of overseas markets were most conspicuous when treaty ports were opened to foreign trade at the end of the Tokugawa period. The price ratio of tradable to non-tradable goods rose most sharply around the 1860s (Shinpo 1995). There was another surge of exports during 1885–97 due to the depreciation of the exchange rate (the price ratio of silver to paper currency) because of international movements in the relative price of gold and silver (Nakamura 1985). Economic growth became fully dependent on exports only during the 1930s, when there was stagnation in domestic demand and the exchange rate depreciated drastically.

Let me add two reservations regarding emphasis on domestic markets. First, the share of exports to GDP increased steadily. However, the level was still low before the 1930s: 4.3 per cent in 1900 and 10.9 per cent in 1920. Second, earning foreign exchange through export promotion was an important policy agenda, partly because of the burden of foreign debt issued to finance military expenditures. This explains why industrial policies at the level of regional economies implemented by the Agriculture and Ministry of Commerce aimed at development of export markets overseas (Sugihara 1995).

4.7 WEALTH AND INCOME DISTRIBUTION

Income and wealth distribution in the Meiji-Taishô system were very unequal. For example, in the fifth general election, in March 1898, voting rights were held only by males over 25 who had paid taxes to the central government of more than 10 yen. This was 4.3 per cent of the male population over 25 (453,000 out of 10,587,000).

Gini coefficients are higher than in the postwar period regardless of the method of estimation, as Table 4.13 shows. Moreover, coefficients had a rising trend throughout the prewar period. Another indicator of income distribution, the income differential between agriculture and non–agriculture, also indicates inequality. As Figure 4.1 shows, the income level of farm households was 50 per cent to 60 per cent of non-

Table 4.13 Gini coefficients, 1891–1990

Year	Gini coefficient	
	I	I'
1891–1900 (1895)	0.476	0.395
1901–1910 (1905)	0.521	0.433
1911–1921 (1915)	0.579	0.481
	II	
1923	0.505	
1930	0.512	
1937	0.547	
	III	IV
1956	0.313	
1959	0.357	
1962	0.382	0.376
1968	0.380	0.349
1974	–	0.344
1980	–	0.337
1985	–	0.359
1990	–	0.372

Notes:

I This series is the average Gini coefficient of 39 cites, towns and villages. Based on Kosûwari tax data, coverage excludes high-income earners.

I' This revises series I to include high-income earners, using national tax data and taking the years in parentheses as benchmark years.

II National-level, all income classes, estimated using national tax data.

III Estimates given in Wada (1975).

IV Estimates given in Mizoguchi and Terasaki (1995).

Source: Minami (1996), Wada (1975), and Mizoguchi and Terasaki (1995).

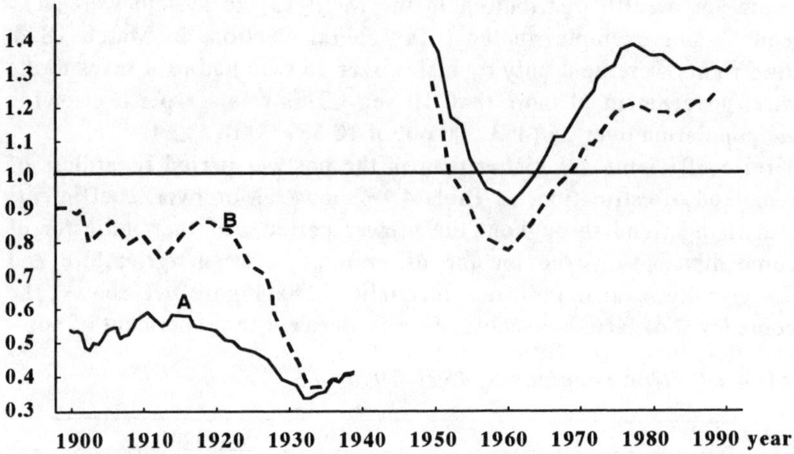

Notes: Series A is a seven-year moving average of the ratios of farm income to non-farm income. Series B is a seven-year moving average of the ratios of farm income deflated by rural consumers' price index to non-farm income deflated by urban consumers' price index.

Source: Minami (1996).

Figure 4.1 Income differentials between farm and non-farm households

farm households. Even if rural and urban differences in the cost of living are taken into account, there remains a 10 per cent to 20 per cent differential. It must be noted, however, that the differential did not increase before the 1930s. This is because of the solid growth of agriculture and indigenous industries during 1890–1920.

Table 4.14 indicates how the assets of a wealthy individual shifted from land (producing rent on tenanted land) to shares in corporations (dividend income). Many rich merchants and industrialists were also large landowners, and although the table represents a single individual, it is representative of landlords and merchants of a developed region such as Kinki. In less developed regions, such as northern Japan, the percentage share of rent generally stayed high throughout the prewar period.

It is important to note both the function of corporate governance led by large shareholders, and venture-capital activities with wealthy individuals playing the role of 'business angels', were possible at least partly because of the concentration of wealth holding.

Table 4.14 Changing composition of a landlord's revenue, 1905–17

	Rent[1]	Interest[2]	Dividends	Other
1905	62.1	5.4	30.7	—
1907	63.9	—	35.5	—
1909	61.2	9.1	29.5	—
1911	43.4	16.0	37.4	3.6
1913	38.8	22.9	34.4	3.5
1915	22.3	6.8	66.4	4.4
1917	19.3	5.9	71.2	3.3
1919	31.0	2.0	63.4	2.8
1921	18.2	3.4	74.7	3.4
1923	14.4	11.0	69.5	3.3
1925	22.9	3.3	67.3	5.7
1927	21.1	12.6	60.3	6.0

Notes: See discussion in text. Nozaki-ke, in the Kinki region, had 613 hectares of farm land in 1917. Excludes temporary income.

[1] Rent from tenanted land; house rent is in Other.

[2] From moneylending and deposits.

Source: Nakamura (1979)

4.7.1 Tenancy

The percentage of arable land rented out (the tenancy ratio) rose until the mid-1910s (Table 4.12). This sometimes is referred to as an indication of rising market power by landlords. Such an interpretation is too simplistic, however. The rise in the ratio until around 1900 is related to the rapid growth of agriculture, where landlords bought or rented in arable lands to cultivate themselves. Landlords led the rural economy through their efforts in diffusing new agricultural technology and in introducing large-scale farming utilizing hired labor. This latter activity, called *jinushi-tezukuri* (direct cultivation by landlords) suffered losses after around 1900 because of the rise in land prices and the wages of hired labor.

Thus, after 1900, direct cultivation by landlords declined substantially. However, until around 1915, small and medium owner-farmers and part-tenant farmers actively rented lands, and expanded their labor and fertilizer-intensive farming. (Part-tenant farmers both owned and rented in land.) This tendency continued until around 1930 and was related to a relative and absolute rise in the land productivity of tenant farmers. This provided incentives for part-tenant farmers to rent additional land. Table 4.15 provides data on land productivity.

Table 4.15 Land productivity, in kilograms of unpolished rice per hectare

	1890	1912
Landlords	4.6	3.0
Owner farmers	2.9	2.9
Tenants	2.7	3.2

Source: Hayami 1986, p. 101, from survey data of Saito Mankichi in Kajii (1961).

Kawagoe (1993) finds that the average labor productivty and average cost of rice production of tenant farmers became almost the same as that of owner-farmers during 1939–41.

The movement of the tenancy ratio in Table 4.12 should be understood against the background of this active behavior by cultivators, which does not have much to do with 'monopoly power' by landlords.

Most active were part-tenant farmers, who comprised 41 per cent of all farmers in 1920. (In that year there were 1,558,000 tenants, 2,244,000 part-tenants, and 1,683,000 owners (including landlords.) Their aggressive management was called *jikosaku-zenshingata* (positive farming by part-tenants) or *chunô-hyojyunka keikô* (standardization of middle-size farmers).

Wataya (1959) analyzes the behavior of part-tenants in terms of land-renting behavior and farming technology. They were heavily dependent on fertilizer inputs and land improvement. Kajii (1961) also gives evidence for the high productivity of part-tenants from the mid-1920s. Teranishi (1982) shows that among the three types, part-tenants were most active in utilizing loans from agricultural cooperatives in order to invest in agriculture.

5. Decline of the Meiji-Taishô economic system

The Meiji-Taishô system, having its heyday during World War I and the first years of Taishô democracy, fell into a decline in the mid-1920s.

After an overview of the decline, the chapter takes up the changes affecting the system in more detail. Specific economic costs related to production efficiency and the financial system, and political costs, in terms of the policy mix, its impact and its limitations, are analyzed. The two government policies that most undermined the institutions of the Meiji-Taishô system are then evaluated.

5.1 OVERVIEW OF THE PROCESS

As firms became increasingly dependent on outside funds, corporate governance led by large shareholders began to malfunction. The concentration of power in zaibatsu hands changed the quality of competition, converting 'the logic of the private sector' into 'the logic of the strong', and from a market-based economy with free play of the private sector into markets dominated by monopolistic powers. As class conflicts, such as tenancy and labor disputes, and inter-industrial conflicts intensified, regional economies failed to work smoothly as an interface between the government and the private sector.

As a backdrop for the emergence of distributive conflicts regarding class interests and inter–industrial interests, during the 1920s there was an emergence and gradual penetration of economic thought supporting intervention by the government, and this became more pronounced in the 1930s. Market failures in resource allocation began to be noticed, especially with respect to infant modern industries. Government intervention in industries was emphasized in the 1930s: government-led competition policy (cartel policy) based on the Regulating Important Industries Act of 1931 (revised in 1936) were introduced, together with various industry-promotion policies An expanded government role was of course inherent in war preparation from the mid-1930s, but even before that impetus, income distribution had attracted attention. Within the private sector, various intermediate organizations representing class, as well as inter-industrial interests, emerged.

5.2 ECONOMIC COSTS

From the viewpoint of efficiency, one of the main reasons for the fall of the Meiji-Taishô system was the weakening of the production system. The fragility and under-development of the financial system were additional reasons for inefficiency.

Among the three main productive sectors of the economy – agriculture, indigenous and light industries, and heavy and chemical industries – agriculture went into gradual decline after the spread of better technologies had reached its limits, at first during 1900–1910, and decisively in the 1920s. The newly established heavy and chemical industries experienced hard times during the 1920s because of keen competition waged by strong Western competitors. Even in the late 1930s, these industries had yet to acquire international competitiveness. From the mid-1920s, light and indigenous industries, except cotton-spinning, suffered seriously due to credit crunches.

Security markets in which professional dealers and wealthy individuals participated, fulfilled effective risk transfer among investors, and after the 1910s, international security transactions enabled risk transfer to overseas investors to some extent. However, the risk-reduction function performed by the banking sector became increasingly inadequate. This was because business groups based on *kikan-ginko* (often translated as organ banks), plus interlocking ownership and directorships, delayed effective diversification of bank portfolios, eventually resulting in accumulation of unredeemable non-performing loans. Moreover, it was not easy for the system to be equipped with adequate short-term money markets, so the financial system was under constant threat of maturity transformation risks on the macro level.

5.3 POLITICAL COSTS

Saddled with the rise in economic costs, the fall of the Meiji-Taishô system became inevitable when political costs also rose sharply. As distributive conflicts became multi-dimensional, the government was obliged to adopt a policy mix that took a neutral stance with respect to class conflicts, an anti-agricultural policy with respect to conflicts between agriculture and industry, and an anti-heavy and chemical industry policy with respect to the conflicts within the modern sector. The key for success of the policy mix was revival of regional economies based on indigenous production and commerce. However, the government ultimately failed to revive the regional economies. When the regional economies were finally in ruins and party politics had broken down, the Meiji-Taishô economic system, based on interest representation by means of regional economies, collapsed.

5.4 CHANGES AFFECTING THE SYSTEM

This section looks at changes in corporate governance, the nature of competition and the government's response, class consciousness, class-related conflict, and inter-industry conflict.

5.4.1 Corporate Governance

Let us examine the changes in corporate governance. The dependence on outside funds deepened in two respects: increasingly new shares were subscribed not by existing shareholders but by new, outside investors, and bank lending tended to be supplied to firms directly, rather than through the intermediation of wealthy individuals. The higher dependence on bank borrowing, with the lack of information disclosure, resulted in a closer firm–bank relationship, and hence in the formation of *kikan-ginko* (banks tied to specific firms through interlocking shareholding and directorships). These played the role of conduits of funds from depositors to specific firms. A larger ratio of shares held by new, outside shareholders caused a breakdown in the cooperative relationship among existing shareholders, leading to moral hazard by controlling shareholders and exploitation of other shareholders.

Table 5.1 shows the tendency toward dispersion of stock ownership and dependence on outside shareholders with respect to representative large firms. Both the number of outstanding shares and of shareholders increased in all the firms from 1915 to 1934. The average number of shares held increased from 1915 to 1920 for four firms, but fell for all the firms from 1920 to 1935. In other words, reliance on small investors increased during 1920 to 1935.

Moral hazard by large shareholders and managers controlled by them became a serious social issue. There were frequent cases of inadequate and illegal account settlements, such as dividend payments by compa-

Table 5.1 Number of shareholders and shares outstanding for large corporations (thousands)

	Tokyo Electricity	Daido Electricity	Toho Electricity	Nihon Oil	Osaka Marine	Nihon-Yûsen	Kansai Marin	Japan Electricity	Japan Hypothec Bank	South Manchurian Railroad
1915										
Share (a)	1,000	—	30	400	495	880	400	—	200	1,600
Shareholder (b)	4.3	—	0.3	3	5.4	4.2	1.8	—	3.7	7.6
(a)/(b)	231	—	102	134	92	212	217	—	55	211
1920								—		
Share (a)	2,480	2,000	90	800	2,000	2,000	900	1,000	800	3,800
Shareholder (b)	8.8	14.7	0.5	8.3	23.7	21.0	5.8	7.5	3.8	10.0
(a)/(b)	282	136	182	97	84	95	155	134	212	380
1934										
Share (a)	8,591	3,520	4,000	1,600	2,000	2,125	1,600	2,800	2,175	16,000
Shareholder (b)	62.3	37.4	30.0	25.3	30.1	23.7	22.0	21.1	36.5	54.7
(a)/(b)	138	94	133	63	67	90	73	133	60	293

Note: For Japan Hypothec Bank in 1915 and Toho Electricity in 1920, (a)/(b) are not the same as in the source; they are calculated by the author on the assumption that the data for (a) and (b) are correct.

Source: Masuchi (1936).

nies with deficits, manipulation of stock prices by managers, and sh-phoning–off of profits through affiliates. In a book titled *The Corporate Ruining of the Country*, published in 1930, Takahashi Kamekichi recommended unlimited liability for managers to prevent these activities, and even argued that, with regard to pernicious managers, not only fines, but also physical punishments were needed. Takahashi (1891–1977) was a well-known, freelance economic journalist who served as chief editor of *Toyo Keizai Shinpo* during 1924–26.

These moral hazards, however, gradually subsided during the 1930s. This was because institutional investors (banks and insurance companies) and non-financial corporations increased their holdings and became actively involved in corporate governance. As Table 4.1 shows, the share of stock held by corporations reached 56.4 per cent in 1936. As a result, some firms tended to behave as shareholding companies, and cross-shareholding became prevalent among zaibatsu firms (Teranishi 1994a).

5.4.2 Nature of Competition

Changes occurred in the quality of competition. At first, this was a result of an increase in the market power of zaibatsu and other large corporations. This was later exacerbated by intensification of government intervention in private economic activities in order to cope with market failures caused by the behavior of the zaibatsu. In other words, the competitive mechanism that characterized the Meiji-Taishô economic system deteriorated as competition resulted in hegemony of zaibatsu, which in turn provoked government intervention.

The rise of zaibatsu hegemony is most clearly seen by the sharp increase in market share of the five largest banks after the financial panic of 1927 (Table 4.5, p.101). With overwhelming market shares, zaibatsu banks exerted considerable influence on macro policy, as well as on banking and financial-sector policies.

Zaibatsu also acquired significant power in product markets. However, with respect to the manufacturing sector as a whole, and cotton-spinning in particular, the share of large firms (defined as those with more than 1,000 employees) in the number of workers and in production decreased during the 1930s (Nakamura 1993a). The decline in concentration seems to be closely related to the cartel movement. Cartel activities in the form of production and sales control became prevalent in heavy industries, chemical industries and textile industries during the depression years of the 1930s, and zaibatsu firms, especially the general trading company in each group, took a leading role in organizing and managing them (Takahashi 1933, Hashimoto 1984).

5.4.3 Government Response

To cope with the changes in the market mechanism, the government introduced two measures.

First, it became involved in bailing out firms, especially non-zaibatsu firms, through lending by the Industrial Bank of Japan (IBJ) and Japan Hypothec Bank. (Note that although these were privately funded, they were subject to government regulation through special legislation, and their governors were appointed by the government.) The operation, which had started from the rescue of exporters at the time of World War I, became a daily matter after the postwar recession (*handô-kyôkô*) in 1920. Funds came from the Bank of Japan (BOJ) and the Deposit Bureau of the Ministry of Finance (MOF). MOF extended funds obtained through postal savings to lending to private firms in general, as well as to municipal governments (Teranishi 1995a). These had previously been confined to purchase of government bonds and support of private firms engaged in colonial development.

IBJ, which had been unable to obtain various privileges due to opposition by the private sector at the time of its establishment, began to be actively involved in policy-based lending through bailing out private firms. Its loans, accompanied by dispatch of bankers to the boards of directors to monitor the borrowers, were directed to large non-zaibatsu corporations in manufacturing, electricity, electric railroads and marine transportation, among others. (After World War II, many of these firms established a relationship with the reorganized IBJ by becoming members of what is called the Kogin-keiretsu (Kawakami 1960).)

The second measure was to intervene in cartel activities that were led by zaibatsu firms. The landmark was promulgation of the Regulating Important Industries Act (*Jyûyô Sangyô Tôsei Hô*) in 1931 as a part of the industrial rationalization policy conducted by the Minseitô cabinet of Hamaguchi Osachi. The aims were to 'avoid waste and instability due to competition' through promoting cartels and to 'supervise from a public viewpoint the self-government agreements [that is, cartels] of the private sector' through monitoring cartels. Under the act, cartel agreements, authorized and monitored by the government, were introduced in many industries and, in the process, industrial associations were organized and strengthened.

5.4.4 Class Consciousness

The income-distributional consequences of capitalism had drawn attention from early on. As in other advanced countries, there was nothing noteworthy in the way of a social insurance system, although various possibilities for social policies regarding workers and peasants were actively explored and, to some extent, enforced by bureaucrats at the Social Bureau of the Ministry of Internal Affairs and the Bureau of Agricultural Policy of the Ministry of Agriculture and Commerce. (Japan's social insurance system started as health insurance and retirement annuities for public servants were introduced in 1868. Health insurance was extended to workers at private firms in 1927, except for smaller firms, and to farmers in 1938. In 1942 firm-level retirement annuities were introduced.)

Among the general populace, socialism gradually gained influence, effectively diffusing the concept of redistribution among classes, but socialist movements had been severely suppressed by the government from the 1910s. Enactment of the Maintenance of the Public Order Act (*Chian Iji Hô*) in 1925, and its revision in 1928, dealt near-fatal blows to the movements by escalating suppression. However, during the 1920s Marxism was an intellectual fashion and an important ingredient in the culture among students. Among such an intellectual climate, so-called innovative bureaucrats (*kakushin-kanryô*) emerged after the outbreak of war in 1937.

5.4.5 Class-related Conflict

The role of regional economies as intermediary organizations changed significantly after the mid-1920s. The changes were inevitable, partly because the cities and towns, originally envisaged by Yamagata Aritomo and Hara Takashi (Hara Kei) as regional economic units representing distributive interests, became relatively too small as units, because the whole economy had developed and the size of markets became larger. But the changes were mainly because distributive conflicts became multi-dimensional, and new patterns of interest representation by means of class as well as by means of industry had emerged.

A new pattern of representation of distributive interests based on class interests manifested itself in the form of labor and tenancy disputes and the growth of worker and tenant organizations. The number of labor union members increased sharply, from 126,000 in 1923 to 309,000 in 1928, and continued to increase until the mid-1930s.

Membership in farmers' associations increased from 164,000 to a peak of 347,000 in 1927.

As Table 5.2 shows, labor disputes had previously been negligible in terms of both size and frequency, but rapidly became prevalent,

Table 5.2 Labor and tenancy disputes and participants (thousands)

Year	Labor disputes[1]		Tenancy disputes	
	Number	Participants	Number	Participants
1913	47	5	–	–
1914	50	8	–	–
1915	64	8	–	–
1916	108	8		
1917	398	57	85	–
1918	417	66	256	–
1919	497	63	326	–
1920	282	36	408	35
1921	246	58	1,680	146
1922	250	42	1,578	126
1923	270	36	1,917	135
1924	333	55	1,532	111
1925	293	41	2,206	135
1926	495	67	2,751	151
1927	383	47	2,052	91
1928	397	46	1,866	75
1929	576	77	2,434	82
1930	906	81	2,478	59
1931	998	65	3,419	81
1932	893	55	3,414	61
1933	610	49	4,000	48
1934	626	50	5,828	121
1935	590	38	6,824	113
1936	547	31	6,804	77
1937	628	124[a]	6,170	63
1938	262	18	4,615	53
1939	358	73	3,578	26
1940	271	33	3,165	39

Notes:
[1] For 1919–23, includes only disputes that resulted in a strike (*domei-higyo*). From 1924, includes incidents of sabotage (*domei taigyo*). From 1927, also includes lockouts (*kojo-heisa*). Gordon (1985, p. 440) provides data on just strikes and number of strikers for 1897–1940.
[a] The large number of participants and incidents in 1937 is probably related to increased sabotage of private railways and bus companies.

Source: Rôdô Undô Shiryô Iinkai (1959) and Nakamura (1993b).

reaching 497 incidents with 63,000 participants in 1919, before receding in the 1920s. The length of the dispute period also decreased. Militancy declined in part because 'leftist' members in total union membership, which was 100 per cent in 1923, decreased to 28.8 per cent in 1927 and to 6.7 per cent in 1936 (Nishida 1991). (Here, 'leftist' means anarchists, communists and left-wing social democrats. Nishida analyzed issues of the Ministry of Internal Affair's *Labor Yearbook* (*Rôdô Undô Nenpô*) and other sources that provide classification of unions by the ideological tendencies of their membership.) In addition, labor unions began to explore labor–management cooperation within a firm system, especially after 1932 (Banno 1991). The number of labor disputes and their size rose quickly during the Showa Depression (1930–31), which merged into the global Great Depression. From peaks in 1930–31, the numbers subsequently decline.

Many of the labor disputes before World War I were aimed at gaining 'respect for workers' personal rights'. The early disputes centered on large factories belonging to zaibatsu, with the case of the Nagasaki Shipyard of Mitsubishi during 1917–19 being representative. Later, their major arena shifted to small and medium firms. In these disputes, demands centered on defensive items such as opposition to wage reduction and dismissals (Nishinarita 1988).

Tenancy disputes increased rapidly toward a peak in 1926, with 2,751 occurrences and 151,000 participants. After a temporary decrease, the figures rose again after 1930, reaching a maximum number of disputes (6,824) in 1935. Tenancy disputes, in contrast to labor disputes, continued to be militant and leftist, with the time they lasted becoming longer. Nishida (1991), using sources and techniques similar to those mentioned above for labor unions, found that the share of leftist members in total tenant union membership was 100 per cent in 1924 and 73.3 per cent in 1927. He argues that the militancy of tenancy disputes was due to the improvement of economic conditions of tenants, who had diversified their income sources to non-agricultural sources such as part-time labor or indigenous production. Diversification of income sources enhanced the bargaining power of tenants against the threat of eviction from the land they farmed.

5.4.6 Inter-industry Conflict

Representation of distributive interests by means of inter-industrial conflicts appeared at the time of the Russo-Japan War (1904–1905) when conflict between agriculture and non-agriculture intensified. The land tax rate was increased to finance the war but, because of opposition by farmers, the increase was compensated by a new duty on rice imports. The Seiyûkai passed the tariff at the request of the Imperial Association of Agriculture (Teikoku Nôkai). This generated a heated controversy between Nôkai, which claimed it was protecting small farmers, and the Chamber of Commerce (Shôgyô Kaigi-sho), which objected on the basis of the tariff's impact on industrialization and workers (Mochida 1954).

This friction between agriculture and non-agriculture was apparently new in view of the fact that previous conflicts over the land tax rate had taken place between the government and farmers. The conflict over business tax and land tax in the 1880s was also of a similar nature. Strife between agriculture and non-agriculture was repeated with respect to the promulgation and enforcement of the Rice Act (*Beikoku Hô*) in April 1921, especially regarding government intervention to 'adjust supply and demand', and thus rice prices, through inventory management (Miyazaki 1980).

Inter-industrial conflicts also occurred within the non-agricultural sector. For example, when the Tanaka cabinet (1927–29) tried to promote domestic production of pig iron by raising the import duty, the policy was opposed by the steel and cotton-spinning industries. The former feared for high input prices and the latter was concerned about trade friction with Indian competitors. The policy to lower dye prices to promote dyeing and weaving as a leading export sector invited opposition from advocates of an import-substitution policy to promote a domestic chemical industry producing synthetic dyes.

Further, with regard to the policy regarding the gold embargo (whether to return to the gold standard), there was a clear conflict of interest between heavy industry on the one hand and the light, trade, and financial industries on the other, regarding the costs and benefits of the policy. With regard to agriculture, the Ministry of Commerce and Industry, which aimed to promote the fertilizer industry through protective measures, encountered strong opposition by agricultural associations and the Ministry of Agriculture (Tsuchikawa 1994/95).

Organizations of inter-industrial interests advanced rapidly when organizing industrial associations among small and medium firms was encouraged from a social-policy viewpoint after enactment of the Industrial Associations for Important Export Goods Act (*Jyûyô Yushutsuhin Kôgyô Kumiai Hô*) in 1925, and especially after revision of the Industrial Association Act (*Kôgyô Kumiai Hô*) in 1933. The dramatic increase in the number of associations after 1938 (see Table 5.3) is because they became in charge of rationing materials.

Table 5.3 Number of industrial associations, 1925–40

1925	1931	1932	1937	1938	1940
20	152	212	1173	2836	6580

Source: 1925–31, Shôkô Gyôseishi Kankôkai (1954–55) (*chûkan*) p. 234; after 1932, Tsusho Sangyo-sho, 1963.

5.5 PRODUCTION EFFICIENCY

Agriculture maintained a high rate of growth until around 1920, partly owing to active farm management by medium farmers, especially by part-tenant farmers (that is, farmers who both owned and rented in land). Nevertheless, agriculture fell into apparent stagnation in the 1920s, as seen in Table 4.11.

There are three reasons for this: first, diffusion of indigenous technology reached saturation point; second, the effect of the expansion of domestic and international markets had worn off; third, government policies disadvantageous to agriculture, especially rice production, were enacted. The influence of these factors manifested itself as a decrease in the residual growth rate (technological progress) of the primary sector, as shown in Table 4.11 (p. 112).

Stagnation of agriculture could be offset by industrial growth. However, this did not happen because industries were also in a serious situation, except cotton-spinning, the leading industry of interwar Japan. In particular, firms in steel, shipbuilding, electrical machinery and chemicals, newly established or expanded during the World War I boom, faced severe competition from Western competitors after the war. Company histories of these firms for this period invariably show intense competition with overseas competitors as a main motif. Prolonged periods of loss were common even among large companies, and several were forced to stop production or go into bankruptcy.

The predicament faced by firms in heavy and chemical industries was partly due to difficulty in learning to utilize advanced technology in a short period, and partly due to policy factors. The policy atmosphere of the time was primarily free-trade oriented, so industries were only slightly protected by tariffs and promoted by subsidies.

Figure 5.1 compares the actual yen-dollar exchange rate and an estimate of the equilibrium rate. The yen was significantly overvalued during the 1920s. This was because a return to the gold standard at the prewar parity was regarded as an imperative policy objective, so that

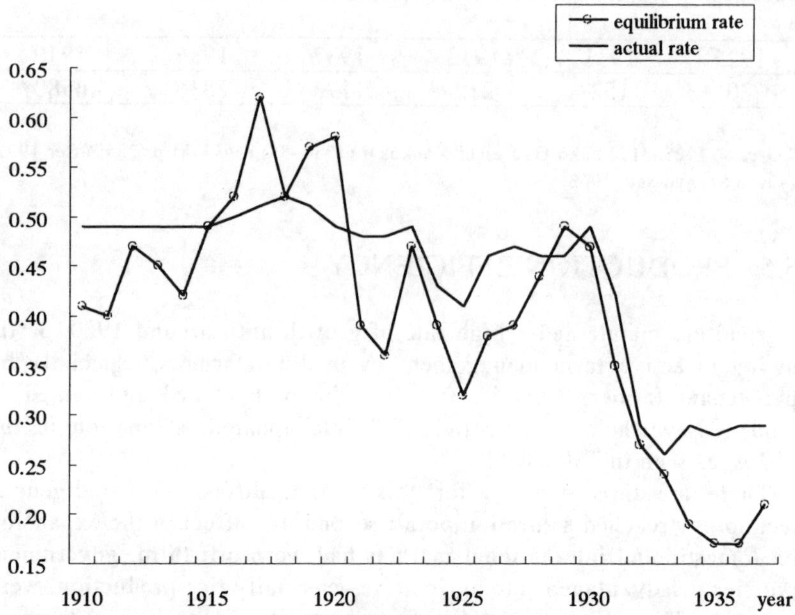

Notes: Vertical axis shows dollar/yen exchange rate, so that the higher is this value, the more appreciated (overvalued) is the exchange rate.

Japan left the gold standard on September 12 1917. (Strictly speaking, from that date shipment of gold coin and bullion required MOF approval, so that gold was effectively embargoed, and that was the same as leaving the gold standard. The United States had taken a similar action on September 10.) On assuming office in July 1929, the Hamaguchi government had pledged return to the gold standard (removal of the embargo) 'at an early date' and on November 21 announced that the date would be January 11 1930. Japan abandoned the gold standard again (re-imposed an embargo) on December 13 1931.

The equilibrium rate is calculated by multiplying the ratio of the general price level of Japan and the United States to the equilibrium real exchange rate, estimated in a macroeconomic model as the rate equating the difference between saving and investment to current account, assuming full employment and the equality of real interest rates between Japan and the US.

Although the figure shows the yen as undervalued after 1932, the authors note that it actually was significantly overvalued if the effects of exports to the colonies financed through policy-based capital exports are taken into consideration.

Source: Okura and Teranishi (1994).

Figure 5.1 Actual and equilibrium value of exchange rate

the exchange rate was anchored to the old parity (about 2 yen per US$1) in spite of serious trade deficits. Economists at the time, such as Ishibashi Tanzan of Toyo Keizai Shinpo-sha, argued for a return to the gold standard at a depreciated parity, but such opinions remained in the minority. If effects of exports to the colonies financed through policy-based capital exports are taken into consideration, the exchange rate during the 1930s remained significantly overvalued.

Under these circumstances, development of heavy and chemical industries through import substitution was not an easy matter. Table 5.4 indicates this by means of net-import levels for major products. Trade in rice, one of the main export goods in early modern Japan, became a net import as early as the first half of the 1890s. Copper and coal, however, continued to be net export goods until the 1920s. Cotton yarn kept the position of main export from around 1895 through to the 1960s. Cotton cloth became a net export good in the first half of the 1910s. Among heavy and chemical products, only steel materials became net export goods before World War II.

Table 5.5 shows how the pattern of trade detected in Table 5.4 is related to comparative production costs or technology level of various industries. The larger the number, the greater the comparative advantage for Japan *vis-à-vis* the United States with respect to the *i*th product, and conversely. It can be seen that, while Japan increased advantage in textiles after the 1920s and lost it in the 1960s, there were no substantial changes in advantage in chemical and metals during the period. Further, farm products lost advantage after around 1911.

In sum, it was not easy for Japan to accomplish import substitution in the heavy and chemical industries during the prewar period. While import substitution in light industries such as textiles was easily carried out, in heavy and chemical industries prewar Japan did not have enough technology infrastructure.

Most heavy and chemical products were sold in domestic markets, and export markets were confined to Manchuria generally and (initially) its Kwantung province (around Port Arthur) in particular, where exports were preferentially financed by capital exports and governmental loans implemented as national policies. For example, in the case of machinery, low-level and small–scale products could be produced domestically, while the supply of high-level and large-scale products relied mostly on imports.

The same applied to chemical products except ammonium sulphate. Through an examination of data compiled by Yukizawa and Maeda (1978), it can be seen that of the 610 million yen increase in exports during 1925–35, 69 per cent (420 million yen) was directed to colonial and semi-colonial regions. Of that, 350 million yen comprised heavy and chemical products (Teranishi 1992). Further, of the 8.65 million yen increase of exports of electrical machinery during 1932–34, 8.59 million was to Manchuria (then a colony, Manchukuo) and China

Table 5.4 Net imports as percentage of domestic production, 1875–1974

	Copper	Coal	Rice	Steel materials	Cotton yarn	Cotton cloth	Passenger car	General machinery
1875–1879	–53	–31	–1	–	585	107	–	–
1880–1884	–37	–41	–1	–	281	69	–	–
1885–1889	–86	–57	–2	–	124	34	–	–
1890–1894	–107	–64	1	–	117	23	–	–
1895–1899	–82	–59	3	–	–114	27	–	–
1900–1904	–79	–47	6	644	–33	21	–	–
1905–1909	–82	–27	8	346	–26	10	–	–
1910–1914	–70	–27	6	172	–31	–29	–	–
1915–1919	–58	–	7	97	–27	–59	–	–
1920–1924	13	–3	10	118	–21	–52	–	–
1925–1929	9	3	17	41	–11	–59	5,820	[a]22
1930–1934	–8	11	17	3	–4	–65	1,491	9
1935–1939	29	12	20	–6	–7	–63	341	–0
1950–1954	–	–	–	–15	–10	–32	83	[b]–0
1955–1959	–	–	–	–9	–4	–37	5	3
1960–1964	–	–	–	–13	–6	–41	–9	3
1965–1969	–	–	–	–21	–2	–33	–20	–3
1970–1974	–	–	–	–25	4	3	–30	–6

Notes: Entries are (imports minus exports) divided by domestic output, times 100. This means positive numbers are net imports as a percentage of domestic output, and negative numbers are net exports as a percentage of domestic output.

[a] Average of 1926–29.

[b] Average of 1951–54.

Sources: Data on copper and coal are from Nihon Tokei Kyokai (1988a) for imports and exports and from Shinohara (1972) for output; on rice, from Shinohara (1962); cotton yarn, cotton cloth, steel, passenger cars and general machinery, from Yamazawa (1984) and Hashimoto (1984).

Table 5.5 Changes in comparative-advantage structure

Period	Farm products	Food	Textiles	Chemicals	Metals	Non-ferrous metals	Machinery
1891–95	0.76	1.17	1.10	1.07	1.00	–	–
1896–1900	0.77	1.20	1.17	0.87	1.04	–	–
1901–05	0.73	1.09	1.17	0.88	1.07	–	–
1906–10	0.76	0.96	1.22	0.81	1.01	–	–
1911–15	0.57	1.01	1.38	0.76	1.05	–	–
1916–20	0.54	1.15	1.19	0.84	0.98	–	–
1921–25	0.49	1.16	1.34	0.99	1.34	–	–
1926–30	0.48	1.04	1.73	0.89	1.23	–	–
1931–35	0.60	0.98	2.10	0.89	1.11	–	–
1936–40	0.54	1.31	2.18	0.89	0.81	–	–
1960–1970	–	0.88	0.91	1.09	1.27[a]	1.08	1.21

Notes:
Each entry is the ratio of the relevant wholesale price index of the United States to that of Japan ($A_{i\,US} / A_{i\,Japan}$), where each A_i is given by

$$Ai = \left(\frac{\text{WPI of } i\text{-th product of period } t}{\text{WPI of } i\text{-th product of base year}}\right) \Big/ \left(\frac{\text{average of WPI in period } t}{\text{average of WPI in base year}}\right)$$

The prewar base is the average for 1880–90; the postwar base is 1960.
[a] Steel.

Sources: Postwar data are from Fujino (1987). Prewar are as follows. The WPI of Japan for each commodity is from Ohkawa (1967), tables 10 and 14; average WPI is from Nihon Ginko Hyakunen-shi Hensan Iinkai (1986). WPI for the United States is from US Department of Commerce (1960). Series E13-24 and Series E1-12 are linked at 1890. Average WPI is that of all commodities.

(where Japan, like the Western powers, had spheres of influence) (Mitsubishi Keizai Kenkyûjyo 1935). Likewise, almost all the exports of engineering machinery, railroad vehicles and telephones were to colonial regions.

5.6 FINANCIAL SYSTEM

The fragility of the financial system appeared in two respects. These are declines in risk–reduction capability through portfolio diverisification and in maturity-transformation capability.

5.6.1 Risk-reduction Capability

First is the decline in risk-reduction capability through portfolio diversification. The aggravation of the problems related to *kikan-ginko* was typical of such fragility. *Kikan-ginko* were managed or controlled by the members of the owner-family of particular firms or groups of firms, and lent to those firms preferentially. Examples are the Nanajyûyon Bank, which had a close relationship with the textile merchant Mogi, Murai Bank with trading and textile businesses run by the Murai family, and Soda Bank with various firms held by the Soda family. Many banks after the Taishô period had traits of *kikan-ginko*, even if they were not so well known as these examples.

The banking practices of *kikan-ginko* were definitely unsound: concentration of lending to particular firms paralyzes the risk-reduction function of banks, leading to the simultaneous bankruptcies of both lenders and borrowers. During slump periods, financial crises caused by the failures of *kikan-ginko* quite often amplified the downward swing of business cycles.

Table 5.6 indicates the risk associated with *kikan-ginko* through various characteristics of the balance sheets of banks that failed during the financial crisis (*kinyû kyôkô*) in 1927, the largest such crisis in prewar Japan. The ratio of deposits to paid-in capital and of lending to deposits, indicators of deposit mobilization capability, are at a comparable level to the average of all ordinary banks. This, however, reflects the fact that these banks had tried to absorb deposits by offering very high interest rates, as revealed by the Bank of Japan's investigation after the crisis.

Even Jyûgo Bank (Peers Bank), closely related to the aristocracy both in its origins and as a cash office of the Imperial Household Agency, had to offer extraordinarily high deposit rates to keep its lending–deposit ratio at 0.97, close to the average 0.94, because the bank was at the same time the *kikan-ginko* of the Matsukata family. The eldest son of the Meiji oligarch, Iwao, was president of the bank; the third son, Kojiro, was president of Kawasaki Shipbuilding.

Further, composition of lending by the type of collateral shows that many of the failed banks either lent without collateral or with real estate

Table 5.6 Financial data on closed bank during the 1927 financial panic

Paid-in capital[1]	Deposits as % of paid-in capital	Lending as % of deposits	Loans, real estate collateral[2]	Loans, no collateral[2]	Loans to share-holders[2]	Loans to bank managers[2]	Loans to related firms[2]	Bank and (prefecture)
161	103	88	61.6	32.7	–	–	–	Kuki Bank (Saitama)
250	66	97	–	–		[a]49.0	–	Kawaizumi Bank (Osaka)
400	48	91	–	68.1	–	30.2	–	Tokatsu Bank (Chiba)
400	67	104	30.7	38.1	–	16.4	–	Nishiebara Bank (Okayama)
700	110	63	19.5	49.8	9.7	–	30.9	Tokushima Bank (Tokushima)
800	78	102	36.1	32.5	–	22.9	–	Kurita Bank (Shiga)
1,000	58	93	31.4	51.4	–	–	–	Kurate Bank (Fukuoka)
1,250	70	140	2.7	89.2	23.0	–	71.4	Nakazawa Bank (Tokyo)
2,000	185	104	–	–	36.1	[b]37.7		Tokyo-Watanabe Bank (Tokyo)
2,300	77	91	–	–	–	18.9	–	Hachijyûyon Bank (Ishikawa)
2,500	55	128	29.9	49.1	–	28.7	–	Imabari-Shôgyô Bank (Ehime)
2,500	87	107	9.7	69.8	9.2	–	31.3	Souda Bank (Kanagawa)
5,000	91	91	25.7	23.4	2.8	–	–	Nakai Bank (Tokyo)
5,125	117	95	11.3	66.0	25.8	–	–	Murai Bank (Tokyo)
6,250	45	103	10.8	42.5	22.5	5.9	–	Dairokujyûgo Bank (Hyogo)
9,375	146	91	12.3	58.6	–	7.7	–	Oumi Bank (Osaka)
49,750	74	97	–	–	1.9	3.5	34.7	Jyûgo Bank (Tokyo)
1,677	61	94	21.0	33.8	–	–	–	Average, of all ordinary banks

Notes:
[1] In thousand yen.
[2] As percentage of total loans.
[a] Includes loans to shareholders.
[b] Includes loans to related firms.

Source: Teranishi (1982) using data on closed banks reported in Bank of Japan 'Causes of Bankruptcy of Closed Banks' (1928).

as collateral. The share of lending to firms related to shareholders and managers or to group firms was significantly high.

5.6.1.1 Spillover effects

The decline in the risk-reduction capability of banks was accelerated because adverse business shocks had spillover effects among related industries through an input–output relationship.

The shocks of the start and end of World War I especially affected trading companies. They obtained huge profits through the export boom during the war, and they also suffered the most from the cease-fire and the recessions in 1920 and 1922. Mid-sized trading companies such as Nomura-shoji, Furukawa-shoji, Kuraha-shôji and Murai-bôeki ran large deficits, and some were forced to dissolve. This was partly because the boom from 1918 through to early 1920 became extremely speculative, and partly because many of the trading companies established during the war did not have enough actual expertise in trading and management.

Because a large part of bank lending was directed to commercial activities, the difficulties faced by the trading companies spilled over to banks, especially medium city banks, related to them. Most of the bankruptcies of medium city banks during the financial crisis were at least partly caused by non-performing loans to trading companies: Ohira-shôkai and Taiwa-shôkai in the case of the bankruptcy of Souda Bank; Murai-bôeki in the case of Murai Bank; Taika-yôkô and Tokai-shoji in the case of Nakazawa Bank; Itochu in the case of Oumi Bank; and Suzuki–shoten in the case of Dairokujyûgo Bank (and Bank of Taiwan).

The failure of trading companies and the decline in exports of indigenous and light-industry products to Asia and Africa spilled into the rest of the economy through two routes. First, the failures caused a liquidity crisis among domestic traders, and then among producers in the regions making the products (Teranishi (1982) emphasizes this route). Second, the decline in exports eroded the revenues and profits of firms involved in marine transportation, shipbuilding, and then steel production (Hashimoto (1992) emphasizes this route).

While both routes brought growth of related industries during the export boom, the same linkages resulted in a downward spiral after the end of the war. The first led to a slump for local banks related to domestic traders and regional producers, and the second led to a slump for medium city banks related to large firms in marine transportation, shipbuilding and steel production.

The first linkage is exemplified by the damage to regional production centers and local banks at the time of the financial crisis: closure of Oumi Bank was caused by the slump of cotton weaving in the Osaka area, Imabari Shôgyô Bank by the decline of cotton weaving in Ehime, and Hachijyûyon Bank by the depression in raw silk and silk weaving in Ishikawa. Examples of the second linkages include Kawasaki Shipbuilding, Kokusai Marine Transportation, and Suzuki Shoten, all hitting Jyûgo Bank heavily, and Asano Cement, Asano Shipbuilding, Toyo Marine Transportation together doing serious damage to Yasuda Bank.

5.6.2 Maturity Mismatch

The fragility of the financial system also manifested itself in the decline of maturity-transformation capability. After World War I, maturity mismatch in the banking sector became serious for three reasons. First, banks had become very dependent on short-term deposits. Second, loans to agriculture also became fixed (in the sense of repeated rollover) and of longer maturity as the sector went into long-term stagnation. Third, the difficulties faced by heavy and chemical industries through competition with foreign producers resulted in the lengthening of the maturity periods of bank loans. Godo and Teranishi (1992) point out that for term loans, the average maturity period (computed as outstanding loans at the end of period divided by new loans and loan repayments during the period) increased sharply during the 1920s and until around 1935.

Lengthening loan maturity and a shorter deposit term meant maturity transformation was an increasing burden for the banking sector. It was addressed in two ways: first, by introducing long-term time deposits at the cost of higher interest rates, and second, by increased utilization of rollover credits by means of accommodation bills.

Thus, the maturity period of time deposits (outstanding deposits at the end of periods divided by new acceptances and repayments of deposits during the period) as well as the ratio of accommodation bills (*tegata kashitsuke*) to the sum of accommodation bills and term loans (*shôsho kashitsuke*) was increased. (Accommodation bills are bankers' acceptances (bills of exchange) based on trade bills, which are bills of exchange accepted by a party other than a bank.)

5.6.2.1 Government response

The government responded to the increased burden of maturity transformation with three policies: promotion of money markets, substitution of long-term loans by banks with policy-based loans, and flexible Bank of Japan credit supply to banks.

None of these was effective enough. With respect to money markets, the attempt by Bank of Japan governor Inoue Junnosuke to establish a market for trade bills to make Tokyo the 'London in the Far East' was aborted when the market ceased to work for various reasons just two years after its inception in 1919 (Teranishi 1991). The nascent commercial paper market, born during the 1920s out of pioneering efforts by bill brokers, ceased to exist when zaibatsu banks waged competition against the bill brokers by discounting the bills of zaibatsu-related firms (Tsurumi 1983).

Efforts to promote efficient money markets within the Ministry of Finance were not successful either. The Ministry, intending to promote money markets, consulted the deliberative council on the financial system (*Kin'yû-seido Chôsakai*), held in 1926, about establishment of a new bill–discounting market, making it the first priority item on the agenda. The council, however, was controlled by members related to zaibatsu banks, and did not meet the Ministry's wishes. A subcommittee submitted a report on 'Concrete measures to promote a bill discounting market', but this draft report was never discussed in the council. Instead, the item was treated only as third priority, after improvement of the function of the Bank of Japan and the reform of the banking system, and the meetings ended without it being deliberated at all.

With respect to substitution of long-term loans by policy-based loans, the activity of the Japan Hypothec Bank was successful to some extent during the 1910s. A cross-prefectural regression of the share of loans with real estate collateral of ordinary and savings banks (a proxy for the non–performing long-term loan ratio) as a dependent variable and loans by the Japan Hypothec Bank as an independent variable, yields a significant negative coefficient for the independent variable in 1915, but the coefficient is insignificant in 1925 and 1935 (Godo and Teranishi 1992). (Loans of Nôkô banks, as well as of Hokkaido-Takushoku Bank are included, and loans are divided by the population of each prefecture.) The result can be construed as saying that, after the mid–1920s, maturity mismatch had become so serious that policy-based loans could not rectify the situation.

Finally, with respect to the role of the Bank of Japan, there had been a long-lasting controversy between those arguing for a commitment to the financing of industrial development, and those for specialization in commercial banking. With the controversy unsettled, equity collateral-financing by the Bank of Japan, one of the most effective tools for industrial-banking activity, was not authorized until the promulgation of a new Bank of Japan Act in February 1942. Further, the Bank of Japan became heavily committed to bailing out banks during the two major recessions immediately after World War I, 1920 and 1922. However, BOJ was obliged to abandon the policy after 1923 because of serious moral hazard by banks that received rescue funds (*tokubetsu yûshi*).

In sum, in the 1920s the Meiji-Taishô system suffered from a rise in economic costs because of both low technological infrastructure on the production side and fragility of the banking sector on the financial side. The financial crisis in 1927 highlighted the weakness.

5.6.3 The 1927 Financial Crisis

There actually were two panics which differ in nature and in terms of what triggered and what ended them, but because they occurred in quick succession, it is usual to speak of them as one crisis. (This summary is drawn from a detailed analysis of daily data of the two panics in Korenaga, Nagase and Teranishi (2001).)

In answer to a question at the Budget Committee of the lower house of the Diet on 14 March 1927, Minister of Finance Kataoka Naoharu incorrectly said that Watanabe Bank had closed, thereby revealing the bank had been in difficulty. (Kataoka was unaware the bank's immediate problem had been resolved.) Its weakness revealed, Watanabe was forced to close the next day.

In spite of the special legislation to allow BOJ to rediscount bills related to earthquake damages enacted on 27 September 1923, *Shinsai-tegata-sonshitsu-hoshô Rei*, the outstanding amount of the earthquake bill did not decrease, so the government intended to pass two additional legislations (earthquake bills) through the Diets, *Shinsai-tegata-sonshitsu-hoshô Hô* and *Shinsai-tegata-zengoshori Hô*. In the process of Diet deliberation of earthquake bills especially after January 1927, it was disclosed that some medium banks were suffering problems not only from loans related to the earthquake damages but also from large amounts of non–performing loans that had nothing to do with the damages of the Kantô earthquake on September 1 1923. As a result, there were large-scale withdrawals from banks in the Tokyo area. This led to the closure of major medium city banks such as Murai, Souda, Nakazawa and Hachijyûyon on March 22. The panic ended when earthquake-bill legislation passed the House of Peers on March 23.

A second panic was triggered by the Privy Council's rejection on April 17 of the government's proposal to bail out the Bank of Taiwan (BOT). BOT was in difficulties due to problems at Suzuki Shoten (a trading company). The government feared BOT's bankruptcy would paralyze the inter-bank call market, on which the banks relied heavily for financing. BOT and Oumi Bank closed on April 18, and there ensued a nation-wide bank run that included closure of Jyûgo Bank (the Peers' Bank) on April 21. The panic was calmed by a moratorium implemented on April 22, suspending withdrawal of deposits of more than 500 yen for three weeks. (The average deposit account at ordinary banks had a balance of 655 yen in 1927.) This was followed up by special legislation passed on May 4, three days before expiry of the moratorium, providing special loans to stabilize the Bank of Taiwan, as well as other banks with large amounts of non-performing loans.

It follows that the first panic was caused by closure of inefficient banks plagued with non-performing loans, while the second was caused by the collapse of the inter-bank call market, and rise of skepticism about the maturity-transformation capability of the banking sector. In other words, the first panic was efficiency enhancing, while the second was a phenomenon quite close to the self-fulfilling panic model in Diamond and Dybvig (1983), in the sense that it was caused by maturity mismatch in the banking sector as a whole.

5.7 POLICY MIX

There is a plethora of literature about the behavior of political parties, bureaucrats and interest groups related to the emergence of the multi-dimensional pattern of distributive conflicts in Japan. The arguments advanced are varied and diverse. Still, when with hindsight, we survey the vast pile of material and summarize it, it can be shown that there was a definite tenet in the government's policy mix.

The entire strategy with respect to the complex patterns of distributional conflicts is as follows. The government had to sacrifice agriculture to carry out industrialization and, at the same time, to defend the nation from the 'contamination' of labor movements and Marxism. So, the rice price was kept low. However, for socio-political stability, the living standard of peasants could not be overlooked, so the government tried to solve the problem by helping regional economies by providing assistance to the budgets of local governments and supporting indigenous industries. The support for indigenous industries resulted in relative neglect of heavy and chemical industries.

Moreover, the government refrained from explicitly favoring particular elements in class conflicts, and instead tried to reduce the conflict itself. Thus, the policy to sacrifice agriculture helped both workers and capitalists, and the policy to subsidize local governments was beneficial both to landlords and peasants.

In sum, the strategy of the government had three pillars: a neutral policy toward class conflicts, an anti-agriculture policy, and an anti-heavy and chemical industry policy. Let me explain how these policies were implemented.

5.7.1 Class Conflicts

With respect to labor and tenancy disputes, the government's stance was basically neutral. Also, it neither helped nor suppressed class movements. Rather than favor one side or the other, it tried to adopt policies supporting both parties in conflicts. In the case of labor disputes, it tried to help both capital and labor by lowering the price of the major 'wage good', rice. In other words, sacrificing the interests of agriculture was the tactic adopted by the government in this case. Likewise, with respect to tenancy disputes, rather than favoring one party, the government took the stance of helping regional economies by adjusting the tax system and increasing public investment. The government believed that, as long as traditional community ties continued to function, its policy stance would satisfy both parties.

5.7.1.1 Labor disputes

As labor disputes spread after the 1920s, the government sometimes attempted half-heartedly to suppress the labor movement, and sometimes sought to encourage cooperative (enterprise-based) unions. A Social Bureau (*Shakai-kyoku*) was established in the Ministry of Internal Affairs in 1921 to take care of labor disputes, and the government virtually gave official acknowledgement to labor unions when the Bureau chose the representatives for a meeting of the International Labor Organization (ILO) in 1924 (Yasuda 1993). At the same time, however, the Maintenance of Public Order Act, a powerful tool for suppressing labor and tenancy disputes, was promulgated in 1925 and revised in 1928. With respect to industrial actions, a Mediation of Labor Disputes Act (*Rôdôsôgi Chôtei Hô*) was introduced in 1927, and the Social Bureau was said to be quite careful in applying the law so as to minimize dismissal and its impact on public security.

The Social Bureau's attempt to legalize labor unions was aborted in 1929, despite the support of the Hamaguchi cabinet and its supporting party, the Minseitô. Major opposition came from capitalist groups. However, these groups, such as the *Nihon Kôgyô*-club and Japan Chamber of Commerce, were not against introduction of labor unions suited to the Japanese company system (Nishinarita 1988). They opposed the proposal of the Hamaguchi cabinet because it seemed to presuppose and, hence, to institutionalize, confrontation between labor and capitalists through introduction of a system of collective bargaining (Ogihara 1983).

5.7.1.2 Tenancy disputes

With respect to tenancy disputes, a group of bureaucrats, related to the Research Committee on the Tenancy System established in 1920 in the Ministry of Agriculture and Commerce, worked actively to protect the rights of tenants. The Mediation of Tenancy Disputes Act in 1924 enabled resolution of disputes on practical terms. A system to create owner-farmers through policy-based lending was introduced in 1926, and subsequent promulgation of the Adjustment of Arable Lands Act (*Nôchi Chôsei Hô*) in 1938 aimed at protection of tenancy rights and circumscription of the rights of landlords. For example, if municipal governments wanted to introduce a policy of increasing the number of owner-farmers, administrative offices had the right to negotiate with landlords regarding sale of land. Further, added constraints were placed on the one-sided cancellation of tenancy contracts by landlords. Kawagoe (1993) evaluates the law as a prelude to the land reform after World War II, although it was not perfectly effective in protecting the interests of tenants.

5.7.2 Sectoral Conflict

With regard to the conflicts between agriculture and non-agriculture, the government apparently took an anti-agricultural policy. This is evident from the stance of the government toward the price of rice. In 1919, the year after the Rice Riot (*kome-sôdô*), the Hara cabinet of the Seiyûkai decided to encourage new cultivation of farmland and the importing of rice from colonial regions (Korea and Taiwan). There was already a tendency toward excess supply in the rice market, so the policy could not be justified by short-run demand–supply conditions.

Nevertheless, the government intended to secure rice from a long-term perspective without any regard to near-term price movements (Nakamura 1980). A fear of the labor movement and communism, felt most deeply by *genrô* Yamagata Aritomo, and recurrent balance of payments crises during the 1920s made it imperative for the government to pursue such a policy. The Promotion of Farmland Cultivation Act, promulgated in 1919, subsidized 25 per cent of the costs from the government budge, and the Rice Act introduced in 1919 in response to a strong request by the Imperial Association of Agriculture (*Teikoku*

Nôkai) was utilized as a tool for lowering rice prices, contrary to the expectation of the Association.

The Takahashi cabinet, which followed the Hara cabinet, tried to cope with the rice price hike in 1921 by means of the inventory controls stipulated the law, as well as the repeal of the import duty on rice. The low price of rice benefited non-agriculture, both labor and capital, at the expense of agriculture.

5.7.3 Inter-industry Conflicts

With regard to inter-industry conflicts within non-agriculture, two facts provide strong evidence of a policy bias against heavy and chemical industries. The first is the substantial overvaluation of the exchange rate throughout the 1920s, as shown in Figure 5.1 (Okura and Teranishi 1994). The second is that there were only modest subsidies and tariff protection.

5.7.3.1 Overvalued exchange rate

Although the high exchange rate helped heavy and chemical industries by lowering the cost of imported machinery and materials, it exerted a more serious effect on competitiveness by forcing up prices, weakening Japanese producers vis-à-vis foreign competition in both domestic and overseas markets. This was especially true for large companies in industries with high proportions of skilled workers, whose wage levels had downward rigidity.

The unfavorable effect of the overvalued exchange rate on heavy and chemical industries can be observed in the attitude of various industries toward the policy regarding the gold embargo after the 1920s. When the Hamaguchi cabinet pledged a return to the gold standard in July 1929 at the prewar parity, which was obviously an overvalued rate, the policy was supported by banks, trading companies, and the silk industry, and opposed by the machine and steel industries. The attitude of the cotton-spinning industry, which relied on unskilled labor but obtained most of its materials from abroad, is not clear (Miwa 1974).

5.7.3.2 Modest protection

Opinions of researchers are diverse regarding protection policies for heavy and chemical industries. Miwa (1976) claims that, except for the Hamaguchi cabinet (1929–31), interwar cabinets generally adopted strong protection policies for these industries. Hashimoto (1984) maintains that it was difficult for the government to pursue a comprehensive protection policy due to the conflicts of interest among industries. Miyajima (1992) asserts that although tariff and subsidy policies were carefully adopted, the main theme in trade policy during the interwar period was the pursuit of the benefits from trade.

I argue that industrial protection for heavy and chemical industries was modest, and this is shown in two ways.

First, trade protection through tariff and non-tariff measures was not strong. Even in the case of the large-scale revision of tariff rates in 1926, when rates on many heavy and chemical products were raised, the stated proposal was to check unfair trade practices by foreign competition rather than explicitly to prevent imports. There was only a single case of quantity rationing: from June 1924 to June 1928 imports of synthetic dyes from Germany were suspended on account of dumping. This was resolved with ratification of a mutual trade treaty (Miyajima 1991).

Second, industrial subsidies were supplied only to industries in which tariffs were not a policy option due to adverse effects on other industries, and, the subsidies invariably came with a strict time limit. Further, implicit subsidies through subsidized credits were not an important policy tool. This is evident from that fact that the Industrial Bank of Japan was unable to persuade the Diet to expand its charter to allow it to supply policy-based financing to industries until 1937, when its debentures were guaranteed by the government with respect to special loans related to the *Rinji Shiken Chôsei Hô*. (However, since the World War I period, it had intermediated in low-interest funds supplied by the Deposit Bureau to bail out industries.)

Among bureaucrats, the concept of industrial-promotion was long-standing – indeed, it was a basic goal of the Meiji government along with the military build-up. However, this was general; only slowly and later did policies aimed at specific industries emerge. For example, in 1927 the Deliberative Council on Commerce and Industry at the Ministry of Commerce and Industry proposed a plan to promote the textile industry as the leading industry, and heavy and chemical industries (synthetic dyes, soda ash, nitrogen fixation (nitrates), machine tools and precision machinery) as key industries.

However, the political parties lacked articulated, let alone coherent, policies regarding protection or promotion of heavy and chemical industries. Kenseikai (Minseitô) was basically against an import-substitution policy for heavy and chemical industries, and supported export promotion through rationalization of industries. The stance of Seiyûkai was mixed: while there were strong proponents for protection of the heavy and chemical industries, such an assertion remained a minority opinion, and quite often mingled with other policies such as promotion of light industries and export industries (Tsuchikawa 1994/95).

5.8 POLICY IMPACT

Let us move on to the impact of the policy mix on regional economies based on agriculture and indigenous commerce and industries. The policy mix oppressed agriculture as an industry. This, however, does not imply that the rural sector or regional economies were oppressed or neglected. Both peasants and landlords suffered from the low-rice-price policy. However, with regard to landlords and large farmers, the policy mix provided preferential benefits in two respects. One was infrastructure investment, the other was transfer of tax revenue from the central government to local governments. It was expected that the two benefits, through activating regional economies, would improve the economic conditions of peasants, and hence bring about socio-political stability in the regional economies.

5.8.1 Infrastructure Investment

Extensive infrastructure investment is seen in policies of the Hara cabinet (1918–21), which devoted huge amounts to railroads, roads, harbor facilities, irrigation, and diffusion of high-level education. Such an emphasis on rural infrastructure was not limited to the Seiyûkai: although Kenseikai (Minseitô) supporters were mainly urban, the party could not neglect demands by rural constituents in view of the importance of the sector.

More than half the income of landlords came from non-agricultural sources (business revenue, dividends and interest) in western areas and prefectures thriving on raw silk production (Nakamura 1979). There is no doubt that such policies benefited them greatly. Owner and tenant farmers had also been obtaining substantial income from non-agricultural wage income. Moreover, the increase in the income of landlords was expected to lower the tax burden of peasants because, as local government regained fiscal soundness through an increase in business and income taxes, it could afford room for reductions of regressive lump-sum taxes such as the *kosûwari*.

5.8.2 Transfer of Tax Revenue

The idea of bringing socio-political stability to regional communities through rehabilitation of landlords' businesses and the fiscal condition of local government is clearly seen in the Seiyûkai policy to transfer land (and business) tax revenue from the central government to local governments. The policy was intended to restore the order of rural communities governed by landlords and *meibôka*. It aroused substantial controversy during the 1920s, and ultimately was not realized. For example, under a bill submitted to the 51st Diet (December 1925–March 1926) by the Seiyûkai, 74 million yen in land tax revenue was to be transferred to local governments, and 30 million yen was to be provided them by introducing a new *kaokuzei* (housing tax). In addition, it was planned to reduce the local tax burden by 63.4 million yen (58 million of *kosûwari*, as well as 5.4 million yen of miscellaneous taxes, local business tax and others) (see Kanazawa 1984, p. 120). The 74 million yen decrease in central government revenue was to be offset by increases of 40 million through tariff revision, issue of government bonds, and other sources. At first, the transfer was concerned only with the land tax, but later, business taxes imposed by the central government were included.

In other words, it was intended to alleviate the tax burden of peasants by reducing *kosûwari* and to restore the local economy by giving local leaders (*meibôka*) free cash flow of 40.6 million yen. (That is, the 74 million in land tax revenue plus 30 million from the *kaokuzei* minus 63.4 million in local tax reductions.) How to spend the free cash flow was not stipulated: it could be a reduction of the tax burden of landlords or investment in local infrastructure.

At any rate, the policy aimed at bringing about a virtuous circle. Strengthening indigenous industries run by landlords would lead to increases in employment and opportunities for subsidiaries to develop. These would allow rehabilitation of the fiscal condition of municipal governments, as well as an improvement in the economic conditions of peasants. That would mean restoration of regional economies as intermediate organizations at the government–private-sector interface.

In sum, in the policy mix of the interwar period, peasants and the rural sector were never neglected or oppressed in spite of adoption of an anti-agricultural policy.

5.8.3 Distributive Conflicts

Restoration of indigenous industries and the rural community led by *meibôka* was clearly an ultimate objective of the policy mix. To see this, let us return to the multi-dimensionality of distributive conflicts. With respect to class conflict, which was one of the new patterns of distributive conflict, the policy mix incorporated a mechanism to alleviate labor–capitalist conflict by lowering the price of 'wage goods', that is, rice. Moreover, appreciation of the exchange rate benefited urban consumers by lowering the cost of imported goods, although high tariff rates were imposed on luxury consumption goods. Therefore, for successful implementation of the policy mix, it was indispensable to resolve the class conflict between landlords and tenants through rehabilitation of the *meibôka* order.

Resolution of inter-industrial conflicts was not a simple matter. The anti-heavy and chemical industries policy meant a preferential treatment of two groups of industries: the export sector, such as light manufacturing and indigenous production, and the non-tradable sector, such as financial industries, foreign trading and public utilities. It is important to note that the interests of the two groups, other than heavy and chemical industries, were not homogeneous.

Especially important is that the interests of large companies in the non-tradable sector were by and large controlled by zaibatsu. As economic stagnation became prolonged after World War I, zaibatsu became increasingly dominant and 'arrogant', giving rise to an anti-zaibatsu atmosphere in society. This provided another reason for emphasis on promotion of indigenous industries in the policy mix. Within the export sector, light manufacturing represented by cotton-spinning retained strong competitive power.

5.8.4 Political Parties

The policy of supporting regional economies was supported by both main parties, the Seiyûkai and Kenseikai (Minseitô), despite their other differences. It is often pointed out that Seiyûkai was more intent on a spending policy, while Kenseikai stuck to a tighter fiscal policy, and Seiyûkai was supported by the rural sector, while Kenseikai was based more on urban constituents. With regard to the policy to help the rural and indigenous economies, however, both took a more or less similar stance, and actually competed with each other with respect to policy tools to accomplish the same policy goal. This similarity is emphasized by Hara (1980) with respect fiscal policy and by Takahashi and Miyazaki (1985) with respect to policy toward China.

With respect to support for the rural sector, Kenseikai proposed subsidizing the costs of compulsory education, and competed with the Seiyûkai policy of transferring part of the land tax to local governments. This was because expenses for compulsory education, especially teacher salaries, comprised a major part of the expenditures of municipal governments (cities, towns and villages), so subsidization by the central government would effect substantial burden alleviation. (School fees had been abolished in 1900.) Initially, Kenseikai also proposed reduction of the land tax in order to alleviate the burden of landlords.

The aim of both Seiyûkai and Keiseikai was rehabilitation of regional economies through restructuring of the fiscal conditions of municipal governments, and the policies of the parties differed only regarding monetary magnitude and methodology: through transferring 74 million yen of the land tax revenue to local governments or by subsidizing costs of compulsory education by 20 million yen.

Furthermore, the two parties came to take quite a similar stance with respect to the policies of channeling benefits to regions. Although such a policy originated with Hoshi Toru in the 1890s, it was by no means peculiar to Seiyûkai. Kenseikai was increasingly committed to such a policy and vied with Seiyûkai.

Take the case of Yamanashi prefecture for example. *Meibôka* members of the Kenseikai (called Dôshikai in Yamanashi prefecture until 1926) changed their stance after World War I considerably. Instead of competing with Seiyûkai with respect to national objectives, the Kenseikai *meibôka* devoted more effort to siphoning off benefits of central government expenditures to the region (Ariizumi 1980). This was partly because the people in the prefecture became increasingly eager to attract central government investment in transportation, other industrial infrastructures, and education facilities in order to keep up with the rapid economic development of the country and widening differentials among regions. Moreover, universal male suffrage was approved in 1925, and it became necessary for the Kenseikai to garner political support among peasants in order to win the general election of March 1928, the first with universal male suffrage.

5.9 LIMITATIONS AND FAILURE OF THE POLICY MIX

The strategy of successive governments to cope with the complex of distributive conflicts ended in a complete failure. The main evidence of this is the rapid impoverishment of the rural sector, especially peasants, in the Showa era, which began in 1926. Ultimately, after the May 15 Incident, an emergency rescue program (*jikyoku kyôkyû jigyô*) was introduced.[1]

The program, undertaken by a 'government of national unity' during

1932–34, was powered by an unprecedented 865 million yen, 13.6 per cent of central government general expenditures, earmarked for rural areas. The major part – 75 per cent of expenditures under the jurisdiction of the Ministry of the Agriculture and 50 per cent of expenditures under the jurisdiction of the Ministry of Internal Affairs – was spent hiring peasants for public works to give them cash incomes (Nakamura 1980).

The rescue is sometimes applauded as a Keynesian spending policy under the *Takahashi zaisei* (Finance Minister Takahashi Korekiyo's fiscal policy). The other side of the coin, however, was a manifestation of the failure of the policy mix during the 1920s. Not only peasants, but also the middle class, comprising urban merchants and industrialists related to indigenous industries as well as mid-size farmers, fell into poverty after around 1930 (Kanazawa 1994).

Why was the carefully contrived strategy to cope with distributive conflicts unsuccessful? Among possible reasons are exogenous shocks such as the impact of the Great Depression, especially on raw silk production (which relied on export to the United States), and the insufficient growth potential of heavy and chemical industries (which lacked adequate technological infrastructure). The most important reason, however, was failure in rehabilitating the indigenous sector. There were two reasons for this: first, the Banking Law, which took effect on January 1 1928, caused a serious credit crunch in indigenous industries due to the merger of small and medium banks, and second, the policy to transfer land tax revenue to local governments was abandoned in April 1929 when preparation for the return to the gold standard made fiscal tightening inevitable.

5.9.1 Bank Consolidation, 1928–32

The Banking Law promulgated in March 1927 had two objectives. The first was to enhance the soundness of banks through strengthening monitoring by the Ministry of Finance (MOF) and the Bank of Japan and limiting the form of business organization for ordinary banks to joint stock companies, which are obligated to disclose information. The second objective was to increase the net worth of banks by defining minimum capital requirements. (These were based on the population of the place in which the head office was located.) The law became effective in January 1928, but banks were given five years, to the end of 1932, to increase capital.

But MOF's goal was not just better-capitalized banks, it was fewer banks. For that reason, the law is commonly called the 'Bank Concentration Act', even though that was not a stated purpose. MOF set out to achieve this in several ways.

In November 1927, MOF announced that a bank could not meet the new requirement by means of an equity issue. This incurred strong opposition on the grounds that only a sound bank could raise additional capital through issuing new shares, and the market should be allowed to make the judgment – or, rather, the banks should be given the opportunity. MOF accepted the criticism, so that, among the 631 banks that did not meet the minimum capital requirement, 50 (8 per cent) cleared the hurdle with new capital issues.

MOF also initiated a powerful campaign to promote mergers and acquisitions across the entire banking sector, involving banks that met the minimum requirements as well as those that did not. This included ordering prefectural governors, who were appointed by the central government and heads of local branches of the Bank of Japan to encourage mergers through implementing 'strict' reassessment of the quality of bank assets.

In the five years from 1928 to 32, the financial community was overtaken by a storm of mergers. Among disqualified banks (those not meeting the capital requirements), 54 per cent (340) were acquired or involved in mergers, and 28 per cent (241) were liquidated. But the data also suggest that among qualified banks (that is, those meeting the requirements), at least 187 were involved in mergers and acquisitions, and another 52 were liquidated (Goto 1970).

The average capital of liquidated banks is far larger for qualified banks (105/52 = 2.0 million yen) than for unqualified banks (64/241 = 0.266 million yen). This presumably reflects the fact that the most seriously ailing banks were middle-sized, rather than small or very large (Teranishi 1982, ch. 6).

Most of the capital decrease from mergers and acquisitions seems to have been used to write off loans by small banks. Presumably the capital of liquidated banks also was written off against bad loans. Writing off bad loans did not proceed smoothly: officially forced mergers and acquisitions did not give enough incentive to do that. As a result, many of the combined banks suffered again from a non-performing loan problem. But beyond that, analysis of the data strongly suggests that bank concentration caused an unprecedentedly drastic credit contraction.

5.9.2 Credit Crunch

The Ministry of Finance (MOF) determined to use the 1928 bank law to reduce the number of banks. This meant eliminating not just banks with poor performance, but also those that met the law's minimum capital requirements. Attention thus must be paid to the effects of MOF's policy on sound banks,

At least three things together strongly suggest that bank consolidation made it more difficult for customers of non-surviving banks to obtain loans, quite often leading to a credit crunch. First, because the larger bank usually controlled management after a merger or acquisition, a surviving bank's relationship with its new customers was usually weaker. Second, many offices of dissolved banks were closed. Third, mergers reflected the interests of the political parties; therefore, it is likely that the credit facility was often reduced based on political interests. As pointed out by Bernanke (1983) for the US case during the 1930s, there is a possibility that the efficiency of financial intermediation was reduced due to the discontinuation of the information network of the banks that were closed. In other words, there is a good possibility that bank concentration dealt a drastic blow to general small and medium banks and indigenous commercial and manufacturing industries.

The conventional way to analyze the financing problems of indigenous commercial and manufacturing industries in the late 1920s is to pay attention to the flight of deposits from small and medium banks at the time of the 1927 crises. (Flight occurred from small and weak banks to large and sound banks, as well as to the postal saving system.) Clearly, there is more to consider than declining deposits.

The amount of credit availability that was lost as a result of bank consolidation can be estimated. According to my calculations (Table 5.7), 830 banks ceased operations during 1928–32, resulting in the loss of at least 396 million yen in authorized capital. Total lending by regional banks during 1928–32 was about 3.2 times total authorized capital. This suggests that lending on the order of 1.267 billion yen was affected in some way.

Table 5.8 presents flow data of deposits and lending of regional banks (ordinary banks excluding the zaibatsu-affiliated five large banks). Lending and deposits both declined in 1927 when the financial crisis occurred, but while deposits recovered in 1928–29, when effects of the crisis had worn off, lending continued to fall. The estimate in Table 5.7 of a loss of 608 million yen in the lending facility in those years is about 76 per cent of the 801 million yen decline in lending.

During 1930 and 1931, the years the gold embargo was lifted, lending was reduced by 1,025 million yen and deposits by 1,194 million yen compared to their levels at the end of 1929. With the lifting of the gold

Table 5.7 Effects of 1928 bank law, 1928–32

	1928–29		1930–31		1928–32	
	No.[1]	Capital lost[2]	No.[1]	Capital lost[2]	No.[1]	Capital lost[2]
Banks that were						
Consolidated[3]	335	109	147	92	537	227
Liquidated, not qualified[4]	89	23	58	12	241	64
Liquidated but qualified[5]	24	58	21	32	52	105
Total	448	190	226	136	830	396
Possible lending reduction[6]	–	608	–	435	–	1,267

Notes:
[1] Number of banks.
[2] Capital of banks liquidated, and reduction in capital as a result of mergers, and acquisitions, in million yen (see note 3).
[3] Merged out of existence or acquired. Computed by the author from data on individual banks in Kin'yû Kenkyû-kai, *Wagakuni ni okeru ginko-gôdô no taisei*, 1934, which. includes both qualified and disqualified banks. Teranishi (2004) contains further details of the estimation method. Note that Goto (1970) reports 527 banks in this category (1928–32); the reason for the difference in the two sources is not clear.
[4] Computed by the author from data in Komiya You, 'Iwayuru Ikken-ikkô-shugi no genri', Zenkoku-chihô Ginko-kyôkai, *Kaihô*, 2 (May 1937).
[5] Calculated as the difference between the total for all liquidated banks given in Goto (1968) and the total for liquidated not-qualified banks (note 4).
[6] In million yen. This is total capital multiplied by 3.2, which is an estimate of the ratio of lending to capital. See the text.

Table 5.8 Changes in lending and deposits of regional banks, 1927–31 (million yen)

Years	Lending	Deposits
1927	–661	–736
1928–29	–801	–128
1930–31	–1,025	–1,194

Note: Entries are the decline in lending and deposits during the year(s) shown. (For example, from the end of 1927 to the end of 1929, lending declined 801 million yen.)

Source: Goto (1970).

embargo came the Shôwa Depression and continued deflationary fiscal policy. Thus, compared to 1928–29, it is reasonable to expect a smaller share of the decline in lending to be attributable to the bank concentration policy. Indeed, the estimated loss of an additional 435 million in lending facility is about 42 per cent of reduced lending.

Considering that outstanding lending by regional banks at the end of 1926 stood at 6.847 billion yen, the effects of the contracted lending indicated in Table 5.8 would have been extremely drastic. In this process, most indigenous commercial and manufacturing industries were struck a disastrous blow. As pointed out in conventional views, one of the causes of contracted lending is the financial crisis in 1927. However, more serious credit contraction occurred due to elimination of small and medium banks under the Banking Act and deflationary policies aimed toward the lifting of the gold embargo.

While the credit crunch just after the 1927 crisis was a short-term phenomenon caused by an increase in risk aversion, malfunctioning of the money market due to the contraction of the call market, and a fall in collateral value, the credit crunch due to enforcement of the Banking Act was long-term. This was because, whenever banks were related to specific firms through a *kikan-ginko* relationship, the merger and acquisition of smaller banks caused the dilution of the effectiveness of cross-shareholding and interlocking directorships, consequently excluding old customers of smaller banks from the lender–customer relationship of the newly combined banks.

The severity of the credit crunch in the process of merger and acquisition is underlined by a survey of small and medium merchants and manufacturers conducted by the city of Tokyo in 1930. Improvement in access to financing was by far the most urgent response, exceeding requests for tax reduction and exemption. For respondents with annual profits of less than 400 yen, the number of responses was: financing 271, tax relief 68. For firms with annual profits of more than 400 yen, responses were: financing 220, tax relief 121 (Kanazawa 1994).

The Chamber of Commerce criticized the merger and acquisition policy, and called on the government to introduce subsidy programs for companies (Yui 1964). The government was not indifferent to the credit crunch, and actively implemented rescue programs, mainly utilizing funds at the Deposit Bureau of the Ministry of Finance collected through the postal saving system. These programs included supplying operating funds to small and medium merchants and manufacturers and to industrial cooperatives in 1928 and again in 1930, the supply of industrial funds during 1932–37, and so on. Such efforts by the government, however, ended by and large unsuccessfully. This was because ordinary banks, assigned the role of intermediating the funds supplied by the Deposit Bureau, were too risk averse and did not have enough information about borrowers (Yui 1964).

5.9.3 Crucified on a Cross of Gold

Another factor that dealt a critical blow to regional economic units was that the bill to transfer land tax and business tax to local governments, the last resort for restoration of regional economies, was shelved in April 1929. The Seiyûkai-backed cabinet of Tanaka Giichi, formed in March 1927, aimed at restoration of regional economies by means of the tax transfer and at lifting the gold embargo after waiting for sufficient appreciation of the exchange rate. The Finance Minister, Mitsuchi Chuzo, however, concluded that abandonment of the tax-transfer bill was unavoidable if the national debt redemption program was to be carried out as part of the preparation for return to the gold standard. The Tanaka cabinet was followed by the Minseitô-backed Hamaguchi cabinet in July 1929. Lifting of the gold embargo was decided by the cabinet in November 1929 and implemented on January 11 1930.

Mitsuchi's conclusion is said to be derived from recognition that, for successful lifting of the gold embargo, replenishment of foreign exchange through issuance of government bonds in overseas markets was indispensable, and that was possible only when the national debt redemption plan had been successfully implemented.

Return to the gold standard was the first priority policy agenda for the governments at the time, and that explains why the tax transfer bill was shelved. To understand why the bill was then abandoned, it is necessary to take into account changes in the policy atmosphere regarding regional economy rehabilitation. As devastation of regional economies went on, and merchants and landlords lost socio-economic control over the regional economies, it became increasingly difficult to restore social order based on *meibôka*. Instead of utilizing the power of *meibôka* and an autonomous rehabilitation mechanism, the government tended to commit to more direct control over regional economic units. Tanaka Giichi, for example, argued for the tax transfer bill on the grounds that 'it is urgently needed to create strong local organizations that can carry out economic war in the era of total wars among nations'.

Government-led plans for 'restructuring of the rural sector' were introduced in various forms thereafter. *Nôsangyoson kôsei keikaku* was the first such attempt, and the production and marketing of agricultural products were increasingly put under a planning system. At the same time, the fiscal policy of Baba Teiichi, finance minister during 1936–37, involved a centralization of the fiscal system. This was to mobilize fiscal resources 'in preparation of emergency for the nation'. The regions thus were deprived of fiscal autonomy.

5.9.4 Other Factors

Endogenous mechanisms also contributed to the malfunctioning of regional economies. First, regional economies as the interface representing distributive interests in the Meiji-Taishô system were composed of cities, towns and villages controlled by *meibôka*. However, as economic development proceeded, the size of markets in which economic activities were carried out expanded beyond the control of *meibôka*. Second, the education system, into which regional economic units and *meibôka* had put so much effort, inherently weakened regional economies through a brain drain. Elites educated locally did not stay there, but instead sought opportunities in the major cities.

5.10 POLICY EVALUATION

Let us re-examine the two policies – the policy to lift the gold embargo which necessitated abandonment of the transfer of taxes, and the policy of implementing the Banking Act – which helped destroy the Meiji-Taishô system.

Both were reasonable in view of economic logic: the return to gold was aimed at revival of the autonomous adjustment mechanism of external and internal equilibrium through utilization of the price mechanism, and the Banking Act was prudent policy aimed at creating sound banking practices. Both policies, however, were costly in the sense of holding back rehabilitation of indigenous industries, as well as the fiscal condition of local governments, and eventually ruined the policy mix that was intended to resolve multi-dimensional distributive conflicts.

Why were policies, reasonable from the viewpoint of economic efficiency but costly in terms of the policy to resolve distributive conflict, implemented? A belief in market discipline and the influence of the zaibatsu, especially their banks are two main reasons.

5.10.1 Market Discipline

An important factor that necessitated implementation of the two policies was the economic thought emphasizing disciplining through competition.

First, market discipline was asserted to avoid moral hazard. The Bank of Japan ceased to supply rescue lending to closed banks after 1922, in view of the serious moral hazard by banks that were closed and bailed out during the crises in 1920 and 1922. For similar reasons, the Ministry of Finance consistently opposed introduction of rescue operations for small and medium firms in general, and establishment of special institutions for financing those firms, during the recession period of the early 1930s.

Second, market discipline was emphasized from the viewpoint of international competitiveness of industries. At the time the gold embargo was lifted, the stance of the Finance Minister, Inoue Junnosuke, was based on this reasoning. The tariff policy of the Hamaguchi cabinet (1929–31) also aimed at similar effects. Generally speaking, by weeding out inefficient firms and banks (*zaikai-seiri*), the aim was to enhance the international competitiveness of industries, and to bring about the benefits of trade.

However, as the military increased its power, the idea of disciplining through competition was replaced by the idea of discipline by government control, and the idea of the pursuit of benefits from trade was replaced by the necessity to prepare for total war. The first step in that direction was marked by the Regulating Important Industries Act of 1931.

5.10.2 Zaibatsu Influence

For one thing, there was a strong influence of zaibatsu-affiliated banks, the 'logic of the strong'. The banking system was composed of three layers: large, modern zaibatsu-affiliated banks; medium banks in cities; and small and medium banks in local areas. The latter two had close relationships with indigenous commerce and manufacturing, while the first layer did not. Instead, it was tightly related to foreign trade, mining, and heavy and chemical industries.

For the large banks, the stability of the exchange rate in terms of its gold value, and attainment of a stable banking system were of vital importance to engage in overseas financial transactions and investment. The policy of lifting the gold embargo was most strongly supported by the banking and foreign trading sector, and the Banking Act was prepared by a committee drawn mostly from the circle of large banks.

Moreover, during the early 1930s, large banks, led by the Industrial Bank of Japan and Mitsui Bank carried out a 'Corporate Bond Purifying Campaign' which required collateralized bond issue. Collateralization discourages the issuance of bonds by small and new firms, while it was expected to bring huge profits to large banks and trust banks that could become trustees of the collateral. Security companies, which could not become trustees, opposed the campaign without success. Collateralization was justified on the basis of protecting bond holders in the event of bankruptcy. It was claimed that the clearing and settling process took much longer and required more effort in the case of uncollateralized bonds. However, this claim was not based on any solid empirical evidence.

It is difficult to deny that the assertions of zaibatsu banks in these cases were based on their own interests, without much consideration of broader, national interests. On many occasions, zaibatsu behaved, or at least were regarded to have behaved, as 'the strong'. For example, Mitsui Bank speculated against the yen by conducting dollar-buying operations during the period when the gold embargo was lifted, and continued in the face of serious criticism by the public.

The actual degree of concentration in commodity markets was not high (Nakamura 1971), and many markets maintained a high degree of contestability in the sense of free entry. However, zaibatsu took a leading role in organizing cartels in various industries, and in general their behavior was considered overbearing and aroused criticism. The view that there was no way to offset the 'arrogance' of zaibatsu other than to extend government intervention in the economy spread rapidly. When 'the logic of the private sector' was replaced by 'the logic of the strong', the Meiji-Taishô system had lost part of its intellectual justification.

Murakami, Kumon and Sato (1979) ascribe the disfunctioning of the Meiji state (considered to have lasted as a governmental system until World War II) to the degeneration of the political system (the coalition system of independent groups and the party cabinet system) as a decision-making organization, and second, to the growth of landlords and zaibatsu, whose behavior as private complexes clashed with state objectives and with the solidarity of village communities.

5.11 CONCLUSION

With the failure of the policy mix, the crisis of the Meiji-Taishô system accelerated.

First, the income-distributive interests of people became divergent from the interests of regional economies as industrialization continued and commercialization of the rural sector continued. With a larger share of income coming from non-agricultural activities such as wage income and indigenous manufacturing production, peasants came to be more conscious of inter-industry interests. With the decline of rice prices in the 1920s, the Agricultural Society (*Nôkai*), under control of landlords, became vocal in asserting the interests of agriculture as an industry. As tenant farmers enhanced their political power through extension of the suffrage, *meibôka* lost motivation to behave as leaders of regional economies. After universal male suffrage was introduced in 1925, 20 per cent to 30 per cent of seats in village assemblies and the Agricultural Society were held by tenant farmers (Ohkado 1993).

Second, decline of indigenous industries resulted in a decrease in the share of *meibôka* in total tax payments: *meibôka* no longer sustained the revenues of the central and local governments (Suzuki 1988). Central government expenditures in the rural sector were part of a shift to a centralized fiscal and government system, which has continued to the present day.

Party politics during the Meiji-Taishô system functioned on the premise that regional economic units led by *meibôka* played the role of the intermediate organization at the government–private-sector interface. When *meibôka* lost both the motivation and the economic power to lead, the parties were obliged to change, also. From 1927 (Tanaka cabinet) to 1932 (Inukai cabinet), when the Seiyûkai and Minseitô were actively vying over foreign and domestic issues, and seeking support from regions, classes and industries, party politics had its heyday.

When it became difficult to resolve the three-dimensional distributive conflicts by means of the policy mix, party politics entered into a decline. With the near-simultaneous onset of three crises – the economic crisis related to the depression caused by the lifting of the gold embargo (from January 1930); the external crisis due to the Manchurian Incident (September 1931) and the international isolation thereafter; and the direct political action undertaken from 1932 by the military after the May 15 Incident (which ended the Taishô democracy period) – each party came to be concerned only with immediate interests, and finally succumbed to the military (Banno 1985).

In sum, the Meiji-Taishô economic system collapsed with the failure of the policy mix and the collapse of party politics, when regional economies were no longer able to develop autonomously, and people had ceased to share development of regional economies as a social norm.

NOTE

1. Calling for a Shôwa Restoration – more direct rule by the emperor – on May 15 1932 a group of junior naval officers, with some army elements, staged a large-scale coup attempt that left the prime minister, Inukai Tsuyoshi, dead. The coup was suppressed, but the participants, widely viewed as patriots, received little punishment in most cases. Usually, this is considered to be the end of party government. However, Banno (1985) points out that there continued to be a strong movement to rehabilitate party politics and, moreover, cabinets continued to be formed primarily from party members until the Hirota Koki cabinet of March 1936.

   To Ariizumi (1984), measures like *jikyoku kyôkyû jigyô* are 'channelling benefits to regions through the bureaucracy', that is, without the intermediation of political parties.

PART III

The high-growth-period economic system

6. Emergence of the high-growth-period economic system

Japan entered the 1950s with three heritages from its 1937–45 wars and postwar occupation: bureaucrats experienced in control; financial institutions and corporate firms that had been essentially bankrupt by wartime losses; and the extinction of large shareholders and landlords. The last two meant the private sector was substantially weakened compared to the prewar period, and the first resulted in the bureaucracy leading the economy with strong confidence in the necessity and effectiveness of its interventions. Among the exogenous conditions, isolated catch-up in East Asia resumed, and there was a strong positive view of the role of government in the economy, which exerted a significant influence on the formation of the system.

From this emerged the high-growth-period economic system, characterized by a division of labor favoring pervasive intervention in the economy by the government, the Japanese-style firm and bank-centered finance in the private sector, and by representation by inter-industry interests at the interface of the government and private sectors.

After transformation during wartime and the turmoil immediately afterward, each sub-system had acquired the new system's characteristics by the mid-1950s, and institutional complementarities among sub-systems had come to work. Establishment of the high-growth-period system thus can be dated to that time. Others date the system differently: Noguchi (1995) and Okazaki and Okuno (1993) claim the system was established during the war. If the role of the government–private interface is ignored – that is, in a narrow economic sense – their assertion is correct.

6.1 OVERVIEW

The origin of pervasive government intervention lies partly in the diffusion of thought emphasizing the role of government in the economy in the years following World War I and intensified by the Great Depression. Significant government intervention in the economy occurred during the war years and occupation, and the bureaucrats in charge of the interventions mostly survived the war intact. As the postwar recovery progressed, they quickly acquired confidence and intensified their orientation toward developmental policies. Helped by the rise and dominance of Keynesian economics during the 1950s and 1960s, ideas viewing intervention favorably gave way to convictions held by society generally.

The enormous shock of defeat shaped the private-sector sub-system. Managerial autonomy by way of cross-shareholding and the main bank monitoring system was established out of the turmoil of corporate governance against the backdrop of the elimination of large shareholders due to wartime regulations and zaibatsu dissolution. The ruin of large asset-holders and the weakened state of the private sector resulted in a highly regulated financial system dominated by banks.

The Japanese-style firm system is characterized by long-term employment, seniority wages, and equal treatment of blue- and white-collar workers. It was born through an evolutionary process in the labor market in close relationship with an evolutionary process in the financial system. The historical emphasis on actual producers (managers and employees) *vis-à-vis* investors resulted in a mechanism to motivate actual producers to invest in firm-specific skills.

This chapter provides a detailed examination of the process of the establishment of each sub-system. After reviewing the war and reconstruction years and their legacy, attention turns to analyzing three features of the high-growth era. These are cross-shareholding by firms and banks, bank-centered corporate finance, and the employment system. Although they are characteristics of the private sector, bank-centered finance was in large part created and sustained by the government, representing a major redrawing of the boundaries of the division of labor. The discussion relates each of the three to its antecedents.

Looking at the government–private-sector interface, the fate of regions and the early postwar labor movement are briefly reviewed as background for the emergence of the *genkyoku* industrial association system as the interface. The chapter concludes with a review of how party politics and class concepts relate to the high-growth-period system's emergence.

6.2 MOBILIZING FOR WAR AND RECONSTRUCTION, 1937–49

The process and consequences of war-related economic controls can be broken down into four phases: the outbreak and early years of the (second) Sino-Japanese War (July 1937–1941); the run-up to, and initial success of, the Pacific War (mid-1941 to 1942); the deterioration of the military situation from 1943; and from surrender in August 1945 to the start of the Dodge stabilization policy in April 1949. Table 6.1 lists major wartime controls, and Table 6.2 lists postwar ones. Fuller discussion of many controls is included later in presenting the antecedents of features of the high-growth-period system. Here just a brief chronological overview is presented.

6.2.1 The War Years

Japan was at war in China from July 7 1937 (the Marco Polo Bridge Incident), and with the Allied Forces in the Pacific from December 8 1941.

Within a month of full-scale hostilities with China, extensive measures were being phased in. Thus, a Temporary Funds Adjustment Act was passed and partly enforced in mid-September, with full enforcement from September 27. The Act regulated lending of funds for equipment, and for purchase of stocks and bonds above a fixed amount, in order to concentrate funds in the munitions and related industries. At the same time, controls were extended to trade and labor areas.

In April 1938 the Diet effectively abandoned much of its authority by voting to vest in the Cabinet broad powers to control the economy. Under this legislation, the National General Mobilization Act (NGMA), the Cabinet would draft imperial directives as needed. Opposition to control measures – which did exist in the Diet, business community, and public at large – thus could be bypassed. Under NGMA, a mobilization plan drawn by the Planning Board (*Kikakuin*) was implemented throughout the economy from April 1938.

From mid-1941 a command system to enforce a planned economy (Okazaki 1991) was instituted by bureaucrats at the Planning Board (*Kikakuin*), through an iterative method that used control associations (*tôsei-kai*) as conduits of information. In the period before and immediately after the outbreak of the Pacific War, production expanded steadily. Although industrial production, including aircraft and ships, managed to maintain high levels until 1944, production in agriculture

Table 6.1 Wartime controls, 1937–45

1937 Sept 10	Temporary Funds Adjustment Act (*Rinji Shikin Chôsei Hô*), promulgated and partially enforced from Sept 15, fully enforced from Sept 27.
1937 Sept 10	Temporary Law on Exports and Imports (*Yushutsu-nyû Hin tô Rinji Soshi Hô*) promulgated and enforced. This placed restrictions on traded goods, so even processing of trade-related goods was affected. Because cotton textiles were the leading foreign-exchange earner, and foreign exchange was needed to pay for war-related imports, raw cotton and cotton yarn were the first items covered.
1937 Sept 10	Application of Munitions Factory Mobilization Act (*Gunjyu Kôgyô Dôin Hô no Tekiyô ni kansuru Hôritsu*) promulgated and enforced. This stipulated application of the Munitions Factory Mobilization Act (promulgated in 1918) to the war with China.
1938 Apr 1	National General Mobilization Act (NGMA, *Kokka Sôdôin Hô*) promulgated. Enforced from May 5.
1939 Apr 1	Corporate Profits, Dividends, and Financing Directive (*Kaisha Rieki Haitô oyobi Shikin Yûzû Rei*) promulgated. Enforced from Apr 10. Upper limits were set on the dividend rates of firms larger than a certain size, and a command financing system (*meirei-yûshi*) for the Industrial Bank of Japan (IBJ) was introduced.
1940 Oct 19	Bank Funds Operating Directive (*Ginko-tô Shikin Un'yô Rei*) promulgated. Mostly enforced from Oct 20, partially after 1941 Jan 1. Provisions of the Temporary Funds Adjustment Act were extended to cover operating capital, and the command financing system was widened to apply to all banks.
1941 Aug 30	Major Industries Associations Directive (*Jyûyô Sangyô Dantai Rei*) promulgated. Enforced from Sept 1. Established control associations (*Tôsei-kai*) after Nov.
1941 Dec 8	Labor Demand–Supply Adjustment Directive (*Rômu Jyukyû Chôsei Rei*). Enforced from 1942 Jan 10. Leaving jobs and firing workers at major factories designated by the Minister of Welfare were put under the supervision of the government.
1942 Feb 24	Revision of the Bank of Japan Act (*Nippon Ginkô Hô*) promulgated. Enforced partially from Mar 20, fully from May 1. Following the example of Nazi Germany's Reichs bank, central bank independence was abolished, and the Bank of Japan's mission was the fulfilment of state objectives.
1942 Feb 25	Labor–Management Directive of Essential Factories (*Jyûyô Jigyôjyo Rômu Kanri Rei*) promulgated and enforced. The wage system was put under control. A uniform wage schedule based on seniority and living costs was introduced in important industries.

Table 6.1 Wartime controls, 1937–45 (continued)

1942 Apr 18	Finance Control Association Directive (*Kin'yû Tôsei Dantai Rei*) promulgated and enforced. Banks were encouraged to merge in order to strengthen their capacity to collect funds and lower their funding costs.
1942 May 23	National Finance Control Association (*Zenkoku Kin'yû Tôsei-kai*) created, with president of Bank of Japan as chair, to provide centralized supervision of lending operations.
1943 Mar 18	*Senji Gyôsei-shokuken Tokurei*. Steel, coal, light metals, ship-building, and aircraft designated as the five important industries.
1943 Oct 31	Munitions Corporations Act (*Gunjyu Kaisha Hô*) promulgated. Enforced from Dec 17. Private firms were designated for munitions production. Initially 150, and ultimately around 600, firms were designated and direct control over their production was imposed. Shareholder rights were drastically curtailed. For example, if ministerial approval was granted, agreement at shareholder meetings was not needed.
1943 Nov 1	Ministry of Munitions (*Gunjyu-shô*) established to administer dirext control over production in order to promote munitions output. The main aim of production expansion was shifted from the five important industries to just aircraft.
1944 Jan 18	Designated Financial Institutions System for Munitions Company Financing (*Gunjyu Yûshi Shitei Kin'yû Kikan Seido*) dicided at a Cabinet meeting. For a smoother provision of funds, a single 'main bank' was designated for each munitions firm.
1945 Feb 26	Munitions Financing Special Measures Act (*Gunjyu Kin'yû tô Tokubetsu Sochi Hô*) promulgated. Enforced from Mar 23. This introduced a system to designate a particular financing institution for firms other than munitions firms.

Notes: *Hô* were acts passed by the Diet. *Rei* were issued by the Cabinet or (usually with Cabinet approval) a Ministry, sometimes in the name of the emperor. *Promulgation* is the official announcement of a law or regulation, with the effective date – *enforcement* – sometimes being later. In general, promulgation of acts passed by the Diet is also the date they were approved by the Diet. Directives originating in the Cabinet sometimes were not promulgated until after they were approved by that body.

Sources: Iwanami Shoten, (1968); Nihon Ginko (Kin'yu Kenkyojyo) (1993), and Tsuchiya and Yamaguchi (1968).
(In English: Cohen (1949, pp. 543–45) alphabetically lists major wartime and postwar laws and ordinances, and discusses them with extensive reference to contemporary descriptions.)

Table 6.2 Occupation-era controls, 1946–7

1946 Feb 17	Emergency Financial Measures Directive (*Kin'yû Kinkyû Sochi Rei*) promulgated and enforced. Old yen deposits frozen and, starting Feb 25, old bank notes were converted into new notes.
1946 Mar 3	March 3 Relative Price System (*Bukka Taikei*) introduced. This involved price control measures using subsidies and anchoring prices of basic commodities were set at 6.5 times a 1934–36 base, and the base monthly wage was set at 500 yen. The gap between the controlled sales price of products and actual production costs was subsidized by the government.
1946 Oct 19	Special Measures for Cancelling Wartime Compensation Act (*Senji Hoshô Tokubetsu Sochi Hô*) promulgated and enforced. Compensation by the government for wartime damage and payments to munitions-producing companies were virtually cancelled. In order to cope with the losses incurred by financial institutions and manufacturing firms, the Financial Institutions Special Rehabilitation Act (*Kin'yû Kikan Saiken Seibi Hô*) and Corporate Special Rehabilitation Act (*Kigyô Saiken Seibi Hô*) were promulgated and enforced from the same day.
1946 Dec 27	Priority Production System (*Keisha Seisan Hôshiki*) is determined by the Cabinet.
1947 Jan 25	Establishment of Reconstruction Finance Bank (RFB, *Fukkô Kin'yû Kinko*). Funds raised by the sales of RFB debentures (mainly to BOJ) were channelled to priority sectors to finance equipment investment. As of March 1949, 60% of loans were directed to four strategic industries: coal, steel, fertilizer, and electricity; 75% of total loans were used to finance equipment investment.
1947 Mar 1	Ordinance for Fund Allocation of Financial Institutions (*Kin'yû Kikan Shikin Yûzû Jyunsoku*) announced. This was the chief measure, together with loans by the RFB, for the priority financing system (*Keisha kin'yû*). It specified that 50% of the new funds of commercial banks, trust banks, and insurance companies were compulsorily rationed to priority industries. The remaining 50% were also controlled so as to be invested in designated financial instruments such as bonds of the central and municipal governments. It was not completely successful. As of October 1947, the loans directed to first-priority industries comprised only 7% of total outstanding loans. This was because private financial institutions preferred to lend to more profitable second-priority industries and unspecified industries (Teranishi 1993a).
1947 Jul 7	July 7 Relative Price System introduced. Prices of basic commodities were set at 65 times a 1934–36 base, and wages of public servants at 28 times.
1947 Dec 13	Temporary Adjustment of Interest Act (*Rinji Kinri Chôsei Hô*) promulgated. Enforced from Dec 15.

Notes and Sources: See Table 6.1.

and services fell after 1943, so that GNP peaked in 1942 (Mizoguchi and Nojima 1993).

From the spring of 1943, losses in shipping capacity caused a decline in imports of goods and raw materials, resulting in a downturn in production. These circumstances led to further realignment of production to give priority to munitions. Steel, coal, light metals, shipbuilding and aircraft were designated the five important industries. From December 1943, a growing list of companies was directed to shift to military production. At these firms, shareholder-rights were drastically curtailed and management was endowed with significant autonomy.

The squeezing of the economy for the war effort, with the resulting widespread regulation of the financial system, labor market and foreign trade, brought about major changes to the industrial structure, as shown in Table 6.3. The shares of heavy industries, particularly machinery, rose sharply. This reflected both significant increases in production for these industries and actual declines in production in consumer-oriented industries such as foodstuffs, textiles, and wood products.

Table 6.3 Distribution of output in the manufacturing sector (per cent)

Product	1932	1937	1941	1944	1945
Foodstuffs	19.8	15.1	12.2	11.2	17.8
Textiles	32.7	29.4	14.7	5.3	4.6
Timber and wood prod. products	3.3	2.7	3.0	2.4	3.0
Chemicals	13.3	17.3	17.5	13.4	11.6
Ceramics	2.4	2.7	2.6	2.1	1.8
Iron and steel	8.4	9.5	12.6	14.6	12.4
Non-ferrous metals	3.8	3.2	2.9	6.6	5.5
Machinery	9.7	14.4	30.2	41.6	40.8
Printing	3.0	2.4	1.9	1.4	1.0
Other	3.5	3.4	2.6	1.6	1.5
Total in billion yen	10.2	17.3	19.0	14.4	6.4
Index of total	100	171	187	141	62

Note: Value of production in 1934–36 prices. Columns may not add to 100 due to rounding.

Source: Computed by the author from yen values in Ohkawa and Shinohara (1979, Table A21).

6.2.2 1945–49

The Emperor announced the termination of the war on August 15 1945, and Japan formally surrendered on September 2. Occupation by the Allied Forces continued until April 28 1952.

A steep inflation erupted after the war because of a fall in production and an increase in the money supply. There was severe war damage to urban housing and ships, but most production equipment was unimpaired. The main reason for the decline in production was the shortage of raw materials.

The ratio of production capacity available in 1945 to the maximum capacity attained before 1944 was 78 per cent for electricity, 100.2 per cent for steel, 89 per cent for nonferrous metals, 52.2 per cent for machinery, 68.9 per cent for chemicals, and 31.2 per cent for textiles. The low figure for machinery is the result of extensive damage from bombing, while that for textiles reflects the compulsory diversion of equipment for military use during the war. Thus, the decline in production after the war was primarily the result of raw material and energy shortages (Teranishi 1993a).

With foreign trade under complete control of the Supreme Commander for the Allied Powers (SCAP), the import of goods, especially raw materials such as coal and oil, was kept to a minimum. As a result, industrial production gradually declined, reaching a trough in January–February 1947 as inventories of basic materials ran out. Imports as a share of GNP in 1946 stood at less than one-quarter of the 1934–36 average (generally taken to be the 'normal' prewar level) and, consequently, the index of industrial production was less than one-third of its prewar level.

Bad weather and input shortages (fertilizers and labor) reduced agricultural production in 1945: the rice crop was less than two-thirds of its prewar level, and the harvest was the worst since 1909. The Priority Production System (*Keisha Seisan Hôshiki*) adopted by the cabinet in December 1946 and fully implemented in mid-1947, aimed at concentrating scarce raw materials in production of basic goods and services: first, coal and steel; thereafter, fertilizer, electricity, and rail transportation.

In contrast to low production levels, nominal demand soared due to an increased money supply. This had two aspects.

First, immediately after the end of the war in August 1945, the money supply expanded substantially as the government tried to meet its war-related commitments (payment of retirement allowances to soldiers and for wartime procurement) using notes issued by the BOJ. To stem the expansion of purchasing power, a deposit freeze was implemented. Given the sharp increase in the supply of BOJ notes, the government in February 1946 ordered that all BOJ notes above a certain denomination be deposited, and forbade withdrawals of deposits except for the minimum needs of living and production activity. Old bank notes were invalidated and new notes issued at the time of withdrawals. Introduction of this measure halved the outstanding currency balance and reduced the sum of currency and deposits to one-third. As a result, the hyperinflation, which had been running at almost 40 per cent per month, was cut by half.

It is, however, also true that outstanding currency returned to its original level in the summer of 1946 and began expanding again. Total money supply (M2) shows a similar pattern, though with a lag. It may be said that deposit freezing helped only in converting near-hyperinflation into high inflation. As economic activity gradually recovered, limitations on withdrawals were relaxed and the measure was formally suspended in July 1948. At that time, all deposits were freed, except those of large corporations, which were eventually used to compensate for war-related losses.

Second, because price subsidies for producers and subsidized credits through the Reconstruction Finance Bank (RFB, *Fukkô Kin'yû Kinko*) were the main tools of the Priority Production System, it became necessary to issue an increasingly large number of new BOJ notes beginning in 1947. In this regard, it must be noted that almost 70 per cent of the financial debentures issued by RFB were purchased by BOJ (116 billion yen out of 167 billion yen during 1946–48). Price subsidies to producers amounted to 204 billion yen during 1946–49, which was 13.9 per cent of government expenditure (*ippan kaikei*) during the period.

Although the priority production system accelerated inflation, it achieved its aim of increasing production, and eventually stabilized inflation (Teranishi 1993a). Thus, the production level in March 1949 had recovered to 1.71 times that of September 1947. Monthly inflation, which had been more than 40 per cent during 1945–46, became less than 5 per cent in 1948, even before initiation of the Dodge Plan stabilization policy.

An orthodox stabilization policy was implemented under the guidance of Joseph M. Dodge (a special economic adviser sent by President Truman) from April 1949. This policy had three pillars: an extremely stringent budget for the fiscal years of 1949 and 1950; introduction of a single exchange rate; and suspension of activities by the Reconstruction Finance Bank. These had a significant effect in the final termination of inflation. It must be noted, however, that the monetary effect of the policy was not necessarily large. This was because commercial banks, under BOJ guidance, were expanding credit, and hence deposits, significantly to mitigate the Plan's deflationary impact on production. Thus, although the Plan caused a drastic reduction in the currency supply, its effect on the growth rate of total money supply (M2) was small. Moreover, the impact of fiscal tightening should be evaluated taking into consideration the 1947 price-anchoring effects (discussed later). (Also see Teranishi 1993a.)

6.3 IMPORTANCE OF THE 1937–49 EXPERIENCE

So far we have summarized the experience and major regulations implemented by the government during wartime and the period immediately after the war. Although this was a unique experience in unprecedented circumstances, it bears special importance for the Japanese economy in two senses. First, regulations were effective in shifting resources, thus helping to sustain the war effort for so long. Second, the bureaucrats who implemented them survived.

6.3.1 Survival of the Bureaucrats

The bureaucrats in charge of wartime economic regulation survived with their power and positions. Yonekura (1993) claims that many of those who led the war economy either were in positions to wield the same control power or were promoted to higher positions after the war. Dower (1999) notes the role of SCAP in forming the bureaucratic-controlled system. He suggests that, by bolstering the roles and prestige of the bureaucracy, the Americans, together with the Japanese, created the highly regulated and bureaucratic model of the Japanese system. Indeed, it is worth noting that the US-led Occupation brought both democracy and administrative 'nationalization'. Especially important were the 'innovative bureaucrats' (*kakushin kanryô*), who graduated from college during the 1920s and were strongly orientated toward a totalitarian, controlled economy (Furukawa 1990). Members of this group were in charge of economic matters at the Planning Board and had a close relationship with the army officers in charge of economic and political matters (*rikugun seikei shôkô*), who were advocates of totalitarianism or the agriculture-first principle (*nôhon-shugi*).

Some people involved in the execution of the war were removed from their positions in January 1946 and January 1947. This included not only military personnel, but also many important businessmen. The removal of bureaucrats, however, was minimal, and was mainly confined to the Ministry of Internal Affairs. Most bureaucrats in charge of economic control stayed in the same positions after the war, with their accumulated experience with respect to economic planning. They began to lead the postwar economy with a strong orientation toward developmentalism and administrative centralization.

6.3.2 Effectiveness of Regulations

The purpose of wartime regulations was to shift resources from consumer industries, called sacrificed industries (*gisei sangyô*), to munitions production. This purpose was by and large realized. With regard to the postwar stabilization policy, regulations were arguably also effective, as detailed earlier.

The industrial composition of manufacturing production underwent a drastic transformation. Previously centered on light industries such as textiles, the production structure was converted to one composed mainly of heavy and chemical industries, especially the machinery industry. As a consequence, a full-set style industrial structure was completed. Although the production of aircraft toward the end of the war was not necessarily successful, this was mainly due to the shortage of raw materials.

6.4 WEAKENED PRIVATE SECTOR

The pervasive government intervention of the postwar period also owes its origin to the weakening of the private sector during and immediately after the war. This resulted from wartime controls, wartime damage and Occupation policies.

6.4.1 Corporations as Organic Units

Shareholder rights were severely restricted from relatively early in the war. The first restriction involved control of the dividend rate. Beginning in April 1939, the Corporate Profits, Dividend, and Financing Directive stipulated that a company wishing to increase its dividend rate needed MOF approval if the current rate was 10 per cent or more (of par value), or if the current rate was higher than 6 per cent and the proposed increase was more than 2 per centage points. The rationale was fairness: the workforce was controlled under the National

General Mobilization Act, so it was deemed fair to control shareholder rights as well (Nakamura 1974).

Control was extended to a comprehensive notion of the mission of corporations under the New Economic Structure (*Keizai Shin Taisei*) during 1940–41. Firms were considered to be organic units comprising capital, management and labor, so that both the control-rights and income-rights of shareholders were restricted in order to accommodate the rights of other stakeholders. Innovative bureaucrats at the Planning Board intended to convert the objective of corporate behavior from the pursuit of profits to the pursuit of public benefits. This was expressed in the New Economic Structure Establishment Outline (*Keizai Shin Taisei Yôkô*) decided at the Cabinet meeting on December 7 1940. This defined a firm as 'an organic unit composed of capital, management, and labor'.

Such a move met severe opposition from business circles, and stirred antagonism with the Ministry of Commerce and Industry, which more or less represented the interests of the capitalist class.[1] The intention of the Planning Board was not denial of profit maximizing behavior but control of shareholder rights, while the Ministry was skeptical that bureaucrats working with the Board would admit the profit motive *per se*.

Partly because of the fall of production below planned levels around 1942, opposition by the Ministry of Commerce and Industry led to a renewed emphasis on maximization of profits, although profits were considered to be shared not only by shareholders but also by other stakeholders. As the military situation deteriorated and the need for compulsory resource mobilization increased, however, shareholder rights were further restricted.

6.4.2 Managerial Autonomy

Under the Munitions Corporation Act promulgated in October 1943 (and the Enforcement Directive of the Act promulgated in December) management ('production administrators') were given substantial autonomy from shareholders. Provided they had ministerial approval, their decisions did not require agreement at shareholder meetings, nor were they obliged to disclose corporate information.

Managers also obtained autonomy from banks. Under the Designating Financial Institution System introduced to realize quick and efficient funding for munitions companies, banks and other financial institutions were in effect forced to lend at the bidding of management. Any monitoring function by banks was virtually paralyzed. Under the

Munitions Financing Special Measures Act of March 1945, this system was extended to cover non-munitions firms as well, and a new one-firm-one-bank arrangement was introduced, in which designated banks were completely subordinated to the managers of firms.

6.4.3 Zaibatsu Dissolution

After the war, the power of the private sector was decisively reduced through dissolution of the zaibatsu. Implemented as part of democratization and deconcentration, dissolution involved two measures. These were transfer of shares to the Holding Company Liquidity Committee (HCLC, *Mochikabu-Kaisha Seiri Iinkai*) and removal of wartime management.

The HCLC, established in August 1946, ordered zaibatsu families, member firms and holding companies to sell it all the securities they held. The shares had a par value of 25.3 billion yen and represented over 57 per cent of the 44.1 billion yen in paid-up capital of all corporate firms at the end of 1945.

They were marketed by the Securities Coordinating Liquidation Committee (SCLC, *Shôken Shori Chôsei Kyôgi-kai*). The sell-off process, called security democratization, began in July 1947. It was based on a set of guidelines under which priority was given to employees, sales to zaibatsu holding companies (and family members) were prohibited, and sales were prohibited to anyone already in possession of more than 1 per cent of the stock of the firms concerned. As a result, the number of individual shareholders rose more than two-and-a-half times, from 1,674,000 in 1945 to 4,191,000 in 1949. The proportion of shares in the hands of individual shareholders increased from 51.9 per cent in 1947 to 69.1 per cent in 1949, while the proportion held by corporate organizations dropped from 24.6 per cent to 5.6 per cent.

Senior managers of major corporations (presidents, vice-presidents and board members) were ousted in July 1947, and forbidden to return for 10 years. With respect to zaibatsu firms, removals were more extensive: in January 1948, the Zaibatsu Family Control Termination Act (*Zaibatsu Dôzoku Shihairyoku Haijo Hô*) was promulgated. With this measure, the elimination of zaibatsu power was completed. (On these points refer to Cohen (1949, pp. 434–36), Hadley (1970, pp. 99–100), Miwa (1993), and Miyajima (1992).)

6.4.4 Land Reform

Land reform had the effect of extinguishing the landlord class, which had represented the power of the private sector in agriculture and had led the regional communities. This was implemented over five years, beginning in 1946 under strong pressure by SCAP. By 1948, about 37.6 per cent of arable land had been purchased by the government and sold on to cultivators (tenant farmers). The price paid to landlords was 1 to 3 per cent of the prewar price. Some 28 per cent of arable land was transferred: 1.93 million hectares, compared to the 1945 total of 5.16 million hectares. The share of tenanted land in total arable land declined from 45.9 per cent in 1945 to 10.1 per cent in 1950 (Kawagoe 1993; Kayo 1958, Table D-C-2).

6.4.5 War-caused Losses and Restructuring

The private sector was crippled by the huge losses suffered by banks and firms that came with loss of the war. At SCAP's direction, munitions companies were not compensated for cancellation of contracts, and insurance companies were not compensated for their payments of claims due to war damage, although the wartime government had obligated itself to do so. Formally, the government did not default: it fulfilled its obligations, but at the same time levied a 100 per cent tax on payments (*Senji Hoshô Tokubetsu-zei*) pursuant to the Special Measure for Canceling Wartime Compensation Act promulgated October 19 1946.

In October 1946, under strong pressure from SCAP, the Special Measures for War-time Compensation Act (*Senji Hoshô Tokubetsu Sochi Hô*) was promulgated, stipulating suspension of wartime compensation estimated at 67 billion yen, suspension of compensation for the losses arising from loans supplied through the command financing system (*meirei-yûshi*), and invalidation of government guarantees on the liabilities of various institutions. Similar measures were applied to business firms, with further deleterious effects.

The legislation aroused fears regarding serious adverse effects on heavily debt-ridden business firms and, eventually, on lenders or financial institutions. Therefore, the balance-sheet items of financial institutions were divided into two categories, old and new. This idea originated in MOF, but a deposit freeze met with initial reluctance from BOJ. SCAP agreed with MOF's position. The plan is outlined in Table 6.4.

Financial institutions were allowed to operate only on new accounts.

Table 6.4 Division of financial institution balance sheets

Accounts	Assets	Liabilities and equity
Old	War-related lending, corporate bonds, equities, other assets	Second-line frozen deposits, other liabilities, capital, retained earnings
New	Cash, government bonds, claims on financial institutions	Free deposits, first-line frozen deposits, deposits of tax revenue, liabilities to financial institutions

Notes: In order to contain the hyperinflation, all cash was ordered to be deposited on February 17 1946 and people were allowed to withdraw amounts necessary to cover living expenses. On August 5, these frozen deposits were divided into two categories: those less than 3,000 yen for households and 15,000 yen for corporations were classified as *first-line frozen deposits*; remaining deposits were *second-line frozen deposits*. Deposits accepted after February 17 were called *free deposits*.

Source: Okurasho (1983, pp. 225–27).

The old accounts were re-evaluated at the end of March 1948, and identified losses were applied against the following, in order of priority: capital gains on assets, retained earnings, 90 per cent of bank capital, and second-line frozen deposits. The pattern of final settlement differed among individual banks, but the loss borne by bank shareholders was enormous. The final results of the re-evaluation for all financial institutions are in Table 6.5.

For non-banks, the problems of war-related losses and recapitalization were exacerbated because restructuring was delayed until 1949 due to confusion regarding the deconcentration policy.

6.4.6 Establishing Control of the Banks

The Banking Bureau of the Ministry of Finance began its 'guidance' of banks in place of the significantly weakened bank shareholders. As the re-evaluation of losses was being settled, MOF issued a circular on May 14 1948 regarding bank loss settlement. Banks were notified that they were not allowed to pay dividends from sources other than current profits, and dividend payments needed to be approved by the chief of the Banking Bureau. This marked the start of government regulation of postwar dividend payments, something maintained throughout the high-growth period.

At the same time, MOF began strict monitoring of expenditures of

Table 6.5 Losses by financial institutions from re-evaluation of accounts (billion yen)

Item	Entire sector	Banks only
Direct losses to shareholders from reduction in:		
Capital gains	8.1	6.2
Retained earnings	1.9	1.3
Bank capital (up to 90% for each bank)	2.0	1.6
Total shareholder losses[1]	12.0	9.1
Depositors' losses (second-line frozen deposits)	20.9	18.0
Subsidies due from the government[2]	12.2	0.4
Total losses	44.7[3]	27.5

Notes: Data are for the situation on March 31 1948.
[1] The loss ultimately borne by shareholders was less than these figures because some non-performing loans later became sound. Final settlement was done on March 31 1957. It was only in 1959 that final resolution was achieved, with the merging of the two accounts, and a new account was created for final adjustment and the remaining loss ascribed to the government.
[2] The loss exceeding the portion allotted to shareholders and depositors was borne by the government. The government financed the expenditure by issuing bonds.
[3] The discrepancy between the total and the sum of individual items is caused by a missing item in the original data for 'city, town, village and agriculture'. Teranishi (1993b) contains a few errors in similar figures, which are corrected here.

Source: Okurasho Ginkokyoku (1953), p. 213.

banks, including wage payments, setting guidelines on the ratio of current expenditures to current revenue. Specifically, wage rates were controlled by the Ministry during 1949–52, and thereafter banks were requested to report their salary schedules to the Ministry before implementing them.

6.5 CROSS-SHAREHOLDING

Cross-shareholding started during the 1930s when zaibatsu needed funds to expand in the heavy and chemical industries without diluting their control. After the war the practice was a way to protect incumbent managers from being dislodged by shareholders.

6.5.1 Prewar

Huge sums were needed for the rapid expansion of capital-intensive industries beginning in the early 1930s. As a device to raise equity capital without diluting group ties, cross-shareholding thus was widely introduced among large corporations. Before developing this, a distinction needs to be made here between the old zaibatsu and *shinkô* (new) zaibatsu (Box 6.1).

BOX 6.1 NEW ZAIBATSU

The new zaibatsu emerged in the 1930s to take advantage of the opportunities offered by the demands of the military, including the latter's distaste for the established zaibatsu. This means that, unlike the old and Taishô zaibatsu, they were founded to engage in 'modern' manufacturing, especially in heavy industries. They were also often involved in Japan's colonies in cooperation with the military. For example, Nissan cooperated with the Manchurian development plan actively, and the founder Ayukawa Gisuke became the president of Manshû-sôgyô.

They were managed by owner-founders, but these founders were not content with expanding as family businesses. Instead they tried quite aggressively to diversify their group activities and to establish a managerial control system. Several methods were used for this purpose. (1) Cross-shareholding was encouraged. (2) Public offering of shares was common (an exception was Nichitsu, which kept a closed shareholding system based on the extraordinarily large patent income it received from Chosen Chisso.) By selling shares of group companies at a price higher than their original purchase price (par value), the founder obtained funds to invest in new companies. (3) Relationships were maintained with a large number of banks, including the major commercial banks, Chosen Bank and the Industrial Bank of Japan (IBJ).

In the case of new zaibatsu, cross-shareholding was pursued as a basic strategy to expand the groups, and was carried out under the leadership of founders. Typical were the Riken and Nisso groups. For the old zaibatsu, it was done on the decision of the top managerial team, mainly composed of hired professional managers. The families were not generally actively involved in management.

It is important to emphasize that the old zaibatsu had two motives for using cross-shareholding. In addition to financial reasons, it was hoped that by converting from pure family businesses to ones in which a broader public could 'share', some of the dislike of the zaibatsu might be mitigated. Thus, equity sales to outsiders were an attempt to adapt to the changing industrial structure and to mitigate anti-zaibatsu sentiment, while cross-holdings within the group diluted the outsiders' voice.

Until the 1920s, the old zaibatsu had expanded by reinvesting profits (Teranishi 1994a). Because they were in highly profitable businesses such as mining and foreign trade, financing this way had been sufficient for growth. But with the demands for heavy investments in capital-intensive modern industries, they were obliged to raise ever-more funds. Cross-shareholding was utilized to tap funds from non-bank financial institutions and other firms within the group to complement the internal funds of the groups expanding capital-goods units.

Shares held by the families and shareholding companies were offered to the public. Although Mitsui was first, it and Sumitomo were rather cautious in this respect, while Mitsubishi was the most active. Apart from its bank, Mitsui's offerings were second-line companies and three affiliates of first-line companies. Sumitomo opened three first-line companies to the public during 1934–37. Major offerings are shown in Table 6.6.

Mitsui Gômei (the holding company) began extensive sales of shares of group companies after 1932, using the proceeds to invest in other companies and to pay taxes. Most of the purchasers were financial institutions in the same group, such as Mitsui Life Insurance, Mitsui Trust, Mitsui Bussan and Taishô Insurance (Kasuga 1987). Similarly, from 1933 Sumitomo Gôshi (the holding company) sold shares of other Sumitomo companies to its group financial institutions, such as Sumitomo Bank, Sumitomo Trust, Sumitomo Life Insurance and Fuso Marine Insurance (Asajima 1983). At Mitsubishi, after initiation of public offerings, overall cross-holdings in the group increased and the composition of shareholders outside the group increased (Teranishi 1994a). In all three cases, most of the shares sold were in companies in heavy and chemical industries, strategic for the group.

The result of such cross-shareholdings during 1930–45 in the zaibatsu groups can be seen in Table 6.7, which presents data from immediately after the war. The degree of cross-shareholding was already as high as 10 per cent to 40 per cent during the war.

Another important change in the financing pattern of zaibatsu was that group banks began to lend to group firms. Before the 1920s, zaibatsu banks had refrained from lending to group firms in order to avoid *kikan-ginkô* practices, and to keep a sound portfolio through asset diversification (Teranishi 1994a).

Table 6.6 Zaibatsu firm stock sales to the public

1917	Mitsui Ginkô[1] (bank)
1920	Mitsubishi Kogyo[1] (mining)
1927	Mitsubishi Ginkô[1] (bank)
1933	Miike Chisso*[2] (nitrates)
1933	Toyo Koatsu*[2]
1933	Toyo Reiyon*[2] (textiles)
1934	Hokkaido Tankô Kisen*[2]
1934	Mitsubishi Jyûkôgyô[1] (machinery)
1934	Sumitomo Hiryô[1] (Kagaku)
1935	Sumitomo Kinzoku[1] (steel)
1937	Mitsubishi Denki[2] (electrical machinery)
1937	Mitsubishi Sôko[2] (warehouse)
1937	Sumitomo Densen[1] (Denko) (electrical wire)
1938	Mitsubishi Shoji[1] (trading)
1940	Mitsubishi-sha (holding company)
1940	Nihon Kasei[2] (a Mitsubishi company, chemical)
1943	Mitsubishi Seiko[1] (steel)

Notes:
* indicates a Mitsui company.
[1] First-line company. These are directly owned by zaibatsu families or by holding companies.
[2] Second-line company or affiliate of a first-line company.

Source: Asajima (1983, 1986, 1987).

Table 6.7 Distribution of shareholding in zaibatsu groups immediately after World War II

Zaibatsu	Number of sample companies	Owner family, holding company	Other firms in the same zaibatsu	Outside the zaibatsu
Mitsui				
First line	10	63.4	11.9	24.7
Second line	13	35.9	17.2	46.9
Mitsubishi				
First line	11	30.3	15.3	54.4
Second line	16	18.4	40.3	41.3
Sumitomo				
First line	17	27.9	16.5	55.6
Second line	16	13.2	30.7	56.1
Yasuda				
First line	20	27.9	17.8	54.3
Second line	12	17.0	15.3	67.7

Note: Second-line companies include affiliates of first-line companies.

Source: Miyajima (1992) and Okurashô (1981).

6.5.2 Postwar

Cross-shareholding was promoted after the war for three reasons: to avoid hostile takeovers, to protect from foreign ownership, and to enhance group ties as *keiretsu*. All three reasons relate to enhancement of managerial autonomy from stockholders.

The selling of large blocks of stock by SCLC was intended to democratize the stock market by encouraging small shareholdings. But the initial, small buyers could sell their shares, and it thus became possible to acquire control of a company through the stock market. Several takeover attempts were made. The main examples include moves to buy Yôwa Fudosan, a Mitsubishi real-estate company, and Taishô Kaijyô Kasai, a Mitsui insurance firm. Shares of these two firms were purchased by individuals who had made huge profits from the Korean War boom. In addition, foreigners requested permission to purchase shares in electrical machinery companies that had been joint-ventures with foreign firms in the prewar period. These included Sumitomo Denko, Fuji Denki, and NEC (Nihon Denki).

Although all these attempts were eventually unsuccessful, managements regarded the loss of stability in the composition of ownership as a crisis. However, the Anti-Monopoly Act (*Dokusen Kinshi Hô*) of April 1947 strictly prohibited firms from holding other firms' shares, and limited financial institutions to 5 per cent of shares. Managements were just regaining confidence and drive, and showed it by launching a strong campaign through such organizations as Keidanren (Federation of Economic Organizations) for this to be revised. In June 1949 the provisions were relaxed, so only owning competitor's shares was prohibited.

However, the prohibition against former zaibatsu firms holding shares in their own groups was only withdrawn after the Peace Treaty in 1952, and cross-holdings grew. Then, components of the major zaibatsu began to form groups, called *keiretsu*, initially identified with their trading companies and later considered centered on their main banks. There was rapid growth in holdings between Sumitomo firms of all types, while Mitsubishi cross-holdings were largely between firms and group banks. The practice did not develop as quickly among Mitsui firms, and then was limited to minor holdings between financial institutions. These intertwined firms strengthened their group identity with presidents' meetings (*shachô-kai*).

In September 1953, the limit on holdings by financial institutions was raised from 5 to 10 per cent. As a result, cross-holdings between banks and firms were growing, including those that were related through a former zaibatsu. Fuji Bank (successor to Yasuda Bank) increased relations not only with firms in the former Yasuda group but also with the former Asano and Nissan groups. Dai-Ichi Bank did likewise with firms of the former Shibusawa, Furukawa and Kawasaki groups. Sanwa Bank increased ties with the former Nissan group and also with companies it had been dealing with after the war. These were largely holdings between banks and firms; there were only a few cases of cross-holdings between different firms, mostly in the Furukawa group.

Capital liberalization began in 1967, encouraging further cross-holdings between firms and between firms and financial institutions, as a way of stabilizing share ownership. Rationing of stock to third parties, by which an underwriter was able to sell new shares preferentially to shareholders designated by the issuing company, was approved in a 1966 revision of the Commercial Code. This practice, called *oyabike*, became widespread during the 1970s, and this also spurred the tendency toward cross-holding. However, the spread of cross-holdings created a risk of monopoly control by banks and general trading companies, and in a 1977 revision of the Anti-Monopoly Law, the proportion of shares that could be held by financial institutions was scaled back to 5 per cent. This was again raised to 10 per cent in 1987, and to 15 per cent when the law allowing bank holding companies was enacted in 1997.

The expansion of share ownership during the *zaiteku* (money-game) boom of the 1980s encouraged ownership of shares purely as assets, and was entirely unrelated to moves to stabilize shareholders. However, this also increased the proportion of cross-holdings.

6.6 PRECURSORS OF MAIN BANKS

The origin of the main bank system lies in the transformation of the economic system into a wartime system after the outbreak of the Sino-Japanese War in 1937. Let us begin by examining how the corporate monitoring system underwent changes in the process of increasing government intervention in fund allocation for war preparation. This is done for two phases; up to July 1941, and the subsequent war period.

6.6.1 Formation of Lending Groups

An interesting phenomenon that occurred in the period after 1939 was the spontaneous formation of a number of 'cooperative lending groups' (loan consortia). These consortia can be considered an embryonic main bank system. The principal reason for setting up consortia was the need to diversify and spread risk by means of loan syndication. The outbreak of full-scale war in Europe in 1939 and the Tripartite Pact between Nazi Germany, Italy and Japan, which was signed the following year, led to widespread nervousness, and many banks became noticeably more cautious in their lending activities. This is clear from Table 6.8, which shows the growth in lending by ordinary banks.

Table 6.8 Lendings, loans and loan accounts of ordinary banks

Year	Increase in outstanding lendings	Outstanding loans (1)	Number of loan accounts (2)	(1)/(2)
1935	259	5,313	992	5.4
1936	571	5,688	1,031	5.5
1937	1,029	6,533	967	6.8
1938	1,057	7,485	917	8.2
1939	2,502	9,531	847	11.3
1940	2,488	12,284	769	16.0
1941	1,640	—	—	—
1942	2,639	—	—	—
1943	4,588	—	—	—

Note: Lendings are the sum of loan and bill discounting. Lendings and loans are in million yen, and the number of accounts in thousand.

Source: Calculated from Goto (1970).

After rapid growth in 1938, 1939 and into 1940, there was a drastic slowing in lending between 1940 and 1941. Moreover, the size of individual bank loans became significantly larger. Compared with 1935, the loan per account had grown almost three-fold by 1940.

As an example of the implications of this, consider loan consortium lending to three Mitsui companies during 1940: Mitsui Kôzan, 180 million yen; Toyo Koatsu, 36 million yen; Mitsui Bussan, 100 million yen (Mitsui Bank 1957, p. 272). This is the equivalent of 20 per cent of Mitsui Bank's total deposits (1,589 million yen) in 1940. This indicates that the need for risk diversification was one of the most important reasons for organizing loan syndication. As the bank's history puts it, 'Cooperating with the government in purchasing national bonds, lending to national-policy firms in colonial areas, and supplying funds to strategic industries – it is already beyond what any single bank is capable of achieving to lend sufficient money to group firms' (Mitsui Ginko Hachijyû-nenshi Hensan Iinkai 1957, p. 272).

At the end of June 1941, 114 firms were involved in 130 syndicates (some firms had more than one syndicate). Lending totaled 1.724 billion yen, accounting for 8.9 per cent of the total lending of 19.328 billion yen by the banking system at the end of June 1941. (For more on the syndicates, see Teranishi 1994a.)

Among the four old zaibatsu, Mitsui was the most active in resorting to loan syndication. This seems closely related to differences in fund-raising capabilities among banks in the years between the start of the Sino-Japanese War (1937) and the Pacific War (1941). Among the four major zaibatsu banks, Mitsui dropped to a distant fourth in terms of deposits, as shown in Table 6.9. The reason seems to be that Mitsui was late entering heavy and chemical industries, and found it difficult to get access to the inter-firm transaction and, hence, deposit business of these industries.

Table 6.9 Total deposits of major zaibatsu banks, 1936 and 1942 (in million yen, except as noted)

	1936	1942	Change (%)	
Sumitomo Bank	1,017	3,530	2,513	(247)
Yasuda Bank	929	3,525	2,596	(279)
Mitsubishi Bank	810	2,774	1,964	(242)
Mitsui Bank	857	2,190	1,333	(155)

Source: Calculated from Goto (1970).

Another reason might be the small number of branches, as the bank claims in its official history (Mitsui Bank 1957, p. 270). However, the number of branches was almost the same as Mitsubishi, so this is not sufficient to explain the slow growth of deposits. It was critical to Mitsui that it failed to make Toshiba a first-line company in 1941 (Sawai 1992, p. 178) so it was unable to have access to the company's deposit network.

6.6.2 Information Problems

Rapid realignment in industrial structure meant that the banks had to deal with new borrowers with whom they had no previous business relations, and lack of information on these borrowers heightened the need to diversify risk.

The problem of lack of information was particularly serious with regard to national-policy firms. They grew quickly in number, from 27 in 1937 at the start of the war to 154 at the end of June 1941. Many were involved in investment financing in colonial areas, and only a few, such as the South Manchurian Railway, were profitable and paying dividends. Indeed, not only were many running deficits, some even refused to disclose corporate information on the grounds of national security, and so lending became an extremely risky venture. Even so, banks were obliged to lend as a gesture of cooperating in national policy.

The food and textile industries included many marketing and exporting cooperatives, and funding these low-priority industries ('sacrificed industries') was possible only with considerable diversification of risk by means of loan syndications.

6.6.3 The Banks as Conduits, 1941–1943

During the period before July 1941, there was a tendency toward managerial autonomy, and the emergence of formal loan syndication in August 1941 furthered it. With syndication, banks and other financial institutions could not play any kind of monitoring role: they simply became conduits of funds into munitions companies.

The vehicles for formalized syndicates were the newly established Emergency Joint-Lending Groups (*Jikyoku Kyôdô Yûshi-dan*), made up of the top-10 ordinary banks and IBJ. The five leading trust banks joined later. In May 1942 the National Finance Control Association (*Zenkoku Kin'yû Tôsei-kai*) was organized. More and more of the lending and mediation of joint-lending groups came under the supervision of this highly active control association, so that in 1942 most lending was carried out through the association.

For commercial banks, participating in joint lending was an important strategy for finding new customers for loans, and they are said to have contested fiercely over lending shares. Some firms and banks had business relations that dated back to the prewar period, but many more new relationships were forged during this period. In view of the heated competition for lending share, the Bank of Japan ordered its branches to monitor and regulate joint-lending activity by banks so as to prevent monopolistic behavior and excessive competition (Nihon Ginko 1984, p. 300).

6.6.4 Direct Controls, October 1943–1945

During the final stage of the war, the basic principle of war economy management changed from a planning system to a direct-control system, and direct bureaucratic intervention in production was intensified. The Munitions Company Act of October 1943 stipulated that 'production managers' were to be under the direct control of the government. With approval of the relevant minister, managers could disregard the decisions of stockholder meetings and decline to disclose information. Moreover, stockholders could not discharge managers without the approval of the relevant minister.

The Designated Financial Institution System for Munitions Company Financing was introduced in January 1944 to give managers an even freer hand. Each munitions company was assigned one or two banks, one of which was designated as a manager bank (*kanji ginko*) based on the history of lender–customer relationships. These banks were allowed to organize loan consortia.

Of the 217 companies covered by the first-round designation of munitions companies, loan consortia were organized for 64. For those companies that already had loan syndicates, consortium members were the same as the members of the loan syndicate. The distribution of manager banks among 217 companies was: IBJ, 63; other special banks, 10; nine large banks, 139; and four local banks, 5.

The fixed relationship between each company and the manager bank is seemingly similar to the subsequent main bank system. However, the two systems are quite different for the following reasons. First, all the loans in this system were supplied in the name of the manager bank, so other banks in the consortium were in practice lending to the manager bank, not to the company. Second, because the financing of munitions companies was an absolute obligation for financial institutions, banks were more or less subordinated to munitions companies, having no choice but to supply as much funding as was demanded.

In March 1945, the system was further modified by the Munitions Financing Special Measures Act. Loan syndication was completely eliminated. Instead, each of about 2,000 companies, including non-munitions companies, was assigned one bank, and that bank was given the role of taking care of all its financing needs. Banks were put under the control of production companies. It is pertinent to consider that at this point a main bank system, even in its embryonic form of loan syndication, ceased to exit. Production managers in this system (*seisan sekininsha*) were almighty: they did not need approval by stockholder meetings when related ministries gave approval, they could refuse information disclosure, and could not be dismissed without agreement of the government.

6.6.5 Postwar Loan Syndicates

During the period immediately after the war, another embryonic main bank system emerged in the form of loan syndication intermediated by the Bank of Japan. This was triggered by termination of the huge policy-based lending during the war and continuing through the reconstruction period immediately after the war. In April 1949, when the orthodox stabilization policy known as the Dodge Plan was initiated, new loans from the Reconstruction Finance Bank (RFB) were suspended, and RFB went into a process of dissolution.

Because most large firms had been accustomed to borrowing heavily from policy-based financial institutions, the impact of the suspension of RFB loans was enormous. As Table 6.10 shows, the sum of loans from the policy-based financial system – IBJ, the Wartime Finance Bank (*Senji Kin'yû Kinko*), and RFB – were more than 30 per cent of the total outstanding loans of ordinary banks during 1943–49.

Table 6.10 Lending by Industrial Bank of Japan, Wartime Finance Corporation, Reconstruction Finance Bank, and ordinary banks (million yen)

End of month	Industrial Bank of Japan (A)	Wartime Finance Bank (B)	Reconstruction Finance Bank (C)	Ordinary banks (D)	(A) + (B) +(C) as % of (D)
1942 Mar	2,559	–	–	15,662	16.3
1943 Mar	9,766	306	–	19,034	52.9
1944 Mar	6,002	999	–	25,054	27.9
1945 Mar	12,106	2,903	–	40,354	37.2
1945 Sept	14,649	3,074	–	56,429	31.4
1947 Dec	–	–	44,210	135,711	32.6
1948 Dec	–	–	111,159	332,006	33.5
1949 Mar	17,970	–	131,965	357,096	42.0
1949 Dec	40,979	–	108,410	588,593	25.4
1950 Dec	69,158	–	89,895	845,510	18.8
1951 Dec	102,964	–	79,247	1,286,780	14.2

Note: Data for ordinary banks in 1945 is as of the end of August, and those for IBJ during 1949–51 are for the end of March of the following year.

Source: Nihon Kogyo Ginko(1957); Ourasho (1955); Nihon Ginko(1947); Nihon Ginko *Economic Statistics Annual*, each year.

The drastic fall in the availability of loans from the usual sources obliged firms to borrow from sources other than policy-based financial institutions, and banks to lend to firms with which they did not have any previous lending relationship. There is no doubt that agency costs due to asymmetric information increased significantly, enhancing the necessity of risk diversification by means of loan syndication, as well as effective monitoring by lead banks.

In addition, the Ordinance for Fund Allocation of Financial Institutions, enacted in March 1947, required banks to supply credit to specified strategic industries. Large banks, accustomed to lending to heavy and chemical industries during the war, felt no difficulty obeying the rules. For local banks, however, the rules were not easy to follow, for two reasons. First, funds had to be supplied in the form of direct lending. Purchasing corporate bonds could not be used to satisfy the requirements, although that had been acceptable under the 1937 legislation. Second, funds other than those supplied to designated industries were also controlled by the government. They had to be invested in government bonds (national, local, or RFB), held as reserves, or used for repayment of Bank of Japan borrowing. There was no way to tap funds through an inter-bank money market.

To help local banks lend to the specified industries, BOJ took on the role of intermediation, actively organizing loan syndications, as requested by large city banks. The number of cases of intermediation (value of loans in billion yen) was 621 (20.0) in 1947, 2,273 (68.9) in 1948, and 2,449 (162.2) in 1949, but had declined to 431 (45.5) during January–March 1950 and continued to taper off thereafter.

Table 6.11 indicates that new lender–customer relationships were formed through the process. With respect to 24 companies in the sample, as the share of loans from policy-based financial institutions and from the wartime-designated financial institutions (that is, their old main banks') decreased, the share of other institutions increased. The decline in the share of old main banks seems to have continued through the first half of the 1950s. According to Kikkawa (1992), the share stabilized at the 20 per cent level in the second half of the 1950s.

The loan syndication intermediated by the Bank of Japan has some similarity to the main bank system in the high-growth era. Thus, local banks participating in the syndicates delegated the monitoring role to the lead city banks, which had requested the Bank of Japan to organize the syndicates.

Although there are similarities between the high-growth-period main bank system and the loan syndications before July 1941, the designated financial institutions during the war, and the postwar loan syndications

Table 6.11 Borrowing by 24 major firms by lenders (million yen, per cent)

Type of financial Institutions	1948 million yen	%	1949 million yen	%	1951 million yen	%
Former designated[1]	6,124	58.5	9,676	34.0	20,845	31.4
Government[2]	3,230	30.7	7,162	25.1	18,918	28.5
Other	1,139	10.8	11,645	40.9	26,630	40.1

Notes: The percentages for each year are the distribution of total borrowing by the firms from the three types of financial institutions, and thus total 100%. The 24 firms comprise 5 in metals, 10 in machinery, 5 in chemicals, and 4 in marine transportation and mining.

[1] Designated banks are explained in the text.

[2] Reconstruction Finance Bank, Hokkaido Colonial Bank, counterpart funds, and Bank of Japan.

Source: Miyajima (1992).

intermediated by the Bank of Japan, none of them has the two principal characteristics of the fully-fledged main bank system. These are reciprocal monitoring and risk-sharing. Reciprocal monitoring means each bank takes the role of monitoring the firms for which it is the main bank, while lending freely to firms for which other banks are main banks. Risk-sharing means that, when a firm falls into financial distress, its main bank provides rescue funds more than proportionally to its lending share.

For emergence of the high-growth-period main bank system, it was necessary that autonomy of managements be established through the progress of cross-shareholding, and banks be a primary source of corporate financing in a bank-centered financial system. We have already discussed the first; the next section is concerned with the second.

6.7 BANK-CENTERED CORPORATE FINANCE

Bank-centered financing (indirect financing), where funding for almost all firms, large as well as small and medium, is dependent on bank borrowing, is a phenomenon specific to the postwar high-growth period. The prewar system was quite different. Small, indigenous-industry borrowers never borrowed directly from banks, instead utilizing intermediated borrowing through merchants. Financing of large firms relied heavily on capital markets: equity and bond financing comprised significant sources of funds. Firms in cotton-spinning, the leading industry, were able to raise funds through money markets utilizing their high reputation; electric utilities issued bonds denominated in foreign currency to tap long-term funds from abroad. Further, financing of zaibatsu firms relied heavily on re-investment of profits until around 1930. Summary figures for the sources of corporate financing in manufacturing during the postwar period are in Tables 6.12 and 6.13. A comparison of this with Table 3.3 regarding the prewar period shows the differences.

Table 6.12 contains data on firms with capital of more than 1 billion yen, and Table 6.13 has figures on manufacturing firms with capital of more than 10 million yen. The difference between the figures in the two tables indicates the financing pattern of small firms with equity capital between 1 billon yen and 10 billion yen. Smaller firms' continued substantial dependence on borrowing after 1980 is the most significant difference between larger and smaller firms in the postwar period.

The rise of bank-centered financing in the postwar period reflects policy-based underdevelopment of capital markets. This had two aspects. First, the regulation of interest rates in bond markets and the

Table 6.12 Compositions of manufacturing sector financing, large firms (equity capital more than 1 billion yen)

Year	Borrowings	Bond	Equity	Retained ernings
1960	36.7	0.0	15.9	15.2
	(54.1)	(0.0)	(23.5)	(22.4)
1970	35.4	3.4	10.6	10.7
	(58.9)	(5.7)	(17.6)	(17.8)
1980	31.7	3.3	6.6	15.6
	(55.4)	(5.8)	(11.5)	(27.3)
1990	16.3	11.1	9.2	28.1
	(25.2)	(17.2)	(14.2)	(43.4)
2000	14.9	8.4	9.9	33.7
	(22.3)	(12.6)	(14.8)	(50.4)

Notes:
Data are year-end values. Entries without parentheses are percentages of total assets. Entries in parentheses are percentages of the sum of borrowing, bonds, equity, and retained earnings, so they do not include trade credits and other items, as Table 3.3 does for the prewar period.

Source: Okurasho, *Hôjinkigyô-tôkei* annual issues.

Table 6.13 Composition of manufacturing sector financing, all firms (equity capital more than 10 million yen)

Year	Borrowings	Bonds	Equity	Retained earnings
1954	26.7	3.2	11.9	24.4
	(40.3)	(4.8)	(18.0)	(36.9)
1960	35.0	0.0	14.0	15.8
	(54.0)	(0.0)	(21.6)	(24.4)
1970	32.6	2.3	9.4	12.3
	(57.6)	(4.1)	(16.6)	(21.7)
1980	31.2	2.1	5.8	15.6
	(57.0)	(3.8)	(10.6)	(28.5)
1990	23.3	7.1	6.9	24.8
	(37.5)	(11.4)	(11.1)	(39.9)
2000	21.8	5.4	7.5	31.0
	(33.2)	(8.2)	(11.4)	(47.2)

Notes and Source: See Table 6.12.

consequent credit rationing held back development of free security markets. Second, the system of creating and rationing long-term funds within the bank-centered system, and the system of smooth rollover of short-term bank loans subsidized by BOJ credit rationing, reduced the need for the capital market as a mechanism to supply investment funds.

6.7.1 Credit Rationing

The reason why credit rationing was established can be understood from the policy environment and prevailing economic theory immediately after the war: the bureaucrats had a strong orientation toward developmental policy, and so intervened in financial markets; most financial institutions were seriously impaired, if not on the verge of bankruptcy; and prevailing economic theory emphasized possible market failures, and thus encouraged rationing and monitoring by the government.

Let us examine the political process in which rationing and interest regulation in the bond markets were introduced and maintained. The regulation on bank lending rates was first introduced when the 7.7 relative price systems (price and wage anchoring started from July 7) were implemented in 1947. Bank lending rates were controlled in order to lower the production costs of firms. However, there was apprehension that the regulation violated the Anti-Monopoly Act of

April 1947. Therefore, the regulation was given clearer legitimacy with the Temporary Adjustment of Interest Rates Act in December 1947. This enabled regulation of deposit and lending rates by the governor of the Bank of Japan after consulting with the interest adjustment committee at the request of the Minister of Finance.

Asset management of banks had been under the regulation of the Ordinance for Fund Allocation of Financial Institutions since March 1947. The ordinance directed that 50 per cent of the targeted increase in the free deposits be lent to strategic areas, and the remainder in securities such as national bonds, municipal bonds and Reconstruction Finance Bank bonds as indicated by administrative guidance.

Financial institutions were in the process of rehabilitation, and the government had been controlling them with respect to current revenue and expenditures. This made it inevitable that the government intervene regarding interest rates on bonds. Rates were set by regulation at a level just sufficient to cover the interest costs of the financial institutions that bought the bonds. The level was determined by the Bond Issuance Adjustment Committee (*Kisai Chôsei Kyôgi-kai*) established in June 1947, whose membership was composed of representatives of the Ministry of Finance, Economics Stabilization Board, Bank of Japan, Reconstruction Finance Bank and major private banks.

Under these conditions, it was natural to expect regulation of interest rates to be abolished when price stability was realized and financial institutions rehabilitated. The program for resolution of the wartime losses of financial institutions was virtually settled by the middle of 1948, by which time prices were also stabilizing. Nevertheless, the regulations were never repealed. Instead, they were maintained throughout the high-growth era, despite the modifier 'temporary' in the act's title.

'Temporary' was construed to mean 'until comprehensive revision of the laws related to the financial sector is finished'. It would have been very disruptive, at least in the short term, to have undone the regulations. This is because interest rates throughout the system were kept lower than the equilibrium level in order to reduce the interest costs of firms. Not only would rates have been higher, but there might have been differentials leading to an allocation of funds different from what was desired by the authorities and the principal beneficiaries of the system. The banks did not oppose the regulation, as the system gave them consistent margins.

6.7.2 Stifling a Bond Market

In March 1949 when General Headquarters (GHQ) asked the BOJ whether it was ready to list bonds on the security exchanges scheduled to reopen in May 1949, BOJ responded that listing would be impossible. Prices of government bonds in (informal) markets were 75 to 85 per cent of their face value, and marking bank bond holdings to market would expose considerable unrealized losses on bank balance sheets. It was asserted that the banks could not absorb such an additional burden (Shimura 1978).

The numbers make the BOJ response reasonable on the surface. Banks as a group held 94.682 billion yen face value of government bonds at the end of 1949. Discounting 15 to 25 per cent would have meant losses of 14.2 billion to 23.7 billion yen, equal to four to seven times the annual net profits of the banking system (all city and local banks), which were 3.3 billion yen in the fiscal year 1948. (It can be argued that the government was not likely to default on the bonds so that, held to maturity, as they mostly were, the bonds led to no losses – other than the opportunity cost of having to accept an artificially low interest rate. However, inherent in having a market for the bonds is the expectation that at least some of them will be traded.)

Here again, the policy prescription was derived from a presupposition that the profitability of the banking sector was the objective of the monitoring and surveillance of the administrative authority. In this way bureaucrats strengthened their grip on banks through a mechanism in which a regulation necessitates another regulation.

6.7.3 Supplying Long-term Funds

Credit rationing and regulation of interest rates hamper the development of capital markets. In the absence of access to well-functioning international financial markets, the lack of domestic capital markets can seriously hinder development policy through a shortage of long-term investment funds. To cope with this, the financial system of the high-growth era was equipped with two mechanisms: the creation and rationing of long-term funds within the intermediated financial system, and the accommodating supply of Bank of Japan credits to banks.

A system for creating and rationing long-term funds within the intermediated financial system was established by the early 1950s. It had three parts.

1. Postal savings and policy-based financing. Deposits in the postal

savings system were invested as long-term, low-interest loans through policy-based financial institutions such as the Japan Development Bank. These institutions could supply long-term loans because postal savings monopolized long-term deposits by keeping their interest rates higher than time deposits of banks for maturities longer than two years (Teranishi 1982, p. 477).
2. Rationed corporate bonds. Bonds issued by large companies in industries such as electricity and steel, as well as financial debentures issued by long-term credit banks, were placed with city banks at yields lower than market rates.
3. Bank of Japan loans with bonds as collateral. City banks could not sell the bonds they held in the secondary markets without incurring capital losses. To alleviate the liquidity shortage, BOJ credits were supplied with the bonds as collateral.

Through this mechanism, deposits at city banks, which were more or less short term during the high-growth era, were converted into long-term investment funds such as corporate bonds and loans by long-term credit banks.

6.7.3.1 Institutions and policies

This mechanism involved creation of several institutions and policies.

First, long-term credit banks were created. Partly because of its belief that the Industrial Bank of Japan (IBJ) and Wartime Finance Bank were utilized for running the war economy, the Occupation strongly opposed long-term banks. It tried to convert the prewar special banks (including IBJ) into ordinary banks on the grounds that long-term funds should be supplied through security markets and the role of commercial banks should be confined to short-term lending financed through deposits. However, the Occupation's position gradually softened as the effective date of the Japan–US Peace Treaty drew nearer, and it finally agreed to allowing banks to issue financial bonds, and such legislation was passed on March 31 1950, effective with the beginning of the new fiscal year on April 1. In February 1952, the Minister of Finance publicized a plan to establish long-term credit banks to alleviate the liquidity problem of banks, and legislation was promulgated in July 1952. A new bank, Japan Long-term Credit Bank (LTCB), was established on December 5 1952 and, on the same day, the Industrial Bank of Japan became a long-term credit bank under the new law.

Second, BOJ and MOF introduced the following system to deal with the banks' illiquid bond holdings.

1. Purchase of government and RFB bonds from banks by BOJ on the condition that banks use the proceeds to finance the long-term credit needs of their customers (the so-called *Himotsuki* Operation).
2. Preferential BOJ lending using specified corporate bonds as collateral, with banks requested to use the proceeds for financing equipment equipment investment.
3. Pre-selection system of bonds qualified for collateral for BOJ credits (*Nichigin Tekikaku Tanpo Shasai Jizen Shinsa Seido*), implemented by two committees – Kisai Kondan-kai, which decided the volume and conditions of bond issuance under the guidance of MOF and BOJ, and Kisai Uchiawase-kai, which dealt with administrative matters for bonds planned to be issued in the following month, the membership of which comprised mainly underwriting banks and security companies.

Of these, the first was directly related to the immediate problem of bank illiquidity, while the other two were an introduction of new institutional devices for credit rationing. Owing to these measures, bond financing was put completely under bureaucratic control. New issuance came to be preferentially rationed to industries selected by bureaucrats, and a secondary market for corporate bonds was left largely underdeveloped.

Third, the Japan Development Bank (JDB) was established through a complicated political process that warrants a section to itself.

6.7.3.2 Establishment of the Japan Development Bank

Reflecting the need for long-term funds, the liquidity problem of city banks, and the orientation-toward-development policy of bureaucrats, there was support for creation of a government-directed development bank. The ongoing liquidity problems plaguing city banks became especially acute as demand for investment funds soared after the outbreak of the Korean War in June 1950. At the same time, the amount of postal savings in MOF's Bureau of Government Funds (*Shikin Unyô-bu*) was rapidly increasing.

Under such conditions, the Minister of Finance, Ikeda Hayato, tried to establish a new governmental bank by resurrecting the Reconstruction Finance Bank. Joseph Dodge agreed in early November 1950, on the condition that the role of the new bank be strictly confined to refinancing, because he had serious concerns over the possible inflationary effects of the bank. GHQ also confirmed this condition (March 9 1951).

However, when legislation to create such a bank, dubbed the Japan

Development Bank, was presented at the cabinet meeting on March 22 1951, the primary aim was to 'supply long-term funds in order to restore the economy and to develop industries'. The JDB started business on May 15 1951 without clearing up the difference in opinion between GHQ and the Japanese government. The exact reason for the occurrence of such an inconsistency is not clear. However, from hindsight, it can be conjectured that the bureaucrats carried out developmental institutional building on the pretext of addressing the liquidity problems of city banks.

It is interesting to compare this process of creating the JDB with that of establishing the IBJ in the Meiji period (see Chapter 3). Had the private sector been as strong around 1950 as it had been in 1900–1905, establishment of the JDB might have met fierce opposition because of its interference with the activity of the private banks. The absence of such an opposition underscores how weakened the private sector was after the war.

6.7.3.3 Bank of Japan accommodation

Let us move on to the accommodating supply of Bank of Japan credits to banks. This mechanism was introduced in 1955. Before that time, BOJ adjusted credits to banks by means of a system of applying higher interest rates, (*kôritsu tekiyô seido*): up to certain limit, BOJ lent at the official discount rate, but, when demand for funds exceeded this limit, it raised rates above the official rate and induced banks to adjust their demand. One reason for this was that to formally change the official discount rate required approval of the Minister of Finance, while informally applying higher rates for additional credits above the limit was possible without such a procedure.

Under monetary policy after 1955, BOJ kept the same discount rate regardless of the demand for credit. At the same time, it controlled lending by banks through 'window guidance' (*madoguchi shidô*). Specifically, BOJ regulated the monthly rate of increase in lending by each city bank. *Madoguchi shidô* was formalized in 1962 as the Regulation on the Maximum Lending Amount (*Kashidashi Gendogaku Kisei*).

In this system, city banks could obtain BOJ credits at given discount rates as much as possible in principle, so long as they obeyed regulations on monthly lending. There was fine tuning: in daily transactions at the window, banks were sometimes asked to reduce their demand for credit by reducing the amount of their deposits (*tsumi no chôsei*) at BOJ (Suzuki 1974). However, apart from this, BOJ took quite a flexible and accommodating stance toward providing for the quite a flexible and accommodating stance toward providing for the liquidity of private banks.

With respect to the effectiveness of monetary policy and the role of *madoguchi shidô,* see Horiuchi (1980) and Teranishi (1982). An extensive description of the mechanics of window guidance is given in Suzuki (1980, p. 166–79).

6.8 THE JAPANESE-STYLE EMPLOYMENT SYSTEM

The Japanese-style employment system, characterized by long-term employment and seniority wages, was formed through the turmoil and confrontation caused by a surging labor movement. It emerged as the class conflicts that flared up immediately after the war were replaced by pursuit of firm growth and inter-industry interests. The decline of conflict was closely related to introduction of an incentive system characterized by a wage system combining a 'livelihood wage' and 'ability to pay', and to the emergence of a homogeneous worker class characterized by equal treatment of blue- and white-collar workers and firm-level unions.

The labor movement in the postwar period went through three phases: a radical phase starting from liberalization of labor laws in 1946; a shift to a cooperative labor–employer relationship from 1949; and convergence of the interests of labor and management, with the concerted pursuit of growth of the firm, after 1955. The emergence of the *shuntô* (spring-offensive) contract-setting system in 1955 was a cornerstone for the beginning of the concerted pursuit of firm growth and the representation of inter-industry interests.

6.8.1 Seniority

The wage system became seniority based. According to Odaka (1993), wages were composed of pay linked to age and to experience (together, *nenrei-keiken-kyû*) and pay linked to job ranking (*shokukai-kyû*). The age-linked component was basic livelihood pay, while experience-linked pay was related to both ability and livelihood. Job ranking depended on age (experience) and ability. Hence, the ultimate determinants of the wage system were age and experience (itself principally a function of age), which is what seniority means, together with considerations regarding ability, especially as regards promotions. The ability element reflects emphasis on an efficiency wage system during the interwar period (Odaka 1993) and on the incentive wage system during the war (Gordon 1985). Thus, using micro-level data, Ono (1989) found that 60 per cent of the differences in wages from initial salaries was related to age, 30 per cent to experience, and 10 per cent to education (his proxy for ability) (based on data for 1970, 1975 and 1984).

This system is considered to have existed in embryonic form among white-collar workers and *kogai* (those trained within the firm) at large companies during the 1920s. Such a system was needed at that time to quarantine workers from contamination by labor movements and to develop and retain skilled workers suitable for heavy and chemical industrialization (Ono 1989).

On the basis of the experience of large companies, the system was formalized during the war (Gordon 1985, pp. 264–74). In order to carry out munitions production efficiently, production firms intended to introduce output wages or incentive wages, and such a move spread rapidly among firms. But the Mobilization Bureau of the Ministry of Munitions and the Ministry of Welfare criticized incentive wages and administratively guided firms to fortify elements of livelihood wages to guarantee workers a stable income. This, it was felt, would raise productivity.

In particular, the Labor Management Directive of Essential Factories of February 1942 introduced wage control based on the seniority principle in major factories, and control was extended to the rest of industry in June 1943. After the war, in the fierce labor-movement period, workers intensified demands for livelihood wages, called *densan-gata*, and for an employment guarantee. Management responded by accommodating livelihood elements while insisting on ability-based pay for the sake of enhancing competitiveness. Thus, as a compromise, the seniority wage system became a universal system.

According to Koike (1991), who conducted a detailed comparison of employment practices between Japan and Western countries, a seniority wage system also exists in the United States and European countries. However, the system applies only to white-collar workers in Western countries. In Japan, seniority wages and internal promotion are applied equally to both white- and blue-collar workers.

6.8.2 Worker Status

The fading of differences between how blue- and white-collar workers were treated began during wartime. In the prewar period, there were clear differences in status and in how the two groups were treated. For example, blue-collar workers received daily pay and rarely enjoyed bonus payments.

The Labor Demand–Supply Adjustment Directive enacted in December 1941 stepped up control over labor allocation by stipulating that all firing and leaving, voluntary or not, initiated by a worker or by the company, was a matter requiring permission of the directors of the National Job Guidance Agencies, and this entailed social policy effects of raising the employment status of part-time workers toward the level of regular workers.

There is no doubt that the status differential between blue-collar and white-collar workers was narrowed significantly during the labor democratizing period after the war.

First, integration of production workers and staff unions spread rapidly, especially those belonging to *Sanbetsu* (the Congress of Industrial Unions), and the demand for status improvements of blue-collar workers was accommodated.

Second, in the process of the diffusion of seniority wages, the internal promotion system became popular as wages became linked more closely with job-ranking and experience. This, by reducing wage differentials, effectively eliminated the difference between blue-collar and white-collar workers.

6.8.3 Lifetime Employment

Let us next examine how long-term or lifetime employment emerged. Some caveats. First, it must be noted that whether employment tenure in Japan is long by international standards is unclear. Second, long-term employment in Japan is only at large firms; employment at small and medium firms is more liquid. Third, the conclusions of different studies are divided. Clearly, more research remains to be done.

6.8.3.1 Varied findings on employment tenure

Koike (1991) asserts that average employment tenure in Japan is longer than in the United States, but not necessarily compared to Europe. The share of the long-term employed increased sharply during the 1960s in Japan compared to the United States. Compared to Europe, while the share of stable employment in Japan was not necessarily larger, the share of liquid employment in Japan was lower.

Chuma and Higuchi (1995) find that, comparing the composition of workers by employment duration between Japan and Europe, the share of short-term (for example, less than two years) is lower, and the share of long-term (for example, 10–19 years) is higher in Japan than in Europe, contradicting Koike's assertion.

One of the conventional views on this point is that the long-term employment system was established during World War II as a response to excess demand for skilled labor. Okazaki (1991) and Okazaki and Okuno (1993), for example, maintain this on the grounds that both the job-leaving rate and the coefficient of employment adjustment were high in the prewar period and low in the postwar period. Hashimoto (1995) criticizes the view, noting that during the war, an initial increase in the labor turnover rate was offset by intensified regulation of labor mobility in 1939–40 and that, immediately after the war, mobility was temporarily very high. Moreover, their conclusion is derived from a comparison between 1927–36 and 1974–85, so it is not certain whether the changes in the variables occurred during or after the war.

Based on his detailed examination of labor mobility during the war, Gordon (1985) concludes that regulation of labor mobility was not necessarily effective, and the turnover rate of skilled labor was not necessarily low during the 1940s. With regard to the effects of legislation such as the 1941 Labor Demand–Supply Adjustment Directive, Gordon's view differs from Hashimoto's. Gordon feels that the intent was to facilitate reallocation of labor rather than to regulate its mobility.

Tsuda (1984) provides a convincing argument about high mobility immediately after the war, attributing it to the reluctance of large firms to offer long-term employment to a large number of employees, confining it to only a small fraction of workers trained within their firms.

Hashimoto (1995) claims that the long-term employment system emerged through the labor movement's reaction to the threat of lay-offs during the Dodge deflation and the ensuing restructuring period, that is after 1949 and into the early 1950s. However, based on a comparison of the share of long-term workers in Japan and the United States, Koike (1991) notes that the share of long-term workers in Japan became higher than in the United States only after the 1960s.

From the evidence, it seems reasonable to consider that the long-term or lifetime employment system was established as a set of rules, including the seniority wage system and equal treatment of white- and blue-collar workers, during the period around 1950.

6.8.4 Interactions

Practices such as long-term employment are usually established as an equilibrium rule of games, which are determined by changes in the incentives of both employers and employees. Although there might be some influence from regulation, it is likely to disappear when the rules are removed, especially if the rules are inconsistent with other forces. Incentives change in response to the state of skill formation by employees and to evolution of the wage and promotion system.

For example, as the seniority wage system is established, workers are induced to stay longer and to invest in firm-specific skills, while employers consider it profitable to subsidize firm-specific investments. As the long-term commitment by both employers and employees is enhanced, the possibility of the hold-up problem and related inefficiencies is decreased. (The hold-up problem is when one person has to keep their commitment before the other, with the possibility that the other person will then not do so. More formally, due to transaction costs, contracts are usually incomplete. When contracts are incomplete, it is possible one party will opportunistically renege. In this instance, an incomplete contract means it is difficult for workers to invest in firm-specific skills because the employer can renege on the promise of wage rises after the worker has incurred the investment costs.)

Comparing the Stolper–Samuelson model and the specific-factor model, we noted causality from firm-specific skill to labor immobility in Chapter 2. Here, we emphasize an inverse causality from labor immobility to skill formation, where labor immobility is a result of the wage system. Gilson and Roe (1999), on the other hand, consider that labor immobility is caused by the lack of external markets in Japan, which prevented opportunistic behavior by employees. Their assertion, however, seems to depend on an unconventional assumption that even if skills are firm-specific, employees could find employment in other firms if 'an external market is available'.

Through a careful investigation in the historical process of skill formation by workers, Koike (1997) argues convincingly that a key element in worker skill in the context of firm-specific skill is the capacity to deal with accidents and uncertain events, and that such a skill element is most effectively formed through an OJT (on-the-job-training) system that covers diversified jobs by frequent rotation. Such periodic and comprehensive rotation became widespread among large companies during the late 1950s and into the 1960s as a response to fluctuations in demand, and the problem of absentee workers.

6.9 REGIONS

The Meiji-Taishô system was characterized by the autonomy of regional economies, and the fiscal and financial systems were designed so as to be consistent with that autonomy. However, the position of local and regional economies was weakened by institutional changes as the country moved toward a war economy in the 1930s. With war, a centralization mechanism was introduced with the definite intention of mobilizing resources for the war. In addition, during the war and the turmoil immediately afterward, local economies finally lost their wealthy and benevolent leaders, the *meibôka*.

After the war, with the ending of resource mobilization, there was no necessity for centralization. Nevertheless, the centralized system was retained and maintained, complementing the catch-up-type economic policy led by bureaucrats. The centralization of the fiscal and financial system, discussed in the next sections, precluded the possibility of autonomous and spontaneous development of regional economies.

During the high-growth era, there were occasional voices calling for the promotion of regional economies, based on depopulation or environmental issues. Policy recommendations derived from such assertions, however, emphasized the role of central government in resolving the problems, consequently instituting a stronger grip on the local governments. Few recommendations were concerned with autonomous movement by local communities or with local initiatives.

For example, consider the Comprehensive National Land Development Plan (*Kokudo Sôgô Kaihatsu Keikaku*) drawn up by the Ikeda cabinet in 1962. It aimed at coping with socio-economic issues arising from migration from rural areas to the major cities in the Pacific Coast Belt Zone (that is, from Tokyo along the coast through Nagoya and Osaka to Fukuoka). The fact that some areas were experiencing depopulation, and industrial development was concentrated was considered a problem that had to be solved. For this purpose, a massive national land plan was conceived. It involved constructing highways, bullet-train routes, harbors and airports. In addition, 15 New Industrial Cities and six Special Areas for the Development of Industry were designated.

In 1969 a New Comprehensive National Development Plan (*Shin-Zenkoku Sôgô Kaihatsu Keikaku*) was developed. This time the emphasis was on conservation of nature and making rural living standards comparable to urban levels.

The basic idea in both cases, however, was promotion of the central administration as the engine to carry out renovation of regional economies. There was little concern for local initiatives.

Similar to this was the Restructuring Plan of the Japan Archipelago (*Nihon Retto Kaizo-ron*) put forward in a book by Tanaka Kakuei (prime minister from July 1972 to November 1974) published in June

1972 (in English, Tanaka 1972). The plan intended to resolve the problems of air and water pollution in cities and the depopulation problem by diminishing 'disadvantageous centralization'. As a concrete measure, the plan advocated relocating factory areas and promoted cities with populations of about 250,000. While some local communities, suffering from a lack of employment opportunities, seem to have welcomed the plan, its execution relied completely on central government-led and direct interventionist tools. Quite often, environmental considerations were disregarded, and control by the central government was strengthened further (Masamura 1985).

6.10 FISCAL CENTRALIZATION

Let us examine the move toward centralization on the fiscal side. At the 70th Diet in 1937, the Hirota Koki cabinet placed a tax bill designed by Baba Eiichi, Minister of Finance, on the agenda. The bill aimed at two things. First, to establish a system for mobilizing fiscal resources in preparation for emergencies and, second, to put the revenue and expenditures of local governments under the control of the central government in order to restore the social order of local communities. The Baba plan failed to pass due to the collapse of the cabinet in February, but it was gradually incorporated into the tax system during the fiscal 1937–39 budgets, and was realized in full in the 1940 tax reform. The central government thus had a strong grip on local governments by controlling both taxation standards and tax rates. The main components were as follows.

1. The income tax levied by the central government became the core of tax revenues.
2. To facilitate control of the public's purchasing power, a withholding tax system was introduced with respect to the proportional part of the tax. (Personal income taxes were in part proportional (classified tax) and in part progressive (comprehensive tax).)
3. Most taxes independently imposed by local governments, including consumption taxes, were abolished. In their place, surtaxes were established on national taxes such as the land tax, house tax and business tax, and the revenue was passed on to local governments in accordance with the amount raised in each municipality. These were termed refund taxes (*kanpu-zei*). In addition, part of the income tax, corporate income tax, admission tax and amusement taxes was apportioned to local governments in accordance with the

fiscal conditions of each municipality. These were redistribution taxes (*haifu-zei*).

4. Issuance of local government bonds was put under central control.
5. Public services by the local governments were put under the control of the central government. This made some sense since the central government funded expenditures in excess of the refunded surtaxes.

As emphasized by Jinno (1987) and Noguchi (1995), the 1940 tax system bears a strong resemblance to the postwar system. First, the criteria for the introduction of new taxes require approval of the Minister of Home Affairs within the provisions of the Local Tax Act. Local tax rates are under strict regulations with regard to ceiling rates and lump-sum taxes. Second, more than one-third of local government revenue is from the central government in the form of tax-sharing grants (*chihô kôfu-zei*), specific purpose grants (*kokko shishutsu-kin*), and specific revenue grants (*chihô jyôyo-zei*). Third, issuance of local government bonds was under a strict screening system until 1994.

The revenue of the central government, as well as the share of local government revenue transferred from the central government, increased dramatically after 1940, and the resulting division of revenue has been maintained at similar levels in the postwar period. Table 6.14 shows the composition of central and local government revenue during 1931–60.

6.10.1 The Shoup Report

In May 1949 seven tax experts arrived in Japan at the request of SCAP to make recommendations on the tax system. Called the Shoup Mission after its chair, professor Carl Shoup, it duly issued its report in September 1949. This was the foundation for the extensive tax reform of 1950, and much of the postwar tax system. However, not all its proposals were retained for long, despite SCAP's intention that the system would not require changes for several years (Yamamura 1967, p. 32, which also lists the six basic elements of the Report).

The 1950 budget was drafted following the proposals of the report, but the idealistic reform proposed by Shoup was emasculated in many respects soon afterwards. Thus, in an April 1951 White Paper on the Tax System, the government set out its own course. For example, looking at some of the national-level proposals, despite the principle of comprehensive income taxation, various special treatments were introduced during the 1950s. These included preferential treatment of

Table 6.14 Percentage distribution of central government tax revenue and local governments revenue

	Central government tax revenue			Local government revenue		
	Personal income tax	Corporate income tax	Other taxes[1]	Local taxes	Transfers[2]	Other[3]
1931	15.1	4.5	80.4	26.4	8.0	65.6
1932	14.2	5.4	80.4	22.8	12.3	64.9
1933	14.4	6.9	78.7	18.2	10.1	71.7
1934	14.8	8.5	76.7	21.6	10.7	67.8
1935	14.4	10.1	75.5	23.1	9.3	67.6
1936	14.3	12.0	73.7	19.8	7.0	73.2
1937	18.8	14.6	66.6	23.7	9.9	66.4
1938	21.1	15.8	63.1	23.8	10.8	65.4
1939	20.5	15.1	64.4	23.0	14.9	62.1
1940	40.8	5.0	54.2	20.6	21.2	58.1
1945	37.0	11.4	51.6	18.4	41.9	39.7
1950	49.2	18.7	32.0	34.6	40.8	24.6
1955	36.1	24.9	39.1	32.8	41.0	26.1
1960	24.9	36.6	38.5	35.6	39.3	25.1

Notes:
[1] Includes land tax, business tax (until 1945), inheritance tax, liquor tax, sugar consumption tax, tariffs, and the like.
[2] From the central government.
[3] Includes fees and charges, business revenue, municipal bonds, and the like.

Source: Nihon Ginko (1966).

interest income (for the sake of encouraging savings) and of dividend payments (for the sake of promoting reserve accumulation by firms). Further, various tax exemptions were introduced (Ishi 1986).

Our concern here is with the effect on local governments. As one of its major points, the Shoup Report called for fiscal autonomy of local governments. Based on a detailed survey on the fiscal system of local governments, Shoup had a clear understanding of how local communities were deprived of freedom in the decision on fiscal revenues and were delegated excessive administrative obligations by the central government (Suzuki 1960). Shoup proposed the following specific reform measures.

1. Abolition of the *haifu-zei* and introduction of a general equalization transfer (*iippan heikô kôfu-kin*) in its place.

2. Integration of many of the existing subsidies into a general equalization transfer.
3. Determination of the amount of the general equalization transfer on the basis of an assessment of the actual needs of local communities.
4. Respect by the central government of the spirit of autonomy of local communities.
5. Restraint in intervention through imposing conditionality on the use of transferred money.

However, the general equalization transfer system was converted to grants (*chihô kôfu-zei*) in 1954, and the system of transferring a given fraction of the income tax was revived. In addition, tied subsidies increased significantly after the signing of the Peace Treaty.

6.11 FINANCIAL SYSTEM CENTRALIZATION

The financial system was converted into a centralized system during the 1930s: local savings were mobilized to finance munitions industries directly and to invest in government bonds. After the war, the focus of mobilization of funds shifted to financing the equipment investment of the large-firm sector. Local savings were concentrated in the center, and a fraction of the funds were channeled back into the regions through city banks and policy-based financial institutions.

6.11.1 Prewar Financial System Centralization

The first step was the regulation of fund allocation by means of the Temporary Funds Adjustment Act in 1937 and the Bank Funds Operating Directive in 1940. The former was concerned with financing of investment funds and issuance, underwriting and subscription of securities greater than certain amounts, and the latter with financing of operating funds and other liquidity needs. Both regulations aimed at concentrating funds in munitions industries and closely related basic industries, and suppressing financing of industries with excessive production capacity or producing non-essentials (such as luxury goods).

Approval of related ministers was required for financing activities and BOJ took on the role of adjusting the allocation of funds. As a result, local banks, which had been lending mainly to indigenous industries such as textiles, were obliged to curtail such loans and to invest in government securities.

Further, the government intensified the pressure for concentration beyond the drastic mergers under the 1927 Banking Act (Chapter 5). In particular, Finance Minister Baba promoted local mergers of banks in order to facilitate financial control, announcing in 1936, 'In ordinary prefectures, the ideal number of banks should be one or two'. The policy aimed at reducing the cost of funds of local banks through mergers in order to accommodate huge government bonds to be floated for war financing. For this purpose, large city banks were requested to reduce the number of local branch offices, avoiding competition with local banks.

In the financial market up to the 1920s, local banks were the deficit sector and relied heavily on borrowing from large banks and the BOJ, while large city banks were the surplus sector and invested their idle money in the call market. The situation was reversed in the late 1930s. Another reason for the increase in deposits at local banks was the increase of central government expenditures in local areas due to the compulsory purchase of rice from 1933 (*Beikoku Tôsei Hô*) and public works intended to alleviate local distress. The ratio of lending to deposits of city banks began to rise from around 1940, while that of local and *sôgo* banks decreased. Likewise, the net position of city banks in the inter-bank money market changed from surplus to deficit in 1942. Data are in Table 6.15.

The concentration of funds in the city and industries for the sake of war financing was inherited after the war by the Ordinance for Fund Allocation of Financial Institutions in 1947 in order to control the flow of funds to facilitate the Priority Production System. Local banks, facing difficulty in finding borrowers, relied on loan syndicates organized by BOJ, as discussed earlier.

6.11.2 Postwar Flow of Funds Imbalance

For the period after postwar reconstruction – that is, after 1950 –we need to pay attention to the phenomena of imbalance in the flow of funds (*shikin henzai genshô*). This involved financing from inter-bank money markets by city banks, the major deficit sector, and investment in inter-bank money markets by local and other banks (including *sôgo* banks, *shinkin*, and credit cooperatives), the surplus sector.

The direct causes for the flow pattern were differences between the two groups in branch policy and in specialization requirements for lending areas. Until the early 1980s, deposit rates were controlled at levels less than market rates but, although the nominal interest rate on loans of more than one million yen was regulated, due to the widespread practice of compensating balances (that is, required deposits),

Table 6.15 Inter-bank flow of funds

	City banks		Local banks		*Sôgo* banks	
	(A)	(B)	(A)	(B)	(A)	(B)
1930	3.3	63.0	−10.3	74.2	−2.6	46.8
1935	5.7	52.2	−7.1	56.1	−1.8	53.5
1940	3.3	60.9	−0.3	38.8	−0.4	37.4
1945	−36.9	93.3	−8.7	28.4	−1.5	36.0
1950	−16.9	90.1	−8.0	86.3	−0.5	51.9
1955	−6.2	77.3	3.0	78.8	0.9	52.0

Notes: Local banks include ordinary banks other than city banks and saving banks, and now are called first-tier regional banks. *Sôgo* banks were *mujin* before 1951, and correspond to contemporary second-tier regional banks. Data are fiscal-year-end values, which means March of the year following.

(A) Inter-bank loans as a percentage of deposits. An inter-bank loan is defined as call loans plus bills purchased plus loans to financial institutions minus call money minus borrowings from financial institutions minus bills sold.
(B) Lending as a percentage of deposits.

Source: Calculated by Nihon Ginko, *Economic Statistics Annual* for each year and company history of each bank.

effective lending rates were flexible. This resulted in a considerable interest margin between lending and deposit rates.

Thus, the larger the amount of deposits when borrowers were available, the larger bank profits were. When deposit rates are regulated, and the perceived difference in the safety of banks is small – in Japan's case, partly owing to the implicit protection by the government of inefficient banks – the amount of deposits is determined largely by the availability of branches. Moreover, as many econometric studies have confirmed, average costs were decreasing with the scale of bank activity during the high-growth era. MOF policy was to be generous in permitting branching by local and other banks and less generous to city banks, as revealed in the rate of increase in the number of branches of each group (Teranishi 1982, Table 8.22). MOF branch policy thus had the effect of suppressing the deposits of city banks and of expanding the deposits of local and other banks.

There was a clear difference in lending opportunities between the two groups. City banks were allowed to lend to any type of borrower, while local and other banks were narrowly specialized. Thus, local banks were allowed to operate mainly in specific prefectures. *Sôgo* banks and *shinkin*, as well as (urban) credit cooperatives, lent particularly to groups of firms specified by size and the like, which meant they dealt with small and medium firms in some way. Agricultural credit cooperatives were allowed to lend only to agriculture. As a result of the difference in lending specialization, city banks faced a larger demand for funds than local and other banks. Together with the difference in deposit mobilization caused by branch policy, this resulted in the imbalance phenomenon. As a result, in the inter-bank money market, city banks – the deficit sector – borrowed, while local and other banks – the surplus sector – lent.

6.11.2.1 Effects of the imbalance

The imbalance in the flow of funds entailed three effects.

First, monetary policy became effective in spite of interest rate regulation and credit rationing. Monetary policy in the high-growth era involved two mechanisms: an accommodating supply of low-interest credits from the Bank of Japan and control of bank lending through window guidance. What is important is that both mechanisms worked most effectively when applied to individual banks separately.

Window guidance was applied to banks individually and privately. An accommodating supply of BOJ credits was also applied to banks individually, because the purpose was to replenish liquidity in response to individual banks' risk of maturity mismatch and the availability of liquid funds (deposits at BOJ, *tsumi no chôsei*). Such a monetary policy applied to individual banks separately was most effectively implemented when a small number of large banks, city banks, were net borrowers from BOJ. Teranishi (1982) shows how window guidance applied to city banks was effectively transmitted to lending by local and other banks, so that total bank lending was controlled by window guidance under Bank of Japan's accommodating supply of credits.

Second, the concentration of local savings in city banks had the effect of spreading the development policy centered on equipment investment of large firms to the local level, consequently causing a concerted approach to economic growth at the national level. Local and other banks could obtain reasonable profit margins by lending deposits to city banks through the call market. While they enjoyed a trickle-down of the fruits of the high-growth policy in this way, such an easy profit margin reduced incentives for them to search for and monitor innovative local firms, and thus to contribute to the development of regional economies.

Third, some part of local savings was invested back in the local economies. This was typically seen in loans by the Japan Development Bank. The JDB loan category 'local area development' was introduced in 1955, and such loans increased considerably during the 1960s, amounting to 17.3 per cent of total loans during the fiscal year 1966 (38.5 billion of 222.9 billion yen in flow terms). It was the second largest category, after 'marine transportation'. In the main, these were syndicate loans with city banks and were mainly for equipment investment by large firms in low-wage areas.

6.12 LABOR RELATIONS, 1946–55

The defeat in the war triggered fierce confrontations between workers and management. This was partly because the Occupation encouraged labor movements. To that end, it promulgated a new labor law in December 1945, which came into effect in March 1946. The number of unions increased from 386 in December 1945 to 4,849 in December 1946, and the movements became extremely radical.

At every large company, a management committee was organized by the union and management, where negotiations were carried out regarding the guarantee of employment and status improvement of blue-collar workers, as well as introduction of the *densan-gata* wage system (livelihood wages, based on age-linked pay and family allowances, as discussed earlier). Such committees implemented production management at companies such as *Yomiuri Shinbun* (a leading daily newspaper), Nihon Kokan, Mitsubishi Kogyo, Mitsui Kozan, Kurashiki Boseki, Asahi Kasei, Toshiba, Toho and Keisei Dentetsu.

The movement was led by two confederations: *Sôdômei*, related to the Japan Socialist Party, and *Sanbetsu-kaigi*, related to the Japan Communist Party. In particular, *Sanbetsu-kaigi* spearheaded radical actions: in the offensive of October 1946 it organized more than 100 strikes, mobilizing 180,000 workers.

Activities on the management side were severely handicapped as a result of policies such as zaibatsu dissolution, the Asset-Freezing Ordinance, removal of top management, the Anti-Monopoly Act, and the Elimination of Excessive Concentration of Economic Power Act. However, Japan Committee for Economic Development (*Keizai Dôyû-kai*) was established in April 1946 by young managers (50 was the maximum age) and asserted 'the right to manage' in the framework of modified capitalism. In March 1948, the Federation of Management Organizations (*Keieisha Dantai Rengô-kai*) established in May 1947 was reorganized into *Nikkei-ren* (*Nihon Keieisha Dantai Renmei*, Japan Federation of Employees' Association), and intensified its anti-labor stance.

After the general strike of February 1 1947 was suspended on the order of SCAP, the radical labor movement, especially its revolution-targeting component, retreated, and the left wing of the Japan Socialist Party seized leadership. The focus of union activities shifted from the status of blue-collar workers and the right to manage production to wage bargaining and employment security.

Two factors seem to be responsible for such changes: the start of the Cold War and restored management confidence. With the Cold War, the aim of Occupation policy shifted from democratization to conversion of Japan into a stronghold against communism. Meanwhile, management gradually regained confidence in exercising control as the restructuring of firms and banks proceeded and the production level recovered. The control power of firms came to be in the hands of corporate managers, especially after the revision of the labor laws in June 1949, the ensuing dismissal of communists, and general mass firing of workers.

During the 1950s, the labor movement was obliged to retreat and accept defeat in its pursuit of a labor–capital cooperative system. Disputes continued to occur quite frequently, however, as management accelerated its offensive against labor, asserting the necessity of rationalization and production efficiency, while labor responded with demands for higher wages.

After its 1952 strike, *Densan* (the labor union of the electric power industry) was forced to dissolve. In the coal-mining strike of the same year, worker demands to link wages to the cost of living, not to productivity, failed in the face of strong resistance by management. In the 1953 strikes at Nihon Seiko and Nissan, and in 1954 at Nikko (Muroran), management succeeded in undermining the solidarity of the labor union by organizing second unions, led by white-collar workers. In 1954, following passage of a tight budget in the Diet, *Nikkei-ren* announced 'three principles of wage determination', and took a tough policy of no wage hike (Inoki 2000).

Faced with the limitation of wage-hike struggles by individual unions, in 1955 labor union organized *shuntô kyoto kaigi* (a spring-offensive concerted operation committee). Under the leadership of Ota Kaoru of Gôka Rôren, the committee was composed of eight federations (Gôka Rôren for synthetic chemicals, Tanrô for coal mining, Shitetsu Sôren for private railways, Densan for the electric power industry, Kamipa Rôren for paper and pulp, Zenkoku Kinzoku for metals, Kagaku Gômei for chemicals, and Denki Rôren for electric machinery). Many of these were also members of the Sôhyô confederation.

6.13 *GENKYOKU*–INDUSTRIAL ASSOCIATION SYSTEM

Just as *shuntô* was based on a confederation of labor unions from a range of industries, a similar industry-level adjustment system, composed of three elements, emerged at the government–private-sector interface: industrial associations, *genkyoku*, and deliberative councils.

Each element originated independently during the prewar or war periods. An interactive and complementary relationship between the elements emerged during and immediately after the war. The relationship, which was concerned only with the collection and transmission of information about industries during the war, was converted into one concerned with adjustment of inter-industry interests regarding income distribution during the high-growth era.

6.13.1 Precursors

Let us start with an examination of the historical transition of the individual elements of the system. The origin of industrial associations can be traced to the late 19th century, and there were a number of voluntary associations during the late 1920s. At the national level there were 222 such associations in 1936. According to Kikkawa (1991), these had been playing two functions: first was control of competition among firms through cartels, and second was cooperatively purchasing materials, securing workers, selling finished products, and so on.

Under the 1941 Major Industrial Associations Directive these voluntary associations were reorganized into *tôsei-kai* (industry-controlling associations) for the purpose of promoting the wartime economy. The directive was promulgated on August 29 after considerable dispute and discussion with private-sector firms. In November, 12 *tôsei-kai* were designated in nine industries, including steel, coal, industrial machinery, metals and shipbuilding. In the second rounds, nine were established in six industries, including cotton, staple fibers, wool, chemicals and light metals.

The chair of a *tôsei-kai* was endowed with strong powers, and assigned the role of drawing disaggregated plans regarding material purchasing, production and distribution of products, on the basis of aggregate plans drawn by the government. In a feedback, the government plan drew on information provided by *tôsei-kai* (Yonekura 1993). In this way *tôsei-kai* fulfilled an indispensable role in the 'directed planned economy' under the New Economic Structure (*Keizai Shin Taisei*) led by the Planning Board (Okazaki 1993b).

The *genkyoku* system dates from June 1939 when the major bureaus in the Ministry of Commerce and Industry were reorganized into four *genkyoku* classified by the industry concerned: mining, chemicals, machinery and textiles. After the Ministry was converted into the Ministry of International Trade and Industry (MITI) in May 1949, this industry-based system was maintained. After the reorganization of July 1952, there were five *genkyoku*: heavy industry, light industry, machinery, mining and coal. The last two were added as a result of the abolition of the Resources Agency (Suzuki 1995).

The origin of deliberative councils lies in the Council on Agriculture, Commerce and Industry (Nôshôkô Shingi-kai) at the time of the 1894–95 Sino-Japanese War. Thereafter, there were several important councils, such as Keizai Chôsei-kai in 1916, Shoko Shingi-kai in 1927, and Rinji Sangyô Shingi-kai in 1930. Each was organized, on the initiative of the government, in response to particular economic conditions, and had pre-set durations. More important, the members of these councils rarely included representatives of industrial associations (Okazaki 1993a). Most council members were Diet members and representatives of zaibatsu and general economic organizations such as the Chamber of Commerce. Council members were assigned the role of coordinating economic activities 'beyond the frame of individual industries'. In other words, the major role of the councils was to resolve problems from the viewpoint of development of the national economy.

The composition of council membership underwent a drastic change after the war. An examination of three major deliberative councils – Fukkô Shingi-kai, Sangyô Gôrika Shingi-kai, and Sangyô Kôzo Shingi-kai – by Okazaki (1993a) finds that Diet members and representatives of general economic associations decreased, and there was a substantial increase in the number of representatives of industrial associations. In the postwar period, each council usually has had subcommittees in charge of each industry, and most major councils were standing committees without a predetermined period of duration.

6.13.2 Becoming a Sub-system

Each element of the *genkyoku*–industrial association system has an independent origin and, initially, its own role. Let us next discuss how the three came together to fulfill the role of a sub-system in the high-growth era system. Under the wartime economy, *tôsei-kai*, based on existing industrial associations, and *genkyoku* were matched in each industry, and the flow of information between the planning agency of the government and private sector industries was facilitated through the *tôsei-kai* system. Deliberative councils were not utilized during the war period because policies were determined from above, by the military and Planning Board (*Kikakuin*).

In the high-growth era, when *tôsei-kai* was abolished, the *genkyoku*–industrial association system came to fulfill another role: adjusting distributive interests between industries. This new role became important as labor become immobile among industries. This immobility was partly due to formation of firm-specific skills by workers, so that people tended to form coalitions according to their industry. The *genkyoku*–industrial association system provided a useful mechanism for such interest representation. The system came to work as a mechanism to distribute policy-induced rents among industries. A detailed expla-nation of this mechanism is provided later.

In sum, the *genkyoku*–industrial association system, originally established as a tool for information flow during the wartime planned economy, came to fulfill a role of adjusting inter-industry interests, in addition to a informational-conduit role for industrial policy. Such a change occurred partly because the traditional government–private-sector interface based on regional interests had ceased to work due to the centralization of the economic system, the disappearance of wealthy leaders, and so on.

Another reason for inter-industrial representation was the failure of class representation to dominate the interface. And that failure explains why a social-democratic regime did not prevail in the politics of Japan. This is taken up in the next sections.

6.14 NO SUSTAINED CLASS CONCEPT

Recalling the period before the stormy strike at Mitsui Kôzan's Miike mine in 1960, Nakamura (1993a) concludes that the 1950s was the era of politics and that the labor movement operated in a framework of class confrontation between labor and capital. The period from the end of the war into the 1950s saw the government–private-sector interface represented by class interests gather strength, and it came to dominate in place of the prewar interface based on regional interests. However, unlike in Western European countries, class conflict never became a dominant pattern of distributive conflict in Japan. The rise of one-party dominance and limp party politics is closely related to this.

There are several reasons that the concept of class was not widely accepted, and when it was expressed, its hold was short-lived.

In the prewar period there was significant government suppression of 'leftist' thought and of urban labor movements. In agriculture, it simply was not articulated: there were only a small number of hired workers, so a true confrontation between 'haves' and 'have nots' never prevailed in Japanese agriculture before the war. Thus, in 1921, the number of farm households classified as agricultural labor is estimated at 120,000, or just 2.2 per cent of the 5.5 million farming households (Takigawa 1994, p. 290). Tenants were another matter, but in the postwar period land reform eliminated most of the reason for politically active class consciousness.

The Japan Farmers' Cooperative (Nihon Nômin Kumiai) was established in 1922 by Sugiyama Motojiro, Kaga Toyohiko and others as a class organization for peasants. Originally a moderate organization aimed at enhancing the solidarity of tenant farmers, after 1923 it became politicized and radicalized as a proletariat movement oriented toward resolving farm problems through revision of the capitalist system. With oppression by the authorities, and under the influence of ideological friction within the labor movement, however, it had declined toward the end of the 1920s through a repeated process of alignment changes.

After the war, the farmers' cooperative movement revived explosively with membership of 2.0 million to 2.5 million, resulting in a surge of tenancy disputes. This time, however, the movement was effectively calmed by implementation of thorough-going land reform. Farmers with their own land became interested only in securing their own economic well-being. The number of farmers' cooperatives decreased drastically, and most were absorbed into agricultural cooperatives. (Postwar, cooperatives were established by the Agricultural Cooperative Act (*Nôgyô Kyôdô Kumiai Hô*) in 1947 on the basis of the prewar farmers' co-ops and landlord associations (*Nôkai*).)

6.14.1 No Class Party

The ultimately weak influence of class concepts in the postwar period lies in part in the failure of the Japan Socialist Party (JSP) to forge an alliance between labor and peasants after the JSP formed its first cabinet (albeit in coalition) following elections in April 1947. According to a detailed study by Hiwatari (1991), this failure was caused by difficulty in resolving conflict regarding rice price policy – farmers demanded price increases while labor demanded decreases. There was also discord between the Economic Stabilization Board (*Keizai Antei Honbu*), eager to lower rice prices in order to curb inflation, and the Ministry of Agriculture, aiming at an increase in food production. (The JSP, *Nihon Shakaitô*, also is now the SDP (Social Democratic Party).)

After the failure to form an alliance, the labor force were obliged to retreat in the face of an offensive by management, and farmers lost incentives for class movements under the influence of agricultural cooperatives, which pursued the interests of agriculture as an industry. Hiwatari (1991) maintains that in this way the possibility of a two-party system had disappeared even before establishment of the 1955 system and, thereafter, there was parliamentary politics in name only. The Liberal Democratic Party (LDP, *Jiyû Minshutô*) was established through the merger of various conservative parties in 1955. Party politics fell into disfunction and the LDP continued in power until 1993.

During 1955–93 there was no room for active participation by the JSP in economic policy. It barely found a *raison d'être* in disputes regarding national security, such as re-armament, the relationship with the United States, and the constitution. This was because it claimed to be a class-based party, at a time the actual government–private-sector interface was represented by inter-industry interests and not by class interests. Because party politics did not function in economic conflicts for more than 40 years, adjustment of inter-industry interests was left to LDP *zokugiin* – Diet members with special stakes in particular industries. The dual-decision mechanism (government and LDP) was a consequence of the malfunctioning of party politics.

NOTE

1. For example. The Ministers of the Ministry quite often came from business circles; Ikeda Shigeaki from Mitsui Bank, Fujiwara Ginjiro from Ôji Seishi, and Kobayashi Ichizo from Hankyu.

7. Mechanism and performance of the high-growth-period economic system

This chapter examines how the high-growth-period economic system worked and looks at its performance. Institutional complementarity is essential for the successful functioning of a system, and we begin with the various ways in which elements of the system reinforced each other. After a brief review of the stunning performance of the Japanese economy during the heyday of the system, attention turns to factors contributing to that performance. Having a long view was a key factor in shaping the system's mechanisms and propelling the economy forward. Controlling competition was also an element of the system. The final sections address income distribution.

7.1 RECAPITULATION OF THE SUB-SYSTEMS

Before taking up institutional complementarity, let us summarize the main contents of the three sub-systems.

The sub-system of the private sector is composed of the bank-centered financial system and the Japanese-style firm system.

The bank-centered financial system is characterized by the main bank system and the mechanism for supplying long-term investment funds. The mechanism for supplying long-term funds comprises rationing corporate bonds and long-term credit bank debentures, rationing policy-based credits financed through the postal saving system, and a flexible and accommodating supply of Bank of Japan credits to facilitate the maturity transformation of banks.

The Japanese-style firm system is characterized by corporate governance led by management and the Japanese-style employment system. Managerial autonomy in corporate governance is sustained by cross-shareholding among group firms. The Japanese-style firm system is composed of three elements: seniority wages as a mixture of livelihood wages and ability wages, equal status of blue- and white-collar workers, and long-term employment. Further, the seniority wage system was complemented by the internal promotion system, which applied equally to both blue- and white-collar workers and provided a basis for a firm-based labor union, with membership of blue- and white-collar workers.

The government–private-sector interface is composed of an interactive mechanism between government *genkyoku* and private-sector industrial associations, and deliberative councils organized according to issues related to industries. The *genkyoku*–industrial association system fulfilled the role not only of a conduit of information between individual industries and the related government bureaus but also as an adjustment mechanism for inter-industrial income distributive conflicts.

Whenever government intervenes in the competitive conditions of individual industries, policy-induced rents and, hence, the level of value-added in the industry, are influenced by the policy. The effectiveness of this mechanism was enhanced by the full-set characteristics of the industrial structure.

The division of labor between the government and the private sector is characterized by a high degree of government intervention in the economy in the form of regulations regarding competitive conditions of industries – that is, industrial policy. Government intervention in the form of redistribution policy, such as social insurance, was not very important, unlike in economies where distributive interests are represented by class interests.

7.2 INDUSTRIAL POLICY

Industrial policy can be classified as two types: direct intervention in the competitive conditions of industries, and indirect intervention through tax subsidies and rent transfers.

Direct intervention, implemented mainly through the *genkyoku*–industrial association system, was composed of policies such as cartel agreements, entry control and trade policy. Cartel agreements were implemented through exemptions possible under the Anti-Monopoly Law, and affected production, prices, and equipment investment. Entry control was implemented to promote infant industry, adjust the production area, reorganize the 'inter-industry order', and regulate foreign capital inflow. Trade policy involved such measures as tariffs, import quotas and import approval.

Industrial policy also involved special tax exemptions, explicit provision of subsidies, and manipulation of rent transfers through rationing of policy-based credits and foreign exchange rationing. Rationing of foreign exchange, one of the most powerful tools for import control in the period immediately after the war, resulted in a transfer of income from exporters to importers. The rationing of low-interest, long-term funds to strategic industries – that is, policy-based financing – effected a transfer from depositors to borrowing firms. The *genkyoku*–industrial association system, centered on MITI, exerted influence on this type of policy. So did MOF, through its Budget Bureau, which was in charge of fiscal policy, and the Fiscal Investment and Loan Program (FILP, *Zaisei-Tôyûshi*).

Note that industrial policy as defined here can be implemented not only for efficiency reasons – that is, as a means of coping with possible market failures – but also, and quite frequently, for political reasons related to distributive conflicts. (For a more detailed examination and classification of industrial policy, refer to Komiya, Okuno and Suzumura 1984.)

7.3 STRUCTURE OF THE *GENKYOKU* SYSTEM IN ITS HEYDAY

Table 7.1 depicts the organization of the Ministry of International Trade and Industry (MITI) in 1972. The ministry is composed of two kinds of bureaus, *chôsei-kyoku* (coordinating office) in charge of overall issues and *genkyoku* in charge of issues related to each industry.

Chôsei-kyoku functions are primarily administrative: coordinating, budgeting, planning, and monitoring Ministry activities. Most *chôsei-kyoku*, therefore, do not have close contact with many industrial associations. The number of industrial associations related to foreign trade and trade promotion is large because they were in charge of matters related to smaller firms.

Each *genkyoku* has an interface with industrial associations and deliberative councils. Other ministries with close ties to specific industries have similar relationships: the Ministry of Transportation functioned as de facto *genkyoku vis-à-vis* the transportation industry; the Ministry of Welfare with the pharmaceutical industry; bureaus of MOF with the banking, insurance and securities industries; Posts and Telecommunication with the communication industries; and the Ministry of Agriculture with agriculture.

7.3.1 Pluralism or Corporatism?

The system of interest representation by *genkyoku*–industrial associations has been called both pluralism and corporatism. Pempel and

Table 7.1 MITI: Organizational structure 1972

Bureau	Councils[1]	Associations[2]
Total	35	614
	(Chôoseikyoku)	
Minister's Secretariat	2	0
International Trade Bureau	1	28
Trade and Development Bureau	3	87
Industrial Policy Bureau	5	10
Environmental Protection and Safety Bureau	3	3
	(Genkyoku)	
Heavy Industry Bureau (includes iron and steel, industrial machinery, electronics, data Processing, electrical machinery, vehicles, aircraft, and ordnance)	5	161
Chemical Industry Bureau (including ceramics and construction materials, and fertilizers)	1	111
Textile and General Merchandise Bureau (including fiber and spinning, and paper and pulp)	1	133
Minerals, Oil, and Coal Mining Bureau (includes non-ferrous metals)	5	44
Public Utilities Bureau (excludes telephone)	1	20
	Related agencies *(Gaikyoku)*	
Patent Office	2	3
Small and Medium Enterprise Agency	4	9
Agency of Industrial Science and Technology	2	5

Notes:
1 Deliberative Councils (*Shingikai*).
2 Industrial Associations (*gyôkai dantai*).

Sources: Tsûsan Hando Bukku Henshû Iinkai (1972) and (for the formal English names) Japan Institute of International Affairs, White Papers of Japan, 1971–72, pp. 442–45.

Tsunekawa (1979) called it 'corporatism without labor'; Inoguchi (1983) 'bureaucratic-led, mass-inclusionary pluralism'; Sato and Matsuzaki (1986) 'channelled pluralism', Muramatsu and Krauss (1987) 'patterned pluralism'; Aoki (1988) 'bureau pluralism'; and Otake (1999) labeled it 'meso-corporatistic'. However, neither of these poly-scientific categorizations is satisfactory. Schmitter (1979) provides comprehensive definitions of both terms, as shown in Table 7.2.

Table 7.2 Corporatism and pluralism contrasted

	Corporatism[1]	Pluralism[1]
Number of constituents	Limited	Unspecified
Properties of constituents:		
Representation by	Single unit	Multiple units
Participation	Compulsory	Voluntary
Competitition among units	Non-competitive	Competitive
Order	Hierarchical	Non-hierarchical
Relationship with the state:		
Representation	Monopolistic	Not monopolistic
License	Needed	Not needed

Note:
[1] As defined by Schmitter (1979).

The *genkyoku*–industrial association system fits six of the seven characteristics of pluralism, and only one of corporatism. The number of categories in the system is not pluralist because it is given by the number of *genkyoku* in the bureaucratic system, which roughly corresponds to the number of industries in the country.

There was no representation of interests in the system other than interests of industries; interest groups such as consumers, environmentalists, religious groups, and so on are excluded. It is argued below that the exclusion of these groups, especially consumers, or, more precisely, the inability of the system to accommodate the interests of groups other than inter-industrial groups, resulted in the increase in the political costs of the system during the 1980s.

7.4 SMALLER FIRMS

There have been significant differences between the large-firm sector and the small- and medium-enterprise sector (SMEs) within the private sector sub-system.

First, ownership and management are not often separated at SMEs, so managerial autonomy is a characteristic specific to the large-firm

Second, the Japanese-style firm system applies mainly to large firms: long-term employment and internal labor markets are by and large specific to such firms; employment at SMEs has been liquid and market based.

Third, SMEs are not part of the main bank system. Most SMEs borrow from only one specific bank. That is called its main bank, but the bank's function as such is not the same as for a large firm.

7.5 INSTITUTIONAL COMPLEMENTARITY

A sustainable economic system requires compatible sub-systems. Ideally, they are self-reinforcing. This is what is meant by institutional complementarity among the sub-systems, and it is explored in the next two sub-sections.

7.5.1 Complementarities Related to *Genkyoku*–Industrial Associations

Elements of the Japanese-style firm system (seniority wage, internal promotion system, commitment to long-term employment) gives workers incentives to invest in firm-specific skills, effectively avoiding hold-up problems from investment sunk in specific skills. The internal promotion system, together with wages linked to experience gave an incentive for workers to engage in investment in firm-specific skills, and provision of opportunities for on-the-job training (OJT) through job rotation, signaled managerial commitment to long-term employment. In this internal labor market, Aoki (1988) considers that rank hierarchy provides incentives for workers to expend more effort and invest in human capital.

When skills of workers become firm-specific and the cost of investment is sunk, labor mobility is reduced. In this case, people tend to be motivated to organize coalitions based on inter-industrial interests, so the *genkyoku*–industrial association system becomes an effective interface to adjust distributive conflicts.

The internal labor market in the Japanese-style firm system, and the mechanism for distributing policy-induced rents through the *genkyoku*–industrial association system, are complementary in determining income distribution within firms. The *genkyoku*–industrial association system determines policy-induced rents (value-added) for each industry. This mechanism, coupled with the determination of the wage level of each industry through the *shuntô* wage negotiation process, determined the division of value-added into wages and profits. Aoki (1999) also emphasizes institutional complementarity and co-movement between the *genkyoku*–industrial association system (which he calls bureau pluralism) and the Japanese-style firm.

Government intervention in the competitive conditions of industries is facilitated by the functioning of industrial associations, which work as a conduit of information flow between the government and firms within an industry. The power of an industrial association increases as the government intensifies intervention, because an increase in policy-induced rents enlarges the room for the activity of industrial associations with regard to the distributive interests of industries.

7.5.2 Complementarities Related to Government Intervention

Government intervention in capital markets resulted in the bank-centered financial system. Two complementarities developed that successfully fulfilled roles generally played by capital markets. These were supplying long-term funds and monitoring.

Under-development of capital markets due to regulation did not result in a shortage of long-term funds because the supply of long-term funds, supported by an accommodating supply of Bank of Japan credits, enabled a smooth supply of long-term funds and rollover of short-term funds.

The under-development did, however, require adjustments to monitoring and governance mechanisms. Monitoring of managers normally falls on both equity and debt holders, each with their own somewhat different concerns. However, monitoring by outside shareholding was institutionally discouraged, and few firms even had bondholders. Moreover, at large firms generally, and at keiretsu firms in particular, the position of managers *vis-à-vis* outside shareholders was bolstered by cross-shareholding. This made shareholders largely irrelevant to governance.

The tasks thus fell to the banks. As the conduit for most investment funds, main banks could discipline corporate managers who were excessively self-indulgent or inefficient by threatening to cut off access to loans, and even cause their replacement. At that point, monitoring can be said to become governance. Studies showing a correlation between low profitability and a higher probability of new directors from a banker or of management turnover include Kaplan and Minton (1994) and Morck and Nakamura (1999). Thus, main banks fulfilled tasks of monitoring and governance, making those systems complementary with the employment system. Because banks took on the major role in monitoring primarily as a result of government intervention, government intervention and the bank-centered financial system were also complementary. (Also see Aoki 1994, pp. 12–26.)

Once a bank-centered financial system established itself, it could be maintained because its ability to discipline corporate managers and to supply long-term funds provided justification for government intervention in capital markets. In addition, government control of banks was justified in part because it was one of the elements of the *genkyoku*–industrial association system as applied to the banking industry, and partly because it was related to monitoring of the corporate sector through the main bank system.

The government had a grip on private-sector economic activity directly through controlling competitive conditions in each industry, and indirectly through control of banks. Further, in this system, the capital market was left under-developed, and the financial system was dominated by banks partly because of strict regulation on security markets and partly because of weak investor rights due to cross-shareholding.

Under-development of capital markets has quite often been a target of criticism because of the constraints it puts on shareholder decision-making regarding resource allocation. To the extent that the under-development was caused by cross-shareholding, however, it was the other side of the coin of ample investment made in specific skills by actual producers (managers, workers, suppliers). Because relation-specific investment was the main engine for the active (production) process and product innovation by Japanese manufacturers, the evaluation of the under–development of capital markets is related to the choice between organizational efficiency through relation-specific investment and allocational efficiency through shareholder decision-making.

It must be emphasized that the failures and negative aspects of high-growth-period banking policy are not simply the result of MOF bungling of specifics. For several generations of participants, the overall system seemed to work well, so they, and many outside observers, were lulled into overlooking its shortcomings and, more importantly, the evolutionary changes in the economy. One can argue that as the problems became obvious, MOF bureaucrats exhibit an extreme reluctance to adapt, and even that their reluctance was self-serving, but this all reflected a broader problem. That is, the most important reason was the inadequacy of the *genkyoku*–industrial association system as a whole in an era of post-catch-up rapid change in technology and industrial structure.

7.6 PERFORMANCE

As is well known, the high-growth-period economic system realized extraordinarily high growth during 1955–73, and relatively high rates of growth until the mid-1980s. Japan has grown to be the second largest economic power from the ashes of wartime destruction, and at the same time has realized a highly equal income distribution. (See Tables 1.1 and4.13.)

The system was significantly dependent on domestic demand, especially equipment investment. The share of investment in GDP was more than 25 per cent after 1961, and attained a peak of 39.1 per cent in 1973. The share of exports of goods and services was less than 10 per cent until 1973. Although the share then went up until 1985, the highest value was still only 14.4 per cent (Teranishi 1994b). The Meiji-Taishô system was also dependent on domestic demand, but an important difference should be noted. Although the main part of domestic demand comprised investment during the high-growth-period system, consumption was a major component during the Meiji-Taishô system.

7.6.1 Efficiency and Growth

Let us discuss in what sense the high-growth-period system contributed to allocational efficiency and growth. However, for two reasons, it is not necessarily easy to provide a clear cut answer.

First, high growth was started and driven by two main engines: technology imports to fill the wide technological gap, and the existence of abundant, cheap, educated labor and engineers. During World War II the technological gap between Japan and Western countries widened again, but as there was a large number of engineers who had been in charge of locally developing new technology, the ceasefire and peace provided a perfect chance to re-start catch-up growth (Goto 1993). Moreover, immediately after the war, there existed a large pool of workers who had finished compulsory education and experienced learning modern technology in the military. Until the mid-1960s semi-skilled labor was flexibly supplied from the rural sector, and thereafter labor with higher levels of education was amply supplied as more youngsters in rural areas went to high schools and colleges.

With the strong political power of the agricultural sector as a background, massive public investment was poured into rural areas. Income levels rose, and a significant part of the increased income was spent on the education of farm children. This is shown in Box 7.1

BOX 7.1 INVESTING IN RURAL EDUCATION

A cross-section regression on all 48 prefectures, with the ratio of public investment per capita to GDP(I) of each prefecture during 1960–74 as a dependent variable, and per capita income (y) of each prefecture as an independent variable yields (t-values in parentheses):

$$I = \underset{(12.67)}{1.59} - \underset{(-3.87)}{0.57}y : R^2 = 0.24$$

This shows that public investment was concentrated in poor rural areas.

Another cross-prefecture regression, with changes in the percentage of junior-high school students who proceeded to high school during 1960–70 (A) as the dependent variable, and the growth rate of per capital GOP (G_y) as an independent variable, yields

$$A = \underset{(11.27)}{37.06} + \underset{(5.84)}{21.47}\, G_y : R^2 = 0.44$$

This suggests that increases in rural income were invested in education.

Second, to arrive at the net efficiency and growth effects of an economic system, we need to compare the case of alternative systems. In the context of this book, the alternative to the high-growth-period system is a socio-democratic system.

In the socio-democratic system adopted in Western Europe during the 20th century, and especially after World War II, distributive interests were represented by class interests, and government intervened by means of social-welfare policies and macroeconomic incomes policy. Japan, on the other hand, was organized on the lines of distributive interests represented first by regions and then, in the postwar high-growth-period, by inter-industrial interests. Government intervention took the form of industrial policy, or intervention in the competitiveness of industry. Besides the direct influences on allocational efficiency and growth, the difference in systems had significant indirect effects. These related to the effects on the stability of the socio-economy related to the difference in methods of dealing with income-distributional issues.

To arrive at a proper understanding of the growth and efficiency effects of the high-growth-period system, it is necessary to control for these other variables related to efficiency and growth as well as for the opportunity costs related to the alternative system. This, however, must be left as a task for future research. In the next two sections, as a preliminary analysis, the focus is on two aspects of system efficiency: informational efficiency and long-term maximizing behavior.

7.7 INFORMATION EFFICIENCY

Let us examine whether the high-growth-period system contributed to growth and efficiency through a superiority in information-processing capability. As is often argued, there is a possibility that the various special information-processing mechanisms installed in the system, such as the main bank and policy-based financing systems, had positive effects on allocational efficiency through mitigation of market failures due to asymmetric information. It is necessary to examine this from two angles: opportunity costs and the efficiency of the information flow. A plethora of literature has been written on the second without yielding a significant consensus. Several of the studies are reviewed here.

7.7.1 Opportunity Costs

We first address the opportunity costs of policy-based financing and the main bank system. The main bank system is part of a bank-centered financial system that gave little place to capital markets. A developed capital market, with effective information disclosure, disciplined auditing and accounting, and high-quality legal infrastructure, can be efficient not only in corporate governance with stockholder sovereignty, but also in enhancing innovating activity.

Both approaches have demerits. Capital markets might not be good at risk-sharing, long-term maximizing behavior, and giving proper incentives to corporate managers for corporate growth. Costs associated with main bank relationships and policy-based financing are discussed in the next section. The same function can be performed by quite different markets and institutions, so that the performance of a financial system should be evaluated not only from the viewpoint of competitive efficiency, but also from a broader context including risk sharing, as is argued in Allen and Gale (2000).

Aoki (1994) examines the information efficiency of the main bank system in terms of its alternative costs, and concludes that the advantage of the system depends on the stage of economic development. Teranishi (1991) argues that each catching-up country should have a financial system tailored carefully for its initial conditions in terms of demand and supply of information, and the term structure of investment funds.

Horiuchi and Sui (1993) and Fukuda, Teruyama, Kamiya and Kei (1995) examine the value of a policy-based financial system by comparing the information-processing role of policy-based financial institutions with that of private banks. Horiuchi and Sui consider loans of JDB and main banks are substitutes, while Fukuda et al. maintain they are complementary. Specifically, Horiuchi and Sui claim that the signaling effects of Japan Development Bank (JDB) loans are of a similar nature to those of main banks, so JDB loans are redundant as regards information about borrowing firms. On the other hand, Fukuda et al. maintain that JDB and main banks are producing different kinds of information about the future performance of firms and industries. Moreover, the information produced by main banks is monopolized by them, so even if there is overlap, information production by JDB is useful from a national-economy viewpoint.

7.7.2 Main Banks and Agency Costs

It is claimed that the level of agency costs between borrowing firms and their main bank are kept at a minimum. This is true in part because of three key elements of the system.

1. Main banks are the largest lenders to firms. This factor, and the next, directly enhance the motivation of main banks to invest in monitoring activity, which can involve significant fixed sunk costs.
2. The lender–customer relationship is long term.
3. There is a reciprocal monitoring system between banks. This helps to avoid duplicating expenses because each bank is assigned the role of monitoring firms for which it is a main bank, but can lend to firms for which other banks are the main bank. In other words, in the mechanism of reciprocal monitoring, monitoring is exclusive but lending is not. In this system, lending to a firm by its main bank plays the role of signalling the presence of monitoring, so that other banks lend to the firm following the signal.

In addition, the degree of information asymmetry is reduced by other aspects of the system.

1. The main bank's holding of transaction balances provides a major source of internal information of a firm's daily activities.
2. The fact that the dispatching bankers are members of the board of directors provides direct access to information about the firm.

There are a number of empirical studies with respect to the information efficiency of the main bank system. Hoshi, Kashyap and Sharfstein (1991) estimated investment functions for two groups of firms (firms that belong to keiretsu and firms that do not), and found that the coefficient of internal funds (cash flow and security holdings) is smaller for the investment function of the former. If we assume there is a pecking order of financing in an imperfect financial market (that is, the agency costs of financing are lowest for internal funds, next lowest for equity, and highest for bank borrowing), then a smaller estimated coefficient for internal funds in the case of keiretsu firms than for non-keiretsu firms implies that a keiretsu firm has mitigated agency costs between itself and providers of external funds.[1]

However, with respect to the estimation by Hoshi, Kashyap and Sharfstein, there is a criticism by Hayashi (2000) and a counter-argument by Hoshi, so there is no consensus so far. Diverse results are found in the studies inspired by Hoshi, Kashyap and Sharfstein. For example, in an estimation in which firms are classified into two groups according to whether a firm has a main bank or not, Horiuchi and Okazaki (1992) find that the effect of a main bank relationship in mitigating the constraint of bank borrowing is small, even if statistically significant.

7.7.3 Bank Monitoring

The monitory capability of banks is considered to be enhanced by various investments in information channels by banks. Such an investment is motivated by the opportunity to profit from information rents. There are other arguments, however, that the information processing capability of banks is closely related to government policies toward banks.

A typical example is the financial restraint hypothesis advocated in Hellman, Murdock and Stiglitz (1997) as an antithesis to financial-repression theory. The latter – often called the McKinnon–Shaw hypothesis – pointed out the detrimental effects of deposit-rate controls that were widely implemented in developing countries until the 1970s (McKinnon 1973; Shaw 1973). That policy aimed at promoting investment by lowering interest rates, but financial-repression theory claimed it had the effect of retarding investment through its detrimental effect on the mobilization of savings through financial institutions. Repression theory provided the background for the Washington Consensus, and hence the IMF–World Bank policy of market liberalization in developing countries.

In opposition, Hellman, Murdock and Stiglitz claim that policy-induced rents arising from regulating deposit interest rates at a level lower than market rates give incentives for banks to invest in monitoring capability. Their arguments are as follows. The opportunity to pursue rents increases the franchise value (charter value) of banks, defined as the value of being a going concern. Since an increase in franchise value is beneficial to bank stockholders, banks have an incentive to behave with a long-term view and thus to invest in branch networks and monitoring capability. The authors derive their theory in part from their understanding of the experience of high-growth Japan.

The Japanese case, however, does not fit their model well in several respects.

First, it is true that policy-induced rents arising from deposit-rate regulations gave incentives to expand deposits for the sake of long-term profit maximization. However, this does not mean that banks were led to pursue maximization of franchise value as an intermediate objective. This is so because administrative guidance regarding approval of new activity areas, branching, and so on were applied mainly according to existing deposit size, so there is a possibility that banks expanded their deposit base in order to be treated favorably by the Ministry of Finance.

Second, banks are typical Japanese-style firms with internal labor markets and managerial autonomy, so it is not necessarily the case that managers aimed to maximize bank franchise value, and hence the put option value of bank equities. Instead, managers might simply have maximized bank size in order to secure promotion opportunities for peer employees and job opportunities for retired bankers.

Finally, the argument that policy-induced rents were invested in monitoring capability is open to question. The wage level of bank workers has been significantly higher than that of other workers. It is possible to argue that, most probably, the rents were spent to raise wages, which is not necessarily related to efficiency-enhancing investment. In addition, there is strong evidence for the over-employment of labor service, especially with respect to city banks, and over-investment in capital goods with respect to regional banks. This was found by Honma, Godo and Teranishi (1996) following the model of Barnett and Hahm (1994) and Hancock (1991). They argue that such over-employment and over-investment are closely related to the rent opportunity caused by regulations on deposit interest rates. Specifically, they estimated a translog multi-product profit function with respect to city banks and regional banks for 1961–64 and compared the actual levels of inputs with optimum levels on the frontier.

Hellman et al. are well aware of these criticisms, and argue that the policy to provide rents to banks must be 'supported by appropriate ownership and governance' (1997, p. 173). However, it is difficult to know from their argument what the concrete mechanism to assure appropriate ownership and governance is.

Further, banking policy during the high-growth era had aspects other than provision of policy-induced rents related to franchise value. The policy was often described as a 'convoy system'. This refers in part to the setting of deposit rates at a level low enough so that even the most inefficient banks would make profits. Moreover, in the convoy system, banks were given an implicit guarantee by the government that they would be bailed out in case of insolvency. This policy was fully in place until the mid-1980s when liberalization of the financial system was started, and survived into the mid-1990s. With hindsight, the most important consequence of the convoy system was the lack of market discipline in the industrial organization of the banking sector.

Policy-induced rents were also produced by strict regulation of competition among financial institutions in different categories. For example, categories of banks, such as long-term credit banks, trust banks, local banks, *sôgo* banks, and shinkin were regulated so as to keep their activities within stipulated areas, instruments and customer groups. It is now apparent that this considerably held back the growth and innovation potential of financial industries.

In short, the financial-restraint hypothesis should be carefully examined before it is applied to the understanding of the high-growth-period financial system.

7.7.4 Monitoring and *Amakudari*

Amakudari (retired bureaucrats 'descending from heaven' into a job in an industry they had been monitoring) has had both positive and negative effects. Senior MOF bureaucrats moving to jobs at private financial institutions has been common, and at least into the early 1990s it was increasing. Thus, there were 70 instances during 1968–69; 221 during 1970–74; 233 during 1975–79; 254 during 1980–84; 274 during 1985–89; and 247 during 1990–93 (Yamori and Fujiwara 1995). For context the number of MOF employees throughout the period under consideration was 65,000 to 68,000.

The negative effects of this are emphasized by Shimizu and Horiuchi (2000). They maintain it occurs as a result of a collusion between the monitoring agency (MOF) and the banks, and MOF allowed banks to commit risky scale-maximizing behavior in exchange for a share in policy rents through *amakudari*. More positively, Okimoto (1989) argues that *amakudari* is a mechanism for informal consensus-building between the private sector and the government. This position is shared by Aoki (1988) and Van Rixtel (2002), who both claim that it helps to reduce information differentials between large and small banks because smaller banks are able to have effective informational channels with the bureaucracy by accepting *amakudari*.

If the consensus-building argument is correct, *amakudari* bureaucrats are hired into management or the planning section of banks in order to make the most of their capability in coordinating private-sector behavior with governmental regulations. However, according to data on the jobs taken by *amakudari* at *shinkin* (Yamori and Fujiwara 1995), the most popular section for retired bureaucrats is monitoring and auditing. Of 259 retired bureaucrats during 1968–93, 159 were hired into these two sections; the rest went into general affairs, accounting, survey and planning, and so on. This finding favors the negative view: *amakudari* was accepted by smaller banks because it induced MOF auditors and inspectors to make allowances for them.

Shimizu and Horiuchi (2000) shows that the ratio of capital to total assets is significantly low statistically at local banks that accepted *amakudari* than at banks that did not. Specifically, they found that accepting *amakudari* had a statistically significant relationship to a reduced capital–asset ratio one year later. However, it is possible that MOF sent *amakudari* to risky banks because it foresaw difficulties, and the problems would have been even worse otherwise.

There is no direct evidence that when banks accepted *amakudari*, monitoring by MOF tended to become lax, inducing banks to commit risky behavior. Even if bank performance deteriorates and the ratio of capital to total assets becomes low, this does not necessarily lead to risky behavior. This is because shareholder control is imperfect in Japan, and it is difficult to see how bank shareholders could influence bank management in the direction of risky behavior. Also, the deterioration of bank performance discussed in Shimizu and Horiuchi needs to be examined against alternative hypotheses such as bank behavior controlled by insiders during the bubble period, and the like.

7.7.5 Conclusions on Main Bank Information Efficiency

This survey of the major arguments related to the informational efficiency of the main bank system and banking policy is not exhaustive of the literature, but the points covered are sufficient to convey the main thrust of the arguments. Controversy remains. It seems fair to say, however, that even if the main bank system is informationally efficient theoretically, the efficiency does not seem to have been realized in its pure form, but instead has been offset by various side-effects distorting bank behavior. These include insider control, excessive dependence on real estate collateral, and inflexibility of banking policy innate in the *genkyoku*–industrial association system, among others.

Likewise, with respect to the informational role of banking policy, the positive effects of financial restraint and *amakudari* seem to have been by and large offset by the negative effects caused by the convoy system and other policies.

7.7.6 Information Efficiency and Other Institutional Devices

Let us now discuss the information efficiency of other institutional devises of the high-growth-period system. The informational effects of industrial policy, including policy-based financing, are especially important. In this regard, it is essential to know how information about promising industries was produced.

Most information about industries was produced by MITI. During the 1970s, a view prevailed that MITI had selected promising and strategic industries according to their growth potential: that is, their income elasticity of demand and rate of technical progress. This view was even endorsed by the US Department of Commerce (1972), which praised the positive role of the Japanese government in selecting strategic industries.

Although the coordinating role of the Japanese government is highly regarded in many circles, it seems doubtful it behaved with any coherent criteria for selecting industries. Rather, it seems that all new industries were welcomed from the viewpoint of maintaining a full-set type of industrial structure. This is because the *genkyoku*–industrial association system works well as a mechanism to distribute policy-induced rents only when such a structure is maintained. This is not to deny the effectiveness of industrial policy in mitigating market failures in such areas as infant industry protection.

Yonekura (1993) and Okimoto (1989) emphasize the role of Industrial associations as conduits of information between the government and the private sector. Industrial associations played the role of both gathering information within the industries and disseminating information from and about the government.

During the early part of the high-growth era, when there was a clear idea of what industrial structure should be, it seems undeniable that the *genkyoku*–industrial association system realized an efficient information flow between the government and the private sector. Promising industries were more or less known to everyone during the catch-up period because of the model of advanced countries, so it was sufficient for the government to fulfill the coordinating role from the viewpoint of efficient utilization of resources and avoidance of congestion. For this purpose the *genkyoku*–industrial association system was highly useful as a conduit of information flow.

It seems reasonable to conclude that, in terms of informational efficiency, the high-growth-period system did not provide any significant benefit. However, it also seems safe to assert that the system contributed significantly to economic growth through encouraging behavior of firms based on a long-term view, at least until the 1980s.

7.8 BEHAVIOR BASED ON A LONG-TERM VIEW

The Japanese are said to have routinely taken the long-term view. This generally refers to two things. First is the long-term economic horizon: Japanese firms are concerned more with long-term profit, or probably more precisely, scale maximization, than with short-term fluctuations in profits. Second is relationships: long-term relationships enable reputation-building, and hence reduce agency costs. These were contrasted to what was perceived as excessive concern by US companies with short-term signals such as stock prices (quarterly earnings) and a casual view of the durability of business relationships. The successes of Japan's high-growth era were related to this long-term view, and thus reinforced it.

Behavior based on a long-term outlook enabled firms to commit to capital-intensive production and relation-based investment by employees and suppliers. That is, it enhanced investment by workers in firm-specific skills and by suppliers in relation-based equipment and R&D. Such investment was the engine for process and product innovation by Japanese firms. To what degree it explains the growth rate during the high-growth era is not clear. However, when advanced technology was readily available, and demand was growing based on expectations of income growth, a virtuous circle of high investment and high efficiency was realized.

A long-term view was made possible by several, interrelated factors.

1. Price controls in the *genkyoku*–industrial association system induced firms to maximize scale of operation.
2. The government provided various institutions to finance long-term investments.
3. The risk-sharing relationship between banks and firms enabled mitigation of short-term business fluctuations.
4. Under the Japanese-style firm system, workers had incentives to invest in firm-specific skills.

7.8.1 Scale

When prices of both outputs and intermediate inputs are more or less under government control, as in the *genkyoku*–industrial association system, firms have an incentive to maximize their scale of operation as long as the cost function is decreasing. Maximization of scale requires firms to use a longer-term view than in the case of instantaneous profit maximization.

A typical example is the banking sector. During the high-growth period, deposit rates, the price of the main input of the industry, were controlled by the government, and banks, especially city banks, faced a large demand for loans, so the conditions for at least non-decreasing returns to scale prevailed. In fact, as confirmed in various studies (Tsutsui 1988; Royama and Iwane 1973), banking exhibited significant scale economies. These conditions induced banks to maximize scale.

Murakami (1984) emphasizes that firms under the *genkyoku*–industrial association system behaved so as to maximize their scale of operation because the long-term cost function 'as a social entity' tends to be decreasing when the degree of uncertainty is low.

7.8.2 Supplying Long-term Funds

Let us move on to the role of the mechanism to supply long-term funds. Investment funds during the high-growth era were supplied in two ways.

First was the rollover of short-term bank loans. This can cause maturity mismatch, but the accommodating supply of Bank of Japan credits mitigated the problem considerably.

Second was policy-based financing, including rationing of long-term loans and bonds. Empirical research indicates that the supply of long-term funds has significant effects on total factor productivity and the investment level. This hypothesis was emphasized by Teranishi (1982) and others. Horiuchi and Otaki (1987) conducted an econometric test of the hypothesis using causality analysis between a long-term funds index and total factor productivity by industry. They found significant causality from the former to the latter for some industries, and causality was strong during the period before the first oil shock (that is, before 1973).

Takei and Teranishi (1991) maintain that the supply of long-term funds improved total factor productivity through facilitating learning-by-doing, as well as formation of learning capability.

Arrow (1962) emphasizes the role of learning-by-doing in economic development by noting the technical progress achieved through the experience of production. Further, Stiglitz (1988) maintains that, for learning to be effective, the capability of learning needs to be established, or learning-by-learning is necessary. In other words, R&D investment and the experience of learning enhances the learning capability of a society. This experience, in turn, makes learning-by-doing production more fruitful.

Takei and Teranishi (1991) consider that learning capability is accumulated only through the time-consuming experience of learning. They tested a hypothesis that, in order to accomplish the learning process, the availability of long-term funds is crucial. In a panel-data regression using three-year average data for 10 industries, the ratio of long-term funds to total assets has significantly positive effects, together with the R&D variable, on the total factor productivity of industries during 1961–72. Table 7.3 shows the results.

Fukuda (2001) examines whether the mechanism of supplying long-term funds encouraged investment activity of firms through mitigating incentives for excessive liquidation by commercial banks. He finds it did for major heavy industries during 1972–84. Specifically, through a panel-data regression of the investment ratio of individual firms on the ratio of long-term funds to total debts, together with other control variables including Tobin's Q, Fukuda obtains significant positive coefficients for the long-term funds ratio.

Fukuda conducted similar regression analysis for two groups of firms – those belonging to keiretsu and those not – and found no significant difference between the groups. This suggests that the role of long-term funds is qualitatively different from rollover credits or relation-based credits related to the main bank system or keiretsu system.

Table 7.3 Regression of total factor productivity on long-term funds ratio

Independent variable	1961–72	1973–84
Constant	−0.19	−10.5
	(−0.15)	(−0.89)
Long-term funds ratio	2.72	0.13
	(2.05)	(0.15)
R&D index	71.31	14.60
	(3.52)	(2.69)
R^2	0.95	0.99
. use R^2	0.36	0.56
.	0.67	0.61

Notes: The dependent variable is the total factor productivity of industry. . is the autocorrelation coefficient of disturbance term stacked by three years. Figures in parenthesis are *t*-values.

The regression equation is $\ln TFP(t) = \alpha_0 + \alpha_1 LB(t) + \alpha_2 I(t) + \alpha_3 \ln L(t) + u$, where *TFP* is total factor productivity (estimated as $\ln(Q/L) - b\ln(K/L)$ using a Cobb–Douglas-type production function $Q(t) = T(t)K(t)^b L(t)^a$), *LB* is the long-term funds ratio (defined as the ratio of long-term borrowing and bonds to total assets), *L* is the number of employees, *K* is capital stock, and *I* is an R&D index (estimated as the ratio of R&D expenditure to sales). For details on the estimation method, see Kmenta (1971).

The industries are food, textiles, pulp and paper, chemicals, steel, non-ferrous metal, metal products, general machinery, electrical machinery and transportation machinery.

Source: Takei and Teranishi (1991).

7.8.3 Risk-sharing

One role of the main bank system was to contain the damage of a firm's financial distress by means of an implicit insurance contract. It is sometimes claimed that main banks adjusted the interest charged to client firms depending on the financial condition of firms: in bad times interest payments were lowered, which is compensated by higher interest payment in good times.

Horiuchi and Fukuda (1987) tested this mechanism through an examination of the co-movement of financial costs and operating profits for 63 companies in the chemical industry. They found a positive relationship only for one-third of the companies, and so concluded any risk-sharing mechanism of this type was not strong. Such risk-sharing behavior can be regarded as part of state-contingent interdependence between main banks and client firms. For example, Morck and Nakamura (1999) examined dispatching of bankers by main banks to the board of directors of client firms, and found dispatching is related to liquidity shortage.

Further, from the mid-1960s main banks were involved in bailing out financially distressed firms (Hoshi, Kashyap and Sharfstein 1990). When a client defaulted, its main bank bore the refinancing of debts proportionally more than its share in pre-distress debt. Moreover, main banks played a significant role in debt negotiation, organizing cooperative financing, sending in managers, and formulating and implementing recovery plans (Sheard 1994).

Risk-sharing between main banks and client firms is efficiency enhancing whenever it prevents bankruptcy of otherwise sound firms in a temporary liquidity crisis. However, during the 1990s banks were driven to fulfill risk-sharing obligations and were committed to bailing out customers at significant costs. Many of the firms, especially those in construction and real estate, were not sound.

The risk-sharing relation is based on an implicit contract and does not have any legal background (Ramseyer 1994). Because the contracts are not written, there is always a question of whether it is a sharing relationship on an equal-footing or a biased exploitative relationship between a bank and a firm. Through a comparison of firms that belonged to the six largest keiretsu and firms that did not, Nakatani (1984) points out that the former had lower profit rates and growth rates, and inferred that a main objective of keiretsu lies in risk-sharing in order to realize stable profit rates and a high wage level for employees. (Although this can be considered a positive aspect of keiretsu, Nakatani criticizes the system from the viewpoint of exclusiveness and fairness of competition.)

7.8.3.1 Sharing risks or exploitation?

Weinstein and Yafeh (1998) maintain that, during the period before liberalization of financial markets, the foregoing facts imply exploitation of client firms by main banks, and consequent inefficiency due to stifling of innovative activity by firms. In particular, they say the data show that the performance of main bank clients of bank-centered keiretsu was worse than that of other firms in the same industry. Clients were obliged to pay higher interest rates on non-bond debt and to adopt more capital-intensive technology. Both the profit rates and growth rates of main bank clients are lower, suggesting firms were forced to adopt projects preferred by banks, who are usually interested only in repayment of their loans with interest (that is, the lower tail of the probability distribution of a project's return). This was possible because, when alternative financial sources through capital markets are not available, banks tend to have monopoly power over client firms because they have substantial private information about the clients. Relatedly, Rajan (1992) points out that after an investment is undertaken, banks have control power through the threat of liquidation: banks can affect the level of effort by managers, extract information rents from firms, and even force firms to adopt projects desirable from the bank's viewpoint.

Two comments are in order about Weinstein and Yafeh's exploitation hypothesis.

First, their interpretation depends on the assumption that banks had a strong liquidation incentive and used liquidation as a threat against firms. This assumption does not necessarily hold during the high-growth era. The maturity-transformation risk of the banking sector was substantially reduced after 1962 when the Bank of Japan adopted an accommodating stance regarding credit supply to banks. In other words, although liquidity was a constraint on banks, it was not so much of a problem that firms would view it as a credible reason to liquidate a loan.

Second, it is important to note the characteristics of a catch-up economy. Confidence in high profits was high if long-term investments ran their course without being liquidated part-way. Corporate managers usually did not have to pay much attention to the possibility of alternative investment opportunities, because it was optimal for them simply to follow the model of the industrial structure of developed economies. Therefore, from the viewpoint of firms, long-term credit was definitely a desirable measure of financing and a secure rollover of short-term credits was vital. However, from the viewpoint of banks, the supply of long-term funds or a secure pledge regarding rollover had costs not only because of a maturity-mismatch risk but also because of possible moral hazard at the borrowing firm, such as loss of incentive to avoid bad states.

In such a situation, it is optimal for both banks and firms to be involved in risk-sharing regarding the profit from long-term capital formation. Banks obtained higher-than-market interest rates in exchange for the pledge to rollover short-term credits. Whenever firms fell into short-term financial distress, banks were ready to help prop them up. Firms would not pursue short-term, high-profit rates, but instead aim at long-term profits in cooperation with their main banks. Firms would invest heavily in capital-intensive technology to make the most of financing availability and try to obtain a competitive edge both domestically and internationally.

Phenomena such as high interests and high capital-intensity at keiretsu firms, pointed out by Yafeh and Weinstein (1998) as evidence of exploitation of clients by main banks, are also congruent with the risk-sharing hypothesis applied to a catch-up economy.

7.8.4 Worker Incentives

Japanese-style firms inherently behave with a long-term view. Because of the internal promotion system, managers are obliged to direct their attention to promotion opportunities, as well as job opportunities after retirement for peer employees and themselves. This provides a strong incentive to pursue scale maximization. In a similar context, Aoki (1988) shows that managers, as intermediators of the conflict of interests between stockholders and employees, pursue a higher growth rate of sales than the level that short-term stock price maximization would warrant. As to workers, life-time employment and a seniority wage system that included efficiency considerations provides a strong incentive for investment in firm-specific skills. Compared with the prewar period and other countries, equal treatment of blue- and white-collar workers gave the former a strong incentive to invest in firm-specific skills.

In the prewar Japanese economy, which was based on a market mechanism, the emphasis on the role of actual producers and relative neglect of investor rights resulted in emphasis on managerial skill, as is suggested by the high share of profits that went as bonus payments to managers, while in postwar Japan, emphasis was put on the production skill of workers. This is evidenced by the residual income right of workers in the form of bonus payments, and the low level of remuneration of corporate managers relative to line workers.

7.8.5 Relationship Investing

Let us now turn to the relationship among skill formation by workers, process innovation, and the growth mechanism. Koike (1997) argues that firm-specific skill by Japanese workers is characterized by the capacity to deal with unexpected outcomes in the production process. Such a capability was formed through on-the-job training (OJT), including rotation among various jobs. Such an OJT style was originally introduced during the late 1950s and 1960s to operate production processes efficiently in response to demand fluctuations.

Aoki (1995) calls firm-specific skills 'contextual skills', and says they were formed through the activity of small groups in which information is shared horizontally. Production by small groups diffused in the economy as ability-wages spread among firms (Gordon 1993).

Because the seniority wage system as a mixture of experience wages and livelihood wages emerged and was adopted widely, incentives for long-term employment were created, leading to the formation of firm-specific skills. Otaki (1994) claims that firm-specific skill formation necessitated a seniority wage system in order to facilitate recovering the costs of acquiring the skills.

Economic growth during the high-growth era owes much to technology imported from Western countries. When importing foreign technology, Japanese firms added process and product innovations, and realized high production efficiency. Such innovation is closely related to the seniority wage system and long-term employment system, which mitigated the hold-up problem and gives incentives to invest in firm-specific skill formation.

Relation-specific investment was extensively implemented among related firms (Asanuma 1989). Especially important was the product innovation realized by coordinating R&D activities among related firms.

In sum, relationship-based investment by both workers and suppliers enabled process and product innovation, and the prospect of such innovation and the consequent growth of quasi-rents is closely related to the behavior of Japanese firms based on a long-term outlook.

7.9 CONTROLLING COMPETITION

Regulation of competition results in prices that are higher than a competitive level. When competition in almost all industries is controlled in some way, both input and output prices are at higher-than-competitive levels for each industry. The level of output is thus a function of the controlled prices. It also follows that the value-added of each industry is controlled by the competition-preventing measures. Both input and output prices are affected by the policy-induced rents caused by the regulations. If the rents included in the output price are higher than the rents in input price, the value-added of the industry is higher than a level determined through perfect competition, and lower if the rents are less.

Table 7.4 shows the state of various competition-preventing measures for each industry in 1965 and 1990. In 1990, 14.1 per cent of value-added in manufacturing was insulated from competition by some measures, and 25.9 per cent of total protected value-added was in manufacturing. All production is under some kind of regulation not only in public utilities (electricity, gas and water), which are highly regulated in most countries, but also in mining and construction. Although we do not touch upon this here, almost all the regulations are justified by special legislations. Note that from 1965 to 1990 the share of protected value-added in agriculture increased by 1.4 percentage points. Political importance and protection are highly correlated in most countries, and that is the case here as well.

Table 7.4 Regulation on industries

Industry	value-added (1990, billion yen)	Percentage of regulated areas in value-added of the industry[1]	
		1965	1990
Agriculture, fishery and forestry	10,219	85.7	87.1
Mining	1,145	100.0	100.0
Construction	41,131	100.0	100.0
Manufacturing	115,395	23.4	14.1
Wholesale and retail trade[2]	57,481	–	–
Financial insurance and security	21,963	100.0	100.0
Real estate	42,004	2.6	7.5
Transportation and communication	27,510	98.8	97.3
Electricity, gas, water, and heat	10,782	100.0	100.0
Services[3]	101,672	72.8	55.6
Public services	14,487	0.0	0.0
Others	2,330	0.0	0.0

Notes: Industry value-added is given to indicate the relative importance of industries.
[1] Regulated areas imply commodities and services in the input–output table on which any kind of regulatory legislation exists, so that changes in the content of the legislation do not affect the percentage.
[2] Regulations are placed with respect to the size of traders as well as commodity traded.
[3] Includes education, medical and welfare.

Source: Hashimoto, Hasegawa and Miyajima (1998). Original data were calculated by the Economic Planning Agency.

The degree of regulation in transportation and communication is high at 97.3 per cent. Part of the reason is that these were overwhelming government-owned activities at the time. Privatization of the railroads and telephone network has occurred since, but as public services the industries remain highly regulated.

The various regulatory measures established through the years are implemented by the *genkyoku* with the help of the industrial associations. Table 7.5 outlines the number and nature of the associations.

Table 7.5 Classification of industrial associations, 1996

	All	Nation-wide
Total associations	15,391	3,127
By sector		
Primary	1,524	341
Manufacturing	4,433	1,793
Service	9,434	993
By legal status[1]		
Voluntary	9,655	1,987
Approved	2,223	793
Based on the special laws of cooperatives	3,513	347

Note: There are two *types* of associations: core and umbrella. Core associations are the central group for a narrowly defined industry at either the national or regional level, and have firms as members. Umbrella associations are composed of several core associations on a national level or in a more broadly defined industry, that is, they have other associations as their primary members, and firms are members through those associations. It is umbrella groups that provide information on the industry as a whole to member firms and to ministries.

[1] An association assumes full legal status when it registers and obtains an 'approval license' from the regulating ministry, except for those based on the special laws of cooperatives. An approved association is either a corporation (*shadan hôjin*) or a foundation (*zaidan hôjin*).

Source: Schaede (2000), from data reported to the Japan Fair Trade Commission.

In some cases, such as the formation of a cartel, the role of industrial associations is particularly important in coordinating firm behavior in the industry, quite often utilizing government regulatory functions. Schaede (2000) provides a detailed analysis on this through an institutional and legal investigation in the role of Japan's Fair Trading Commission in enforcing the anti-monopoly law and the self-regulating behavior of industries led by industrial associations.

7.9.1 Trade Restrictions

Until 1977, many products were protected from competition by foreign products. Trade liberalization began in Japan in 1960 when an Overall Plan to Liberalize Foreign Trade (*Bôeki Kawase Jiyûka Keikaku Taikô*) was announced by the Cabinet after its June 24 meeting. Under the plan, MITI consulted with 217 industrial associations and drew up a detailed schedule for trade liberalization regarding 230 tradable items. Table 7.6 shows the process. Almost all formal trade restrictions were abolished by 1977. At that time, 27 items were still under quota systems, mainly agriculture-related products.

Table 7.6 Step-wise implementation of trade liberalization

Year	Percentage share of liberalized goods	Number of goods still under quota system AIQ	IQ	Main goods liberalized during the year
1960	44			Coffee beans, movie films
1961	70			Raw cotton, instant coffee, watches, radios
1962	88	254		stockings, sheet glass, fountain pens, crude oil
1963	92	192	155	Bananas, crude sugar
1964	93	162	123	Lead, zinc, kaoliang (forage), generators
1965	93	161	122	Passenger cars
1966	93	167	124	Cocoa, streptomycin
1968	93	164	121	Perfume, cream
1969	93	161	118	Brandy
1970	94	133	90	Wine, margarine, machine tools, generators (more than 400 KWH), chassis with engines, 400 KWH), woollen goods
1971	95	87	40	Pork, candy, tea
1972	95	86	33	Ham, bacon, sugar, heavy and light oil
1973			31	Electric cash registers, calculators, some fishery products
1974			29	Malt, integrated circuits (more than 200 elements)
1975			27	Computers
1977			27	Tobacco

Note: IQ indicates the number of tradable items still under import quota for each year. AIQ shows the number of tradable items for which imports were formally rationed but flexibly approved on application.

Source: Yamazawa (1984).

7.10 MECHANISM OF INCOME DISTRIBUTION

It is not easy to give a coherent theoretical analysis of the mechanism of income distribution. The theory must capture the complicated interaction among the information and negotiating power of *genkyoku* and of industrial associations, the role of *zokugiin* (special-interest politicians), the structure of internal labor markets, and so on. Moreover, income flow is influenced not only by the policy-induced rents caused by competition-prevention policies implemented by *genkyoku*, but also by information rents obtained by the bureaucracy and main banks, as well as quasi-rents caused by the specific investment of workers. Further, as a more fundamental element, income distribution is influenced by macroeconomic demand and supply in labor markets. The wages of smaller firms, in particular, are strongly influenced by market forces.

That said, the high-growth-period system significantly affected income distribution through government intervention in competitive conditions of industries via the *genkyoku*–industrial association system and the wage-determination system based on internal labor markets and *shuntô*. The mechanics of this are fairly straightforward. Before analyzing them, let us review each of the two features.

7.10.1 *Shuntô*

The *shuntô* system determined the wage level for each industry. More exactly, through the *shuntô* process, the standard wage (*sôba chingin*), or standard base-up rate for each industry, was determined. Given the previous year's wage level, determining the current year's base-up rates is synonymous with determining the current year's wage level. At first, the standard wage was determined in key industries at major firms (such as the five largest companies) called 'pattern-setters'. From 1955 to 1980 steel was the key industry; after 1981 the key industries included such industries as electric machinery, automobiles, shipbuilding and chemicals. Then the wage level of industries related to the key industries through the input–output structure was determined. For example, wage levels in metal industries were determined in reference to wages in the steel industry; wages in pharmaceuticals and paint in reference to basic chemicals; and so on. Further, wages of smaller firms were determined using the wage level of large firms in the same industry as standard wages, although wages of smaller firms were more significantly influenced by labor market demand and supply conditions.

Although the standard wage set at pattern-setters and adjusted through labor union federations such as *Sôhyô* was the standard wage for each industry, wage bargaining was carried out at each company (Koike 1991, p. 208). In other words, once the standard base-up rate was settled for an industry, each firm in the industry determined its own base-up rate considering its profit condition. In many industries, such as steel, firms in the same industry chose the same base-up rate (*yoko narabi*), while in some industries, such as automobiles, wages differed substantially among firms depending on their profit condition. The wage rate for each worker in a firm was determined in an internal labor market largely on the basis of a seniority system.

7.10.2 The *Genkyoku*–Industrial Association System's Role

The MITI *genkyoku* listed in Table 7.1 and the de facto *genkyoku* of other ministries controlled competitive conditions through various measures.

First, they controlled the cartel behavior of each industry, especially industries composed of smaller firms. The policy was based on the Stabilization of Small and Medium Enterprises Act (*Tokutei Chûshô Kigyô Antei Rinji Sochi Hô*) promulgated in 1953. Following the 1953 revision of the anti-monopoly law to allow cartel behavior in the event of depression and for the purpose of rationalization, smaller firms could organize adjustment cooperatives in order to adjust production and invest in equipment. Protective policy by means of competition-prevention measures was also included in the 1956 Department Store Act (*Hyakkaten Hô*) and the 1959 Retail Commerce Act (*Kouri Shôgyô Chôsei Tokubetsu Sochi Hô*), which regulated large-scale firms in retail trade as regards size, hours, and the like.

Second, *genkyoku* intervened in capacity and equipment adjustment in declining industries.

Textiles are a typical case. The Textile Manufacturing Equipment Act (*Sen'i Kôgyô Setsubi Rinji Sochi Hô*), promulgated in 1956 just before liberalization of raw cotton imports, required the registering and scrapping of redundant spinning machines, which were purchased with government funds. A 1964 act (*Sen'i Kôgyô Setsubi to Rinji Sochi Hô*) introduced equipment adjustment on the principle of scrap-and-build. Then, to cope with structural depression, in 1967 the Structural Improvement of Specific Textile Manufacturing Industries Act (*Tokutei Sen'i Kôgyô Kôzô Kaizen Rinji Shochi Hô*) stipulated comprehensive measures such as scrapping excess equipment, modernizing remaining equipment, adjusting firm size, and the like.

To cope with declining industries after the oil crises and yen appreciation, a series of special laws was introduced: the 1973 Improving Industrial Structure Act (*Tokutei Sangyô Kôzô Kaizen Rinji Shochi Hô*), the 1978 Stabilizing Special Declining Industries Act (*Tokuan Hô, Tokutei Fukyô Sangyô Antei Rinji Shochi Hô*), and the 1983 Smooth Restructuring of Industrial Structure Act (*Sangyô Kôzô*

Tenkan Enkatsu-ka Rinji Sochi Hô). These facilitated scrapping excess refinery capacity through subsidization (specifically, tariff exemption and employment adjustment). Aluminum refining during the 1980s was forced to contract because high Japanese electricity costs made the industry globally uncompetitive. Partly owing to employment absorption by related *keiretsu* firms, the aluminum companies successfully accomplished a quick withdrawal – lasting about five years (1978–83).

Third, with respect to new industries, *genkyoku* intervened for the sake of infant-industry protection. For example, in 1951 the MITI Science Bureau announced a policy of promoting the petrochemical industry. In 1954, a deliberative council on the technology of the petrochemical industry was formed, with its main role being to control new entry. In the same year, a petrochemical industrial association was organized, through which the MITI Heavy Industry Bureau, a *genkyoku*, began to apply various preferential measures.

7.10.3 The Mechanics

The *shuntô* system and the *genkyoku*–industrial association system together functioned as a mechanism to determine the value-added of each industry and to distribute it between profits and wages. That is, because the system's competition-preventive policies yield policy-rents, the value-added determined in this way is higher than a competitive level in industries with stricter regulations, and lower than a competitive level in industries with milder regulations. The *shuntô* system helped determine distribution of the rents.

For such a mechanism to function smoothly at the national level, internal labor markets and immobility of labor are indispensable. In addition, the following zero-sum condition needs to be satisfied. An increase in the product price of an industry causes an increase in the production costs of other industries that utilize the product as an input. Conversely, an increase in the product price of other industries that produce inputs for this industry causes an increase in the production costs of the industry. An industry whose output prices are affected more favorably than its input prices obtains positive policy-induced rents, and an industry whose input prices rise more than its output prices as a result of a competition-preventing policy obtains negative rents. The zero-sum condition means that the sum of policy-induced rents is zero in the whole production sector in an economy.

The zero-sum condition is necessary for the social approval of the mechanism of lobbying in pursuit of inter-industrial interests. This is because the condition means that the income-distributive effects of industrial policy are contained within the production sector, without any significant spillover effects to economic agents outside the sector (that is, without causing any serious complaints from other members of society). That, in turn, means negotiations through the *genkyoku*–industrial association system are nothing but a hunt for rights and concessions between the government and interest groups, and such interest-group behavior is built into the system.

During the high-growth era the zero-sum requirement was satisfied because of three conditions.

First was the full-set style industrial structure, established during the war period. The term 'full-set' industrial structure was coined by Seki (1993). Its origin is in a concept of *keiretsu* behavior developed by Miyazaki (1966): each *keiretsu* sought to establish a firm in each new industry so as to have 'one-set' of industries in the *keiretsu*. Because everything from clothing to aircraft, and all the necessary intermediate products, were produced in the country within this industrial structure, all the effects due to changes in competitive conditions are contained within the country, so that the effects on macro variables such as the balance of payments and the exchange rate were kept at a minimum.

The second condition is that consumers did not complain about the income-distribution process. Consumers purchased consumption goods from the production sector but sold nothing to the sector. Households do sell labor service to the production sector and through wages thereby received policy-induced rents. However, we assume the decision process regarding the supply of labor was independent of the decision regarding purchase of consumption goods. Even if producers of consumption goods were treated favorably in interest group politics, and prices of consumption goods went up, the system could be maintained in as much as consumers were not vocal and did not complain.

The third condition was that the behavior of *genkyoku* did not influence macroeconomic variables because, in the early postwar years, the Budget Bureau of the Ministry of Finance maintained independence from the distributive conflicts among industries. This meant it was rare for subsidies and preferential tax treatment to be targeted at particular industries. When *genkyoku* negotiated with related interest groups, the industrial associations, they had to resort to tools unrelated to macro budget conditions, namely regulations on competitive conditions.

In the 1980s the first two conditions ceased to be satisfied for two reasons.

First, the increase in the trade surplus *vis-à-vis* the United States triggered intense criticism against the full-set industrial structure, which arguably ignores comparative advantage. The flying geese hypothesis, that leading industries follow a product cycle, is a characteristic of prewar Japan. It is important to note that this hypothesis does not apply to the postwar high-growth era when the international division of labor based on comparative advantage was negated by maintaining a full-set industrial structure. The United States escalated its offensive against what it deemed non-tariff trade barriers. Although there had been trade disputes between Japan and the US regarding individual industries such as textiles, steel and automobile since the 1960s, during the 1980s the disputes became comprehensive and were concerned with issues regarding overall industrial structure and macroeconomic issues.

Second, the significant yen appreciation after the 1985 Plaza Agreement brought to light the considerable disparity between international and domestic prices of consumption goods. Consumers, led by a middle class with a new consumption orientation, became critical of the excessive protection of consumption-goods producers. This expanded into severe criticism of the competition-prevention measures widely employed by the bureaucracy. These points are discussed in detail in the next chapter.

The distributive game of the *genkyoku*–industrial association system and *shuntô* system was carried out with consideration of the international competitiveness of product prices. Sako (1997) clarifies this in an interesting analysis of *hasshakon*. Established in the mid-1970s after the first oil shock, this was a forum for coordinating wage negotiation among representatives of four major labor union federations (steel, shipbuilding, automobiles and electric machinery) and managers from the eight major companies in the four industries. (*Hasshakon* translates as eight-company meeting.) In the negotiation, wages were determined through careful consideration of inter-industrial input–output relationships so as to minimize the detrimental effects of wage hikes on the international competitiveness of industries.

7.10.4 Agriculture as an Example

The agriculture sector provides a typical example of the influence on income distribution exerted by industrial associations. The sector intensified its political ties with conservative political parties in the 1950s, and its political leverage was enhanced through the vote-mobilizing mechanism of agricultural cooperatives (Hiwatari 1991). The cooperatives, as the powerful industrial associations of the agricultural sector, opposed trade liberalization of rice, utilized a food-control system as an income-compensating mechanism, and transformed the structural reform program of the government into a generous subsidy-distribution system in the rural sector.

In particular, the conversion of the rice-price determination system from a parity system to a production-cost income-compensation system (*seisanhi shotoku hoshô hôshiki*) in 1960 is worth noting. This changed the rice-price determination from a price linked to the cost of purchased inputs (fertilizer and agricultural machines) to a price linked to the labor-input of farmers valued at the wages of urban workers. As a result, not only did the consumer price of rice become higher than the international price, the producer price became higher than the consumer price, leading to a huge deficit in the special account of the food control system.

The strong political power of the agricultural sector is not specific to Japan. Honma (1994) conducted regression analysis on panel data for 14 countries and eight years (carried out at five-year intervals). He concludes that as the share of agriculture declines in the process of industrialization, the political influence of the sector increases, and international competition tends to be prevented (that is, protection increases).[2]

The political power of the *genkyoku*–industrial association system depends not only on the political power of industrial associations but also on the *genkyoku* (bureaucratic) side. For example, developmental bureaucrats might be motivated to promote industries that are receptive because of unstable conditions. Thus, from an examination of MITI policy toward high-tech industries, Okimoto (1989) argues that the level of government intervention is high with respect to industries in the initial phase of growth, as well as in the declining phase, but is low for other industries. Similarly, Aoki (1999) argues that the *genkyoku*–industrial association system (bureau pluralism in his terminology) functions as a system of income transfer from growing industries to declining ones such as agriculture, small and medium firms, construction, and so on.

7.10.5 Effects on Value-added

The income distributive mechanism through the *genkyoku*–industrial association system had systematic effects on the difference in value-added among industries. In particular, the system seems to have exerted significant effects on the competitive conditions of industries. As Okimoto and Aoki suggest, the political power of declining industries, and of the indigenous sector with its small firms, seems to be stronger than other industries.

The system's effects on the manufacturing sector are shown in Tables 7.7 and 7.8. Let us examine the period 1965–70 as typical of the high-growth era. Based on the small standard deviation and coefficient of variation in Table 7.8, the growth rates of the value-added of the different industries are quite uniform: all are in the 12 to 17 per cent range, except for food and general machinery. This uniformity suggests an inverse correlation between the growth rate of labor productivity and the growth rate of the product price. This suggests that, within the manufacturing sector, the difference in productivity growth is offset by changes in product prices. Possible scenarios are as follows.

1. As an industry matures, defined as a decline in the rate of growth of productivity, the industry can utilize its accumulated political power to lobby for competition-preventing measures, so that the product price is increased.
2. When an industry has strong lobbying power, or the bureaus in charge of the industry (*genkyoku*) are intent on protective measures, competition-preventing policy results in a higher rate of increase in product price for the industry. Because the industry is accustomed to protection, efforts to improve productivity are reduced.

Whatever the scenario is, the table suggests that, during the high-growth era, light and indigenous industries such as food, textiles and ceramics were in a less competitive environment, and the rate of increase in their product prices were higher, than modern heavy industries such as steel, non-ferrous metals and machinery.

Beason and Weinstein (1996) claim that the industrial policy of postwar Japan consistently targeted declining industries: the ex-post growth rates of industries are negatively correlated with share of Japan Development Bank loans in the total debt of the industry, or with the degree of preferential tax treatment. A similar bias toward low-growth industries is found with respect to tariff protection and subsidy rates.[3]

Teranishi (1994b) finds that during 1961–70 the ratio of policy-based financing to equipment investment was very high for declining industries (47.9 per cent for agriculture, 39.9 per cent for mining, and 50.9 per cent for marine transportation), while it is clearly low for growing industries (3.6 per cent for steel, 7.1 per cent for chemicals, and 9.5 per cent for machinery). It must be noted that emphasis on low-growth and declining industries is a characteristic only of the high-growth period. Before then, and especially during the period of rehabilitation following the war, industrial policy, especially policy-based financing, lent great weight to industries considered key to re-

Table 7.7 Value-added, price, and productivity for industries

	1960–65				1965–70				1970–73			
	(1)	(2)	(3)	(4)	(1)	(2)	(3)	(4)	(1)	(2)	(3)	(4)
Food	9.9	3.3	6.6	98	8.7	3.7	5.0	87	14.7	6.5	8.2	87
Textiles	9.3	6.9	2.4	100	15.9	9.8	6.1	100	25.7	10.5	15.2	100
Paper & Pulp	12.5	7.7	4.8	104	14.0	13.8	0.2	92	23.3	11.6	11.7	102
Chemical	11.2	10.2	1.0	141	12.8	15.6	–2.8	121	20.1	11.5	8.6	116
Ceramics	9.9	7.8	2.1	112	14.2	11.0	3.2	105	20.2	10.2	10.0	100
Steel	8.7	10.8	–2.1	169	16.8	17.5	–0.7	135	20.3	13.4	6.9	121
Non-ferrous metal	9.4	8.9	0.5	139	13.7	13.5	0.2	124	24.3	12.9	11.4	128
Metal products	11.5	–	–	124	15.2	14.9	0.3	102	16.9	11.9	5.0	97
General machinery	9.6	3.7	5.9	129	18.3	15.7	2.6	125	14.5	12.5	2.0	128
Electric machinery	4.6	6.2	–1.6	171	15.9	20.6	–4.7	152	14.3	17.6	–3.3	133
Transportation machinery	10.9	–	–	167	14.8	13.6	1.2	138	14.1	12.0	2.1	110

Notes:
Figures in columns headed 1, 2, and 3 are per cent; columns headed 4 are indices with textiles as 100.
(1) = rate of growth of value-added per employee
(2) = rate of growth of (physical) labor productivity
(3) = (1) – (2) = rate of growth of product price
(4) = ratio of long-term funds (bond, long-term borrowings from financial institutions, and equity) to total fixed assets. Index with textile as 100

Source: Teranishi (1982) statistical appendix.

Table 7.8 Value-added per employee

	1960–65	1965–70	1970–73
Mean growth rate (annual average, in %)	9.77	14.60	18.95
Standard deviation	1.96	2.48	4.30
Coefficient of variation (= standard deviation/mean)	0.20	0.17	0.23
Growth rate correlation coefficient (see text)	−0.59	−0.83	−0.73

Note: For each set of years, the mean growth rate entry here is the mean of the growth rates given for the 11 industries in Table 7.7, column 1.

covery such as electricity, steel, and fertilizer (chemicals) (Teranishi 1994b).

While policy-based loans were directed to declining industries, long-term private funds, such as long-term loans by city banks and long-term credit banks, corporate bonds and equities, were supplied mainly to growing heavy industries during the high-growth era. Both private funds and policy-based lending of government financial institutions are included in the long-term funds of Table 7.7. Because the absolute size of the former is far larger than the latter, the long-term funds ratio is higher for growing industries in spite of the bias of policy-based funds toward declining industries.

There is a strong correlation between the growth rate of productivity and the ratio of long-term funds to fixed assets. The correlation coefficient is 0.45 during 1960–65, 0.78 during 1965–70, and 0.83 during 1970–73. This suggests that long-term equipment funds were concentrated in growing industries as a whole, and especially heavy and chemical industries. In other words, they were preferentially treated with regard to the rationing of long-term funds compared with declining industries. Rationing of long-term funds was most pronounced during the 1960s, and became ineffective after the mid-1970s (Teranishi 1982). This helped offset the fact that heavy industries faced less-protected and more-competitive markets.

7.11 INCOME DISTRIBUTION

Let us discuss two important consequences of the working of the *genkyoku*–industrial association system, combined with *shuntô* and internal labor markets, on the income distributional aspect of the socio-economic system of the high-growth era. These are the remarkable equity of income distribution and, relatedly, the huge relative size of the middle class.

7.11.1 Significant Equality

Japan has remarkable equality of income distribution. As Table 4.13 (p. 117) shows, Gini coefficients of income distribution in postwar Japan are consistently lower than those in the prewar period, and declined until around 1980. A similar trend can be found with respect to wage differentials between large and small firms and among industries.

Table 7.9 show the ratio of the wage level of firms with 10–99 employees to the wage level of firms with more than 1,000 employees. The differential by firm size tended to decline until the mid-1970s.

Table 7.9 Wage differential by firm size

Year	Fixed, in cash	Variable[1]	Total
1960	59	—	—
1965	76	37	46
1970	78	44	52
1975	76	47	53
1980	75	44	50
1985	72	41	47

Notes: Wages refer to average wages paid in cash by firms with more than 30 employees. Entries are the wages of firms with 10–99 employees as a percentage of firms with 1,000 and more employees.
[1] Includes bonus payments.

Source: Nihon Tokei Kyokai (1988b, Table 16-10).

Table 7.10 shows the ratio of the wage levels of the three industries with the consistently lowest wage levels relative to the industry with the highest during 1955–85. The ratios show consistent rising trends until 1980. It is worth emphasizing that the decline in wage differential was more persistent in the inter-industrial comparison than in the firm-size case. Wage differentials between agriculture and non-agriculture also declined sharply in the postwar period (Figure 4.1, p.118).

As the equalization of income distribution proceeded, the perception of the people underwent significant changes. Almost the entire population considers itself middle class (*ichioku sô chûryû-ka*). From 1958 to 1973 the percentage describing itself as lower or lower-middle income dropped from 49.0 to 27.6 per cent. In 1973, 90.2 per cent called itself middle income. This peaked at 91.3 per cent in 1979 (Imada 1989, statistical appendix). Table 7.11 presents further survey data on self-perceptions of income-class.

Table 7.10 Wage differential by industry, 1955–85

	Construction	Apparel	Trade, Dining[1]
1955	54	32	66
1960	59	33	64
1965	66	37	61
1970	67	38	64
1975	66	40	68
1980	75	41	71
1985	72	38	64

Note: Wages refer to average wages paid in cash by firms with more than 30 employees. Entries are the wages in the listed industry as a percentage of the wages in the public utility industry (electricity, gas, heat supply, and water).

According to the Monthly Labor Statistics (*Maitsuki Kinrô Tôkei Chôsa*), the time series of the wage level of firms (*jigyô-sho*) with more than 30 employees indicates that, among the 21 manufacturing industries covered, wage levels in public utilities are consistently the highest. Those in construction, wholesale and retail trade, eating and drinking places, and apparel have usually been the lowest.

[1] Wholesale and retail trade, eating and drinking places.

Source: Nihon Tokei Kyokai (1988b, Table 16-8).

Table 7.11 Percentage distribution of self-assessed income class

	1958	1973	1979	1987
Middle (all levels)	72.0	90.2	91.3	89.6
Lower and lower-middle	49.0	27.6	27.0	36.9
Detail				
Upper	0.2	0.6	0.6	0.6
Upper-middle	3.0	6.8	8.5	7.1
Middle-middle	37.0	61.3	60.6	52.5
Lower-middle	32.0	22.1	22.2	30.0
Lower	17.0	5.5	4.8	6.9
Unidentified	10.8	3.7	3.3	2.9

Source: Imada (1989) based on public opinion surveys on living conditions conducted by the prime minister's office.

This corresponds to the phenomenon of increasing status inconsistency in the cluster analysis of the SSM (social stratification and mobility) survey. (Status consistency is the state where all indices comprising the class status of an individual are at the same level. Status inconsistency means different indices have different levels.)

Defining social class as upper or lower using four indices (education, income, occupation and prestige), those in the upper category in all four indices belong to the 'consistent upper class', and similarly for a 'consistent lower class'. In postwar Japan, the percentage of 'inconsistent class' (the percentage excluding 'consistent upper class' and 'consistent lower class') rose significantly from 1955 to 1975, while the percentages of 'consistent lower class' declined steadily. Data are in Table 7.12.

Table 7.12 Percentage of population with 'inconsistent class', 1955–85

Year	Tominaga series	Imada series
1955	45.1	48.2
1965	57.6	59.5
1975	60.4	65.2
1985	—	69.6

Note: See the text for an explanation of 'inconsistent class'. Although the two researchers have somewhat different numbers, the trends are the same. Thus, both show an approximately one-third increase in those with 'inconsistent class' from 1955 to 1975.

Source: Tominaga (1988) and Imada (1989).

Imada (1989) finds that the correlation coefficients between education and income, prestige and income, and education and occupation all declined from 1955 to 1975, another indicator of status inconsistency.

Defining social mobility as the movement of individuals among jobs with different status, Erickson and Goldthorpe (1992) examined nine European countries, the United States, Australia and Japan during the 1970s. They find structural change in the sense of inter-generational mobility from routine laboring positions toward professional, administrative and managerial positions in all the countries except Japan. Whether this is related to the difference in the government–private-sector interface in Japan and in other countries is an interesting topic for future study.

7.11.2 The Middle Class

Until the 1920s, the middle class was composed of small and medium landlords, the larger self-cultivating farmers, merchants, and industrialists in local economies, plus government bureaucrats, teachers, and the like. From the 1920s, as more people had attained higher levels of education, a new group became middle class: white-collar workers at government bureaus and large firms. (The relative size of the new middle class in the prewar period is estimated in Hara (1979), and its role and behavior are examined in Ito (1993).)

As social and income equalization proceeded in postwar Japan, the phenomenon of the 'whole population becoming middle class' emerged as people originally classified as 'consistent lower class' collectively experienced social ascent (Tominaga 1988). As part of this huge middle class, the prewar new middle class of managers and administrators of large companies plus bureaucrats expanded and transformed into a central power of the socio-economy. They played the role of leaders in high-growth-period society as self-conscious proponents of the system, and came to embody the social norms of the society during the period.

Considering that promotion of individuals in companies, growth of companies, and an expansion of industries are organically interrelated and have an instrumental value for the development of the socio-economy, the new middle class found social values in hierarchical promotion within companies. Economic groups such as the Federation of Economic Organizations (Keidanren), an organization of large firms, behaved as top leaders of the socio-economy, actively voicing their views not only about economic, but also socio-cultural matters. It was in such a context that the behavior of industrial associations, maximizing the interests of individual industries, as well as the government–private-sector interface based on the *genkyoku*–industrial association system, attained justification in society.

The full-set industrial structure of the postwar period was born in response to the shock of World War I and was fully organized in the industrial restructuring during World War II. As such, it almost completely neglected the logic of comparative-cost advantage. An important reason why such an artificialness, that is, neglect of comparative advantage, went without serious criticism, or even much notice, during the high-growth era lies in the fact that value-added and wage rates, and hence profit rates, of industries were adjusted not in markets but rather within the framework of the *genkyoku*–industrial association system, so as to keep all industries alive and sharing the fruits of overall economic growth. As a result, an illusion that all industries could have international competitiveness persisted for some time.

The bureaucracy tended to function in order to maintain the interests of existing industries. Further, political power, expressed as vote-mobilizing power, is usually stronger for declining and mature industries than for growing and new industries.

NOTES

1. In Japan, where stockholders have *de jure* control over dividends (the amount needs to be approved by shareholder vote), the difference between internal funds and stock is not so large. In such a case, the major difference in agency cost might be between bank borrowing and other funds (internal funds and equity), rather than between internal funds and other funds (equity and bank borrowing). To take this point into consideration, it is necessary to conduct a regression analysis taking the sum of internal funds and equity as an independent variable.
2. With a nominal protection rate on rice, defined as the difference between the producer price and the international price, as the dependent variable, Honma shows that the share of agriculture in GDP, representing the political power of the agricultural sector, has a significant positive coefficient, and the square of the share has a significant negative coefficient. Other independent variables include the comparative advantage of agriculture, the international terms of trade, per capita agricultural GDP, and a dummy representing regional economic alliances.
3. It should be noted that industrial policy in advanced democratic countries has traditionally been as much or more about delaying the sunset than hastening the sunrise of industries. This reflects political realities. A multi-country study of this, which includes Japan, is Patrick (1991).

8. Decline of the high-growth-period economic system

The 1980s witnessed a sea-change in the exogenous conditions that had provided the framework of Japan's economic systems for a century. The catch-up process had been completed. Rapid economic growth had started in neighboring countries. Economic thought on the relationship between government and market was undergoing a drastic change, giving birth to a worldwide movement toward marketization of planned economies, privatization of state enterprises, and deregulation. The movement toward markets was reinforced by evolution in market mechanisms attributable to developments in information technology.

The changes had already occasioned adaptations by the high-growth-period system: administrative reforms accompanied by privatization and deregulation, reform of corporate governance followed by unwinding of cross-shareholdings and emphasis on shareholder control rights, increased mobility in labor markets (especially with respect to middle-aged and older workers and new graduates), and intervention by *zokugiin* politicians in the mechanism of adjusting inter-industrial conflicts.

But even with the adaptations, the high-growth-period system was becoming costly in terms of both economic efficiency and political decision-making. Moreover, the social value system that emphasized high economic growth was weakening.

This chapter looks at the changing nature of relationships in Japan's economy and society. The changes were both caused by and affected the high-growth system. This is especially true of the financial sector, so the limitations of bank-centered finance and deregulation receive considerable attention. Ultimately the changes have led to higher political and economic costs, especially as regards the mechanism of the government–private-sector interface. Simply, the populace shifted toward consumerism from acceptance of a producer-oriented system. Although the mechanism of the interface remains largely in place, it is dysfunctional.

8.1 THE CHANGED ENVIRONMENT

Completion of catch-up and changes in the nature of technological development (particularly the role of information technology) increased uncertainty regarding which new technologies and new industries to develop.

During the high growth of the catch-up phase, changes in industrial structure and even technology were reasonably foreseeable. Design of the industrial structure merely followed the experience of developed countries. The role of government was simply coordinating the import of advanced technology and industries, and the private sector was willing to delegate such a role to the government. Because Japan had maintained a full-set type of industrial organization since the World War I period, there was no need for choice among new industries. All that was needed was the sequencing of transplanting them. Such a practice faced serious difficulties as Japan reached the cutting edge in the 1980s.

Almost simultaneous with achieving catch-up, a fundamental change occurred in the nature of technological development. The speed of new product development increased, as did the speed of diffusion of new technologies and new products (Nihon Ginko 2001). This has given rise to competition in global markets among producers from all over the world. Much of the change relates to information technology (IT), both as an industry in its own right and (more importantly) as a tool used by other industries.

It was inevitable for the government–private-sector interface based on the *genkyoku*–industrial association system to face serious difficulties under these conditions. Both economic and political costs have resulted. Three cases of how the *genkyoku*–industrial association system became dysfunctional are examined in the following sections.

8.2 THE CHANGING NATURE OF RELATIONSHIPS

The high-growth-period system relied heavily on relationship-based investment and knowledge capital among people, firms and banks. However, the direction of technological change in both manufacturing and finance tends to downplay such institutions. Market-oriented economic relationships are more *ad hoc* and impersonal, and less committed. Japanese firms are obliged either to reduce their overall relationship-intensity or to change the nature of their relationships. The retreat of traditional relationship-based transactions and the rise of arm's-length transactions in both manufacturing and financial technology have so far undermined the high-growth-period economic system.

8.2.1 The Effects of Commodified Products

In manufacturing, there has been increasing modularity of products. Modularity is an architecture of design, first seen extensively in computer products, in which complex systems are decomposed into parts called modules with standardized interfaces allowing them to work together. Innovation can be carried out with respect to each module, as well as to the total system.

Modularity has two main advantages: it has economy of specialization because it enables coordination of jobs at each module (Aoki 2002); it facilitates response to uncertainties efficiently because the reduction in interdependence and flexibility of connection among modules enlarges the manageable range of complicated outcomes (Baldwin and Clark 2000).

Modularity has come to have widespread impact as IT develops. Even in industries such as automobiles, which previously were considered unsuitable for modularity-based production because of the necessity to adjust parts by human hand, modularity-based technology is penetrating in the areas of designing and component supply (Fujimoto 2002).

The technology change related to modularity has come to have significant effects on economic institutions.

First, it tends to promote specialization of production units, so that scale-maximizing firm behavior by means of diversification and subsidiaries might become inefficient.

Second, it can reduce the importance of relation-specific investment among firms based on supplier relationships because more parts tend to be acquired through out-sourcing in arm's-length transactions.

Third, it can reduce the role of firm-specific skills because an increased degree of modularity implies a decrease in the need for adjustment by human hands in the production process (Chuma 2002).

8.2.2 Changing Nature of Financial Markets

There is an increased diversity of financial products as a result of unbundling traditional products into components that can be rebundled into new products. The driving force has been to satisfy a wider range of investor preferences. Product offerings are more tailored to varying investor preferences, but are more impersonally offered – often via computer or telephone – to a large public, rather than through a person-to-person client relationship. This practice (technology) was born during the 1970s, and mainly developed in the United States during the 1980s. It has come to be the core of financial innovation.

Securitization of mortgages, credit-card loans, lease credits and project loans is a common application of such technology. Typically, this makes the bank into a fee-earning match-maker rather than an intermediary in the traditional banking sense of depending on the spread between its borrowing and lending rates for earnings. For example, a special-purpose company purchases specific loans (mortgages, and so on) from a bank and issues new securities backed by the collection of loans. These are sold to investors seeking higher returns in exchange for holding a risky, relatively undiversified, asset. The special-purpose company earns a fee for servicing the underlying loans. The bank benefits by regaining liquidity, which allows a new round of lending that can be securitized.

Further, financial derivatives such as options, swaps and futures are produced through unbundling and rebundling the volatility of exchange rates, interest rates and stock prices. The original products are converted into new ones that have risks that are hopefully more easily understood and controlled by investors.

Examining trends in financial technology, Allen and Santomero (1998) argue that the traditional role of financial intermediaries such as banks in reducing the frictions of transactions and asymmetric information is becoming smaller. Instead, risk transfer has become the mainstay of the financial business. Risk transfer is defined as packaging assets with certain levels or types of risks, and then selling the package to investors with a preference for such a package.

There is no doubt that drastic reductions of transaction costs in the financial markets, enabling efficient risk transfer through unbundling and rebundling existing financial products, has realized a sea-change in financial technology and the industry. However, whether information asymmetry between banks and clients and between banks and depositors, among others, can be reduced significantly by the development of information technology is still an open question. Although the risk of a firm related to a particular project can be segregated by project loans, the risk specific to the firm still remains. Likewise, while the risk of a bank related to particular loans is segregated by loan securitization, there still remains information asymmetry with respect to the bank. After passing on risks of particular projects or loans, whether or not the specific risk of the firm or the bank increases is not necessarily clear. In eliminating many sources of specific risks, the risk of the firm or the bank might actually increase because of the decrease in the benefits of diversification.

While transaction costs and information asymmetry decrease, Allen and Santomero (1998) also point out that new financial products are getting more and more complicated, to a point beyond the understanding and control of ordinary individual investors. The rise in participation costs in sophisticated financial markets for ordinary investors makes intermediation by institutional investors such as insurance companies, trust banks and mutual funds more indispensable. Kitamura, Suto and Teranishi (2004) maintain that the effects of the rise in participation costs is crucially related to the distribution of wealth-holding by investors, or size of stakes held by investors.

8.3 LIMITATIONS OF BANK-CENTERED FINANCE

The bank-centered financial system of the high-growth-period system has shown serious technological limitations in the face of new manufacturing and financial technology. These relate to information procurement and processing, including the speed and effectiveness with which these are done.

8.3.1 Producing Information

First, the traditional strategies and practices of Japanese banks are not particularly suited for the era of uncertainty regarding technologies and industries. Banks are usually concerned about the liquidity and short-term solvency condition of firms, and have unique advantages in producing information about firms through monitoring daily movement of transaction balances, but these mechanisms do not work at the level of industries.

Japan Development Bank (JDB) is often said to have produced information about industries and technologies to compensate for other banks' inability to do so. This, however, is not correct. JDB did not produce information about new industries and technologies by itself. Instead, allocation of JDB loans to various industries was dictated to it. The original plan was drafted at the Economic Planning Agency on the basis of information provided by MITI and other industry-related bureaus and ministries. This was presented to the government at the cabinet level as a 'basic plan of fund allocation' (*unyô no kihon hôshin*).

The final allocation plan was sent down to the chief of the MOF

Banking Bureau, who passed it on to JDB.

JDB did have a powerful information-related section, but its main function was to produce information about firms and industries that were already borrowing, not about new industries. During the high-growth era, loans by JDB worked as a signal, called the 'cowbell', to indicate implicit government approval of lending, as well as the general direction of industrial policy regarding loans, tax benefits and other measures. The cowbell called the herd of private banks together to join JDB in loan consortia for industries and specific firms. Fukuda et al. (1995) examined the signaling effect of JDB loans on allocation of loans among various industries by the banking sector. Using an impulse-response function with quarterly data for 1953–93, they conclude the signaling effect was in fact not strong.

Okazaki (1995) examines the allocation of loans of city banks and long-term credit banks among industries, and concludes that the allocation traced industries with high growth rates and profit rates adequately until around 1975, but failed to do so thereafter. Table 8.1 re-examines this hypothesis by use of panel data based on annual loan allocation of city banks. The results are by and large in accordance with our hypothesis. During the high-growth era, banks chose industries with high growth rates, partly following the general guidelines of industrial policy, but after the 1980s banks were unable to target promising industries. Note that banks did not much care about profit rates in the allocation of funds among industries.

Although the analysis in Table 8.1 is still preliminary, and many things, including the impact of financial liberalization after 1980, need to be taken into consideration, it suggests that the choice of industries had become a serious issue that reflected the limitations of the banking industry and the bank-centered financial system. Promising technology and industries were no longer evident from the model of advanced countries, so a mechanism of government-led loan allocation following that model no longer worked well.

8.3.2 Adjustment Speed

A second limitation of the bank-centered financial system is the speed with which banking practices adjust to changes in the technological and industrial landscape. Information processing by banks about their clients is characterized by the indivisibility of information. Information is not useful unless it is accumulated to a certain level, and then kept current. To do this, banks need to invest in establishing information channels with clients, as well as to devote resources to daily monitoring

Table 8.1 Analysis of loan allocation among industries by city banks, 1960–94

	Period	Industry set A[1]	Industry set B[2]
Profit rate	1960–64	-0.111(1.875)	0.076 (0.744)
Sales growth rate		0.050(3.816)	0.030 (1.872)
R^2		-0.177	0.408
Profit rate	1965–69	-0.085(-1.251)	-0.073 (1.930)
Sales growth rate		0.023 (1.516)	-0.000 (0.028)
R^2		-0.143	0.335
Profit rate	1970–74	0.186(1.952)	0.084 (1.562)
Sales growth rate		0.085(2.486)	0.006 (0.320)
R^2		0.113	0.569
Profit rate	1975–79	-0.009(-0.161)	-0.001(-0.017)
Sales growth rate		0.014 (5.938)	-0.008 (0.934)
R^2		0.046	0.631
Profit rate	1980–84	-0.136(-2.894)	-0.121(-3.330)
Sales growth rate		0.070 (4.883)	0.063 (5.925)
R^2		0.165	0.711
Profit rate	1985–89	-0.155(-0.879)	0.040 (0.306)
Sales growth rate		0.013 (0.408)	-0.011(-0.452)
R^2		0.128	0.340
Profit rate	1990–94	-0.042 (-0.812)	0.040 (0.306)
Sales growth rate		0.021 (1.196)	-0.011 (-0.452)
R^2		-0.112	0.340

Notes: Figures in parentheses are *t*-values; R^2 is the correlation coefficient adjusted for degrees of freedom.

[1] Through 1974, 14 industries, then 23.

[2] Through 1974, 13 industries, then 22. This set excludes retail and wholesale trade as an outlier.

The dependant variable is the share of loans to the *i*th industry in total loans in year *t*. Independent variables are the average profit rate (operating profits divided by total assets) and average growth rates of sales during year $t + 1$ to year $t + 5$. Other control variables include year dummies and the log-transformed value of total asset of the *i*th industry.

The regression is conducted by use of a random effect model on the two data sets. The following interesting observations are obtained.

- During the period 1960–65 to 1980–84, the coefficients of sales growth rates are mostly positive and statistically significant in the case of set A, and positive with low significance in the case of set B.
- After 1985–89, the coefficients of sales growth rates are insignificant with a positive sign in the case of set A, but are negative in the case of set B.
- The coefficients of profit rate are generally either negative or insignificant.

Source: Computed by the author from data in the Japan Development Bank data base.

activities.

When bank borrowers find alternative, less-expensive sources of funding and shift toward them, the indivisibility of information can cause disastrous problems. This happened in the 1980s, when deregulation of the euro–yen bond market caused massive shifts of large-firm financing from domestic bank loans to off-shore bond financing. Banks were obliged to seek new borrowers, and the most willing were small and medium firms, and firms in real-estate-related areas. The banks did not have sufficient information on such firms to make sensible lending decisions.

Further, after the burst of the real-estate related bubble and especially during the latter half of the 1990s, banks were unable to lend anywhere and had to accumulate idle balances lest they should lose depositors' trust and cause serious financial disintermediation. This occurred because of the common belief that most of the heavy and chemical industries had been losing international competitiveness in the era of information technology and knowledge capital. Part of such a belief seems to have been based on pessimism about the international competitiveness of Japanese manufacturing with respect to managerial organization and governance issues and not, necessarily, with respect to technological capability.

In such a situation, skepticism prevailed about the value of the information and expertise accumulated by banks: it was concentrated in 'old' industries. *Kashishiburi* (bank reluctance to lend) during the 1990s seems to have occurred because both bank managers and shareholders were caught up in this skepticism.

When technology and desirable client industries are changing rapidly, it is difficult for banks to adjust quickly and efficiently. Risk reduction or risk sharing based on careful evaluation of project risks and pricing of projects are not easy. Accumulated information about clients easily becomes obsolete. Risk transfer through capital markets can be a more suitable method of financing in such a situation.

8.4 COSTS OF THE *GENKYOKU*–INDUSTRIAL ASSOCIATION

As the high-growth era progressed, there was a significant increase in the political costs of the system. Especially important was dysfunctioning of the government–private-sector interface. As a result, the adjustment of inter-industrial conflicts has become very costly, giving rise to inefficient economic policies and administrative muddles.

In the *genkyoku*–industrial association system, the distributive interests of various social strata are represented by industrial associations, and systematically adjusted by the bureaucracy, which includes various *genkyoku*. Although the political system is institutionally the superstructure above the bureaucracy (Muramatsu 1981), issues regarding economic interests were separated from political confrontation under the Liberal Democratic Party (LDP) power monopoly and put under the control of the bureaucracy. Political confrontation was confined mainly to national security issues, and politicians devoted themselves to dealing with grass-roots issues such as induction of public works in their electoral districts (Inoguchi and Iwai 1987).

The mechanism for inter-industrial adjustment in the high-growth system is conditional on either continuation of the existing industrial structure or predictable changes. As a new industry is born and begins to grow, it usually sets up an industrial organization and engages in lobbying related government bureaus. However, the response of the government is usually not quick enough to accommodate the urgent needs of new industries. Moreover, the government is liable to face counter-lobbying by existing competing industries. Further, such a situation tends to invite *ad hoc* intervention by *zokugiin*, leading to increases in the costs of political and administrative decision-making.

For the successful working of the *genkyoku*–industrial association system, three conditions have to be satisfied.

1. People find their social values in a company-based society, and approve the representation of distributive interests through inter-industrial interests.
2. The system is inclusive, encompassing declining sectors and weak segments of the economy.
3. Distributive interests are completely adjusted by the bureaucracy without any significant spillover effects to groups representing interests other than inter-industrial interests.

As the high-growth era ended and exogenous conditions underwent fundamental changes, the conditions ceased to be met. Let us first examine how and why the third condition has become incongruent and tended to raise political costs of the economic system.

8.4.1 Spillovers

In the bureaucratic system of The high-growth era, the inter-industrial interests of most industries in manufacturing were represented by MITI bureaus, and those of financial industries by MOF bureaus. Most inter-industry conflicts were kept within the manufacturing sector or within the financial sector. Adjustments of interests were quickly and effectively carried out within either MITI or MOF. When there was rivalry among MITI bureaus or inter-industrial conflicts involving related bureaus, *chôsei-kyoku* fulfilled the role of adjusting interests from the standpoint of public policy (Aoki 1988). (*Chôsei-kyoku* are coordinating offices in charge of overall issues within ministries such as MITI and MOF; see Table 7.1.)

This adjustment mechanism has been obliged to confront conflicts beyond its original scope: inter-ministerial turf battles and disputes involving interests outside the industrial sector. The system has been inefficient, even ineffective, in dealing with them.

There have been issues that required adjustment across the boundaries of MITI and MOF, and among more than two ministries. That is, coordination by the government (cabinet) was needed. In so far as the cabinet has sufficient capability, and adjustment is motivated by considerations of fairness and efficiency for the whole economy, the *genkyoku*–industrial association system could function adequately. Quite often, however, adjustment became time-consuming and ineffective because each ministry asserted not only the interests of the client industry but also the interests of the ministry. Moreover, ministries tried to justify their positions through use of deliberative councils.

A typical example was the policy muddle regarding reform of information and communication systems. This required coordinating three industries and two ministries: computers, broadcasting, communications, MITI, and Posts and Telecommunications. Serious conflict occurred between the ministries. Moreover, the coordination role of deliberative councils was not effective because of the strong voice of existing companies. As a result, it took more than 10 years to divide NTT (Nippon Telegraph and Telephone Corp) into two local (initially monopoly) companies and one long-distance company (which still dominates its industry).

Financial liberalization is another example. This has involved conflicts between MOF, in charge of banks and other financial firms, and the Ministry of Posts and Telecommunications, in charge of the postal savings system. Liberalization of deposit interest rates took over 15 years – from 1979 to 1994 for implementation of changes, plus several years of debate before the first change.

The *genkyoku*–industrial association system has also faced serious difficulties when distributive conflicts emerged that were related not only to inter-industrial interests but also to interests outside the industrial sector. Such cases increased in number as the value system of the public diversified. In this situation, adjustment by the cabinet is not effective: adjustment within the LDP becomes necessary, partly because the activity of *zokugiin* expands across the boundary of ministry jurisdictions.

Inoguchi and Iwai (1987) emphasize the difference between two types of *zokugiin*: the *banken-gata* (watch-dog-type) work mainly for the interests of particular industries and related bureaus, while *ryôken-gata* (hunting-dog-type) work across ministerial boundaries, trying to benefit through intermediation of various industries. The benefits could be for themselves, for their factions, or for the LDP.

Political decision making becomes time consuming and ineffective because dual decision–making – that is, within the government and within the LDP – is needed. Public investment in highways is a typical example. This not only concerns agriculture (represented by the Ministry of Agriculture, Forestry, and Fishery) and the construction industry (Ministry of Construction), but environmental groups and consumer movements have also become concerned.

Let us examine two cases to see how the *genkyoku*–industrial association system became dysfunctional. These are allocation of public works and the delays in financial liberalization including deregulation of the bond market in particular.

8.4.2 Allocation of Public Works

The allocation of public investment in Japan was carried out following the efficiency principle (that is, equality of the marginal productivity of social capital across regions) during the 1960s, so that the government invested heavily in regions where private capital stock was large. After the 1970s, however, the efficiency principle came to be neglected, and excessive government investment poured into low-income regions with low private capital stock. (See Asako and Sakamoto 1993; Asako et al. 1994; Mitsui, Inoue, and Takezawa 1995; Iwamoto et al. 1996.)

To justify government-investment policy after the 1970s, it is often pointed out that it was allocated from the viewpoint of income equalization between regions, as represented by the well-known slogan 'balanced development of the country'. However, mere construction of physical infrastructure is neither sufficient nor necessary to induce true development of backward regions in either a material or cultural sense. Although increased highway capacity does typically create demand (generates traffic), utilization of the roads built in local areas has been quite low, for example. Moreover, income disparity between urban and rural areas is widening despite government investment.

One reason for the bias toward low-income regions in allocating public works is the subsidy policy of the central government. The availability of subsidies has meant projects have been undertaken by localities simply to obtain subsidies. However, the projects have resulted in large deficits for many local governments because they have to bear some of the costs.

The basic reason for the inefficient allocation of public investment seems to be in the limitation of the government–private-sector interface. Unlike under the Meiji-Taishô system, the allocation of public investment was not an agenda item at the government–private-sector interface, so under the high-growth-period system it should be dealt with from a purely national economic viewpoint, such as the efficiency criterion in land utilization. (Tanaka's 1972 Japanese archipelago rebuilding plan was in line with this globally widely used approach to efficient land use.) However, because land utilization is jurisdictionally under several ministries – including Construction, and Agriculture and Fishery, as well as the National Land Agency and the Environment Agency – the issue was converted into inter-ministerial rivalry.

Moreover, as rivalry intensified, *zokugiin* became involved: *nôrin-zoku* (agriculture) and *kensetsu-zoku* (the construction industry). Their intervention had two effects. First, inter-regional rivalry with regard to public investment issues were added to inter-industrial and other inter-ministerial conflicts. Second, decision-making became a dual system, with both the bureaucracy and the LDP involved as a patronage-dispensing political party.

8.5 DELAYS IN FINANCIAL LIBERALIZATION

The drawback of the *genkyoku*–industrial association system, in the sense of failing to coordinate distributive conflicts related to more than two ministries, is clear in the delays in financial liberalization.

Securitization, which involves the unbundling and rebundling of existing products, is possible only when there are no significant barriers between ministries and bureaus – in particular, the MOF Banking Bureau, MOF Securities Bureau, and the Ministry of Posts of Telecommunications in charge of postal savings.

There were two objectives for liberalization when it was initially advocated in the last half of the 1970s. The first was to establish a more market-oriented system for the purpose of achieving greater efficiency through use of the price mechanism and market discipline, as well as conducting monetary policy more effectively on the basis of efficient markets. The second was to catch up in financial technology and to vitalize the financial industries, mainly by introducing financial innovations appearing in the United States.

Reviewing the process, it is quite noteworthy that government bureaus have put less emphasis on the second objective. In other words, government authorities, together with most economists, did not regard the financial sector as a promising industry nor did it promote its development by introducing new products and technology. For example, Hamada and Horiuchi (1987) note that the government tried to control the introduction of new IT technology in order to maintain specialized areas for each type of financial institution.

Aggressive moves toward financial innovation started only in 1997. Thus, Japan's version of the Big Bang trailed London's by a decade and came more than two decades after deregulation had begun. There is no doubt that such a policy stance resulted in fragile, backward financial industries.

Diversification of banks away from commercial lending is still limited in Japan. In contrast, US banks increased their non-interest income rapidly after around 1979 (Hoshi and Kashyap 2001; Allen and Santomero 1998), and it now amounts to almost half of bank operating income (44.3 per cent in 1996 based on the data of 25 major bank holding companies according to Radecki (1999).) In Japan, the share of fees (*yakumu-torihiki tô shûeki*) and other non-interest income in bank current revenue is only a few per cent. (Fees were 4.2 per cent, and other non-interest income 15.2 per cent, in 1996 based on the data of all banks (*zenkoku-ginko*).) (Fee and non-interest income in the US case includes: foreign exchange dealings, service charges on deposit accounts, credit card fees, insurance fees, fiduciary activities, fees from securitization, venture capital revenues, and so on. Much of this is from business areas closely related to payment settlement services, which is the original banking business (Radecki 1999).)

Financial liberalization (deregulation) in Japan was biased toward mobilizing savings (bank's liability side); liberalization on the asset side was not as extensive. (Comprehensive listings of deregulatory measures are, for 1976–91, Kitagawa and Kurosawa (1994, p. 92, 125–28), and, for 1975–2001, Hoshi and Kashyap (2001, pp. 259–63).

Deregulation was triggered by the issue of massive amounts of government bonds to finance budget deficits beginning in 1975, and was motivated mainly by the necessity to respond to demands by asset holders – that is, the new middle class as depositors. In other words, priority was placed on accommodating the desire by households and corporate firms to diversify asset holdings. As a result, liberalization of the lending areas of specialized financial institutions was left untouched, consequently maintaining barriers among financial institutions.

Liberalization as regards savers started with introduction of NCD (negotiable certificates of deposits) in May 1979, but with a 500 million yen minimum (over $2 million at the time). Then, in 1981 new instruments were introduced, and a steady stream of introductions continued through the 1980s. However, interest rates were still effectively fixed throughout the decade, although there was liberalization starting in 1985.

8.5.1 Deregulation of Bond Markets

The deregulation of bond markets which occurred during the 1980s deserves special attention. This is because foreign pressure, backed by the interests of US financial firms, played an important role in breaking the stalemate in inter-industrial conflicts. The deregulation of the euro-bond market, implemented under strong foreign pressure, had significant effects on the Japanese economy: deregulation of domestic bond markets became inevitable. The resulting shift of funding by large firms from bank borrowing to bond financing triggered expansion of real-estate–related loans, and hence the late 1980s bubble in land prices.

Through the 1970s into the early 1980s, liberalization proceeded slowly. The necessity to deregulate became more urgent, however.

First, deregulation was needed to maintain the effectiveness of monetary policy: as liberalization of interest rates proceeded, monetary policy effected by direct controls on bank lending (window guidance) was expected to become less efficient, so a shift to policy measures utilizing market mechanisms more fully was considered inevitable.

For example, liberalization of impact loans (non-yen – usually euro–dollar – loans to Japanese firms), which had been monopolized by foreign banks before the liberalization, was implemented in 1979. The change did not have much immediate effect because of regulations requiring foreign exchange transactions to be trade-related (the real-demand principle, *jitsuju gensoku*). However, as the real-demand principle was abandoned beginning in 1980 with revision of the foreign exchange law and ending with repeal of yen-conversion regulations in 1985, it became difficult to exert significant influence on the bank loan market. This is because impact loans were not included in the targets of window-guidance on bank loans. As a result, BOJ and MOF felt it necessary to introduce market-based monetary policy.

Second, the international activities of Japanese banks were expanding rapidly as the external assets of Japan doubled every two or three years from 1976 to 1985. At first, international business was confined to servicing overseas affiliates of clients based in Japan. As the banks extended into mergers and acquisitions and other financial transactions, and competed with foreign banks, however, the need to catch-up in financial innovation through further deregulation became urgent if the banks were to be competitive.

The report of the Yen–Dollar Committee in 1984 had an enormous effect on Japanese financial markets, both in propelling internationalization and in liberalizing the corporate bond market. The measures were:

1. Expansion of the euro–yen market: liberalization of short-term euro–yen loans, relaxation of guidelines on euro–yen bond issue by residents, and the like.
2. Expansion of business areas of foreign banks in Japan: dealing in government bonds, trust banking, membership in the Tokyo Stock Exchange, and the like.
3. Ongoing deregulation of deposit rates.
4. Promotion of internationalization of finance: creation of yen-denominated banker's acceptance market, repeal of regulations on yen-conversion of foreign exchange, relaxation of regulations on yen-denominated foreign bonds, and the like.

Almost all the measures called for in the report were realized during 1985, partly due to having a follow-up committee. Also, the yen–dollar rate did not change significantly until the drastic yen appreciation following the September 1985 Plaza Agreement.

What was even more important, however, was a side effect of these measures: Japan was obliged to deregulate its domestic bond market. In the wake of the 1985 liberalization, there was a drastic expansion of euro–yen bond issues by large firms. The bonds were mostly purchased by Japanese investors such as insurance companies, so this was regarded as a hollowing of the domestic bond market, and MOF was obliged to deregulate it. Specifically, the eligibility condition of un-collateralized bond issuance was relaxed considerably. This is seen in Table 8.2.

8.5.1.1 Foreign pressure

What is interesting from the viewpoint of the analysis of inter-industrial

Table 8.2 Number of firms eligible for issuing bonds

	1979 Mar	1984 Apr	[a]1987 Feb
Uncollateralized ordinary	2	16	120
Convertible	2	97	240

Notes:
[a] Orders of magnitude.
Companies that could issue ordinary bonds could also issue convertibles, and so are included in the entries for convertibles.

Source: Nomura Sogo Kenkyujyo (ed.) (1989), *Kôshasai-yôran*, pp. 115–17.

conflicts through the *genkyoku*–industrial system is that foreign pressure through the Yen–Dollar Committees worked quite effectively to realize a breakthrough in the stalemates caused by *zokugiin* activities. Without the Yen–Dollar Committees, liberalization of the euro-market would not have been implemented so smoothly, and without the liberalization of the euro–yen market, deregulation of the domestic bond market would not have proceeded so quickly.

Whether utilization of foreign pressure was intentional is an interesting question. Horiuchi (1994), for one, argues convincingly that MOF intended to use foreign pressure to break the stalemate over liberalization arising from rivalry among ministries. The agreement to have the committee was reached between President Ronald Reagan and Prime Minister Nakasone Yasuhiro in 1983 when Reagan was in Japan. The primary purpose was to realign exchange rates – induce yen appreciation and dollar depreciation – in order to avoid a hard landing of the US economy, which was ailing from fiscal and trade deficits. However, the main reason for the misalignment was huge fiscal deficits and a high real interest rate in the United States, so it was difficult to see how deregulation of international financial transactions could have significant effects on the problem.

Theoretically, deregulation of international financial transactions could affect the yen–dollar rate. This is because liberalization could increase demand for yen held as transaction balances. However, given the interest rate differential between the United States and Japan at the time, for firms and investors to hold yen stably, it was necessary for there to be an expectation of yen appreciation, and in order to induce information of such an expectation, the current level of the yen would usually have to be depreciated.

It must be noted that foreign pressure was motivated by, and represented the needs of, the US banking industry. In other words, this case corresponds to the third category described in section (8.4.1): inter-industrial conflicts affected by interests of a third party.

During the early 1980s US banks became highly confident in their international competitiveness based on new products and strategies cultivated through innovation during the 1970s. They intended to establish global financial networks, operating 24 hours a day, in order to profit from the expanding international fund flow. For this purpose, the opening of the Tokyo market and the internationalization of Japanese financial markets were crucial.

Japanese branches of foreign banks were suffering seriously from the decline in the spread between the interest rate on dollar call loans (beginning in 1972) or euro–dollars and the interest rate on impact loans (dollar-denominated loans to Japanese firms), which was their main revenue source. The interest rate on impact loans was decreasing due to liberalization, but Japanese banks were still benefiting from regulated deposit rates, so foreign banks were eager to speed up liberalization. This point is underlined by the lecture, at the American Center in Tokyo on March 24 1984, by Donald Regan, the US Secretary of Treasury, who deplored the lack of progress in opening Japanese markets to foreign financial institutions in the three years since opening had been requested. He further claimed that internationalization of the yen had become an urgent issue in order to realize yen appreciation.

8.5.2 Effects of Financial Deregulation

It is well known that the deregulation of the bond market had an enormous impact on the domestic banking industry. Deregulation of euro-bonds, as well as of the domestic bond market, caused large firms to massively shift funding from bank loans to bond financing. Banks responded by lending to new areas such as real estate and small and medium enterprises (SMEs) so as to maintain their level of total loans. This was partly caused by the governance pattern of banks: as a typical Japanese firm controlled by insiders, bank managers needed to expand to find room for promotion and jobs after retirement for their peer employees.

The share of loans of city banks and long-term credit banks directed to SMEs, which had an increasing trend since around 1970, soared after 1985 (Hoshi and Kashyap 2001). Likewise, the share of loans to real estate increased during the second half of the 1980s for all types of financial institutions, in particular trust banks and long-term credit banks (Ueda 2000). A considerable part of these loans became non-performing after the bubble burst.

The bubble in real estate occurred not only because of the behavior of real estate firms, but also through the speculative real-estate investment of ordinary firms. In particular, many SMEs engaged in real-state transaction. The speculative behavior of large firms was mainly related to stocks and other financial markets.

8.5.3 Reasons for Relative Backwardness

Liberalization and deregulation have been implemented in many industries since the 1960s, and many of the firms had Japanese-style management systems. Why, then, did only the banking sector fail at liberalization? Why did Japanese financial firms become relatively backward and lose international competitiveness? Two reasons are presented below: lax management and malfunctioning of the *genkyoku*–industrial association system.

Another, more immediate, reason for the non-performing loans of the early 1990s is that, after 1984, the liberalization of the bond market was carried out with unprecedented speed and under foreign pressure, which made it something of a surprise to the banking sector. Thus, the banks did not have time to prepare for it. In other cases, trade for example, liberalization was implemented after careful planning by the *genkyoku*–industrial association system, as discussed in Chapter 7.

8.5.3.1 Lax management

Lax management of banks played a major role in the industry's problems. Banks were accustomed to lending based on real estate as collateral, without carefully evaluating project risks, and to soft budgeting cushioned by huge unrealized profits from holdings of real estate and stocks. Banks had implicit contracts regarding risk-sharing with most of their large, mature clients, and when many clients in heavy and chemical industries all lost competitiveness at the same time and began to decline, the burden on banks was too great for them to shoulder the risks.

Banks should have transferred these risks to the capital markets, both domestic and international, before the firms fell into difficulties. A variety of risk transferring measures existed. Why did the banks not use them?

First, there was a misunderstanding by participants about the efficiency of Japan's traditional risk-sharing. It can be economically efficient when it bails out firms that are temporarily in financial distress but profitable in the long-run. However, in a period of drastic changes in industrial structure, to conduct risk-sharing with many non-innovative firms indulged in rent-seeking is beyond the capability of banks.

Second, banks in Japan did not have enough expertise in the technology of risk transferring. This backwardness was due to the stalemate of inter-industrial competition, and inter-ministerial rivalry with the participation of *zokugiin*. This was beyond the capability of the *genkyoku*–industrial association system. The sub-system of the government–private-sector interface had simply become obsolete by the end of the 1980s.

8.5.3.2 Malfunctioning of the system

The malfunctioning of the *genkyoku*–industrial association system played a major role in the era when distributive conflicts came to be related to more than two industries and bureaus. Because interest rates on financial instruments, as well as fees on security transactions, were regulated, profits of a financial institution became higher as more funds were mobilized through the institutions. In such a situation, together with the incentives arising from the insider control of institutions, financial institutions' behavior was motivated largely by maximization of asset size.

When liberalization began in the 1970s, the greatest concern of financial institutions was the shift of funds across institutions. They could compete fiercely for larger shares by introducing attractive new financial instruments. Instead, the *genkyoku*–industrial association system was utilized to keep relative shares constant.

This was so because inter-industrial conflict and competition was not manageable within the system, but had to be coordinated by politicians, *zokugiin*, who knew little about trends in financial innovation and had only limited concern for the growth of financial industries. For the politicians, it was preferable in terms of vote mobilization that the industries remain in a mature and stable stage, similar to the case of agriculture. Neither rapid innovative growth nor a decline of existing industries, the inevitable consequence of competition, were the choices of the politicians.

The postal saving system has a huge group of *zokugiin* called *yûsei-zoku*. The banking industry does not have such a group, but the banking industry was the largest donor to the LDP.[1] At the time of the revision of the banking law in 1991, the association lobbied fiercely, donating directly to individual LDP Diet members instead of to the party (Inoguchi and Iwai 1987). The security industry has also a *zokugiin* group, although not as powerful as *yûsei-zoku*.

As a result, financial liberalization was carried out so as to minimize the disturbance to the relative share of financial institutions, which in practice meant that competition was suppressed as much as possible. A typical example is the licensing of a series of new financial instruments introduced in 1981. The government followed a *yokonarabi* approach, with each industry segment getting at least one new product.

Thus, in July 1981 the government approved introduction of time deposits with designated maturities for banks, of a new type of loan trust fund (BIG) for trust banks, of a new financial debenture (WIDE) for long-term credit banks, and postal savings consolidated accounts (*yûbin sôgô kôza*) for the postal saving system. That October the *yokonarabi* approach was completed with introduction of a new national-bond fund for security companies, a new fund trust and synthetic security service for trust banks, a synthetic financial debenture account for Bank of Tokyo, and the treatment of special money trust funds for insurance companies, trust banks and security companies.

8.6 THE INTERFACE COLLAPSES

In the government–private-sector interface of the high-growth-period system, if all the players were producers, the input–output interaction of all the industries resulted in a sort of zero-sum game. However, when the interactions are not completed within the producer sector, and some groups excluded from the interactive mechanism feel dissatisfaction with the income distribution, there is a possibility the mechanism will lose legitimacy, and even collapse. The two principal disaffected groups were depositors and consumers: both were excluded from the *genkyoku*–industrial system, so they could not combat unfavorable prices through lobbying and burden shifting. As workers, the new middle class benefited from the high-growth-period system, but as depositors and consumers, they paid higher prices.

The criticism against competition-preventing regulations by depositors and consumers, either in the form of exit or voice, gradually came to be shared by other segments of the economy, and a movement emerged to reconsider the *genkyoku*–industrial association system itself. When the 'company society' supported by the new middle class as workers declined as a normative value, and was replaced by consumerist values, one of the main building-blocks of the high-growth-period system crumbled. The new middle class became disunited, with various (overlapping) parts – such as company men, depositors, consumers and environmentalists – each with its own motivations and agenda.

The remainder of this chapter explains how this happened. I argue that the company society, originally admired as being endowed with instrumental values, came to be criticized from the viewpoint of consumerist values.

8.6.1 Depositors

Deposits are the main input of the financial industry. The industry could lobby the government to realize low input prices (low deposit rates), and high output prices (high loan returns). Depositors, however, had no means to shift the costs of low deposit rates to some other industry. When households and firms feel dissatisfaction with the situation, the *genkyoku*–industrial association system is destined to malfunction. In so far as household interest income was relatively small compared to wage income (and interest revenue was small compared to operating income for non-financial firms as depositors), this did not cause much dissatisfaction. However, as the accumulation of financial assets by households and firms proceeded, the regulated low deposit rates aroused serious opposition.

Let us examine the relationship between depositors and regulations on financial industries. New instruments such as NCDs (negotiable certificates of deposit, from May 1979) and treasury bills (one-month, with free rate, from October 1978) expanded share in the total money market, going from 20.4 per cent in 1975 to 42.7 per cent in 1980. Free interest rate deposits such as MMCs, large denomination deposits, and foreign currency deposits increased share in total deposits from 11.6 per cent at the end of the fiscal year 1985 to 73.6 per cent at the end of the fiscal year 1989, according to BOJ data.

The secondary market of government bonds developed around the same period. The trading volume of government bonds in 1976 was only 0.1 per cent of the outstanding amount, and had grown to just 2.3 per cent in 1980 when regulation of issue prices (distributing government bonds to banks at prices higher than market prices) was virtually abolished. In 1990 it was 15.6 per cent.

At the same time, the regulations on lending areas and specialization requirements were weakened. For example, city banks were allowed to enter the market for long-term deposits when a 30-month time deposit was approved in 1971. *Sôgo* were allowed to deal in foreign exchange in 1973. Security companies were allowed to deal with *chûkoku*-funds (a *de facto* deposit substitute) in 1980. Banks were allowed to sell government bonds to customers in 1983.

The dissatisfaction of depositors about low, regulated deposit rates was a strong driving force in liberalization. In other words, the regulation-avoiding behavior of firms and households caused a shift of funds among financial instruments, and thus made it inevitable that the authorities would further liberalize the markets. The movement was manifest in the behavior of households that had accumulated significant financial assets as a result of high economic growth. Households shifted their portfolio into contractual assets such as annuities and *de facto* term deposits (sold by insurance companies), especially from the late 1970s to early 1980s, and this made the low regulated deposit rates more difficult to maintain. The percentage of insurance (mostly term-deposit-type contracts) and annuities in personal financial asset holdings was 14.8 per cent at the end of 1970, 12.7 per cent 1975, 18.0 per cent 1980, and 28.9 per cent 1985.

The corporate sector also shifted its liquid assets, moving from trade credits to financial assets. Trade credits had been necessary when bank credit was not sufficiently available to small and medium enterprises (SMEs), as they have sales-promotion effects for creditors (large firms). As *sôgo* and *shinkin*, the traditional lenders to SMEs grew, the availability of bank credits increased. At the same time, as large firms increased their retained earnings, they wanted to invest in financial assets rather than trade credits.

As a place to invest short-term funds, the *gensaki* market emerged during the late 1960s. (Gensaki are comparable to reports (repurchase agreements).) An NCD market was created in 1979 to further accommodate such a need. The *chûkoku*-fund at security companies was created in 1980 and grew rapidly as a place for short-term investments by SMEs.

The deregulation of financial markets proceeded mainly as a gradual response to changes in the needs of economic agents, who were more and more dissatisfied with regulated interest rates and sought more profitable market-based opportunities.

8.6.2 Consumers

Another group excluded from the adjustment mechanism was consumers. Firms producing and trading consumer goods lobbied for competition-preventing measures, and were able to maintain prices that were high by international standards. For some time, consumers accepted this for several reasons.

First, during the high-growth era when the incomes of urban workers were rising rapidly and the urban–rural income differential increased, urban consumers tolerated high food prices, including for rice, as a compensation mechanism. Second, consumers were mainly concerned with quality, rather than quantity, and believed that the higher relative prices they paid were largely justified by quality differences. Third, possible dissatisfaction was mitigated by the ample supply, and rapidly declining prices, of consumer durables produced by large manufacturing firms.

An eruption of consumer dissatisfaction was triggered by the drastic appreciation of the yen in late 1985 after the Plaza Agreement. The appreciation clearly showed that Japan's consumer goods prices were extraordinarily high by international standards.[2]

The growth rate of wage income had already passed its peak, and consumers were seeking high-quality consumption with their internationally top-level incomes. As consumers came to realize that the high prices were caused by competition-prevention measures caused by the *genkyoku*–industrial association system, they became skeptical of the fairness of the system, and actively criticized it. The dissatisfaction of urban consumers became a main driving force in the deregulation of prices of consumption goods.

The significant divergence between domestic and international prices of consumption goods as a result of yen appreciation cast light on the huge effects of competition-preventive regulations. The divergence occurred between tradables and non-tradables. A typical example was the price differential between domestic and international traveling costs, which were pointed out as clear evidence for the inefficiency of service industries and the competition-preventing policies behind it.

Another divergence occurred between tradables facing and not facing competition-preventive measures. In spite of liberalization since the 1960s, many food and agricultural products were subject to significant competition-prevention measures. As the yen appreciated rapidly, the wholesale prices of products without such measures declined in tandem with import prices, but the wholesale prices of protected products did not change. Figure 8.1 shows this.

8.6.2.1 Competition prevention

The mainstay of competition prevention was non-tariff barriers, including price supports, import quantity rationing and entry prevention. With respect to 47 commodities with domestic and international price differentials of more than 5 per cent and total imports of more than one billion yen in 1989, Sazanami et al.(1996) investigated to what extent non-tariff barriers were responsible for price differentials and estimated welfare costs of the barriers. Table 8.3 shows that price

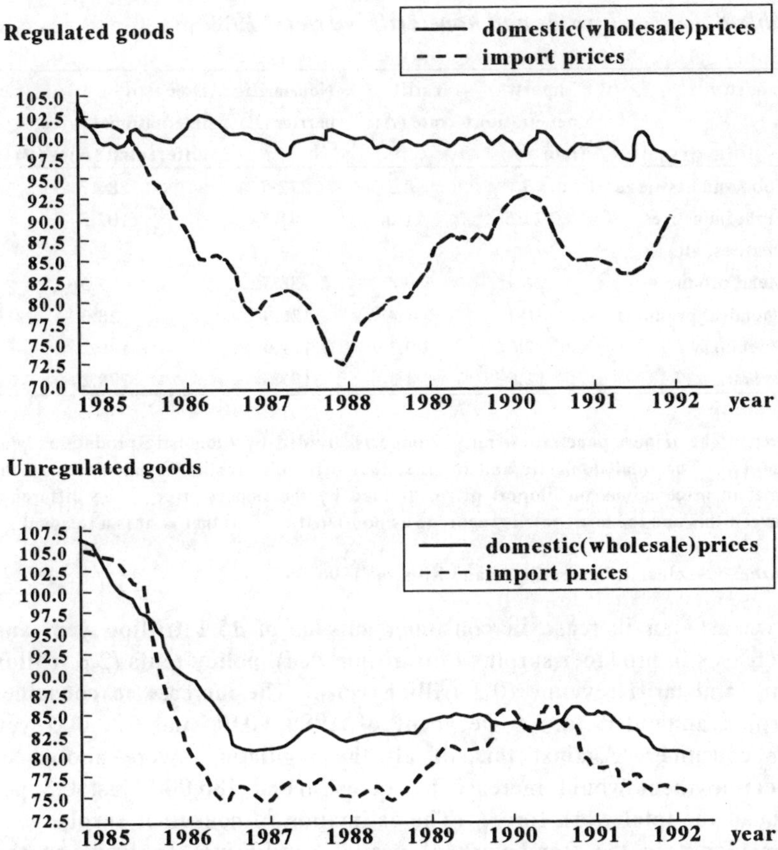

Note: The sample is 78 goods that are included in both the domestic wholesale price index and the import-price index of the Bank of Japan. The goods are classified in two groups, regulated and unregulated. Regulated goods are those subject to price supports, import quantity rationing, or entry regulation. There are 10 of these: milk powder, unrefined sugar, tobacco, whisky, wine, brandy, raw silk, wheat, beef and pork. The other 68 goods are unregulated.

Source: *Keizai Kikaku-chô* (Bureau of Prices 1992).

Figure 8.1 Domestic prices and import prices of regulated and unregulated goods

differentials are mostly explained by non-tariff barriers, and products with large price differentials have low import-penetration ratios.

The authors concluded that if all the trade and non-trade barriers were abolished, total welfare would increase by 2.4 trillion yen. This breaks

Table 8.3 Tariff rates and non-tariff barriers, 1989

Industry	Import penetration rate	Tariff rate (A)	Non-tariff barrier (B)	Domestic international price differential (A) + (B)
Food and beverage	9.4	8.2	272.5	280.7
Light industries (textiles, etc)	21.5	11.0	91.5	102.5
Metal products	36.1	0.8	58.7	59.5
Chemical products	10.1	1.4	126.9	128.3
Machinery	7.6	0.3	139.9	140.2
Overall	11.6	4.7	173.5	178.2

Note: The import penetration rate is imports divided by (domestic production plus imports). The total domestic and international price differential is calculated as the domestic price minus the import price, divided by the import price. The difference between this and the tariff rate is regarded as non-tariff barrier; that is, it is a residual.

Source: Sazanami, Urata, Kawai and Kimura (1996).

down as: an increase in consumer surplus of 15.1 trillion yen, and decreases in producer surplus (9.6 trillion yen), policy rents (2.8 trillion yen), and tariff revenue (0.3 trillion yen). The increase in consumer surplus amounted to 3.8 per cent of 1989 GDP, and 122,000 yen per consumer. Against this, if all the regulations were abolished, unemployment would increase by an estimated 180,000, just 0.3 per cent of the total work force. (The estimation of consumer surplus was carried out in the framework of partial equilibrium analysis, so the spread of effects among industries and dynamic effects is not taken into consideration.)

The clear evidence for competition-prevention measures in the industries producing and distributing consumption goods provoked serious domestic criticism. It also aroused foreign response, leading to the Japan–US Structural Impediment Initiative, organized in 1989. The final report of the committee, released in June 1990 as an agreement of the two governments, spelled out various competition-promoting measures Japan should undertake. These included reducing restrictions on large-scale retail stores, shortening the examination period of patents, and raising the penalties assessed under the anti-monopoly law. With respect to the United States, policies such as reduction of fiscal deficits were called for.

In particular, the US government, confident in a competitive advantage in large-scale distribution, was enthusiastic about entry – particularly in the case of a large-scale toy retailer. Criticism and evasion of regulations spread throughout the country. First, there were arguments against various regulations and the vested interests of industrial associations. Nakakita, Urata and Harada (1993) asserted the necessity for more open markets and the improvement of the distribution industry for the sake of consumers. Ito (1992) argued for the importance of consumer sovereignty through an examination of competition-prevention regulations in such areas as air transportation, real estate transactions, distribution and communications.

More importantly, there was widespread evasion of regulations by consumers and retailers. Department stores and chain stores developed new supply channels, importing directly from overseas producers without intermediation by import agents. Imports by individual consumers and small retailers were widely carried out. Even re-importing of exported goods was undertaken when it reduced prices below domestically sold goods. Development of new distribution channels was costly, of course. The domestic–international price differential caused by the yen appreciation, however, was large enough to cover the costs. As a consequence, the share of manufactured products in total imports rose from 22.8 per cent in 1980 to 50.4 per cent in 1990.

8.6.3 Reform from Above

As context, it is important to note that there has been a series of administrative and fiscal reform activities by the government – 'reform from above' – since the early 1980s. This has brought about privatization and deregulation in various fields. The Temporary Administration Survey Committee (*Rinchô, Rinji Gyôsei Chôseikai*) established in 1981 and presided over by Dokô Toshio aimed at fiscal disciplining through fiscal and administrative reforms. With the slogan 'rehabilitation of the fiscal balance without a tax increase', and in the atmosphere of world wide privatization and marketism, the committee actively implemented privatization of major state enterprises.

- 1985 Japan Monopoly Corp converted to a private company, Japan Tobacco Industry Inc.
- 1985 Public Communications Act (*Koshû Denki Tsushin Hô*), which stipulated a monopoly by NTT, repealed, opening the way for the reorganization of NTT and new entry in telecommunications.
- 1986 Reform of National Railway Act passed (in November), lead-

ing to national railways being divided into regional private companies (1987 April).

- 1987 Japan Airline Act repealed, leading to privatization of JAL through the sale of shares held by the government.

The Deliberative Council on Administration Reform (*Gyôsei Kaikaku Shingikai*), established in 1983 as the successor to the *Dokô-Rinchô*, proposed an action plan of deregulation in 10 industries in four areas – finance, energy, transportation and urban renovation – in its 'Methods for Promoting Deregulation'. The deregulation of the financial system agreed by the Yen–Dollar Committee, as well as liberalization of distribution industry proposed by the Japan–US Structural Impediment Initiative, represent the movement toward deregulation driven by foreign pressures.

Criticism of the *genkyoku*–industrial association system and the movement toward deregulation affected the high-growth-period sub-system in a number of ways. Deregulation inherently means reconsidering the division of labor between government and the private sector. Not just the ends, but also the means were subject to debate, as acceptance of deregulation 'from above' was hardly universal. At the interface, excluded groups expressed dissatisfaction. In particular, the system was being criticized by the new middle class, previously faithful and devoted proponents of the system. Within the private sector there was confrontation between urban consumers as the new middle class, and consumption-good producers and distributors comprising farmers and small and medium firms.

8.6.4 Divergent Interests

Let us discuss why the confrontation between the farmers and small and medium producers on the one hand, and the new middle class on the other, represents criticism of the *genkyoku*–industrial association system from within the system. For this purpose it is convenient to compare our model with Murakami's schema. Murakami (1984) summarized social dynamics in Japan since the 1970s as the collapse of the new middle class and the rise of a new middle mass.

As a political system based on class ideology (conservatives versus progressive) lost popularity and instrumental value and rationality (which had supported industrialization) were exposed to criticism, Murakami felt the new middle class was gradually declining. This was evidenced by the rise of new left-wing movements. The new middle mass intensified its anti-bureaucracy sentiment and support for the new liberalism, as it experienced internal conflicts between conservatism and a critical stance based on a preference for consummatory values. Murakami characterized the two groups as follows.

New middle mass
1. Beneficiaries of vested special interests and tax benefits ('people related to industrial associations, farmers, retail-traders, and workers in the bureaucracy and professional groups').
2. Conservativeness and preference for consumerist values.
3. Passive adapters to industrial society.

New Middle Class
1. Managerial and administrative in a broad sense.
2. Mid-level asset holders.
3. Self-conscious supporters of the instrumental value system supporting industrialization.

From this, it is evident that the new middle mass encompasses all economic groups other than high-ranking bureaucrats and workers in large companies (managers, white-collar workers, and blue-collar workers alike).

Murakami's characterization of a 'class related to special vested interests' is not difficult to understand given that the price disparity of consumption goods was caused mainly by the behavior of farmers, retail-traders, and consumption-service producers, together with their related industrial associations, through assertion of inter-industrial interests. The favorable competitive conditions realized through their strong political power meant that agriculture and the small and medium-firm sector enjoyed significant gains in income.

It must be noted, however, that, during the high-growth era, not only the new middle mass but also all those related to large companies in heavy and chemical industries tried to benefit from pursuing inter-industrial interests. Further, it is an over-simplification to consider that the new middle class was in opposition to the new middle mass. Rather, the new middle class became frustrated with the wide disparity between domestic and international prices of consumption goods.

8.6.5 A Frustrated Middle

There is a crucial difference between Murakami's schema and my understanding of Japan's social-economic structure since the 1970s. Murakami considers the new middle class an important stratum in a social class structure composed of labor, capitalist and new middle class. To him, the new middle class played the role of a cushion or partition between the labor and capitalist classes, and contributed stability to the class structure. In this sense, his scheme is based on the assumption that Japan is a class society. He thus incorporates both Weberian and Marxian traits: Weberian in emphasizing the spread of bureaucratization and the growth of white-collar workers, Marxian in the sense of emphasizing the intermediate position of the middle class between the capitalist and labor classes. (See Mackenzie (1982) on the comparison of Weberian and Marxian views, and Wright (1986) for the intermediate position of the new middle class within 'exploitation location'.)

However, I have emphasized that class structure as a system of representation of distributive interests was not a dominant element in the high-growth-period system. Rather, not only was the new middle class the major proponent of the system, it was also the largest beneficiary. Specifically, the new middle class and the large-firms sector in which it worked were the largest recipients of policy rents accruing from government interventions. Finding instrumental values in a system that utilized firms and industries as the basis for coalitions at the government–private-sector interface, the new middle class led economic development in the era of government intervention in the economy.

It was during the 1970s that competition-prevention measures and policy rents allocation biased to large firms in capital-intensive industries were gradually reduced, and policy emphasis shifted to sectors such as agriculture and small and medium enterprises (SMEs). In this sense, Murakami's new middle mass was the last social strata to participate in the benefits of high growth and in the rent-generation mechanism of the *genkyoku*–industrial association system. His assertion that the new middle mass supported new liberalism and took an anti-bureaucracy stance is not correct. Actually, the new middle mass of small producers lobbied intensively in the 1970s for application of competition-preventive measures. Last in line, the group worked to have the old forms applied to benefit it, even as earlier beneficiaries began to see the forms as a cost to themselves. The system responded favorably: for example, with the 1973 law restricting large-scale retailers. Yoshikawa (1999) notes that since the mid-1970s protection of SMEs and the self-employed has intensified, and the number of small producers has increased.

It was the new middle class that intensified an anti-bureaucratic stance and supported the rise of neo-liberalism. In particular, it was they who proclaimed most loudly the importance of consumer sovereignty, as the domestic–international price differential widened in response to the appreciation of the yen from 1985. It was also this group (in particular the 'wealthy class' of businessmen retired from large firms) that supported financial liberalization, motivated in part because their lump-sum retirement payments made them major depositors.

It is true the new middle mass also participated in the bubble economy of the late 1980s, but this was only passive and did not relate to instrumental rationality. Thus, because many export- and import-competing industries included a large number of SMEs, the late 1980s easy monetary policy, intended to offset the effects of yen appreciation, was strongly supported by the new middle mass. In other words, the policy to slow down the yen's appreciation represented a 'national consensus' (Noguchi 1992) that included strong advocation by the new middle mass. It is suggested in Kosai, Shirakawa and Okina (2001) that the policy atmosphere to resist yen appreciation after the Plaza Accord or exchange rate targeting based on the February 1987 Louvre Agreement worked as a constraint on monetary policy. Nevertheless, it was the new middle class that supported the neo-liberalism and criticized the *genkyoku*–industrial association system.

Why did the new middle class come to be skeptical about the *genkyoku*–industrial association system? There are three reasons.

First, as an integral view of human beings weakened, the class tended to find values in activities other than being 'company men'. The three major groups within the new middle class – managers of large corporations, large depositors, and high-quality consumers – became separated from each other.

Second, as the policy rents accruing to large firms decreased due to various liberalization measures and to growth of the heavy and chemical industries, the incentive to support the system waned.

Third, as the high-growth era ended, and the decline of promotion opportunities and job opportunities after retirement became foreseeable, the instrumental values attached to the growth of firms and industries decreased.

The frustration of the new middle class, as a group oriented to high-level consumption, was directed mainly at the producers of consumption goods and services. It rose against the social norm that emphasized the instrumental values of the growth of firms, and of promotion within the firm, as bases for socio-economic development. This amounted to a revolt against the high-growth-period system. The very success of the system in creating a country that was largely middle class meant the system had sold itself the rope with which it was hanged. But many of the high-growth-period system's parts are viable, and in the concluding chapter these are explored.

NOTES

1. In 1986 there were 403 firms and associations that donated more than 5 million yen to LDP through *kokumin-seiji kyôkai*, the organization for political funds of LDP. The percentage share by industry is 22 per cent for the banking industry, 12 per cent for the construction industry, 8 per cent for the insurance industry, 7 per cent for the steel and metal industry, 6 per cent for the electrical machinery industry, 6 per cent for the automobile industry, and so on (Tsujinaka 1988 p. 130).
2. The appreciation was the delayed adjustment of the exchange rate to the equilibrium rate that reflected Japan's high-productivity growth in the tradable sector (Yoshikawa 1999). The delay was due to the misalignment of exchange rates caused by US fiscal and monetary policy to expand domestic demand under the Reagan administration. In this sense, it was an inevitable consequence of the accomplishment of high growth. McKinnon and Ohno (1998), on the other hand, argue that actual yen appreciation was caused by monetary or expectation-related factors, such as the generation of a yen-appreciation syndrome in response to pressure by the United States' related trade frictions, and to a deflationary bias in the monetary policy of BOJ.

PART IV

9. Conclusion

Since the bubble burst in the late 1980s Japan has been going through a transition in which many parts of the high-growth system have shown themselves to have costs greater than their benefits. These are primarily in the government–private-sector division of labor and the interface between the two sectors.

The former reflects a global shift in emphasis toward markets that began in the 1970s, just as in the 1930s there was a global shift away from markets toward an increased role for the government. Japan is obliged to reconsider the division of labor between the government and market in the direction of deregulation or a larger role for markets. It is also vital to take the evolution of markets into consideration.

The latter reflects a shift from an interface that considers only the interests of industries to a more broadly based interface. It is necessary to examine not only the distributive interests of various industries and producers but also of other groups such as consumers and environmentalists. The concept of stakeholder society must be enlarged.

The next section looks at some other approaches to understanding aspects of Japan's economic development and its economic system's evolution. Attention then turns to the transformation the high-growth-period system is undergoing. I conclude by identifying some topics beyond the scope of this volume relating to the system's future evolutionary process.

9.1 ASPECTS OF THE SYSTEM'S HISTORICAL DEVELOPMENT

In seeking to explain Japan's postwar economic development and system, several views have been advanced that need to be examined. These are the effects of the wartime economy and theories of monotonic development.

9.1.1 Emergence of the High-growth-period Economic System

Let us first summarize the process of the emergence of the high-growth-period economic system.

The main reason for the emergence of the high-growth-period economic system lies in the advent of the era of government intervention in the economy as an external change in economic thinking and the inability of the Meiji-Taishô economic system to accommodate the changes. Faced with this new external condition, the existing Meiji-Taishô economic system, already in trouble due to declining economic performance, fell into serious difficulty. The decline of the economic performance was caused partly by the exhaustion of growth potential of indigenous industries, and partly by the difficulty of the so-called secondary import substitution. The heavy and chemical industries, started during World War I owing to the windfall profit opportunity provided by the warfare in Europe, were obliged to be involved in tough competition with Western producers after the 1920s. The threat of socialist revolution after the establishment of the Soviet Union in 1917, and the perception of the beginning of the era of total war, amplified the impact of the changes in economic thinking. Bureaucrats began to intervene in the economy with various motivations such as developmental orientation, redistributive intention, or planning purpose. People reacted to the maximizing opportunities provided by the government interventions. To distributive conflicts involving regional rivalry were added inter-industrial conflicts and class struggle, and this was beyond the capability of the Meiji-Taishô economic system, designed on the classical role of the government in supplying public goods. The intervention of the government reached a peak at the time of World War II and the reform activities immediately after the war, and the Meiji-Taishô economic system finally gave way to the emerging high-growth-period economic system. The high-growth-period economic system became a stable equilibrium system when it was equipped with the government–private-sector interface representing inter-industrial interests by means of the *genkyoku*-industrial association system, and when workers and managers were motivated to invest in firm-specific skills.

The process of the emergence of the high-growth-period economic system was composed of three phases. First, various ingredients of the new system emerged in very nascent form during the 1920s and 1930s. With respect to the sub-system of the division of labour between the government and the private sector, various measures were introduced to control the behaviour of private-firm activities and to promote important industries. With respect to the sub-system of the private sector, embryonic forms of the seniority wage system and long-term employment emerged in large zaibatsu firms. Syndicated loans was born in order to facilitate monitoring of war-related lendings. With respect to the sub-system of the representation of distributive interests at the government–private-sector interface, industrial associations were born and gradually developed close contact with the government.

All these movements were accelerated and intensified in the second phase, during and immediately after the war. Government started economic planning and direct control of the economy utilizing *tôseikai* (former industrial associations) as conduits of information and directives. Shareholder rights were significantly curtailed, and bank lendings were put under the direct control of the government and, finally, of munitions companies. Employment and wage systems were controlled so as to implement munitions production smoothly; the seniority wage system was formalized and became universal among large firms. The defeat in the war and the reforms implemented by the occupation forces perpetuated, and sometimes, intensified, the wartime system and trend. Intense economic control was maintained until 1952, and zaibatsu and landlords were in effect deprived of their wealth.

In the third phase, institutional complementarity began to work among the three sub-systems. The bureaucracy wielded significant power in the regulation of economic activities. The bank-centred financial system was maintained partly due to the government regulations on the financial markets that repressed the price mechanism, and partly due to the weakened control power of investors. In the absence of large wealth holders and due to the progress of cross-shareholding, cooperate managers obtained their autonomy, and long-term employment was established, giving rise to incentives to invest in firm-specific skills. As the mobility of labour decreased, the government–private-sector interface was converted into one where inter-industrial interests were adjusted through the *genkyoku*–industrial association system. The high degree of government intervention in the economy by means of various regulations became institutionally complementary with the government–private-sector interface based on inter-industrial representation of interests. Industrial policy was facilitated by the *genkyoku*–industrial system, and the latter was justified as the interface in the presence of the former. Further, immobility of labour and firm-specific skills of labour provided basic conditions for the representation for distributive interests by means of inter-industrial groups, and not through groups based on economic class. In this way, the Japanese-style firm system characterized by long-term employment also became institutionally complementary with the government–private-sector interface representing inter-industrial interests during the early 1950s. It could be said that at this stage the high-growth-period economic system was finally established.

9.1.2 Effects of the Wartime Economy

The analysis here casts doubt on some of the popular theories about the effects of the wartime economy on the emergence of the high-growth-period system. The assertions of principal advocates of the hypothesis, such as Noguchi (1995) and Okazaki and Okuno (1993), are derived mainly from consideration of the sub-system of the division of labor between the government and the private sector. Because the shift in economic systems was caused by changes in economic thought regarding this sub-system, it is reasonable for them to focus on it. However, it was the interaction among the three sub-systems, and especially the conversion in the sub-system of the government–private-sector interface, that finally completed the establishment of the high-growth-period system. The assertion by these authors is based on neglect of the fact that the effects on the division of labor between the government and private sector interacted with the government–private-sector interface: industrial policy in the division of labor sub-system was embedded in the whole economic system when it became institutionally complementary with the *genkyoku*–industrial association system. This probably gave rise to the system of 'embedded autonomy' maintained in Evans (1995).

The argument of Okazaki and Okuno (1993) is carefully constructed in encompassing the transformation in the private-sector sub-system, such as changes in firm behavior during wartime. However, such a transformation should be construed carefully: the changes were not caused by firms' rational behavior or by a shift in the equilibrium in the evolutionary game. Okazaki and Okuno seem to have confused apparent changes with real changes. For example, during wartime, the zaibatsu still held huge potential power. Although investor rights were curtailed and significant, formal control of firms was usurped by regulations and controls, many of them labeled temporary, and private firms were not nationalized. Although there was intense dislike of the old zaibatsu in many circles, especially military ones, new zaibatsu were created with the encouragement and cooperation of the government. In other words, outside the context of a wartime economy and control by military-related bureaucrats, large stockholders and zaibatsu families were still the ultimate owners, with potential control rights of the firm system.

This situation was quite different from that of the period after zaibatsu dissolution, when curtailment of investor rights through active cross-shareholding was implemented by corporate managements as a result of maximizing behavior of the firm sector. It was either a strategy to maximize firm value through encouraging investment in firm-specific skills by workers or a rational behavior of managers to maximize private benefits through entrenchment, and could have been intended to do both. In this sense, I cannot agree with the assertion of Okazaki and Okuno, even if they refer not only to the changes in the division of labor between the government and the private-sector but also to the transformation in the private-sector during wartime.

It must be noted that this is not to deny the importance of war-related shocks and reforms after the war. Many ingredients of the high-growth-period system had their origins in the period before the war: seniority wages, industrial policy, industrial associations, and so on. Without the experience of the war and occupation, the economic bureaucrats with a developmental mentality would not have had the opportunity to become so dominant in society. Moreover, defeat in the war meant the disappearance of the wealth of zaibatsu families and the landlord class. This had enormous consequences. Not only did it bring about the final termination of the government–private-sector interface based on regional representation (*meibôka*-based social order), it resulted in there being little opposition and few alternatives to a shift toward the government in the division of labor. It also laid the base of a postwar society with unprecedented equality in wealth and income distribution.

One needs to give due consideration to the continuity between the prewar and postwar period, such as in the development of protection policies regarding tenancy rights since the 1920s, and criticism of zaibatsu during the 1930s, with the consequent changes in zaibatsu behavior. Even considering these points, however, this book suggests that the importance of the shocks of the war is difficult to ignore.

9.1.3 Monotonic Development

One of the focal issues in the controversy about the emergence of the economic system of the high-growth period is whether it resulted from a monotonic transformation from the prewar period; that is, has the system evolved monotonically toward the high-growth-period system, characterized by various 'Japanese-style' properties?

To determine this, it is not sufficient to examine the evolutionary process of particular properties of the system and to point out some embryonic form of them in the prewar period, as proponents of monotonic explanations generally have done. Mere continuity of a particular property since the prewar period does not justify claiming that the economic system-building of modern Japan is characterized by a simple-minded pursuit of creating an economic system characterized by the property. It is imperative to evaluate the importance of the embryonic forms of the system's properties in the full structure of the economic system existing during the prewar period, as has been done in the previous chapters.

In a number of studies of Japan's development written in the 1970s and 1980s, especially by Westerners, it was claimed that Japan has monotonically behaved so as to establish a 'Japanese-style' economic system from the time when construction of a modern state started in the mid-19th century. Such behavior is considered either unintentional in the sense of being guided by cultural characteristics, or intentional in the sense of rational behavior by the state and corporate firms taking advantage of latecomer status. Representative, and most influential among the intentional school, are Dore (1973) on the employment system and Johnson (1982) on industrial policy. Both focus on the examination of particular properties of the high-growth period, and their research is presented in a way that implies that the particular aspects studied are the core or essence of 'the Japanese economic system', so that they are liable to be interpreted as theories regarding the evolution of the whole economic system.

Dore (1973) describes the formation of the Japanese-style employment system as a continuous and monotonic process of cooperative 'organization-oriented' evolution following the early Meiji period. In his analysis, pursuit of a Japanese-style employment system started with the state enterprises related to ordnance production and shipbuilding in the 1870s. Through a trial-and-error process, the prewar Japanese system, which was characterized by corporate paternalism, was established during World War I and the 1920s, and this was transformed further to the welfare corporatism of the postwar period. The driving force for institutional evolution did not lie in cultural factors, but rather in the maximizing behavior of the private sector in pursuit of organizational efficiency. Further, comparing the evolution of the employment system in prewar Japan with that of Great Britain in the mid-19th century, Dore points out that such a pursuit of an efficient system was successful because of the realization of latercomer advantage.

Johnson (1982) sees the evolution of the Japanese economic system as the simple-minded pursuit of a powerful developmental state. He claims that 'plan rationality', as opposed to market rationality, was an invariable policy motif of the Japanese government, and that such a pursuit started in the late 1880s, and culminated in the postwar 'economic miracle' led by industrial policy largely created by the Ministry of International Trade and Industry (MITI). Johnson is aware of the existence of a relatively free and market-based economy around the 1910s, but he refers to it only as an aberration in the basic trend, or as just an interlude.[1]

Although much of what Dore and Johnson assert is correct when interpreted as hypotheses on particular properties of the high-growth period, if it is construed as hypotheses regarding the economic system as a whole, it is not congruent with the evidence and conclusions presented here. In fact, the system prior to the high-growth-period system, the Meiji-Taisho system, is quite different from the images conjured up by Johnson and Dore, and the emergence of the high-growth-period system is closely related to the vicissitudes of the Meiji-Taishô system.

That is, as shown in this book, the high-growth-period system emerged as a result of the failure of the Meiji-Taishô system to adapt to the changes in exogenous conditions. Intensification of industrial policy and a cooperative employment system emerged because of the inability of the incumbent system to resolve distributive conflicts, which provided economic agents (politicians, bureaucrats and entrepreneurs) with incentives to seek a new system suitable for an era of government intervention (and a wartime economy). If one looks at what is going on only in the sub-system of government–private-sector division of labor, or only in the sub-system of the private-sector, one might see a monotonic development of industrial policy or Japanese-style employment system. Behind such monotonic processes, however, there were significant interactions between the three sub-systems and the consequent rise and fall of economic systems as a whole.

9.2 TRANSFORMATION OF THE HIGH-GROWTH-PERIOD SYSTEM

The high-growth-period economic system is considered to have prevailed not only in the high-growth era (1955–73) but also in the stable- to low-growth period thereafter. However, in the face of slower and more uncertain growth prospects, a system that was by name predicated on, and associated with, high-growth cannot be expected to function as well it once did. Thus, the system changed substantially and has begun its decline with respect to the government–private-sector division of labor and industry–based government–private-sector interface.

There are two main views regarding reasons for the changes. One is the simultaneous changing of the three exogenous conditions that had formed the basic framework of the economic system. The other is convergence, which is often related to advocacy of 'structural reforms' as a way of restoring Japanese economic growth. The two views are not mutually exclusive. However, changing exogenous conditions do not require convergence to some global standard. Also, the changing-conditions view is not congruent with traditional modernization theory, while a globalization and standardization view by definition involves convergence, and is the core of traditional modernization theory.

After briefly contrasting the two views, the focus here is on how transformation is taking place on the basis of the exogenous-conditions view.

9.2.1 Convergence and Structural Reform

As deflation and lack of demand plagued the Japanese economy in the 1990s, ways were sought to restore growth. Among the remedies has been structural reform. Structural reform as currently used with reference to Japan relates to the argument that the main drawback of the current system is a lack of market discipline, and partly related to the view that the high-growth-period system is a continuation of bureaucratic controls imposed during wartime. Thus, structural changes in the form of liberalization and deregulation – 'reform' – are fficient to replace the system, or get it back on the 'right' track. However, the evidence shows that the ongoing changes in the economic system are broader than this.

Advocacy of structural reform reflects a view that the evolution of Japan's economic system is a process of modernization, which essentially means convergence to some form of Western economic system or global-standard system. Thus, Japan is seen as moving from a premodern and backward system to a modern Western system, and the high-growth-period system that is so 'Japanese' was simply a digression in the process. Modernization as Westernization goes back to the 19th century, but just what Westernization means has changed through time: most recently it has led to reference to a global-standard system.

The globalization of the world economy and standardization of institutions argument runs as follows. Financial markets around the world are significantly integrated, and competition in commodity markets is global. Under these conditions, it is necessary for various institutions to function with common rules. The rapid development of outsourcing and of global choice of factory location induces standardization of taxation and accounting systems. Firms are pressed to adopt similar governance mechanisms, and financial institutions to follow similar prudential regulations. Also, it can be further argued that the global standards are becoming closer to the Anglo–American system which emphasizes the role of impersonal and arm's-length transactions, and less involvement by the government in the economy. Under these conditions, it is possible to say that the economic system of Japan, characterized by relation-based transactions and emphasis on the role of government, needs to be transformed so as to adapt to global standards.

The model in this book is also useful in explaining the reasons for structural changes that are currently taking place in Japan. It follows that convergence to some global-standard system is not the only hypothesis that explains such changes. I do not deny the validity of the globalization hypothesis, but I want to note that its applicability and scope are significantly more limited than is considered in conventional views.

9.2.2 Changes in Exogenous Conditions

The second view, which is suggested from the analysis of this book, is that the incumbent economic system is changing because the three exogenous conditions that have conditioned Japan's economic systems for most of the time since it began to modernize were changing, and this was happening all at once in the 1980s.

Let us look at each of the conditions. First, the catch-up process begun in the 19th-century Meiji era was completed by the mid-1970s. This meant Japan could no longer grow rapidly simply by mimicking the industrial structure of advanced nations: it had become one of the advanced economies. Second, the situation of Japan being the only industrialized economy in East Asia disappeared in the early 1980s. Japan now needs to reorganize its quasi-autarchic (full-set type) industrial structure, which has ignored the international division of labor. Third, the economic thought emphasizing the role of government and market failures, which became globally dominant during the depression of the 1930s and remained so into the 1970s, was replaced by an intellectual climate that recognized the extensiveness of government failures and emphasized the role of markets.

9.3 CHANGES TO THE SUB-SYSTEMS

Changes in the exogenous conditions affected each sub-system directly, and then the adjustments and adaptations of the sub-systems have interacted through institutional complementarity.

9.3.1 Division of Labor

Change in the sub-system concerning the division of labor between the market and the government was triggered by widening government deficits caused by the slow-down of economic growth, and propelled by the need to accommodate the evolution of markets and to cope with competition in the globalizing economy. The basic background for this was the drastic changes in economic thought about the relative costs of failures by the market and by the government. Compared to other economies, expansion of the welfare state and wasteful rent-seeking were not major reasons for reconsideration of Japan's division of labor. Rather, it was over-expansion of the regulatory role of the central government or the concern about the costs of its failures, which suppressed not just the working of the private-sector but initiatives of local governments as well. This explains why, so far, deregulation has been given first priority in Japan in adapting the government–private-sector division of labor to the changes in exogenous conditions. (Deregulation policy is also justified on the ground of modernization view.)

Assertions of 'excessive' intervention by the government in the economy have become prevalent in the theory of economic policy since the 1980s based on three factors. The first is fiscal deficits, which became serious in most developed countries after the 1970s oil shocks and the ensuing slowing of growth. Expansion of the public sector in redistributive areas, as well as in provision of quasi-private goods, rose as an important reform agenda. The second factor is the realization that, just as there are market failures, so are there government failures and the latter can be quite as deleterious and common as the former. Industrial policies came to be criticized because of the resources lost to rent-seeking and an innate inefficiency of bureaucratic control. The third factor was the evolution of the market. The drastic reduction in information and communication costs and the new competitive environment, owing to the realization of a borderless economy in financial and other areas, has enhanced the competitive advantages of the market mechanism.

9.3.2 Interface

The sub-system of the government–private-sector interface is seriously ailing.

First, the *genkyoku*–industrial system has become unable to resolve distributive conflicts in the post-catch-up period, especially as other Asian economies also move quickly toward catch-up. Representation of distributive conflicts through inter-industrial interests is unable to accommodate new types of distributive interests such as those of consumers, environmentalists, regions, and foreign industries.

Second, partly due to the narrow coverage of the old system and partly due to the dual-decision process (LDP and the government), the speed of policy decisions and the flexibility of institutional design has seriously deteriorated. Enormous amounts of time and energy are needed to reach a consensus among bureaucrats and politicians. Consequently, the Japanese economic system has difficulty in responding quickly to rapid changes in circumstances.

Needless to say, the basic reason for the malfunctioning of the interface based on inter-industrial interest representation is the decline in the role of government in coordinating economic activities. Industrial policy is now obliged to retreat. The intervention by the government in the distributive conflicts by means of control of competitive conditions among industries has now become almost impossible to implement. In this sense the transformation in the sub-system of the government–private-sector interface is proceeding in close relationship with the changes in the sub-system of the government–private-sector division of labor.

9.3.3 Private Sector

The sub-system of the private sector is also changing to accommodate changes in external conditions. To adjust to a more market-based economy, Japanese firms are changing their management and production systems so as to make quick decisions and swift responses to demand and supply conditions. As for growth in Asia, Japanese firms are actively involved in establishing a division of labor between China and other countries through such measures as foreign direct investment (FDI) in production facilities of low- and middle-grade products. With respect to completion of catch-up, firms are obliged to restructure so as to specialize in areas in which Japan has comparative advantage and to devote considerable resources in R&D activities. The adaptation to exogenous conditions by the private sector has been flexible and successful so far. It seems that through the adjustment process the private sector is rediscovering its flexibility in organizational reform as well as its strength in process and product innovation.

The private sector is trying to adapt not only to changing external conditions but also to the transformation of the two other sub-systems. As government regulations are repealed or mitigated, the bank-centered financial system, which came into existence partly because of regulation of capital markets and partly because of the weak control-rights of investors due to cross-shareholding, is undergoing significant changes. Further, in the government–private-sector interface, as the role of *genkyoku*–industrial associations in representing distributive interests has weakened, relation-specific investment by employees in firm-specific skills is affected and, hence, so is the mobility of labor.

9.4 THE ROLE OF SOCIAL NORMS

Contemporary Japan is said to be in an era of diversification of individual values (value pluralism), and this was so also in the 1920s when 'Taishô Democracy' blossomed. Disintegration of the value system can become a cause for the loss of sustainability of an economic system, and the latter can intensify the former. Stated positively, for the smooth and sustainable functioning of an economic system there needs to be an 'adjustment of values' among people, giving rise to a consensus as to the social norms suitable for the system. While paying respect to the values of each individual, people must obey the agreed social norms in their socio-economic behavior, and this requirement is a cost of having a sustainable economic system. In this sense, a sustainable new economic system must be attractive enough to induce people to pay such costs.

As Gerschenkron (1962) emphasizes, the process of a great and sudden industrialization, or of a concerted effort to catch up, cannot be started merely by an improvement of resource allocation or profit opportunity. Rather, 'a New Deal in emotion' or a change in intellectual and ideological climate are essential. Social norms had a significant influence on the rise and fall of the two successive economic systems that characterized Japan's catch-up phase.

Thus, in the Meiji-Taishô economic system, contributing to the development of the region where someone lived was a major social norm, and the system was obliged to decline as this norm weakened, which occurred as distributive conflicts became dependent not only on inter-regional interests but also on class and inter-industrial interests.

In the high-growth-period system, people recognized an instrumental value in the growth of the industry or firm to which they belonged, and the current trouble with the system is closely related to the weakening of that social norm.

Having achieved catch-up, however, it is not easy to judge whether Japan needs an over-riding common social norm. One can plausibly argue that the Japanese should liberalize themselves from the constraints of a common social value. The answer hinges on two points.

First, to be viable in the global context a country finds itself in, there needs to be a consensus about basic principles when constructing a new economic system. In Japan, opinions are divided with respect to the adequate division of labor between the government and markets, and to the role of group and collective behavior. Unless a consensus is reached, it is not easy to coordinate expectations, and thus to realize economic growth. Further, in as much as the future role of the government is not confined to the supply of pure public goods, its activity is not free from influencing income distribution. This means it is necessary to consider what the government–private-sector interface of the new system will be. That, in turn, is closely related to the social norms of the system.

Second is whether a maximization of consumption utility is an adequate norm for the construction of an economic system. From the viewpoint of economic philosophy, it is possible to conceive of an economic system based on non-utilitarian criteria (Shionoya 1994). It could be argued that Japan's economic system should not aim at a high rate of economic growth, but instead aspire to high cultural value some form of. If economic growth is not necessarily needed, and distributive conflicts such as rural–urban disparity and inter-generational inequality are disregarded, it is not necessary to worry about consensus-building regarding the social norms of the future economic system.

9.5 FOR FURTHER DISCUSSION

We have deliberated the question of why and how the high-growth-period system has been changing since the 1980s. Because of the limited scope of this book, it is not possible to capture all the changing aspects, although the investigation was done as coherently as possible. To take into consideration the aspects not directly touched, it is necessary to expand the framework to accommodate global institutional changes, and to tackle the convergence issue more broadly. This, however, is left for future study. Moreover, I have not touched on the normative issue of how the high-growth-period system should be changed.

Although these are issues beyond the scope of this book, let me add three remarks as spurs to further discussion.

First, with respect to whether Japan is converging to some global standard, the evidence is ambiguous. Regarding the normative question of whether the Japanese economic system *should* converge, however, the key issue seems clear. Global convergence of economic systems certainly would be efficiency enhancing – in terms of *static* allocation of resources. However, static benefits in resource allocation should be carefully compared to the possible dynamic gains arising from a diversity of economic systems. Such gains pertain not only to diversity in economic systems but also to cultural values.

Second, one should note the meaning of the shock of World War II on the economic system. Because of the enormous dislocations caused by preparation, execution, defeat and occupation, the decline of the Meiji-Taishô system was accelerated, and an eventual 'hard landing' was unavoidable. However, one can conjecture that, in the case of the high-growth-period system, change can be a gradual transformation, or 'soft landing'. This is true despite the extent of the external changes that have undermined the system. In particular, the transformation can be accomplished in a way that maintains the merits of the private-sector sub-system in the high-growth-period system.

Finally, let me touch on the issue of the sources of future economic growth. This book has emphasized that the economic growth of Japan over its entire modern period owes much to relation-specific investment by tenant farmers and mobilization of resources to corporate management, which enabled adaptation to new technologies, and by workers and suppliers, which enabled process and product innovation by Japanese firms. In the face of drastic changes in the sub-systems of division of labor and the government private-sector interface, how to restructure the private-sector sub-system so as to retain technological capability is an important task to be undertaken by Japan from now on.

NOTE

1. Subsequent research and evidence seem to have shown that Johnson's view of MITI, especially any prowess at 'picking winners', was over-generous. See Okimoto (1989) and Patrick (1986).

References

Abe, Takeshi (1989), *Nihon ni okeru Sanchi Men-orimono-gyô no Tenkai*, Tokyo: University of Tokyo Press.

Abramovitz, Moses (1986), 'Catching Up, Forging Ahead, and Falling Behind', *Journal of Economic History*, **46** (2), 385–406.

Abramovitz, Moses (1990), 'The Catch-up Factor in Postwar Economic Growth', *Economic Inquiry*, **28** (1), 1–18.

Alesina, Alberto and Dani Rodrick (1994), 'Distributive Politics and Economic Growth', *Quarterly Journal of Economics*, **109**, 465–90.

Alesina, Alberto and Howard Rosenthal (1995), *Partissan Politics, Divided Government, and the Economy*, Cambridge and New York: Cambridege University Press.

Allen, Franklin and Anthony M. Santomero (1998), 'The Theory of Financial Intermediation', *Journal of Banking and Finance*, **21**, 1461–85.

Allen, Franklin and Douglas Gale (2000), *Comparing Financial Systems*, Cambridge Mass: MIT Press.

Aoki, Masahiko (1988), *Information, Incentives, and Bargaining in the Japanese Economy*, Cambridge and New York: Cambridge University Press.

Aoki, Masahiko (1994), 'Monitoring Characteristics of the Main Bank System: An Analytical and Developmental View', in Masahiko Aoki and Hugh Patrick (eds), *The Japanese Main Bank System*, Oxford and New York: Oxford University Press, pp. 109–41.

Aoki, Masahiko (1995), *Keizai Shisutemu no Shinka to Tagensei*, Tokyo: Toyokeizai Shinpo-sha.

Aoki, Masahiko (1999), 'Kanryô-sei Tagenshugi Kokka to Sangyô Soshiki no Kyôshin-ka', in Masahiko Aoki, Masahiro Okuno and Tetsuji Okazaki (eds), *Shijyô no Yakuwari Kokka no Yakuwari*, Tokyo: Toyokeizai Shinpo-sha, pp. 3–27.

Aoki, Masahiko (2001), *Towards a Comparative Institutional Analysis*, Cambridge and London: MIT Press.

Aoki, Masahiko (2002), 'Sangyô Âkitekuchua no Mojyûru-ka – Rironteki Intorodakushon', in Masahiko Aoki and Haruhiko Ando (eds), *Mojyûru-ka – Atarashii Sangyô Âkitekuchua no Honshitsu*, Tokyo: Toyo Keizai Shinpo-sha, pp. 3–34.

Aonuma, Yoshimatu (1965), *Nihon no Keieisô – sono Shusshin to Seikaku* (Nikkei Shinsho), Tokyo: Nihon Keizai Shinbun-sha.

Ariizumi, Sadao (1980), *Meij Seiji-shi no Kiso Katei*, Tokyo: Yoshikawa Kobunkan.

Ariizumi, Sadao (1983), *Hoshi Toru*, Tokyo: Asahi Shinbun-sha.

Ariizumi, Sadao (1984), 'Shôwa Kyôkô-ki Zengo no Chihô Seijishi Jyôkyô – 1929–1934 Nen', in Kindai Nihon Kenkyû-kai (ed.), *Nenpô Kindai Nihon Kenkyû (6) – Seitô Naikaku no Seiritsu to Hôkai*, Tokyo: Yamakawa Shuppan-sha, pp. 233–56.

Arrow, Kenneth J. (1962), 'The Economic Implications of Learning by Doing', *Review of Economic Studies*, (29), 155–73.

Asahi Shinbun (1930), *Nihon Keizai Tôkei Sôran*, Tokyo: Asahi Shinbun-sha.

Asai, Yoshio (1975), 'Seiritsu-ki no Nihon Kogyo Ginko', *Tochi Seidoshi-gaku*, **68**, 32–51.

Asai, Yoshio (1983), 'Nihon Kogyo Ginko', in Toshihiko Kato (ed.), *Nihon Kin'yû-ron no Shiteki Kenkyû*, Tokyo: University of Tokyo, pp. 231–50.

Asajima, Shoichi (1983), *Senkan-ki Sumitomo Zaibatsu Keiei-shi*, Tokyo: University of Tokyo Press.

Asajima, Shoichi (1986), *Mitsubishi Zaibatsu no Kin'yû Kôzô*, Tokyo: Ochanomizu Shobo.

Asajima, Shoichi (ed.) (1987), *Zaibatsu Kin'yû Kôzô no Hikaku Kenkyû*, Tokyo: Ochanomizu Shobo.

Asako, Kazumi and Kazunori Sakamoto (1993), 'Seifu Shihon no Seisan Kôka', *Finansharu Rebyû*, (26), 97–101.

Asako, Kazumi, Jun Tsuneki, Shin-ichi Fukuda, Hiroshi Teruyama, Takashi Tsukamoto and Masanori Sugiura (1994), 'Shakai Shihon no Seisanryoku Kôka to Kôkyô Tôshi no Kôsei Sonshitsu', *Keizai Bunseki*, **135**, 1–90.

Asakura, Kokichi (1961), *Meiji Zenki Nihon Kin'yû Kôzô-shi*, Tokyo: Iwanami Shoten.

Asanuma, Banri (1989), 'Manufacturer–Supplier Relationships in Japan and the Concept of Relation-Specific Skill', *Journal of Japanese and International Economics*, **3** (1), 1–30.

Baldwin, Carliss Y. and Kim B. Clark (2000), *Design Rules: The Power of Modularity*, vol. I, Cambridge and London: MIT Press.

Baldwin, Robert E. (1984), 'Rent-seeking and Trade Policy: An Industry Approach', *Weltwirtschaftliches Archiv*, **120** (4), 662–77.

Banno, Junji (1971), *Meiji Kenpô Taisei no Kakuritsu*, Tokyo: University of Tokyo Press.

Banno, Junji (1982), *Taishô Seihen*, Tokyo: Mineruva Shobo.

Banno, Junji (1983), 'Fukokuron no Seijishi-teki Kôsatsu – 1974–81 (Meiji 7–14 Nen) –', in Mataji Umemura and Takafusa Nakamura (eds), *Matsukata-zaisei to Shokusan Kôgyô Seisaku*, Tokyo: University of Tokyo Press, pp. 37–52.

Banno, Junji (1985), 'Seitô Seiji no Hôkai', in Junji Banno and Masahito Miyaji (eds), *Nihon Kindai-shi ni okeru Tenkanki no Kenkyû*, Tokyo: Yamakawa Shuppan-sha, pp. 349–401.

Banno, Junji (1991), 'Senzen-ki ni okeru Shakai Minshu-shugi, Minshu Shakai-shugi, Kigyô Minshu-shugi', in Tokyo Daigaku Shakai Kagaku Kenkyujyo (ed.) *Gendai Nihon Shakai (4) Rekishiteki Zentei*, Tokyo: University of Tokyo Press.

Barnett, William A. and Jeong-Ho Hahm (1994), 'Financial–Firm Production of Monetary Services; A Generalized Symmetric Barnett Variable-Profit-Function Approach', *Journal of Business and Economic Statistics*, **12** (1), 33–46.

Beason, Richard and David E. Weinstein (1996), 'Growth, Economies of Scale, and Targeting in Japan (1955–1990)', *Review of Economics and Statistics*, **78**, May, 286–95.

Becker, Gary S. (1983), 'A Theory of Competition Among Pressure Groups for Political Influence', *Quarterly Journal of Economics*, **98** (3), 371–400.

Bernanke, Ben (1983), 'Nonmonetary Effects of the Financial Crisis in the Propagation of the Great Depression', *American Economic Review*, **73** (3), 257–76.

Binswanger, Hans P. and Klaus Deininger (1997), 'Explaining Agricultural and Agrarian Policies in Developing Countries', *Journal of Economic Literature*, December, **35** (4), 1958–2005.

Chuma, Hiroyuki (1987), 'Nihon-teki Koyô-kankô no Keizai Gôriseiron Sai-kentô – 1920 nendai no Nichibei Hikaku no Shiten kara', *Nihon Keizai Kenkyu*, **38** (4), 307–20.

Chuma, Hiroyuki (2002), 'Mojyûru Sekkei Shisô no Yakuwari – Handôtai Rokô-sôchi Sangyô to Kôsaku-kikai Sangyô o Jirei toshite', in Masahiko Aoki and Haruhiko Ando (eds), *Mojyûru-ka – Atarashii Sangyô Âkitekuchua no Honshitsu*, Tokyo: Toyo Keizai Shinpo-sha, pp. 211–46.

Chuma, Hiroyuki and Yoshio Higuchi (1995), 'Keizai Kankyô no Henka to Chôki Koyô Shisutemu', in Takenori Inoki and Yoshio Higuchi (eds), *Nihon no Koyô Shisutemu to Rôdô Shijyô*, Tokyo: Nihon Keizai Shinbun-sha, pp. 23–56.

Cohen, Jerome B. (1949), *Japan's Economy in War and Reconstruction*, Minneapolis: University of Minnesota Press.

Crafts, Nicholas (2000), 'Globalization and Growth in the Twentieth

Century', Washington, DC: IMF Working Paper WP/00/44.

Crafts, Nicholas and Gianni Toniolo (1996), 'Postwar Growth: An Overview', in Nicholas Crafts and Gianni Toniolo (eds), *Economic Growth in Europe in 1945*, Cambridge: Cambridge University Press, pp. 1–37.

Diamond, Douglas and Dybvig Philip (1983), 'Bank Runs, Deposit Insurance, and Liquidity', *Journal of Political Economy*, **91** (3), 401–19.

Dixit, Avinash (1996), *The Making of Economic Policy*, Cambridge, Mass: MIT Press.

Dore, Ronald (1973), *British Factory–Japanese Factory: The Origin of National Diversity in Industrial Relations*, Berkeley: University of California Press.

Dower, John (1999), *Embracing Defeat: Japan in the Wake of World War II*, New York: W.W. Norton: New Press.

Erickson, Robert and John H. Goldthorpe (1992), *The Constant Flux: A Study of Class Mobility in Industrial Societies*, Oxford: Clarendon Press.

Evans, Peter (1995), *Embedded Autonomy: States and Industrial Transformation*, Princeton NJ: Princeton University Press.

Fei, John C. H. and Gustav Ranis (1964), *Development of the Labor Surplus Economy: Theory and Policy*, Homewood, Ill: R. D. Irwin.

Fujimoto, Takahiro (2002), 'Nihon-gata Sapuraiyâ-shisutemu to Mojyûru-ka – Jidôsha Sangyô o Jirei to shite', Masahiko Aoki and Haruhiko Ando (eds), *Mojyûru-ka – Atarashii Sangyô Âkitekuchua no Honshitsu*, Tokyo: Toyo Keizai Shinpo-sha. pp. 169–202.

Fujino, Shozaburo (1987), 'Sengo Nihon no Kokusai Shûshi', Discussion Paper (148), Tokyo: The Institute of Economic Research, Hitotsubashi University.

Fujino, Shozaburo and Juro Teranishi (2000), *Nihon Kin'yû no Sûryô Bunseki*, Tokyo: Toyokeizai Shinpo-sha.

Fukuda, Shin-ichi, Hiroshi Teruyama, Akihiro Kamiya and So Kei (1995), 'Seizôgyô ni okeru Seisaku Kin'yû no Yûdô Kôka', *Keizai Bunseki*, (140).

Fukuda, Shin-ichi (2001), 'The Role of Long-term Loans for Economic Development: Empirical Evidence in Japan, Korea, and Taiwan', a paper presented at the Conference on Designing Financial Systems in East Asia and Japan, held by Hitotsubashi University (Center for Economic Institution) and IMF in Tokyo Sept. 24–25, 2001.

Furukawa, Takafumi (1990), 'Kakushin Kanryô no Shisô to Kôdô', *Shigaku Zasshi*, **99** (4), 1–38.

Gerschenkron, Alexander (1962), *Economic Backwardness in*

Historical Perspective, Cambridge, Mass: Belknap Press of Harvard University Press.

Gilson, Ronald J. and Mark J. Roe (1999), 'Lifetime Labor Peace and the Evolution of Japanese Corporate Governance', *Columbia Law Review*, **99** (2), pp. 508–40.

Godo, Yoshihisa and Yujiro Hayami (1999), 'Accumulation of Education in Modern Economic Growth,' *ADB Institute Working Paper*, 4, Tokyo: Asian Development Bank Institute

Godo, Yoshihisa and Juro Teranishi (1992), 'Kôgyôka to Ginko no Kikan Henkan Kinô', in Akiyoshi Horiuchi and Naoyuki Yoshino (eds), *Gendai Nihon no Kin'yû Bunseki*, Tokyo: University of Tokyo Press, pp. 123–39.

Gordon, Andrew (1985), *The Evolution of Labor Relations in Japan*, Cambridge, Mass: Harvard University Press.

Gordon, Andrew (1993), 'Contests for the Workplace', in Andrew Gordon (ed.), *Postwar Japan as History*, Berkeley and Oxford: University of California Press, pp. 373–94.

Goto, Akira (1993), 'Gijutsu Dônyû: Sengo Nihon no Keiken', in Yutaka Kosai and Juro Teranishi (eds), *Sengo Nihon no Keizai Kaikaku*, Tokyo: University of Tokyo Press, pp. 237–54.

Goto, Shin-ichi (1970), *Nihon no Kin'yû Tôkei,* Tokyo: Toyo Keizai Shinpo-sha.

Goto, Shin-ichi (1968), *Honpô Ginko Gôdô-shi*, Tokyo: Kin'yû Zaisei Jijyô Kenkyûkai.

Hadley, Eleanor M. (1970), *Antitrust in Japan*, Princeton, NJ: Princeton University Press.

Hamada, Koichi and Akiyoshi Horiuchi (1987), 'The Political Economy of Japan: The Political Economy of the Financial Market', in Kozo Yamamura and Yasukichi Yasuba (eds), *The Political Economy of Japan vol. 1: The Domestic Transformation*, Stanford, California: Stanford University Press, pp. 223–60.

Hancock, Diana (1991), *'A Theory of Production for the Financial Firm'*, Boston: Kluwer Academic Publishers.

Hara, Akira (1979), 'Kaisô Kôsei no Shin-suikei', in Yoshio Ando (ed.), *Ryô-taisen-kan no Nihon Shihon-shugi*, Tokyo: University of Tokyo Press, pp. 325–64.

Hara, Akira (1980), '1920 Nendai no Zaisei Shishutsu to Sekkyoku, Shôkyoku Ryô-rosen Seisaku', in Takafusa Nakamura (ed.), *Senkan-ki no Nihon Keizai Bunseki*, Tokyo: Yamakawa Shuppan-sha, pp. 77–109.

Hashimoto, Juro (1984), *Dai-kyôkô-ki no Nihon Shihon-shugi*, Tokyo: University of Tokyo Press.

Hashimoto, Juro (1992), 'Zaibatsu no Koncherun-ka', in Juro Hashimoto, Haruhito Takeda and Hosei Daigaku Sangyô Jyôhô-sentâ (eds), *Nihon Keizai no Hatten to Kigyô Shûdan*, Tokyo: University of Tokyo Press, pp. 91–148.

Hashimoto, Juro (1995), '1940 Nen Taisei wa Genzai to Chokketsu shiteinai', *Ekonomisuto*, **73** (19), 64–9.

Hashimoto, Juro, Shin Hasegawa and Hideaki Miyajima (1998), *Gendai Nihon Keizai*, Tokyo: Yuhikaku.

Hayami, Yujiro (1973), *Nihon Nôgyô no Seichô Katei*, Tokyo: Sobun-sha.

Hayami, Yujiro (1986), *Nôgyô Keizairon*, Tokyo: Iwanami Shoten.

Hayashi, Fumio (2000), 'The Main Bank System and Corporate Investment: An Empirical Reassessment', in Masahiko Aoki and Gary R. Saxonhouse (eds), *Finance, Governance, and Competitiveness in Japan*, Oxford and Tokyo: Oxford University Press, pp. 81–97.

Hayashi, Takehisa (1963), 'Meiji-zenki no Kabushiki Kaisha', in Shinzo Kaji (ed.), *Dokusen Shihon no Kenkyû*, Tokyo: University of Tokyo Press, pp. 189–220.

Hellman, Thomas, Kevin Murdock and Joseph Stiglitz (1997), 'Financial Restraint: Toward a New Paradigm', in Masahiko Aoki, Hyung-ki Kim and Masahiro Okuno-Fujiwara (eds), *The Role of Government in East Asian Economic Development*, Oxford: Clarendon Press, pp. 163–208.

Hiwatari, Nobuhiro (1991), *Sengo Nihon no Shijyô to Seiji*, Tokyo: University of Tokyo Press.

Honma, Masayoshi (1994), *Nôgyô Mondai no Seiji Keizaigaku*, Tokyo: Nihon Keizai Shinbun-sha.

Honma, Tetsushi, Yoshihisa Godo and Juro Teranishi (1996), 'Kôdo Seichôki no Wagakuni Ginkogyô no Kôritsusei', *Keizai Kenkyû*, **47** (3), 248–69.

Horiuchi, Akiyoshi (1980), *Nihon no Kin'yû Seisaku – Kin'yû Mekanizumu no Jisshô Bunseki*, Tokyo: Toyo Keizai Shinpo-sha.

Horiuchi, Akiyoshi (1994), 'Kin'yû Kokusai-ka to Kin'yû-kisei', in Akiyoshi Horiuchi (ed.), *Kôza, Kôteki Kisei to Sangyô (5) Kinyû*, Tokyo: NTT Shuppan, pp. 267–300.

Horiuchi, Akiyoshi and Shin-ichi Fukuda (1987), 'Nihon no Mein Banku wa donoyôna Yakuwari o Hatashitaka?', *Kin'yû Kenkyû*, **6** (3), 1–27.

Horiuchi, Akiyoshi and Masayuki Otaki (1987), 'Kin'yû – Seifu Kin'yû to Ginko Kashidashi no Jyûyôsei', in Koichi Hamada, Masahiro Kuroda and Akiyoshi Horiuchi (eds), *Nihon Keizai no*

Makuro Bunseki, Tokyo: University of Tokyo, pp. 123–48.

Horiuchi, Akiyoshi and Ryuko Okazaki (1992), 'Kigyô no Setsubi-tôshi to Mein Banku Kankei', *Kin'yû Kenkyû*, **11** (1), 37–59.

Horiuchi, Akiyoshi and Qing-Yuan Sui (1993), 'Influence of the Japan Development Bank Loan on Corporate Investment Behavior', *Journal of Japanese and International Economies*, **7**, 441–65.

Hoshi, Takeo, Anil Kashyap and David Sharfstein (1990), 'The Role of Banks in Reducing the Costs of Financial Distress in Japan', *Journal of Financial Economics*, (27), 67–88.

Hoshi, Takeo, Anil Kashyap and David Sharfstein (1991), 'Corporate Structure, Liquidity, and Investment Evidence from Japanese Industrial Groups', *Quarterly Journal of Economics*, **106** (1), 33–60.

Hoshi, Takeo and Anil Kashyap (2001), *Corporate Financing and Governance in Japan*, Cambridge, Mass: MIT Press.

Howe, Christopher (1996), *The Origins of Japanese Trade Supremacy*, London: Hurst and Company.

Imada, Takatoshi (1989), *Shakai Kaisô to Seiji*, Tokyo: University of Tokyo Press.

Imuta, Toshimitsu (1976a), *Meiji-ki Kabushiki-kaisha Bunseki Jyosetsu*, Tokyo: Hosei Daigaku Shuppan-kyoku.

Imuta, Toshimitsu (1976b), *Meiji-ki Kinyû-kôzô Bunseki Josetsu*, Tokyo: Hosei Daigaku Shuppan-kyoku.

Inoguchi, Takashi (1983), *Gendai Nihon Seiji Keizai no Kôzô: Seifu to Shijyô*, Tokyo: Toyo Keizai Shinpo-sha.

Inoguchi, Takashi and Tomoaki Iwai (1987), *Zokugiin no Kenkyû*, Tokyo: Nihon Keizai Shinbun-sha.

Inoki, Takenori (2000), *Keizai Seichô no Kajitsu 1955–1972 (Nihon no Kindai 7)*, Tokyo: Chuo Koron Shinsha.

Inoki, Takenori (2001), *Jiyû to Chitsujyo*, Tokyo: Chuo Koron Shinsha.

Ishi Hiromitu (1986), *Zeisei Kaikaku o dô Susumeruka*, Tokyo: Nihon Keizai Shinbun-sha.

Ishii, Kanji (1978), 'Sangyô Shihon Kakuritsu-katei no Kabunushi-sô', in Takahito Sakai, Jun Hoshi, Naoshi Sekiguchi and Kanji Ishii (eds), *Nihon Shihon Shugi – Tenkai to Riron*, Tokyo: University of Tokyo Press, pp. 83–98.

Ishii, Kanji (1983), 'Nihon Ginko', in Toshihiko Kato (ed.), *Nihon Kin'yû-ron no Shiteki Kenkyû*, Tokyo: University of Tokyo Press, pp. 27–51.

Ishii, Kanji (1997), *Nihon no Sangyô Kakumei*, Tokyo: Asahi Shinbun-sha.

Ishii, Kanji (2000), 'Hashigaki', in Kanji Ishii, Akira Hara and Haruhito Takeda (eds), *Nihon Keizaishi (2) Sangyô Kakumeiki*,

Tokyo: University of Tokyo Press, pp. v–ix.

Ito, Akihiro (1993), 'Kôtôkyôiku Kikan Kakujyû to Shin-chûkan-sô Keishiki', in Junji Banno, Masato Miyaji, Naosuke Takamura, Hiroshi Yasuda and Hiroshi Watanabe (eds), *Gendai Shakai eno Tenkei (Nihon Kindai-shi 2)*, Tokyo: Iwanami Shoten, pp. 145–79.

Ito, Takatoshi (1992), *Shôhisha Jyûshi no Keizaigaku*, Tokyo: Nihon Keizai Shinbun-sha.

Iwamoto, Yasushi, Satoshi Ouchi, Satoshi Takeshita and Tadashi Bessho (1996), 'Shakai-shihon no Seisansei to Kôkyô Tôshi no Chiikikan Haibun', *Finansharu Rebyû*, (41), 1–26.

Iwanami Shoten (1968), *Kindai Nihon Sôgô Nenpyô*, Tokyo: Iwanami Shoten.

Jinno, Naohiko (1987), 'Gendai Nihon Zeisei no Keisei Katei (1), (2)', *Keizaigaku Zasshi*, **88** (2, 3), 116–43, (5, 6), 58–80.

Johnson, Chalmers (1982), *MITI and the Japanese Miracle*, Stanford California: Stanford University Press.

Jorgenson, Dele W. and Mieko Nishimizu (1978), 'US and Japanese Economic Growth, 1952–1974: An International Comparison', *The Economic Journal*, **88**, December, 707–26.

Jorgenson, Dele W., Masahiro Kuroda and Mieko Nishimuzu (1987), 'Japan–U.S. Industry-Level Productivity Comparison', *Journal of the Japanese and International Economies*, **1**, 1–30.

Kagaku Gijyutsu-cho (1984), *Kagaku Gijyutsu Hakusho*, Tokyo: Okurasho Insatsu-kyoku.

Kaizuka, Keimei (1984), 'Seifu Shishutsu Kôzô no Henka', *Keizai Kenkyû*, **35** (25), 171–75.

Kajii Isoshi (1961), *Nôgyô Seisan-ryoku no Tenkai Kôzô*, Tokyo: Kobundo.

Kanazawa, Fumio (1984), 'Ryôzei Ijyô-ron Tenkai-katei no Kenkyû – 1920 Nendai ni okeru Keizai Seisaku no Tokushitsu', *Shakai Kagaku Kenkyû*, **36** (1-6), 67–146.

Kanazawa, Fumio (1994), 'Taishô Demokurashî Jyôkyô no Tenkan to Keizai Seisaku', in Samon Kinbara (ed.) *Taishô Demokurashî*, Tokyo: Yoshikawa Kobun-kan, pp. 225–54.

Kaplan, Steven M. and Bernadette A. Minton (1994), 'Appointments of Outsiders to Japanese Boards: Determinants and Implications for Managers', *Journal of Financial Economics*, **36** (2), 225–58.

Kasuga, Yutaka (1987), 'Mitsui', in Shoichi Asajima (ed.), *Zaibatsu Kin'yû Kôzô no Hikaku Kenkyû*, Tokyo: Ochanomizu Shobo, pp. 15–93.

Kataoka, Yutaka (1988), 'Meiji-ki ni okeru Kabunushi to Kabunushi-sôkai', *Keieishigaku*, **23** (2), 33–58.

Kataoka, Yutaka, Junko Maru and Juro Teranishi (1989), 'Meiji-kôki ni okeru Kabushiki Shijyô no Kôritsusei no Bunseki', Discussion paper Series A (191), Tokyo: The Institute of Economic Research, Hitotsubashi University.

Kawagoe, Toshihiko (1993), 'Nôchi Kaikaku', in Yutaka Kosai and Juro Teranishi (eds), *Sengo Nihon no Keizai Kaikaku*, Tokyo: University of Tokyo Press, pp. 153–76.

Kawakami, Tadao (1960), 'Dai-ichiji Taisen-ki ni okeru Kôgin no Sangyô Kinyû (1), (2)', *Keizai Shirin*, **28** (3) 195–250, (4), 142–86.

Kayo, Nobufumi (1958), *Nihon Nôgyô Kiso Tôkei*, Tokyo: Nôrin Suisan Sangyô Seisan-sei Kôjyô Kaigi.

Keizai Kikaku-cho (ed.) (1992), *Bukka Repôto*, Tokyo: Keizai Kikaku Kyôkai.

Kikkawa, Takeo (1991), 'Senzen Nihon no Karuteru', *Aogaku Keieironshû*, **25** (4), 73–98.

Kikkawa, Takeo (1992), 'Sengo-gata Kigyô-shûdan no Keisei', in Hosei Daigaku Sangyô Jyôhô Sentâ, Juro Hashimoto and Haruhito Takeda (eds), *Nihon Keizai no Hatten to Kigyô Shûdan*, Tokyo: University of Tokyo Press, pp. 255–304.

Kitagawa, Hiroshi and Yoshitaka Kurosawa (1994), 'Japan: Development and Structural Change of the Banking System', in Hugh T. Patrick and Yung Chul Park (eds), *The Financial Development of Japan, Korea, and Taiwan*, New York: Oxford University Press, pp. 81–128.

Kitamura, Yukinobu, Megumi Suto and Juro Teranishi (2004), 'Reflections on New Financial System in Japan: Participation Costs, Wealth Distribution, and Security Market-Based Intermediation', in Joseph Fan, Masaharu Hanazaki and Juro Teranishi (eds), *Designing Financial Systems in East Asia and Japan*, New York: Routledge.

Kiyokawa, Yukihiko (1995), *Nihon no Keizai Hatten to Gijyutsu Fukyû*, Tokyo: Toyokeizai Shinpo-sha.

Kmenta, Jan (1971), *Elements of Econometrics*, New York: Macmillan.

Koike, Kazuo (1991), *Shigoto no Keizaigaku*, Tokyo: Toyo Keizai Shinpo-sha.

Koike, Kazuo (1997), *Nihon Kigyô no Jinzai Ikusei*, Tokyo: Chuo Koron-sha.

Komiya, Ryutaro, Masahiro Okuno and Kotaro Suzumura (1984), *Nihon no Sangyô Seisaku-shi,* Tokyo: University of Tokyo Press.

Korenaga, Takafumi, Takeshi Nagase and Juro Tranishi (2001), '1927 Nen Kin'yû-kyôkô-ka no Yokin toritsuke Ginko Kyûgyô ni kansuru Sûryô Bunseki', *Keizai Kenkyû*, **52** (4), 315–32.

Kosai, Yutaka, Masaaki Shirakawa and Kunio Okina (eds) (2001),

Baburu to Kin'yû Seisaku, Tokyo: Nihon Keizai Shinbun-sha.

Krueger, Ann (1992), *A Synthesis of the Political Economy of Developing Countries*, (*Political Economy of Agricultural Pricing Policy;* edited by Anne O. Krueger, Maurice Schiff, Albert Valdes; *5*), Baltimore: Published for the World Bank by the Johns Hopkins University Press.

Kuznets, Simon (1966), *Modern Economic Growth*, New Haven: Yale University Press

Laffont, Jean-Jacques (2000), *Incentives and Political Economy*, Oxford: Oxford University Press.

Lewis, W. Arthur (1955), *The Theory of Economic Growth*, London: Allen & Unwin.

Mackenzie, Gavin (1982), 'Class Boundaries and the Labor Process', in Anthony Giddens and Gavin Mackenzie (eds), *Social Class and the Division of Labour: Essays in Honour of Ilya Neu Stadt*, Cambridge: Cambridge University Press, pp. 63–86.

Maddison, Angus (1995), *Monitoring the World Economy 1820–1992*, Paris: Development Centre of the Organization for Economic Cooperation and Development.

Masamura, Kimihiro (1985), *Sengo-shi (jyô)*, Tokyo: Chikuma Shobo.

Masuchi, Yojiro (1936), *Wagakuni Kabushiki Kaisha ni okeru Kabushiki Bunsan to Shihai*, Tokyo: Dobunkan.

Mayer, Wolfgang (1984), 'Endogenous Tariff Formation', *American Economic Review*, **74** (5), 970–85.

McKinnon, Ronald I. (1973), *Money and Capital in Economic Development*, Washington: Brooking Institution.

McKinnon, Ronald I. and Kenichi Ohno (1998), *Doru to En*, Tokyo: Nihon Keizai Shinbun-sha.

Meiji Zaisei-shi Hensankai (ed.) (1927), *Meiji Zaisei-shi 12*, Tokyo: Nihon Hyoron-sha.

Mikuriya, Takashi (1980), *Meiji Kokka Keisei to Chihô Keiei – 1881–1890 Nen*, Tokyo: University of Tokyo Press.

Minami, Ryoshin (1992), *Nihon no Keizai Hatten (dai 2 han)*, Tokyo: Toyo Keizai Shinpo-sha.

Minami, Ryoshin (1996), *Nihon no Keizai Hattenn to Shotoku Bunpu*, Tokyo: Iwanami Shoten.

Mitani, Taichiro (1995), *Zôho, Nihon Seitô Seiji no Keisei*, Tokyo: University of Tokyo Press.

Mitsubishi Keizai Kenkyûjyo (1935), *Nihon no Sangyô to Bôeki no Hatten*, Tokyo: Mitsubishi Keizai Kenkyûjyo.

Mitsui Ginko Hachijû-nenshi Hensan Iinkai (ed.) (1957), *Mitsui Ginko Hachijû-nenshi*, Tokyo: Mitsui Ginko.

Mitsui, Kiyoshi, Jun Inoue and Yasuko Takezawa (1995), 'Shakai Shihon no Bumonbetsu Seisanryoku Kôka', in Kiyoshi Mitsui and Kiyoshi Ota (eds), *Shakai Shihon no Seisansei to Kôteki Kin'yû*, Tokyo: Nihon Hyoron-sha, pp. 155–71.

Miwa, Ryoichi (1974), 'Kin-kaikin Seisaku Kettei Katei ni okeru Rigai Ishiki', *Aoyama Keizai Ronshû*, **26** (1, 2, 3), 173–200.

Miwa, Ryoichi (1976), 'Jyû-kagaku Kôgyô-ka to Keizai Seisaku', *Shakai Keizaishigaku*, **41** (6), 593–611.

Miwa, Yoshiro (1993), 'Shûchû Haijyo Seisaku no Keizai-kôka', in Yutaka Kosai and Juro Teranishi (eds), *Sengo Nihon no Keizai Kaikaku*, Tokyo: University of Tokyo Press, pp. 109–30.

Miyajima, Hideaki (1991), '1920 nendai ni okeru Jyûkagaku Kôgyôka to Sangyô Seisaku: Senryô Kôgyô no Kêsu', in Kindai Nihon Kenkyûkai (ed.), *Keizai Seisaku to Sangyô (Nenpô Kindai Nihon Kenkyû 13)*, Tokyo: Yamakawa Shuppan-kai, pp. 79–111.

Miyajima, Hideaki (1992), 'Zaibatsu Kaitai', in Juro Hashimoto, Haruhito Takeda and Hosei Daigaku Sangyô Jyôhô Sentâ (eds), *Nihon Keizai no Hattenn to Kigyô Shûdan*, Tokyo: University of Tokyo Press, pp. 203–54.

Miyazaki, Ryuji (1980), 'Taishô Demokurashî-ki no Nôson to Seitô (1), (2), (3) – Nôson Sho-rieki no Funshutsu to Seitô no Taiô', *Kokka Gakkai Zasshi*, **93** (7, 8), 445–511, (9, 10), 693–750, (11, 12), 855–923.

Miyazaki, Yoshikazu (1966), *Sengo Nihon no Keizai Kikô*, Tokyo: Shin Hyoron-sha.

Mizoguchi, Toshiyuki and Noriyuki Nojima (1993), *1940–1955 nen ni okeru Kokumin Keizai no Ginmi*, Heisei 2–4 nenndo Kagaku Kenkyû Hojyokin Sôgô Kenkyû (A) Kenkyû Seika Hôkokusho, Kunitachi: The Institute of Economic Research, Hitotsubashi Universty.

Mizoguchi, Toshiyuki and Yasuhiro Terasaki (1995)、 'Kakei no Shotoku Bunpu no Keizai, Shakai oyobi Sangyô Kôzô-teki Yôin – Nihon no Keiken', *Keizai Kenkyû*, **46** (1), 59–77.

Mochida, Keizo (1954), 'Shokuryô Seisaku no Seiritsu Katei (1)', *Nôgyô Sôgô Kenkyû*, **8** (2), 197–250.

Monbusho (1966), *Nihon no Kyôiku Tôkei*, Tokyo: Monbusho.

Morck, Randall and Masao Nakamura (1999), 'Bank and Corporate Control in Japan', *Journal of Finance*, **54** (1), 319–39.

Morikawa, Hidemasa (1980), *Zaibatsu no Keieishi-teki Kenkyû*, Tokyo: Toyo Keizai Shinpo-sha.

Morikawa, Hidemasa (1985), *Chihô Zaibatsu*, Tokyo: Nihon Keizai Shinbun-sha.

Murakami, Hatsu (1970), 'Bôseki Kaisha no Shôken Hakkô to

Kabunushi', in Kazuo Yamaguchi (ed.), *Nihon Sangyô Kin'yû-shi Kenkyû Bôseki Kin'yû-hen*, Tokyo: University of Tokyo Press, pp. 69–120.

Murakami, Yasusuke (1984), *Shin Chûkan Taishû no Jidai*, Tokyo: Chuo Koron-sha.

Murakami, Yasusuke, Shunpei Kumon and Seizaburo Sato (1979), *Bunmei toshiteno Iye Shakai*, Tokyo: Chuo Koron-sha.

Muramatsu, Michio (1981), *Sengo Nihon no Kanryô-sei*, Tokyo: Toyo Keizai Shinpo-sha.

Muramatsu, Michio and Ellis S. Kraus (1987), 'The Conservative Policy Line and the Development of Patterned Pluralism', in Kozo Yamamura and Yasukichi Yasuba (eds), *The Political Economy of Japan vol. 1: The Domestic Transformation*, Stanford, CA: Stanford University Press, pp. 516–54.

Nakakita, Toru, Shujiro Urata and Yutaka Harada (1993), *Naze Shijyô Kaihô ga Hitsuyô nanoka*, Tokyo: Mita Shuppan-kai.

Nakamura, James I. (1966), *Agricultural Production and the Economic Development of Japan 1873–1922*. Princeton: Princeton University Press.

Nakamura, Masanori (1979), *Kindai Nihon Jinushisei-shi Kenkyû*, Tokyo: University of Tokyo Press.

Nakamura, Takafusa (1971), *Senzen-ki Nihon Keizai Seichô no Bunseki*, Tokyo: Iwanami Shoten.

Nakamura, Takafusa (1974), *Nihon no Keizai Tôsei*, Tokyo: Nihon Keizai Shibun-sha.

Nakamura, Takafusa (1980), 'Takahashi Zaisei to Kôkyô Tôshi Seisaku – Jikyoku Kyôkyû, Nôson Doboku Jigyô no Sai-hyôka', in Takafusa Nakamura (ed.), *Senkan-ki no Nihon Keizai Bunseki*, Tokyo: Yamakawa Shuppan-sha, pp. 111–33.

Nakamura, Takafusa (1985), *Meiji Taishô-ki no Keizai*, Tokyo: University of Tokyo Press.

Nakamura, Takafusa (1990), 'Makuro Keizai to Sengo Keiei', in Shunsaku Nishikawa and Yuzo Yamamoto (eds), *Sangyô-ka no Jidai (ge)*, Tokyo: Iwanami Shoten, pp. 1–36.

Nakamura, Takafusa (1993a), *Shôwa-shi*, (II), Tokyo: Toyo Keizai Shinpo-sha.

Nakamura, Takafusa (1993b), *Nihon Keizai (Dai 3 Pan)*, Tokyo: University of Tokyo Press.

Nakamura, Takafusa (1994), *Lectures on Modern Japanese Economic History 1926–1994*, Tokyo: LTCB International Library Foundation.

Nakamura, Takafusa and Konosuke Odaka (1989), 'Gaisetsu 1914–37 Nen', in Takafusa Nakamufa and Konosuke Odaka (eds), *Nijyû Kôzô*,

Tokyo: Iwanami Shoten, pp. 1–80.

Nakaoka, Tetsuro, Tadashi Ishii and Hoshimi Uchida (1986), *Kindai Nihon no Gijyutsu to Gijyutsu Seisaku*, Tokyo: United Nations University.

Nakatani, Iwao (1984), 'The Economic Role of Financial Corporate Group', in Masahiko Aoki (ed.), *The Economic Analysis of the Japanese Firms*, Amsterdam: North Holland, pp. 227–58.

Namikata, Shoichi (1972), 'Meiji 20 Nendai Shotô no Dôsan Ginko Setsuritsu Kôsô', *Tochi Seidoshigaku*, (57), 54–67.

Nelson, Douglas (1988), 'Endogenous Tariff Theory: A Critical Survey', *American Journal of Political Science*, **32**, 786–837.

Nihon Ginko (1947), *Senjichû Kin'yû Tôkei Yôran*, Tokyo: Nihon Ginko.

Nihon Ginko (2001), 'Gijyutsu Kakushin to Ginko-gyô, Kin'yû Seisaku – Denshi Kessai Gijyutsu to Kin'yû Seisaku Unei tono Kanren o Kangaeru Fôramu Hôkokusho', *Kin'yû Kenkyû*, **20** (1) 1–73, Tokyo: Nihon Ginko.

Nihon Ginko Hyakunen-shi Hensan Iinkai (ed.) (1984), *Nihon Ginko Hyakunenshi*, **4**, Tokyo: Nihon Ginko.

Nihon Ginko Hyakunen-shi Hensan Iinkai (ed.) (1986), *Nihon Ginko Hyakunenshi: Shiryô-hen*, Tokyo: Nihon Ginko.

Nihon Ginko, Kin'yu Kenkyujyo (1993), *Nihon Kin'yû Nenpyô*, Tokyo: Nihon Ginko.

Nihon Ginko Tokei-kyoku (1966), *Meiji Ikô Honpô Shuyô Keizai Tôkei*, Tokyo: Nihon Ginko.

Nihon Kogyo Ginko (1948), *Gaikoku Kaisha no Honpô Tôshi*, Tokyo: Nihon Kogyo Ginko Gaijibu.

Nihon Kogyo Ginko Rinji Shiryôshitsu (ed.) (1957), *Nihon Kogyo Ginko Gojyû-nenshi*, Tokyo: Nihon Kogyo Ginko.

Nihon Tokei Kyokai (ed.) (1988a), *Nihon Chôki Tôkei Sôran 3*, Tokyo: Nihon Tokei Kyokai.

Nihon Tokei Kyokai (ed.) (1988b), *Nihon Chôki Tôkei Sôran 4*, Tokyo: Nihon Tokei Kyokai.

Nishida, Yoshiaki (1991), 'Senzen Nihon ni okeru Rôdô Undô, Nômin Undô no Seishitsu', in Tokyo Daigaku Shakai Kagaku Kenkyûjyo (ed.), *Gendai Nihon Shakai (4) Rekishi-teki Zentei*, Tokyo: University of Tokyo Press, pp. 263–313.

Nishikawa, Shunsaku and Takeshi Abe (1990), 'Gaisetsu 1885–1914 Nen', in Shunsaku Nishikawa and Takeshi Abe (eds), *Sangyô-ka no Jidai* (Jyô), Tokyo: Iwanami Shoten, pp. 1–77.

Nishinarita, Yutaka (1988), *Kindai Nihon Rôshi Kankei-shi no Kenkyû*, Tokyo: University of Tokyo Press.

Noda, Tsutomu (1963), *Meiji-ki ni okeru Ryûtsû Dankai-betsu, Chiiki-betsu Bukka-sa*, (The Institute of Economic Research, Hitotsubashi Daigaku, Kokumin Shotoku Suikei Kenkyûkai Shiryô, D-28, Tôsha).

Noguchi, Yukio (1992), *Baburu no Keizaigaku*, Tokyo: Nihon Keizai Shinbun-sha.

Noguchi, Yukio (1995), *1940 Nen Taisei*, Tokyo: Toyo Keizai Shinpo-sha.

Nomura Sogo Kenkyujyo (1989), *Kôshasai-yôran*, pp. 115–17, Tokyo: Nomura Shoken.

North, Douglass (1981), *Structure and Changes in Economic History*, New York: Norton.

North, Douglass (1990a), *Institutions, Institutional Change and Economic Performance*, Cambridge and New York: Cambridge University Press.

North, Douglass (1990b), 'A Transaction Cost Theory of Politics', *Journal of Theoretical Politics*, **2** (4), 355–67.

Odagiri, Hiroyuki and Akira Goto (1996), *Technology and Industrial Development in Japan*, Oxford: Clarendon Press.

Odaka, Konosuke (1993), 'Nihon-teki Rôshi Kankei', in Tetsuji Okazaki and Masahiro Okuno (eds), *Gendai Nihon Keizai Shisutemu no Genryû*, Tokyo: Nihon Keizai Shinbun-sha, pp. 145–82.

Ogihara, Susumu (1983), 'Sangyô Hôkoku Tasei no Ichi Kôsatsu', *Shôwa-ki no Shakai Undô (Nenpô Kindai Nihon Kenkyû 5)*, Tokyo: Yamakawa Shuppan-sha, pp. 93–121.

Ohkado, Masakatsu (1993), 'Meibôka Chitsujyo no Henbô', *Nihon Kindaishi (3) Gendai Shakai eno Tenkei*, Tokyo: Iwanami Shoten, pp. 65–108.

Ohkawa, Kazushi (1967), *Chôki Keizai Tôkei 8 Bukka*, Tokyo: Toyo Keizai Shinpo-sha.

Ohkawa, Kazushi (1972), *Differential Structure and Agriculture: Essays on Dualistic Growth*, Tokyo: Kinokuniya Shoten.

Ohkawa, Kazushi (1974), *Kokumin Shotoku*, Tokyo: Toyo Keizai Shinpo-sha.

Ohkawa, Kazushi and Henry Rosovsky (1973), *Japanese Economic Growth: Trend Acceleration in the Twentieth Century*, Stanford, CA: Stanford University Press.

Ohkawa, Kazushi and Miyohei Shinohara (eds) (1979), *Patterns of Japanese Economic Development*, New Haven: Yale University Press.

Okazaki, Tetsuji (1991), 'Senji Keikaku Keizai to Kigyô', in Tokyo Daigaku Shakai Kagaku Kenkyûjyo (ed.), *Rekishi-teki Zentei (Gendai Nihon Shakai 4)*, Tokyo: University of Tokyo Press, pp.

363–98.

Okazaki, Tetsuji (1993a), 'Nihon no Seifu, Kigyô-kan Kankei – Gyôkai Dantai, Shingikai Shisutemu no Keisei ni kansuru Oboegaki', *Soshiki Kagaku*, **26** (4), 115–23.

Okazaki, Tetsuji (1993b), 'Kigyô Shisutemu', in Tetsuji Okazaki and Masahiro Okuno (eds), *Gendai Nihon Keizai Shisutemu no Genryû*, Tokyo: Nihon Keizai Shibun-sha, pp. 97–144.

Okazaki, Tetsuji (1995), 'Sengo Nihon no Kin'yû Shisutemu', in Hidemasa Morikawa and Seiichiro Yonekura (eds), *Kôdo Seichôki o koete (Nihon Keieishi 5)*, Tokyo: Iwanami Shoten, pp. 137–204.

Okazaki Tetsuji (1997), *Kôgyô-ka no Kiseki*, Tokyo: Yomiuri Shinbun-sha.

Okazaki Tetsuji (1999), *Mochikabu Kaisha no Rekishi*, Tokyo: Chikuma Shobo.

Okazaki Tetsuji and Masahiro Okuno (1993), 'Gendai Nihon no Keizai Shisutemu to sono Rekishiteki Genryû', in Tetsuji Okazaki and Masahiro Okuno (eds), *Gendai Nihon Keizai Shisutemu no Genryû*, Tokyo: Nihon Keizai Shinbun-sha, pp. 1–34.

Okimoto, Daniel (1989), *Between MITI and the Market: Japanese Industrial Policy for High Technology*, Stanford, CA: Stanford University Press.

Okura, Masanori and Juro Teranishi (1994), 'Exchange Rate and Economic Recovery of Japan in the 1930s', *Hitotsubashi Journal of Economics*, **35** (1), 1–22.

Okurasho Ginkokyoku (ed.) (1953), *Ginkokyoku Kin'yû Nenpô*, Tokyo: Kin'yû Zaisei-jijyô Kenkyûkai.

Okurasho Showa Zaisei-shi Henshushitsu (ed.) (1955), *Showa Zaisei-shi*, **11**, Tokyo: Toyo Keizai Shinpo-sha.

Okurasho Showa Zaisei-shi Henshushitsu (ed.) (1981), *Showa Zaisei-shi – Shûsen kara Kôwa made*, **2**, Tokyo: Toyo Keizai Shinpo-sha.

Okurasho Shôwa Zaisei-shi Henshushitsu (ed.) (1983), *Shôwa Zaisei-shi – Shûsen kara Kôwa made*, **13**, Tokyo: Toyo Keizai Shinpo-sha.

Olson, Mancur (1965), *The Logic of Collective Action*, Cambridge, Mass: Harvard University Press.

Ono, Akira (1985), 'Borrowed Technology in Iron and Steel; Brazil, India, and Japan', in Kazushi Ohkawa and Gustav Ranis with Larry Meissner (eds), *Japan and the Developing Countries: A comparative Analysis*, New York: Basil Blackwell, pp. 236–46.

Ono, Akira (1989), *Nihon-teki Koyô Kankô to Rôdô Shijyô*, Tokyo: Toyo Keizai Shinpo-sha.

Oshima, Harry T. (1987), *Economic Growth in Monsoon Asia: A Comparative Survey,* Tokyo: University of Tokyo Press.

Otake, Hideo (1999), *Kôdo Seichôki no Seijigaku*, Tokyo: University of Tokyo Press.

Otaki, Masayuki (1994), *Keiki Junkan no Riron*, Tokyo: University of Tokyo Press

Otsuka, Keijiro, Hiroyuki Chuma and Yujiro Hayami (1992), 'Land and Labor Contracts in Agrarian Economies: Theories and Facts, *Journal of Economic Literature*, **30** (4) 1965–2018.

Patrick, Hugh T. (1991), *Pacific Basin Industries in Distress: Structural Adjustment and Trade Industrialized Economies*, in Hugh Patrick with Larry Meissner (eds), New York: Columbia University Press.

Patrick, Hugh T. with the assistance of Larry Meissner (eds) (1986), *Japan's High Technology Industries: Lessons and Limitations of Industrial Policy*, Seattle: University of Washington Press.

Peacock, Alan T. and Jack Wiseman (1961), *The Growth of Public Expenditures in the United Kingdom*, Princeton: Princeton University Press.

Pempel, T. J. and Keiichi Tsunekawa (1979), 'Corporatism without Labor? The Japanese Anomaly', in Philippe C. Schmitter and Gerhard Lehmbruch (eds), *Trends Toward Corporatist Intermediation*, London and Beverly Hills: Saga Publications, pp. 231–70.

Persson, Torsten and Guido Tabellini (1990), *Macroeconomic Policy, Credibility and Politics*, Chur, Switzerland: Harwood Academic Publishers.

Polanyi, Karl (1957), *The Great Transformation*, Boston: Beacon Press.

Radecki, Lawrence J. (1999), 'Banks Payments-Driven Revenues', *Federal Reserve Bank of New York Economic Policy Review*, July, **5** (2), 53–70.

Rajan, Raghuram G. (1992), 'Insiders and Outsiders: The Choice between Informed and Arm's-Length Debt', *Journal of Finance*, **47** (4), 1367–400.

Ramseyer, J. Mark (1994), 'Explicit Reasons for Implicit Contracts: The Legal Logic to the Japanese Main Bank System', in Masahiko Aoki and Hugh Patrick (eds), *The Japanese Main Bank System*, Oxford: Oxford University Press, pp. 231–57.

Ranis, Gustav and Syed Mahmood (1992), *The Political Economy of Development Policy Change*, Cambridge, Mass: Blackwell.

Rôdô Undô Shiryô Iinkai (1959-1975), *Nihon Rôdô Undô Shiryô (Vol. 10 Tôkei-hen)*, in Rôdô Undô Shiryô Iinkai (ed.), Tokyo: Rôodô Undô Shiryô Kankô Iinkai.

Royama, Shoichi and Toru Iwane (1973), 'Wagakuni no Ginko-gyô ni okeru Kibo to Keizaisei', *Osaka Daigaku Keizaigaku*, **23** (2, 3), 117–34.

Saito, Osamu (1983), 'Chihô Reberu no Shokusan Kôgyô Seisaku', in Mataji Umemura and Takafusa Nakamura (eds), *Matsukata Zaisei to Shokusan Kôgyô Seisaku*, Tokyo: University of Tokyo Press.

Sako, Mari (1997), 'Shuntô: The Role of Employer and Union Coordination and the Industry and Inter-sectoral Levels', in Mari Sako and Hiroshi Sato (eds), *Japanese Labour and Management in Transition*, London and New York: Routledge, pp. 236–64.

Sato, Seizaburo and Tetsuhisa Matsuzaki (1986), *Jimintô Seiken*, Tokyo: Chuo Koron-sha.

Sawai, Minoru (1992), 'Senji Keizai to Zaibatsu', in Hosei Daigaku Sangyô Jyôhô Sentâ, Juro Hashimoto and Haruto Takeda (eds), *Nihon Keizai no Hatten to Kigyô Shûdan*, Tokyo: University of Tokyo Press, pp. 149–202.

Saxonhouse, Gary (1974), 'A tale of Japanese Technological Diffusion in the Meiji Period', *Journal of Economic History*, **34** (1), 149–65.

Saxonhouse, Gary (1985), 'Technology Choice in Cotton Textile Manufacturing', in Kazushi Ohkawa and Gustav Ranis with Larry Meissner (eds), *Japan and the Developing Countries*, New York: Basil Blackwell, pp. 212–35.

Sazanami, Yoko, Shujiro Urata, Hiroki Kawai and Fukunari Kimura (1996), *Naigai Kakakusa no Keizaigaku*, Tokyo: Toyo Keizai Shinpo-sha.

Schaede, Ulrike (2000), *Cooperative Capitalism; Self-Regulation, Trade Associations, and the Antimonopoly Law in Japan*, Oxford and Tokyo: Oxford University Press.

Schmitter, Philippe C. (1979), 'Still the Century of Corporatism', in Philippe C. Schmitter and Gerhard Lehmbruch (eds), *Trends Toward Corporatist Intermediation*, London and Beverly Hills: Saga Publications, pp. 7–52.

Seki, Mitsuhiro (1993), Furusetto-gata Sangyô Kôzô o koete, Tokyo: Chuo Koron-sha.

Shaw, Edward S. (1973), *Financial Deepening in Economic Development*, New York: Oxford University Press.

Sheard, Paul (1994), 'Main Bank and the Governance of Financial Distress', in Masahiko Aoki and Hugh Patrick (eds), *The Japanese Main Bank System*, Oxford and New York: Oxford University Press, pp. 188–230.

Shibagaki, Kazuo (1965), *Nihon Kin'yû Shihon Bunseki*, Tokyo: University of Tokyo Press.

Shimizu, Katsutoshi and Akiyoshi Horiuchi (2000), 'Kin'yû Shisutemu no Zeijakusei to Amakudari', in Hirobumi Uzawa and Masaharu Hanazaki (eds), *Kin'yû Shisutemu no Keizaigaku*, Tokyo: University of Tokyo Press, pp. 83–111.

Shimura, Kaichi (1969), *Nihon Shihon Shijyô Bunseki*, Tokyo: University of Tokyo Press.

Shimura, Kaichi (1978), *Gendai Nihon Kôshasai-ron*, Tokyo: University of Tokyo Press.

Shinohara, Miyohei (1962), 'Nijyû Kôzô no Seisei to Shôrai', in Mitsuharu Ito (ed.), *Nihon Keizai no Kiso Kôzô*, Tokyo: Shunjyu-sha, pp. 109–21.

Shinohara, Miyohei (1972), *Chôki Keizai Tôkei 10 Kôkôgyô*, Tokyo: Toyo Keizai Shinpo-sha.

Shinpo, Hiroshi (1995), *Kindai Nihon Keizai-shi*, Tokyo: Sobun-sha.

Shionoya, Yuichi (1994), *Kachi Rinen no Kôzô*, Tokyo: Toyo Keizai Shinpo-sha.

Shôkô Gyôseishi Kankô-kai (ed.) (1954–55) *Shôkô Gyôseishi*, (chû-kan), Tokyo: Shôkô Gyôseishi Kankôkai.

Smith, Thomas C. (1959), *The Agrarian Origins of Modern Japan*, Stanford, California: Stanford University Press.

Stigler, George (1975), *The Citizen and the State*, Chicago: University of Chicago Press.

Stiglitz, Joseph E. (1988), 'Economic Organization, Information and Development', in H. Chenery and T. N. Srinivasan (eds), *Handbook of Development Economics*, vol.1, Amsterdam; Tokyo: North Holland, pp. 93–160.

Sugihara, Kaoru (1995), 'Keiei Hatten no Kiban Seibi', in Mataro Miyamoto and Takeshi Abe (eds), *Keiei Kakushin to Kôgyô-ka, Nihon Keiei-shi (2)*, Tokyo: Iwanami Shoten, pp. 51–90.

Suzuki, Masayuki (1988), 'Nôson Seijishi Kenkyû no Genjyô to Kadai', in Masanao Ito, Masakatsu Ohkado and Masayuki Suzuki (eds), *Senkan-ki no Nihon Nôson*, Kyoto: Sekai Shiso-sha.

Suzuki, Takeo (1960), *Gendai Nihon Zaiseshi*, **4**, Tokyo: University of Tokyo Press.

Suzuki, Tsuneo (1995), 'Sengo-gata Sangyô Seisaku no Seiritsu', in Hiroaki Yamazaki and Takeo Kikkawa (eds), *Nihonteki Keiei no Renzoku to Danzetsu*, Tokyo: Iwanami Shoten, pp. 275–321.

Suzuki, Yoshio (1974), *Gendai Nihon Kin'yû-ron*, Tokyo: Toyo Keizai Shinpo-sha.

Suzuki, Yoshio (1980), *Money and Banking in Contemporary Japan*, New Haven: Yale University Press.

Takahashi, Kamekichi (1930), *Kabushiki Kaisha Bôkoku-ron*, Tokyo: Banrikaku.

Takahashi, Kamekichi (1933), *Nihon Keizai Tôsei-ron*, Tokyo: Kaizo-sha.

Takahashi, Kamekichi (1976), *Meiji Taishô Nôson Keizai no Hensen, (Meiji Taishô Nôsei Keizai Meichoshû 19)*, Tokyo: Nôsan Gyoson Bunka Kyôkai.

Takahashi, Kamekichi (1977), *Nihon no Kigyô, Keieisha Hattatsushi*, Tokyo: Toyo Keizai Shinpo-sha.

Takahashi, Susumu and Miyazaki Ryuji (1985), 'Seitô Seiji no Teichaku to Hôkai', in Junji Banno and Masato Miyaji (eds), *Nihon Kindaishi ni okeru Tenkanki no Kenkyû*, Tokyo: Yamakawa Shuppan-sha, pp. 225–56.

Takei, Yasuhiko and Juro Teranishi (1991), 'Sengo Keizai Seichô to Seisansei, Chôki Shikin', *Keizai Kenkyû*, **42** (2), 106–16.

Takigawa, Tsutomu (1994), *Tônan Ajia Nôgyô Mondai*, Tokyo: Keiso Shobo.

Tanaka, Kakuei (1972), *Building a New Japan: A Plan for Remodeling the Japanese Archipelago*, Tokyo: Simul Press.

Tanimoto, Masayuki and Takeshi Abe (1995), 'Kigyô Bokkô to Kindai Keiei, Zairai Keiei', in Mataro Miyamoto and Takeshi Abe (eds), *Keiei Kakushin to Kôgyô-ka, Nihon Keieishi (2)*, Tokyo: Iwanamni Shoten, pp. 91–138.

Teranishi Juro (1982), *Nihon no Keizai Hatten to Kin'yû*, Tokyo: Iwanami Shoten.

Teranishi, Juro (1983), 'Matsukata Defure no Makuro Keizaigaku-teki Bunseki (Kaiteiban)', in Mataji Umemura and Takafusa Nakamura (eds), *Matsukata Zaisei to Shokusan Kôgyô Seisaku*, Tokyo: University of Tokyo Press, pp. 157–85.

Teranishi, Juro (1990), 'Financial System and Industrialization of Japan: 1900–1970', *Banca Nazionale del Lavoro Quarterly Review*, **174**, 309–42.

Teranishi, Juro (1991), *Kôgyôka to Kin'yû Shisutemu*, Tokyo: Toyo Keizai Shinpo-sha.

Teranishi, Juro (1992), 'Senzen-ki ni okeru Yunyû Daitai-teki Seichô', *Keizai Kenkyû*, **43** (2), 109–22.

Teranishi, Juro (1993a), 'Anteika Seisaku to Seisan Kakudai, Seichô', in Yutaka Kosai and Juro Teranishi (eds), *Sengo Nihon no Keizai Kaikaku*, Tokyo: University of Tokyo Press, pp. 49–66.

Teranishi, Juro (1993b), 'Shûsen Chokugo ni okeru Kin'yû Seido Kaikaku,' in Yutaka Kosai and Juro Teranishi (eds), *Sengo Nihon no Keizai Kaikaku*, Tokyo: University of Tokyo Press, pp. 131–52.

Teranishi, Juro (1994a), 'Loan Syndication in War-Time Japan and the Origins of the Main Bank System', in Masahiko Aoki and Hugh

Patrick (eds), *The Japanese Main Bank System*, Oxford: Oxford University Press, pp. 51–88.

Teranishi, Juro (1994b), 'Japan: Development and Structural Change of the Financial System', in Hugh T. Patrick and Yung Chul Park (eds), *The Financial Development of Japan, Korea and Taiwan*, Oxford: Oxford University Press, pp. 21–80.

Teranishi, Juro (1995a), 'Money Markets in Prewar Japan', in David Cole, Philip Wellons and Hal Scott (eds), *Asian Money Markets*, Oxford: Oxford University Press, pp. 388–408.

Teranishi, Juro (1995b), 'Senzenki ni okeru Seisaku Kin'yû Ginko', *Keizai Kenkyû*, **46** (2), 160–79.

Teranishi, Juro (2000), 'The Fall of the Taishô Economic System', in Masahiko Aoki and Gary Saxonhouse (eds), *Finance, Governance, and Competitiveness in Japan*, Oxford: Oxford University Press, pp. 43–63.

Teranishi, Juro (2003a), 'Review of Hoshi and Kashyap's Corporate Financing and Governance in Japan', *Journal of Economic Literature*, **41,** 566–74.

Teranishi, Juro (2003b), 'Financial Institution Building in Meiji Japan', in Machiko Nissanke and Ernest Aryeetey (eds), *Comparative Development Experiences of Sub-Saharan Africa and East Asia*, Aldershot: Ashgate, pp. 334–56.

Teranishi, Juro (2004), '1927 nen Ginko-hô no motodeno Ginko no Shûchû to Kashidashi,' *Keizai Kenkyû,* **55** (2), pp. 155–70.

Tominaga, Kenichi (1988), *Nihon Sangyô Kaisha no Tenki*, Tokyo: University of Tokyo Press.

Toniolo, Gianni (1980), *L'Economia Dell' Italia Fascista*, Roma-Bari: Gius Laterza.

Tsuchikawa, Nobuo (1994/1995), 'Seitô Naikaku to Sangyô Seisaku: 1925–1932 Nen (1), (2)', *Kokka Gakkai Zasshi*, **107** (3, 4), 313–60, **108** (11, 12), 1113–58.

Tsuchiya, Takoa and Yamaguchi Kazuo (1968), *Nihon Keizai Keieishi Nenpyô*, Tokyo: Nihon Keizai Shinbun-sha.

Tsuda, Masumi (1984), 'Sengo Keiei to Rôshi Kankei', *Bijinesu Rebyû*, **31**, 15–28.

Tsujinaka, Yutaka (1988), *Rieki Shûdan*, Tokyo: University of Tokyo Press.

Tsurumi, Seiryo (1983), 'Dai-ichiji Taisen-chû Tanki Kin'yû Shijyô no Hatten to Biru Burôkâ no Keiei Kidô', *Keizai Shirin*, **51** (1), 29–63.

Tsûsan Hando Bukku Henshû Iinkai (ed.), (1972), *Tsûsan Hando Bukku*, Tokyo: Shôkô Kaikan.

Tsutsui, Masao (1993), 'Nôson no Henbô to Meibôka', in Junji Banno et al. (eds), *Nihon Kin-Gendaishi (2), Shihon Shugi to Jiyû Shugi'*, Tokyo: Iwanami Shoten, pp. 211–55.

Tsutsui, Yoshiro (1988), *Kin'yû-shijyô to Ginkogyô*, Tokyo: Toyo Keizai Shinpo-sha.

Ueda, Kazuo (2000), 'Causes of Japan's Banking Problems in the 1990s', in Takeo Hoshi and Hugh Patrick (eds), *Crisis and Change in the Japanese Financial System*, Boston: Kluwer Academic, pp. 59–81.

U.S. Department of Commerce, Bureau of the Census (1960), *Historical Statistics of the United States, Colonial Times to 1957*, Washington, DC: U.S. Department of Commerce, Bureau of the Census.

U.S. Department of Commerce, (1972), *Japan: Government-Business Relationship*, Washington, DC: U.S. Department of Commerce, Bureau of International Commerce.

Van Rixtel, Adrian (2002), *Informality and Monetary Policy in Japan (The Political Economy of Bank Performance)*, Cambridge: Cambridge University Press.

Wada, Richard O. (1975), 'Impact of Economic Growth on the Size Distribution of Income: The Postwar Experience of Japan', in *Income Distribution, Employment and Economic Development in Southeast and East Asia*, vol. 2, Japan Economic Research Center, Tokyo and Council for Asian Manpower Studies, Tokyo: Japan Economic Research Center, pp. 515–65.

Wagner, Adolf (1892), *Grundlagen der Volkswirtschaft*, in Handbuch der Politischen Oekonomie, 3rd edn, Part 1, Leipzig: C. F. Winter.

Watanabe, Sahei and Shizuya Nishikawa (1957), 'Kahei, Shinyô Seido', in Hiromi Arisawa, Kiyoshi Oshima, Seijiro Usami and Sahei Watanabe (eds), *Nihon Shihon Shugi Kenkyû Nyûmon 2*, Tokyo: Nihon Hyoron-sha, pp. 249–95.

Wataya, Takeo (1959), 'Shihon-shugi no Hatten to Nômin no Kaisô Bunka', in Seiichi Tohata and Kozo Uno (eds), *Nihon Shihon Shugi to Nôgyô*, Tokyo: Nôgyô Sôgô Kenkyûjyo, pp.191–303.

Weinstein, E. David and Yishay Yafeh (1998,) 'On the Cost of Bank-Centered Financial System: Evidence from the Changing Main Bank Relations in Japan', *Journal of Finance*, **53** (2), 635–72.

Wright, Erik Olin (1986), 'What is Middle about Middle Class?', in John Roemer (ed.), *Analytical Marxism*, Cambridge and New York: Cambridge University Press.

Yamamura, Kozo (1967), *Economic Policy in Postwar Japan*, Berkeley: University of California Press.

Yamazawa Ippei (1984), *Nihon no Keizai Hatten to Kokusai Bungyô*,

Tokyo: Toyo Keizai Shinpo-sha.

Yamazawa, Ippei and Yuzo Yamamoto (1979), *Chôki Keizai Tôkei 14 Bôeki to Kokusai Shûshi*, Tokyo: Toyo Keizai Shinpo-sha.

Yamori, Nobuyoshi and Kenya Fujiwara (1995), 'Kantoku Tôkyoku karano Sai-shûshoku to Kin'yû-kikan Keiei', *Keizai Kagaku*, **43** (3), 1–15.

Yasuba, Yasukichi (1979), 'Meiji-ki Kaiun ni okeru Unchin to Seisansei', in Hiroshi Shinpo and Yasukichi Yasuba (eds), *Sûryô Keizaishi Ronshû 2, Kindai Ikôki no Nihon Keizai; Bakumatsu kara Meiji e*, Tokyo: Nihon Keizai Shinbun-sha, pp. 103–31.

Yasuda, Hiroshi (1993), 'Naimusho, Minseito, Sôdômei to Rôdô Seisaku', in Junji Banno (ed.), *Gendai Shakai eno Tenkei (Nihon Kindaishi 3)*, Tokyo: Iwanami Shoten, pp. 181–227.

Yonekura, Seiichiro (1993), 'Gyôkai Dantai no Kinô', in Tetsuji Okazaki and Masahiro Okuno (eds), *Gendai Nihon Keizai Shisutemu no Genryû*, Tokyo: Nihon Keizai Shinbun-sha, pp. 183–209.

Yoshikawa, Hiroshi (1999), *Tenkan-ki no Nihon Keizai*, Tokyo: University of Tokyo Press.

Yui, Tsunehiko (1964), *Chûshô Kigyô Seisaku no Shiteki Kenkyû*, Tokyo: Toyo Keizai Shipo-sha.

Yukizawa, Kenzo and Shozo Maeda (1978), *Nihon Bôeki no Chôki Tôkei*, Kyoto: Doho-sha.

Index

CARDIFF UNIVERSITY PRIFYSGOL CAERDYDD